Exploring the Dynamics
of Second Language Writing

THE CAMBRIDGE APPLIED LINGUISTICS SERIES

Series editors: Michael H. Long and Jack C. Richards

This series presents the findings of work in applied linguistics that are of direct relevance to language teaching and learning and of particular interest to applied linguists, researchers, language teachers, and teacher trainers.

Recent publications in this series:

Exploring the Dynamics of Second Language Writing

Edited by

Barbara Kroll
California State University, Northridge

CAMBRIDGE
UNIVERSITY PRESS

CAMBRIDGE UNIVERSITY PRESS
Cambridge, New York, Melbourne, Madrid, Cape Town, Singapore, São Paulo, Delhi

Cambridge University Press
32 Avenue of the Americas, New York, NY 10013–2473, USA

www.cambridge.org
Information on this title: www.cambridge.org/9780521529839

First published 2003
3rd printing 2008

Printed in in the United States of America

A catalog record for this publication is available from the British Library

Library of Congress Cataloging in Publication Data

Exploring the dynamics of second language writing / edited by Barbara Kroll.
    p. cm. – (The Cambridge applied linguistics series)
Includes bibliographical references and index.
ISBN 978-0-521-82292-3 (hbk.) – ISBN 978-0-521-52983-9 (pbk.)
1. Language and languages – Study and teaching 2. Composition (Language arts) 3.
Rhetoric – Study and teaching. I. Kroll, Barbara. II. Series.Problems,

P53.27 .E97 2003   2002074049
808'.0071–dc21

ISBN 978-0-521-82292-3 hardback
ISBN 978-0-521-52983-9 paperback   •

Contents

Contributors

Yoshiki Chikuma, *College of Charleston*

Ulla Connor, *Indiana University–Purdue University in Indianapolis*

Alister Cumming, *University of Toronto*

Nathalie Duval-Couetil, *Purdue University*

Dana Ferris, *California State University, Sacramento*

Jan Frodesen, *University of California, Santa Barbara*

William Grabe, *Northern Arizona University*

Liz Hamp-Lyons, *Hong Kong Polytechnic University*

Christine Holten, *University of California, Los Angeles*

Ann M. Johns, *San Diego State University*

Ilona Leki, *University of Tennessee*

Paul Kei Matsuda, *University of New Hampshire*

Ruo-Ping J. Mo, *Canton, Michigan*

Martha C. Pennington, *University of Luton*

Charlene Polio, *Michigan State University*

Melinda Reichelt, *University of Toledo*

Tony Silva, *Purdue University*

Stephanie Vandrick, *University of San Francisco*

Gloria Vélez-Rendón, *Purdue University–Calumet*

Sandra Wood, *University of Connecticut*

Acknowledgments

For most of my 35 years of teaching, I have been working to address the needs of writers and to investigate the variables that contribute to differing skill levels in the texts that non-native speakers of English produce. I salute all of my colleagues who have worked to create the field that no one could have named when I started teaching: second language writing studies; they have enriched my life immeasurably with their efforts to establish a discipline and seek answers to our common questions. This book represents the work of several members of that scholarly community, each focusing on a specific aspect of our now very diverse field.

I wish to thank the contributors to this volume; they worked diligently to repeatedly revise their chapters, helping me realize the vision I had for this book. They also dealt gracefully with the feedback given by a variety of anonymous reviewers who read multiple versions of the manuscript. I thank the reviewers for putting in such scrupulous attention to the volume; even when their individual suggestions and concerns contradicted each other, their collective advice proved useful in shaping the final text.

Linda Lonon Blanton graciously volunteered to offer focused and speedy feedback on my own contributions to this volume; I am grateful to her. I also appreciate the hard work of the series editor Jack Richards and all of those at Cambridge University Press who encouraged me during this project and who worked closely with me during a fairly lengthy birthing process: Mary Vaughn, Debbie Goldbatt, Judy Bernstein, and Julia Hough. Many thanks to Regina Paleski, my very efficient production editor, and Patterson Lamb, an eagle-eyed copy editor if ever there was one!

Lastly, my bountiful thanks to Ruth; she knows why.

Barbara Kroll

Abbreviations used

ACT	American College Testing Program
ASTP	Army Specialized Training Program
CCCC	Conference on College Composition and Communication
CLEAR	Center for Language Education and Research
CUNY	City University of New York
EAP	English for academic purposes
EFL	English as a foreign language
ELI	English Language Institute
ELTS	English Language Testing Service
ESL	English as a second language
ESP	English for special [or specific] purposes
ETS	Educational Testing Service
FCE	(Cambridge) First Certificate in English
FL	foreign language
GSLPA	Graduating Students' Language Proficiency Assessment
IATEFL	International Association of Teachers of English as a Foreign Language
IEA	International Educational Achievement
IELTS	International English Language Testing System
IRC	Internet relay chat
JBW	*Journal of Basic Writing*
LAN	local area network
L1	native [or first] language
L2	second language
MELAB	Michigan English Language Battery
MOO	multi-user domain, object-oriented
MUD	multi-user domain
NES	native English speakers
NR	New Rhetoricians
PEG	Project Essay Grader
SAT	Scholastic Aptitude Test
SFL	Systemic Functional Linguistics
SLA	second language acquisition

TESL	Teaching of English as a second language
TESOL	Teachers of English to Speakers of Other Languages
TOEFL	Test of English as a Foreign Language
TWE	Test of Written English
WAC	writing across the curriculum
WAN	wide area network
WSSE	World Standard Spoken English

Series editors' preface

Whereas it is commonplace to talk of English as the language of globalization and international communication, it is appropriate to recognize that it is written English that is the predominant medium for much of this discourse. Second language writing skills play an increasingly important role today in the lives of professionals in almost every field and discipline, creating a challenge to those responsible for the teaching of second language writing. The growing body of research by scholars in the field of second language writing instruction reflects an international response to this phenomenon, much of the results of which are reflected in the present volume.

Exploring the Dynamics of Second Language Writing is a timely collection of original papers surveying theory, research, and practice in the teaching of second language writing. Each of the chapters provides a useful overview of a key topic in second language writing, identifying the major theoretical issues, surveying research findings, and exploring applications to second language teaching.

The book is based on several assumptions:

- The field of second language (L2) writing is an autonomous discipline, though one that draws on a number of related fields, including composition studies, rhetoric, contrastive rhetoric, text linguistics, and genre theory.
- There is a demand today for teachers with a high level of pedagogical understanding and expertise in the different aspects of writing instruction, from curriculum development, to classroom pedagogy, to assessment.
- If teachers, teacher educators, and language teaching professionals are to keep abreast of ideas and developments in this rapidly expanding field, they need access to information on current research theory and practice. Language programs around the world require instructors who can assist international students to meet the complex academic writing demands of a wide range of disciplines.
- The teaching of writing is based on an understanding of the nature of texts, cognitive processes, learners, participants, and learning contexts;

and a variety of different research approaches are needed to explore these variables.

These themes are reflected throughout this book, which draws on theory and research to examine pedagogical issues and to provide a basis for the development of courses in L2 writing. The contributors show how the field has developed in the last 40 years, explain the shifts in theoretical perspectives and teaching approaches that have marked its development, and suggest directions for future research. The book will thus prove an invaluable resource for teachers in preparation, as well as for experienced teachers, researchers on L2 writing, and curriculum and materials developers.

Michael H. Long
Jack C. Richards

Introduction *Teaching the next generation of second language writers*

Barbara Kroll

As a field of academic inquiry, the teaching of writing to second language (L2) learners sits at the junction of the discipline of composition and rhetoric (which concerns itself primarily with identifying the nature of texts and the processes that writers engage in to produce those texts) and the discipline of language learning (which concerns itself with cognitive and affective factors learners engage in as they move toward mastery of a particular linguistic code).[1] No one teaching writing to this population of learners can responsibly serve his or her students without a clear recognition that these two fields intersect, especially at the post-secondary level. This volume is addressed to future L2 writing teachers; the authors of the chapters are steeped in traditions of inquiry central to composition and rhetoric and offer an applied linguistics perspective focused on adult learners.

A growing need for English teachers

If teaching second language skills to populations of adult students who grew up speaking other native languages was ever a simple matter for teachers, it is certainly no longer so in the twenty-first century. The complexity has been intensified by the phenomena known as "globalization" and the Internet revolution. They have brought such an expansion in the use of English throughout the world that one can only partly imagine the still unfolding ramifications, including the changing of the English language itself (Warshauer, 2000). Full participation in the world community, particularly within interconnected economic, technological, and geopolitical realities, can require a fluency in English that goes beyond the spoken language and embraces a variety of uses of the written language as well. Because the English-language cultures (among others) are increasingly literacy-driven cultures (see, for example, Baynham, 1995; Cushman, Kintgen, Kroll, & Rose, 2001; Kern, 2000) and digital-literacy driven (Warshauer, 2001), the pursuit of English entails a pursuit of written English, offering those who acquire skill in this code the possibility for improved life chances. Thus, career options in English-language teaching

1

seem assured for the foreseeable future, and perhaps especially for teachers who focus on teaching writing skills.

To judge by what is going on in the United States, there is a steady increase in the number of learners of English seeking entrance to our institutions of higher education. The Institute of International Education (IIE) has been tracking the number of foreign visa students enrolled in U.S. institutions of higher education since 1949 (Institute of International Education, 2001). That number has continued to increase every year, undiminished in toto by any war or economic disaster impacting a particular population or world area. In the decade from 1990 to 2000, for example, the number of foreign visa students in the United States increased by over 140,000 and surpassed half a million[2] for the first time in the 1999–2000 academic year (Open Doors, 2001). And this says nothing of the vast and ever-growing number of L2 students on U.S. campuses not included in these tabulations (or any other official counts) because they are U.S. residents or citizens and do not hold foreign visas.

Further, countries outside the traditional English-speaking world are increasingly drawn into situations where fluency in English becomes critical for their citizens who wish to participate in the global arena. For example, a report prepared for the then Prime Minister of Japan and issued in January 2000 called for a national discussion on making English Japan's official second language and recommended that English-language teaching be introduced in kindergarten (Tolbert, 2000). The document suggested to the late Prime Minister Keizo Obuchi that increased fluency in English among the Japanese would greatly contribute to reversing the economic stagnation Japan was experiencing at the time, but this fluency could be accomplished only with radical changes in the current methods of delivering English-language instruction in Japanese schools (Tolbert, 2000). On another plane, many in our profession worry about the increasing number of languages dying out around the world, often with English as the replacement tongue (Crystal, 2000; Nettle & Romaine, 2000), and the concomitant need for fluency in English. Regardless of how one views such a phenomenon, it contributes to the increasing use of English in geographic regions where, different from such places as North America, Great Britain, and Australia, English does not have a long tradition. To a certain extent, then, geopolitical realities contribute to the expanding need for English-language teachers outside of English-dominant countries.

So far, I have referred primarily to English-language teaching. The teaching of writing is a specialized component of this instruction, one that has come to occupy a prominent place in research and teaching due in part to the ever-expanding student body and the recognition of changes in global realities. Over the past quarter of a century or so, faculty and researchers in many countries around the world have increasingly recognized that teaching English writing skills to tertiary-level students who come from non-English-speaking backgrounds is a critical part of the higher education system. The growing interest in second language writing as an academic enterprise is attested to by the large number of courses in writing offered to second language students at institutions from community colleges to the most prestigious graduate research institutions; the phenomenal growth in the number of papers on the subject published in books and professional journals; the number of presentations delivered at regional, national, and international conferences sponsored by a wide range of professional organizations; and the founding of a scholarly journal devoted to the topic (the *Journal of Second Language Writing*, established in 1992). The teaching of writing in L2 contexts, once little discussed (see Blanton & Kroll et al., 2002), has come front and center in the profession of applied linguistics.

While this volume is devoted primarily to issues in the acquisition of English-language writing skills, the teaching of second/foreign languages other than English remains a significant part of school and university curricula in many different countries. Indeed, the field of second language writing is an area affecting the lives of hundreds of thousands of students at institutions around the world where they must submit high-quality written work in a language they did not acquire as native speakers; and in fact, multilingualism is alive and well in numerous locales where it might even be considered the norm (Edwards, 1994; Nettle & Romaine, 2000). Many users of second languages other than English need to be able to write fluently in their L2, and books and anthologies on specific classroom practices and issues related to second language writing in a variety of European languages (as well as in English) have begun to proliferate (e.g., Brauer, 2000; Kern, 2000; Scott, 1996). Reichelt (1999) reviews some 200 published works relating to foreign language (FL) writing and research pedagogy in the United States alone, identifying ways in which FL concerns overlap with and differ from concerns in English as a second language/English as a foreign language (ESL/EFL). The discussions in the following chapters may also be of value to future teachers of L2 writing in non-English settings, who can adapt some of the English-specific foci to their own situations and contexts.

Understanding teacher training

With all of these factors, multiple teaching opportunities are likely to await faculty able to provide instruction in L2 writing in a variety of post-secondary settings. A critical question thus becomes how best to prepare teachers to undertake this task. To serve their students well, teachers of L2 writing must be prepared with more than a set of lesson plans, an interest in their students, and strong skills of their own in the target language. To be sure, these are necessary components, but they are not sufficient. As distinguished researcher Arthur Applebee pointed out: "Teachers of English need to make the distinction between knowledge which informs their teaching, and that which should be imparted to the student" (Applebee, cited in Applebee, 1999, p. 362).

So too, teachers of writing to L2 students need to make the distinction between what can be termed "foundational knowledge" – subject matter content that serves them as professionals – and "procedural knowledge" – ideas and techniques that will shape specific lesson plans for their students. For example, as part of building a foundation of knowledge, future teachers must acquire an understanding of how the profession has evolved and what issues form the core of subject matter (as opposed to methodological) concerns – that is, they must know what drives the field forward. Additionally, teachers should come to see that the tools they will use for analyzing their own students' progress (or lack thereof) not only serve their immediate needs on a day-to-day basis and form a component of requisite procedural knowledge but can also provide raw data that might contribute to changes in course design motivated by their foundational knowledge of course possibilities (cf. Graves, 2000).

Because good writing teachers must have a rich understanding of the field to be able to make the best possible choices in their uniquely situated teaching positions, this book is designed to help them acquire such understanding. Knowing the field includes being able to recognize how any given classroom choice speaks to a particular approach toward teaching and/or awareness of student learning issues and/or interpretation of what texts are and what they do. Further, even the most classroom-oriented of teachers should be able to contribute knowledgeably to ongoing professional discussions. The so-called theory–practice divide is undoubtedly an artificial one; I would prefer to conceive of the relationship between research and practice in the field of second language writing as an interactive one. As I have pointed out elsewhere, "Research insights drive practice and concerns for practices that do not seem to be working drive additional research" (Kroll, 2001, p. 230).

Foundational knowledge gives faculty the scholarly background to provide the best of instruction to students in second language writing and guides instructors toward making appropriate curricula and classroom choices. Attaining this scholarly background involves exposure to the accumulated knowledge of the profession and an awareness of what tools are available to expand and refine this knowledge base. It is simply not enough for prospective teachers to focus solely on acquiring information about methods and materials, important though they are. While I do not mean to downplay the significance of being able to learn from the accumulated classroom wisdom ("best practices") of highly experienced teachers, Edge and Richards (1998, p. 571) caution that focusing solely on the search for "best practices" in and of themselves can lead to the "deskilling of teachers, who are [then] seen as the technicians responsible for learning-delivery systems" (p. 571). Rather, teachers must rely on theory to become well-trained professionals responsible for helping their students gain needed mastery. As Stenberg and Lee (2002) point out in regard to training native language (L1) composition teachers, "theory and practice necessarily function in interplay, and pedagogy encompasses both" (p. 328).

In fact, it is the command of basic foundational knowledge in a given field that allows teachers to make principled rather than ad hoc curriculum decisions. In that sense, this volume, which helps to build subject matter background, is truly a teacher-training book even though it does not provide direct guidance on such day-to-day concerns as syllabus design and lesson planning. Identifying what constitutes the "subject matter" knowledge critical for teachers is not without its controversies, however, and the reality is that the topics selected for inclusion in this volume constitute one vision of the parameters of the profession – a vision shaped by the collective experience of the contributors to this volume and our beliefs about areas of knowledge critical for teachers.

This volume is intended primarily to assist in the preparation of new teachers by providing chapters that offer overviews of key issues, discussions of the relevance of prior and ongoing research to teachers, and insight into current thinking as presented by leading scholars in the field. Whether teachers are trained in programs allied to applied linguistics, second language acquisition, modern languages (including English as a second/foreign language), or education, they must also learn to be lifelong learners themselves, continually prepared to expand their own knowledge and understanding in the pursuit of sounder teaching practices. Thus, the information contained in this book should be considered a starting point and not the end point for promoting teacher engagement with the field of second language writing.

A note on theory/model-building

Unlike introductions to some other disciplines, this book begins with a historical perspective rather than an outline of theory. In contrast, trainees in some fields, including linguistics, are initiated into and expected to become familiar with well-established theories relevant to their education and training. Although many researchers in the field of second language writing, including several contributors to this volume, are particularly interested in theory-building (e.g., Cumming, 1998;

Grabe, 2001; Matsuda, 1998; Silva, 1993), regrettably at the present time "there is no single theory of writing in a second language" (Gebhard, 1998) capable of explaining the role of and interaction among key variables discussed here. In fact, despite a wealth of information on L2 composing processes and the description of texts produced in L2, "we have very little information on how people actually *learn to write in second languages or how teaching might influence this*" (Cumming & Riazi, 2000, p. 57, italics mine).

In fact, to build a theory of second language writing, we would need to ask whether a theory of *writing* would overlap with or be distinct from a theory of *learning to write*, and to further delineate if, how, and in what ways theories relevant to *second* language writers applied to or distinguished themselves from theories applicable to *first* language writers. Grabe (2001) explains that we turn to theories for their predictive and explanatory properties, and at the moment, most of the information we have about writing and learning to write and writing classrooms is descriptive in nature, thus making theory-building difficult. Even substituting the notion of "models" for theories does not resolve the dilemma. After reviewing a number of models that have been advanced (not theories, really), Cumming (1998) notes, "We are far from seeing models that adequately explain learning to write in a second language or precisely how . . . [L2] writing should be taught" (p. 68). And last, in his recent conceptual overview of L2 writing, Hyland (2002) uses the words "theory" and "framework" interchangeably to review key approaches to the teaching of writing. Thus, volumes such as this cannot present "standard" theory in a neatly packaged format.

We *can* point out that what can pass for theory is sometimes better labeled a methodology or a widely held belief. For example, terms frequently used in discussing writing are "the composing process" and "process theory." When these were first introduced and popularized, many felt that focusing the writing course on the process of writing itself was a *theoretical* breakthrough. In retrospect, a more accurate claim would be that process insights gave rise to a *methodological* breakthrough in the teaching of writing. In fact, process theory, although widely discussed in L1 writing circles, has itself been challenged by many L1 writing theorists who have moved into a so-called post-process period (see, for example, Kent, 1999; Olson & Dobrin, 1994). Clearly, every writer, from the most novice and inept to the most skilled and professional, completes a given writing task by engaging in some sort of process. We should recognize the importance of the methodological breakthrough engendered by insights from research into the composing process of skilled L1 and L2 writers; these findings assist teachers in helping less skilled writers alter their writing behaviors so they can write more successfully. But no matter how much we help student writers "improve" their composing process(es), we are still talking about methods and not theory, and this is just one variable in the multifaceted enterprise known as "writing."

Among other critical variables in the equation of writer, writing task, discourse constraints, and audience expectations is context. Here, too, terms such as EAP (English for Academic Purposes) and ESP (English for Special Purposes), when first introduced, seemed likely to contribute to theory-building; but they turn out to be methodologically based as well. EAP and ESP provide helpful orientations to pedagogy – perhaps more than they do to theory-building – because they suggest that the entire curriculum for a writing course is context-driven; change the context and you need to change how a course is packaged and delivered – not a trivial point, as well discussed by Swales (1990) among others.

Thus, this volume is not about specific pedagogical practices or any given theory per se, but it is a volume that should help teachers to more fully understand the framework of concerns within which the field and its key constituents (teachers and learners) operate.

Overview of this volume

This book has thirteen chapters that collectively offer an orientation to second language writing as a field; they are grouped around five areas that serve as "explorations" into the subject and set out parameters for identifying critical subject matter material, the collective foundational knowledge discussed earlier. Exploring what goes on in writing classrooms is a multifaceted enterprise. Although certain commonalities are to be expected in how teachers and students work together toward the improvement of students' L2 writing proficiency, a single change in one of many variables can alter the specific dynamics of any given class. Some of the variables considered in this volume are related to the student–teacher dynamic; others investigate the specific epistemologies associated with L2 writing as a discipline and various contexts of the writing situation.

Each section of the book is preceded by a short overview of how the chapter or chapters in that section relate to the theme of the section and/or interrelate to each other. These section introductions, by providing additional background not specifically discussed in the chapters themselves, highlight and sometimes interpret key issues in the individual chapters. In the section introductions I highlight the key focus of each chapter by showing how it answers a significant question of concern to second language writing theorists and/or practitioners.

The first section of the book explores the field in broad strokes, noting how we continue to build the bases of knowledge that are specific to the area of L2 writing. It provides a historical orientation (Chapter 1) and a framework for considering the several research paradigms that provide insight into writers, their texts, and the contexts for writing (Chapter 2). The second section of the book explores voices of the two key stakeholders in the teaching of writing – teachers and students. It offers a tour of several English-writing curricula around the world as discussed by the teachers in those settings (Chapter 3) and a presentation and interpretation of several individual L2 writers' personal learning narratives (Chapter 4). The third section of the book explores perspectives on the texts that students produce, including issues related to teacher and peer response to student writing (Chapter 5), factors surrounding grammatical considerations in the analysis of student texts (Chapter 6), and the latest thinking about the assessment of writing (Chapter 7). The fourth section of the book explores some contexts in which to consider texts: defining and understanding how genre interacts with student writing needs (Chapter 8); an up-to-date look at the field of contrastive rhetoric (Chapter 9); drawing connections between texts consulted by writers (readings) and their own evolving texts (writings), that is, reading–writing connections (Chapter 10); and finding a role for literature in the L2 composition classroom (Chapter 11). The fifth section of the book explores technology, discussing the impact of computers and the Internet on L2 writing students and classrooms (Chapter 12). Last, the book concludes with an epilogue (Chapter 13) that raises some interesting and challenging questions about the whole enterprise of teaching writing.

All the chapters have been specifically prepared for this volume and assembled to present a reasonably comprehensive sense of the key issues and questions of major concern to L2 writing specialists today. However, because teaching second language writing skills is a highly situated activity, the chapters focus primarily though not exclusively on teaching English-language writing skills to non-native speakers of English. Additionally, although most of the chapters report on research conducted in a wide range of international settings, they primarily discuss teaching writing in North American university courses. The goal of each chapter is to provide key foundational knowledge primarily for prospective and novice teachers. Most chapters can also function as resource guides by reference to extensive scholarship, with the bibliographical citations useful in promoting opportunities for further investigation. Now is an exciting time to be engaged in teaching L2 writing, and I hope this collection will inspire readers to join the conversation.

Notes

1. I am aware that Matsuda (1998) presents a more complex vision of the disciplinary relationships.

2. The number of foreign visa holders is not the same as the number of L2 speakers, since the tabulation includes native speakers of English (i.e., students from such places as England, Canada, and Australia – plausibly English L1 speakers – are included in the IIE number).

References

Applebee, A. (1999). Building a foundation for effective teaching and learning of English: A personal perspective on thirty years of research. *Research in the Teaching of English, 33*, 352–366.

Baynham, M. (1995). *Literacy practices: Investigating literacy in social contexts.* New York: Longman.

Blanton, L. L., & Kroll, B., et al. (2002). *ESL composition tales: Reflections on teaching.* Ann Arbor: University of Michigan Press.

Brauer, G. (Ed.). (2000). *Writing across languages.* Stamford, CT: Ablex.

Crystal, D. (2000). *Language death.* New York: Cambridge University Press.

Cumming, A. (1998). Theoretical perspectives on writing. *Annual Review of Applied Linguistics, 18*, 61–78.

Cumming, A., & Riazi, A. (2000). Building models of adult second-language writing instruction. *Learning and Instruction, 10*, 55–71.

Cushman, E., Kintgen, E. R., Kroll, B. M., & Rose, M. (Eds.). (2001). *Literacy: A critical sourcebook.* New York: Bedford/St. Martin's Press.

Edge, J., & Richards, K. (1998). Why best practice is not good enough. *TESOL Quarterly, 32*, 569–574.

Edwards, J. (1994). *Multilingualism.* London and New York: Routledge.

Gebhard, M. (1998). Second language writing theory. In M. L. Kennedy (Ed.), *Theorizing composition: A critical sourcebook of theory and scholarship in contemporary composition studies* (pp. 277–280). Westport, CT: Greenwood Press.

Grabe, W. (2001). Notes towards a theory of second language writing. In T. Silva & P. K. Matsuda (Eds.), *On second language writing* (pp. 39–57). Mahwah, NJ: Lawrence Erlbaum.

Graves, K. (2000). *Designing language courses: A guide for teachers.* Boston: Heinle & Heinle.

Hyland, K. (2002). *Teaching and researching writing.* Harlow, UK: Longman.

Institute of International Education. (2001, November 13). Press release. New York: Author. Retrieved February 16, 2002, from the World Wide Web: http://www.iie.org/svcs/pressrel/pr111301a.htm.

Kent, T. (Ed.). (1999). *Post-process theory.* Carbondale: Southern Illinois University Press.

Kern, R. (2000). *Literacy and language teaching.* Oxford and New York: Oxford University Press.

Kroll, B. (2001). Considerations for teaching an ESL/EFL writing course. In M. Celce-Murcia (Ed.), *Teaching English as a second/foreign language* (3rd ed., pp. 219–232). Boston: Heinle & Heinle.

Matsuda, P. K. (1998). Situating ESL writing in a cross-disciplinary context. *Written Communication, 15*, 99–121.

Nettle, D., & Romaine, S. (2000). *Vanishing voices: The extinction of the world's languages.* Oxford and New York: Oxford University Press.

Olson, G. A., & Dobrin, S. I. (Eds.). (1994). *Composition theory for the post-modern classroom.* Albany: State University of New York Press.

Open Doors. (2001). Open doors on the web. New York: Institute of International Education. Retrieved February 16, 2002 from the World Wide Web: http://www.opendoorsweb.org/.

Reichelt, M. (1999). Toward a more comprehensive view of L2 writing: Foreign language writing in the U.S. *Journal of Second Language Writing, 8,* 181–204.

Scott, V. M. (1996). *Rethinking foreign language writing.* Boston: Heinle & Heinle.

Silva, T. (1993). Toward an understanding of the distinct nature of L2 writing. *TESOL Quarterly, 27,* 657–677.

Stenberg, S., & Lee, A. (2002). Developing pedagogies: Learning and the teaching of English. *College English, 64,* 326–347.

Swales, J. (1990). *Genre analysis.* New York: Cambridge University Press.

Tolbert, K. (2000, January 29). English is the talk of Japan. *The Washington Post,* p. A13.

Warshauer, M. (2000). The changing global economy and the future of English teaching. *TESOL Quarterly, 34,* 511–535.

Warshauer, M. (2001). Millennialism and media: Language, literacy, and technology in the 21st century. *AILA Review, 14,* 49–59.

PART I:
EXPLORING THE FIELD OF
SECOND LANGUAGE WRITING

When people set out to explore a previously unknown territory, they typically prepare themselves by studying maps and outfitting themselves with the needed regalia of exploration, such as specialized equipment and a compass. For territories already well explored, new visitors set out with a guidebook. So, too, a person newly drawn to a particular academic area should begin by preparing for his or her own exploration with the appropriate equipment or guidebook to provide some understanding of how the field has evolved and what to anticipate in the new terrain. What exactly should one expect to find in this field of study? What is central to the field? Where is the field moving? What is controversial? These are some of the questions that concern the authors of all the chapters in this volume.

Second language writing is a uniquely characterizable specialty area that has ties to but does not completely overlap with the fields of first language writing instruction, second language acquisition, or second language pedagogy. Perhaps a truism is that certain realities are true for all students in any academic environment whereas others are uniquely true for second language students. Just as linguists today recognize that language is culturally constructed, so too are students – defined by and defining their own place in the educational spectrum. This book is concerned with second language writers, bringing to the table not only their needs as novice writers but also their needs as second language speakers.

The first part of this book lays the groundwork for helping future teachers situate themselves as part of an identifiable scholarly endeavor and for beginning to understand how we make the claims we do about writers and texts. Although many scholars active in publishing in this area are based in countries around the world, Atkinson (2000, p. 318) believes that "an organized academic field is a group of scholars who not only study similar phenomena, but who also share ... common theoretical and practical concerns (and similar research questions)." He finds, by this definition, that the field as such and the scholars who are working collectively to explore it are "substantially North American"

(p. 319), particularly when considered from a historical perspective. The North American perspective is foregrounded by the first two chapters in this volume, and they serve to provide an orientation to the field of study known as second language writing. The first chapter recounts how the field's early scholars came to be identified as a community, and the second chapter offers an interpretation of how we make knowledge in this field through a review of major research paradigms and perspectives to address the similar research questions that continue to drive the field.

From where and how has the field of second language writing come into being?

A very large number of institutions have been offering specialized courses in writing to second language (L2) students for many years, particularly courses in English composition to non-native speakers of English; realistically speaking, however, it wasn't all that long ago that faculty had to argue for the need to consider even native speaker (L1) writing as a discipline worthy of scholarly study. Prior to about 1960, L1 "writing was the most often taught of college subjects and by a great measure the least examined" (Connors, 1997, p. 15). All that has radically changed, and as the field as grown, its initial preoccupation with practice has shifted into a broader-based set of scholarly and theoretical concerns (Kennedy, 1998). But L2 writing draws its current insights from and has its historical roots in more than just the field of L1 writing.

Chapter 1, by Paul Kei Matsuda, provides a historical perspective on second language writing as broadly conceived. He looks into the interdisciplinary relationships between composition studies and second language studies as they have evolved, starting in the latter part of the twentieth century. Although his history draws primarily on specific events that unfolded in the United States, his claims apply to a broad range of geographic locations. Robert Kaplan (2000), whose pioneering work in second language writing is much cited in this volume and elsewhere, takes issue with the characterization of the field in this manner (as first presented by Santos et al., 2000), finding it more international in scope, but Matsuda focuses on the significant part of discipline-building that took place in the United States. This chapter is particularly informative for those newer to the field; an understanding of the interplay between concerns of compositionists and applied linguists should serve to ground them in the discipline of second language writing studies. In providing a particular point of view and interpretation of our history, Matsuda has much to offer more established members of the L2 writing community as well.

How do we go about investigating what we need to know about L2 writing/writers?

Our understanding of second language writers and writing has been the result of painstakingly detailed research using a variety of paradigms common to composition and social science research. This variety is necessitated and perhaps made more complex because objects of inquiry include all or some of the following: the written product, the writing process, the writers' backgrounds and experience, the classroom context, the teacher, the social setting and writing goals outside the classroom, and educational interventions (i.e., teachers interacting with students). As noted by Archibald and Jeffery (2000), in an introduction to a special issue of *Learning and Instruction* featuring research on second language writing:

There has been considerable interplay over the years between research into writing and learning and instruction in writing. Much of the research has had direct repercussions on the classroom, and classroom practice and observation has often been the source of research studies. (p. 7)

Given the interconnection between the classroom and the researcher, it is imperative that teachers familiarize themselves with how research is conducted.

Chapter 2, by Charlene Polio, offers readers the opportunity to understand a variety of research findings in the field that seem critical to the discipline of L2 writing as determined through many research paradigms. She explains the goals for and the methodology of research that uses the following approaches: experimental and quasi-experimental, correlational, causal-comparative, survey, content analysis, historical, participant observation, nonparticipant observation, and ethnographic – in each case citing specific studies in L2 writing that utilize the method in question. The framework she provides helps promote awareness of how to seek out and process additional published research studies about L2 writing with richer understanding.

References

Archibald, A., & Jeffery, G. C. (2000). Editorial: Second language acquisition and writing: A multi-disciplinary approach. *Learning and Instruction, 10,* 1–11.

Atkinson, D. (2000). On Robert B. Kaplan's response to Terry Santos et al.'s "On the future of second language writing." *Journal of Second Language Writing, 9,* 317–320.

Connors, R. (1997). *Composition-rhetoric: Backgrounds, theory, pedagogy.* Pittsburgh, PA: University of Pittsburgh Press.

Kaplan, R. B. (2000). Response to "On the future of second language writing," Terry Santos (Ed.), et al. *Journal of Second Language Writing, 9,* 311–314.

Kennedy, M. L. (Ed.). (1998). *Theorizing composition: A critical sourcebook of theory and scholarship in contemporary composition studies.* Westport, CT: Greenwood Press.

Santos, T., Atkinson, D., Erickson, M., Matsuda, P. K., & Silva, T. (2000). On the future of second language writing: A colloquium. *Journal of Second Language Writing, 9,* 1–20.

1 Second language writing in the twentieth century: A situated historical perspective

Paul Kei Matsuda

Existing historical accounts of studies in second language (L2) writing, which began to appear in the 1990s, usually begin with the 1960s and catalogue pedagogical approaches or emphases (e.g., Leki, 1992; Raimes, 1991; Silva, 1990).[1] It is not historically insignificant that many researchers see the 1960s as the beginning of the discipline, that they focus on pedagogical approaches or emphases, and that historical accounts began to appear in the 1990s because these accounts embody a set of assumptions about the disciplinary and epistemological status of second language writing. That is, these accounts tend to position second language writing as a subfield of second language studies and present the primary responsibility of second language writing researchers as the development of pedagogical knowledge in the service of advancing the field. Yet, a broader view of the history seems to suggest the limitations of these assumptions. Although it is true that writing issues began to attract serious attention from L2 specialists only in the 1960s, historical evidence suggests that L2 writing instruction did not suddenly become an issue in the 1960s (Matsuda, 1999). Furthermore, the rise of historical consciousness in the early 1990s seems to indicate that the nature of second language writing studies began to change around that time.

My goal in this chapter is to provide an understanding of the dynamics of the field of second language writing by considering its development from a broader, interdisciplinary perspective. Specifically, I will be examining how this academic specialty has been shaped by the interdisciplinary relationship between composition studies and second language studies. Understanding the historical context of the field is important both for researchers and teachers because our theoretical and pedagogical practices are always historically situated. Without knowing the context in which certain theories or pedagogical strategies developed, we will not be able to apply them or modify them in other contexts or in light of new theoretical insights. Without an understanding of the history, we may continue to use pedagogical strategies that are no longer appropriate for the changing student population or dismiss some useful ideas or practices for the wrong reasons. In other words, this historical chapter tries to enhance second language writing

15

teachers' understanding of the existing theoretical and pedagogical insights.

The genesis of second language writing issues

Writing was neglected in the early years of second language studies possibly because of the dominance of the audiolingual approach in the mid twentieth century. As I have argued elsewhere (Matsuda, 2001), however, the neglect of writing in second language studies goes even further back, namely, to the rise of applied linguistics in the late nineteenth century. Early applied linguists of that era sought to apply, quite literally, the findings of scientific linguistics – which has until fairly recently focused almost exclusively on spoken language – in the realm of language teaching. Reacting against the perceived dominance of "writing" in L2 learning (i.e., literary texts in such "dead" languages as Latin), the intellectual leaders of early applied linguistics in Europe – most notably, phoneticians Henry Sweet (1899/1964) and Paul Passy (1929) – argued that phonetics should be the basis of both theoretical and practical studies of language (i.e., linguistics *and* applied linguistics) and that the spoken form of language should take precedence over the written form. For the most advanced language learners, the use of free composition – or the production of extended written discourse by reproducing previously learned materials – was recommended as a more desirable alternative to then-traditional translation exercises. However, priority was given to spoken language because writing was defined merely as an orthographic representation of speech and because letter writing was considered to be the highest literacy need for most people.

The view of language teaching as an application of scientific descriptive linguistics – with a strong emphasis on the primacy of spoken language – became influential in many parts of the world. For this reason, writing did not become an important component of L2 teaching until fairly recently. The neglect of written language was most conspicuous in the United States between the 1940s and the 1960s, when the view of language as speech was institutionalized through the work of Leonard Bloomfield and Charles C. Fries.

The rise of L2 studies in U.S. higher education

Although U.S. higher education institutions began to enroll a significant number of international English as a second language (ESL) students starting in the late nineteenth century, the teaching of ESL did not receive serious attention until the 1940s. At this time, the potential threat of totalitarianism coming into Latin American countries made the teaching of English to people from those nations a matter of national security for the United States, especially given their geographic proximity. To provide English instruction and develop pedagogical materials for those Spanish-speaking students, the English Language Institute (ELI), the first intensive language program of its kind, was created at the University of Michigan in 1941 with Charles C. Fries as its director. After World War II, the ELI expanded its scope to provide instruction for international students from other countries.

The curriculum at the Michigan ELI reflected the influence of Sweet's work as well as Fries's strong commitment to the application of descriptive linguistics (Allen, 1973). The production of extended written discourse was not one of the instructional goals of the ELI because Fries (1945), like Sweet, assumed that students would be able to write once they mastered the structure and sounds of a language. Although written script was sometimes used, it was usually to facilitate the learning of spoken language through the use of printed materials developed at the ELI. The ELI also provided professional preparation in the teaching of ESL, contributing to the creation of intensive English programs across the nation (modeled on the ELI) as well as the professionalization of the field of *teaching* ESL (hence TESL) in the United States and abroad. The teaching of writing, however, was not a significant part of the ESL teacher's preparation at least until the late 1950s.

In the context of foreign language teaching, this development was paralleled by the work of Leonard Bloomfield. Because of his strong commitment to the application of linguistics to the teaching of language – which was inspired by the work of Sweet (1899/1964) and Otto Jespersen (1904), among others – his pedagogy, which he had begun to develop as early as 1914, focused exclusively on spoken language. Parallel to these developments, reading had been the primary goal of instruction in the foreign language teaching community since the early twentieth century. Only in the 1940s was Bloomfield's *Outline Guide for the Practical Study of Foreign Language* (1942) adopted by the Intensive Language Program of the American Council of Learned Societies as well as by the Army Specialized Training Program (ASTP).

Later, the ASTP Method – which was informed by Bloomfield's pedagogical work – and Fries's oral approach were consolidated to form what came to be known as the audiolingual approach; this became influential in both ESL and foreign language classrooms. However, the presence of an increasing number of international ESL students in higher education and required college composition courses led to the emergence of instruction in second language writing in U.S. higher education institutions.[2]

L2 issues in English departments

In English departments, which had been offering required first-year composition courses since the late nineteenth century, L2 writing instruction first became a serious concern. After World War II (1939–1945), the number of international students in the United States began to increase rapidly, especially at research institutions. Between 1940 and 1950, the number rose from 6,570 to 29,813 (Institute of International Education, 1961). No longer able to ignore the presence of non-native speakers, teachers and administrators of composition began to create special sections of freshman English courses. Although some institutions labeled these courses remedial, others considered them equivalent to composition courses required of native-English speakers and awarded ESL students college credit for such courses.

Reflecting the increasing recognition of the instructional problem, L2 writing instruction became a significant issue at annual meetings of the Conference on College Composition and Communication (CCCC), which was established in 1949 as the primary professional forum at which teachers and scholars gathered to discuss the field. During the 1950s, ESL panels and workshops at CCCC were attended by composition teachers as well as ESL teachers. Many second language specialists at CCCC recommended the use of materials developed at the Michigan ELI because no other available textbooks for L2 learners were informed by linguistic perspectives. Although these materials were intended for the teaching of spoken language in intensive programs, they were targeted to L2 students, in contrast to available composition textbooks that had been developed for L1 students.

In the late 1950s, concern with L2 writing issues began to shift gradually from composition studies to second language studies. The professionalization of second language teachers, prompted by the creation of the Michigan ELI and other teacher preparation programs, led ESL specialists to argue that L2 students should be taught only by trained specialists (now that such training was available). As a result, many composition specialists of the time lost interest in ESL issues. By the mid-1960s, attendance at ESL sessions of CCCC had become so small that at the 1966 meeting the discouraged members of the ESL workshop decided not to meet there again. In the same year, a new organization was founded to serve the needs and interests of L2 specialists in general: TESOL (Teachers of English to Speakers of Other Languages). Consequently, writing issues were divided into L1 and L2 components, and L2 writing issues came to be situated almost exclusively in second language studies – or more specifically, in the area of Teaching English as a Second Language (TESL). Thus, the *disciplinary division of labor* between composition studies and second language studies was firmly established.[3]

Second language writing as a subdiscipline of TESL

With the continuing increase of international students in U.S. higher education and the creation of the disciplinary division of labor between L1 and L2 composition, preparing international ESL students for required first-year composition courses became an important responsibility for ESL teachers in intensive English programs, which were usually external to college curricula.[4] In other words, the intensive English program began to assume a remedial role in relation to the composition program. When second language writing instruction became part of ESL programs in the early 1960s, however, ESL teachers were not specifically prepared for the new responsibility because their professional preparation, if any, focused almost exclusively on teaching the spoken language. It was clear to many that a pedagogy in second language writing was needed for intermediate ESL students who had completed the oral component of the program but who were yet not prepared for first-year composition courses. For this reason, second language writing emerged as a "subdiscipline" (Ferris & Hedgcock, 1998, p. 5) of TESL with a strong pedagogical emphasis. A number of pedagogical approaches were proposed, each representing a different conception of the nature of writing,[5] several of which are discussed briefly.

Writing as sentence-level structure

In response to the gap between the need to prepare ESL students for free composition – or the production of "an original discourse . . . about some given subject matter" (Erazmus, 1960, p. 25) – and the lack of writing pedagogy, ESL specialists attempted to extend the application of existing principles of second language pedagogy (i.e., the oral approach and the audiolingual approach) to the teaching of second language writing. Edward Erazmus, who at the time was a staff member of the Michigan ELI, attempted to reintroduce the use of free composition exercises as a way of developing fluency in writing. He also suggested the application of Kenneth Pike's tagmemics as an invention heuristic, and this later became influential in the field of composition studies. However, arguments for free composition exercises were dismissed as "naive traditional views" by those who, from the perspective of contrastive linguistics and a behavioral theory of learning, believed that "any free, random, hit-or-miss activity" should be "eliminated wherever possible, so that errors arising from the native-to-target language transfer can be avoided" (Pincas, 1962, p. 185). Instead, the use of controlled composition, an approach that focused on sentence-level structure, was proposed. Informed by a behavioral, habit-formation theory of learning, controlled composition consisted of combining and substitution exercises that were designed to facilitate the learning of sentence structures by providing students with "no freedom to make mistakes" (Pincas, 1982, p. 91).

The limitation of controlled composition soon became clear, however, because sentence-level grammar exercises did not help students to produce original sentences, let alone free composition. For this reason, the use of guided composition, which provided less rigid structural guidance, was devised. In its broadest conception, guided composition "includes any writing for which students are given assistance such as a model to follow, a plan or outline to expand from, a partly-written version with indications of how to complete it, or pictures that show a new subject to write about in the same way as something that has been read" (Pincas, 1982, p. 102). Despite some efforts to provide empirical support for fluency over accuracy (e.g., Brière, 1966), a consensus seemed to have emerged that "composing – writing beyond the sentence – must be guided or controlled" (Slager, 1966, p. 77). Although the teaching of sentence-level structure continues to be a concern in many ESL writing classrooms, its place in writing pedagogy has been a controversial issue (see Ferris, 1999; Truscott, 1996, 1999).

Writing as discourse-level structure

Neither controlled nor guided composition provided adequate preparation for free composition, however, because both focused almost exclusively on sentence-level structures. Observing the discrepancy between students' ability to produce grammatically correct sentences and the ability to achieve "logical organization" as judged by native English speaking (NES) readers, Robert B. Kaplan (1966) argued that the problem stemmed from the transfer of L1 structures beyond the sentence level. He was especially influenced by composition specialist Francis Christensen, whose "Generative Rhetoric of the Paragraph" (1965) extended the analysis of linguistic structure to the level of the paragraph. Drawing on the principles of contrastive analysis and the Sapir-Whorf hypothesis, Kaplan suggested that paragraph structures, like sentence structures, were language and culture specific, a founding principle of the field of contrastive rhetoric (discussed more fully in Chapter 9, this volume, by Connor). Kaplan's suggestion led to a realization that "writing is much more than an orthographic symbolization of speech; it is, most importantly, a *purposeful selection and organization of experience*" (Arapoff, 1967, p. 33).

The emphasis on "rhetoric," narrowly defined as the organizational structure, came to be conceived of as an intermediate step between controlled or guided exercises at the sentence level and free composition at the other extreme. In the 1980s, the development of discourse analysis and text linguistics in the United States and Europe provided various theoretical and methodological frameworks for investigating written discourse systematically, and researchers began to examine structures of written discourse in various languages and their possible influences on L2 texts. Alternative explanations for L2 textual structures were also explored, and the notion of contrastive rhetoric came to be defined less deterministically. In recent years, contrastive rhetoric research has evolved into a field of research of its own, encompassing more than just the organizational structure of written discourse (see Connor, 1996, Chapter 9 this volume; Panetta, 2001). Yet implications of contrastive rhetoric research in the context of the second language writing classroom remain a point of contention (see Kubota, 1998; Leki, 1991; Matsuda, 1997).

Writing as process

Until well into the 1970s, the teaching of second language writing focused mostly on the features of L2 written text – orthography, sentence-level structure, and discourse-level structure – and the way L2 student texts deviated from the L1 norm. In the late 1970s and the 1980s, however, a number of developments in both composition studies and second language studies prompted second language writing teachers and researchers to consider factors other than properties of the texts themselves. In composition studies, the interest had begun to shift from textual features to the *process* of writing itself, with researchers from various philosophical and methodological orientations investigating the processes underlying the production of written discourse (e.g., Emig, 1971; Flower & Hayes, 1981).[6]

The notion of writing as process was introduced to L2 studies by Vivian Zamel (1976), who argued that advanced L2 writers are similar to L1 writers and can benefit from instruction emphasizing the process of writing. Rather than the view of writing as a reproduction of previously learned syntactic or discourse structures, the process-based approach emphasized the view of writing as a process of developing organization as well as meaning. Invention strategies, multiple drafts, and formative feedback – both by the teacher and by peers – also became important parts of writing instruction in many L2 writing classrooms. Although some L2 teachers – following Hairston (1982) and others in composition studies – enthusiastically promoted the process-based approach, characterizing its arrival as a paradigm shift (e.g., Raimes, 1983b), others warned against its uncritical acceptance (e.g., Horowitz, 1986; Susser, 1994). The applicability in the L2 context of pedagogical practices that had been developed for L1 writers also came to be questioned, and researchers began to examine L2 writing processes to see how they were similar to *and* different from L1 processes (for overviews of L2 writing process research, see Krapels, 1990; Sasaki, 2000; Silva, 1993).

Writing as language use in context

The introduction of writing as process was paralleled by a development in second language studies – that is, English for Specific Purposes – which considered language and writing in the specific context of their use (see Johns & Dudley-Evans, 1991) as well as the development of English for Academic Purposes (EAP) (see Jordan, 1997), a major emphasis prompted by an increase of composition courses designed specifically for international ESL students in English-dominant countries. This movement was also fueled by the demand for writing instruction for a growing number of non-native English-speaking graduate students, particularly in the United States.

If instruction that was specific to the context of language use was to be provided, an understanding of the various contexts of writing first had to be developed. For this reason, EAP researchers began to describe various aspects of writing in relation to their specific context of use, including features of academic genre (for a review, see Johns, Chapter 8 this volume) and academic writing needs as well as tasks that are required in courses across the discipline. The reconceptualization of errors in light of their effects on a native English speaking academic audience has also taken place as part of this focus (see Frodesen & Holten, Chapter 6 this volume). As a result of these developments, ESL writing courses at many institutions were reconceived as preparation for writing in academic discourse communities rather than as remediation for required composition courses, although the ability of language teachers to provide domain-specific language instruction has been questioned by some teachers (see Spack, 1988).

The limitations of pedagogical focus

These pedagogical approaches, which were based on differing conceptions of writing, emphasize different aspects of second language writing, but they are by no means mutually exclusive. As Raimes (1983a) writes, few teachers are "so devoted to one approach as to exclude all others" (p. 11). Yet in the professional literature, these approaches have often been pitted against one another, resulting in "a rather unproductive approach cycle" that did not "encourage consensus on important issues, preservation of legitimate insights, synthesis of a body of knowledge, or principled evaluation of approaches" (Silva, 1990, p. 18). Further aggravating the situation was the lack of professional preparation opportunities in the teaching of L2 writing. Until fairly recently, few post-baccalaureate professional preparation programs in TESL or related fields offered a course in second language writing. With few opportunities for professional preparation, teachers of L2 writing often relied on textbooks as their source of pedagogical knowledge coupled with their own classroom experience for most of their preparation in the field. Thus, textbooks and teacher "lore" (North, 1987) were their preparation. However, as Raimes (1986) has pointed out, "new theories and approaches are . . . often slow to find their way into practice" because of the influence of "the oppositions in the field" as well as "publishing and marketing demands" (p. 157).

ESL writing issues in composition studies in North America

While ESL writing pedagogy and research flourished in second language studies, ESL writing issues were conspicuously absent from composition studies for many years because of the disciplinary division of labor (Matsuda, 1998, 1999). Although there were some exceptions, ESL concerns were virtually nonexistent in composition studies between the mid 1960s and the late 1970s. In the meantime, the ESL student population in U.S. higher education continued to grow, as reflected in the annual Open Doors Reports issued by the Institute of International Education. The number of ESL writers was further increased by the advent of open admissions policies in the 1960s and the 1970s, which brought in numbers of immigrant ESL students who had previously been excluded from higher education.

Although the quantity of intensive English programs was also increasing, composition instructors in general continued to face the challenge of working with ESL writers because the number of institutions enrolling international ESL students far outnumbered those that offered special ESL programs. Even when ESL programs were available, L2 writers' "written accent" – L2 textual features that deviated markedly from L1 texts – would not often disappear after a few months of instruction. As a result, many international ESL students seeking a baccalaureate degree – in many cases after completing intensive language courses – were placed in basic writing courses before becoming eligible to enroll in required first-year composition courses.

The field of basic writing,[7] a subfield of composition studies, emerged in the 1970s as a result of open admissions policies at many urban institutions – most notably, the City University of New York (CUNY) – and brought a significant number of traditionally excluded groups of students to U.S. higher education. Although basic writing was concerned with all students who were enrolled in basic writing courses, its primary focus was "native-born" rather than "foreign-born" students because of the differing needs of the two groups. Some institutions, such as Hunter College, created separate courses for NES basic writers and ESL students, but many institutions, because of the lack of resources, placed ESL writers into basic writing courses that were taught by teachers with little or no preparation in working with ESL writers. Thus, the placement of ESL writers in basic writing classes became a point of contention. Many argued that ESL and basic writers should be taught separately because of their differing needs; others – especially those who had background in both ESL and writing – argued that they could be taught together profitably.[8]

Contrary to popular belief that L1 composition influences L2 composition but not the other way around, some insights from second language studies have been applied to L1 composition studies as a way of addressing the needs of NES basic writers. For instance, Mina Shaughnessy, a pioneer in the field of basic writing, suggested that "many of the techniques developed in foreign language teaching seem to be applicable to basic writing" (1976, p. 162) because basic writers, "however different their linguistic backgrounds, are clearly colliding with many of the same stubborn contours of formal English...that are also troublesome to students learning English as a second language" (1977, p. 92). For this reason, a number of basic writing specialists suggested the application in basic writing instruction of theoretical and pedagogical insights from second language studies, including error analysis, vocabulary lists, and controlled composition. Shaughnessy (1977) also tried to improve writing teachers' attitudes toward basic writers by adapting "the view a teacher is more likely to have toward a foreign student learning English" (p. 121). As a result, "writing as a second language" came to the fore as a metaphor for characterizing the difficulties NES writers faced in learning to produce the type of formal writing required in higher education. However, the goal of these borrowed practices usually was to meet the needs of NES basic writers rather than to help ESL writers in basic writing programs (Matsuda & Jablonski, 2000).

Nevertheless, basic writing specialists, with their strong commitment to helping traditionally excluded students gain access to higher education, also welcomed the discussion of ESL issues in their publications. For instance, the *Journal of Basic Writing (JBW)*, established in 1975 and published by CUNY, has featured a number of articles concerning ESL writers. In 1985, the *JBW* officially announced the inclusion of ESL as a topic of interest, and articles focusing on ESL writing increased rapidly. The interest in ESL issues was so intense that in 1991 *College ESL*, also published by CUNY, was established as a journal that focused on "urban immigrant and refugee adults in college and pre-college settings" (editorial policy). The publication of this new journal was significant because it created additional space to discuss issues surrounding the traditionally neglected population of immigrant and refugee ESL writers. Yet it may also have reinforced the disciplinary division of labor between composition studies and second language studies, as the number of ESL-related articles in the *JBW* has dropped noticeably since the founding of *College ESL*.

Although intensive English programs and basic writing courses served a remedial role, composition teachers continued to face the challenge of working with ESL writers because a few semesters of additional language instruction would not usually allow them to achieve native-like writing proficiency. For this reason, ESL issues once again became an issue in composition studies in the late 1970s. As L2 writing issues became more visible and as teachers and researchers from both composition studies and second language studies became involved in second language writing research, the disciplinary boundary between the two became increasingly blurred. Although the collaborative efforts of L1 and L2 specialists have resulted in various publications, and although CCCC has recently adopted an official statement concerning second language writing and writers in North American college composition programs (CCCC Statement on Second Language Writing and Writers, 2001), more efforts need to be made to fully integrate L2 writing issues into composition studies (Matsuda, 1999; Silva, Leki, & Carson, 1997).

The emergence of an interdisciplinary field

As the exchange of insights between composition studies and second language studies has increased, researchers have come to recognize the complexity and multidisciplinary nature of second language writing research and teaching. For instance, Johnson and Roen (1989) pointed out that a "broader, multidisciplinary base is important in examining issues in L2 writing" because "no single theory from a single discipline can account for the complex and interacting social, cultural, cognitive, and linguistic processes involved" (p. 3). Kroll (1990) also writes that "for those engaged in teaching second language [writers], what is needed is both a firm grounding in the theoretical issues of first and second language writing *and* an understanding of a broad range of pedagogical issues that shape classroom writing instruction" (p. 2; italics mine). Consequently, second language writing evolved into an interdisciplinary field of inquiry situated in both composition studies and second language studies simultaneously.

With second language writing recognized as a legitimate field, the number of studies examining it has increased exponentially. Research articles on second language writing issues have become increasingly visible in journals such as *College ESL, English for Specific Purposes, Language*

Learning, and *TESOL Quarterly.* Some journals in composition studies – such as *College Composition and Communication, Teaching English in the Two-Year College, WPA: Writing Program Administration,* and *Written Communication* – have also begun to feature articles related to L2 writing. An increasing number of dissertations are now being devoted to second language writing. Only about a half dozen dissertations on L2 writing were written in the 1960s and about thirty in the 1970s, but this number rose to more than 150 in the 1980s and well over 300 in the 1990s. As the number of studies increased, the shortage of outlets for publication became apparent and the field began to develop its own disciplinary infrastructure to facilitate the creation and dissemination of knowledge about second language writing.

In response to the "explosion of interest in research on composing in a second language" (Leki & Silva, 1992, p. iii), the *Journal of Second Language Writing* was established in 1992, indicating "the maturing of scholarly communication in the field" (Tannacito, 1995, p. v). The number of books on second language writing also increased, including monographs (e.g., Connor, 1996; Fox, 1994; Johns, 1997; Li, 1996; Pennington, 1996; Rodby, 1992; Swales, 1990; Tucker, 1995) and edited collections (e.g., Belcher & Braine, 1995; Connor & Johns, 1990; Harklau, Losey, & Siegal, 1999; Kroll, 1990; Severino, Guerra, & Butler, 1997; Silva & Matsuda, 2001b) as well as collections of reprinted articles (e.g., DeLuca et al., 2002; Leeds, 1996; Silva & Matsuda, 2001a; Zamel & Spack, 1998). Textbooks for second language writing teachers also began to appear (Campbell, 1998; Ferris & Hedgcock, 1998; Grabe & Kaplan, 1996; Hyland, 2002; Leki, 1992; Reid, 1993). With the increase of scholarship in the field, bibliographic sources focusing on second language writing have also become available. *A Guide to Writing in English as a Second or Foreign Language: An Annotated Bibliography* (Tannacito, 1995) features annotations of articles, books, and conference presentations that were published before 1994. Since 1993, the *Journal of Second Language Writing* has been providing annotated bibliographies of recent related scholarship on a regular basis. A five-year compilation of this bibliography has also been separately published (Silva, Brice, & Reichelt, 1999). In addition, Polio and Mosele (1998) have developed an online bibliography that focuses on the teaching and learning of writing in second languages other than English.

Several conferences focusing solely on second language writing issues have been held, each resulting in an edited collection of essays and research reports. The first of these conferences, called Second Language Acquisition and Writing: A Multi-Disciplinary Approach, took place in the summer of 1996 at the University of Southampton (United Kingdom). Papers from that conference appear in Archibald and Jeffrey (1997). Additional edited collections resulting from recent conferences include papers from the Ohio State Conference on Reading-Writing Connections (Belcher & Hirvela, 2001) and papers from the first Symposium on Second Language Writing held at Purdue University (Silva & Matsuda, 2001b). The Symposium on Second Language Writing has now become a biennial event. In addition to specialized conferences, presentations and workshops focusing on second language writing issues have become increasingly visible at related conferences, such as those of the American Association for Applied Linguistics, the Conference on College Composition and Communication, and Teachers of English to Speakers of Other Languages, among others.

Opportunities for professional development have also increased in recent years. In the latest edition of *The Directory of Professional Preparation Programs in TESOL in the United States and Canada, 1999–2001* (Garshick, 1998), an increasing number of professional preparation programs in TESOL have indicated the availability of coursework in second language writing or writing in general. A few programs are even beginning to offer a specialization in second language writing that integrates coursework in both composition studies and second language studies. At a number of institutions – such as Indiana University of Pennsylvania, Northern Arizona University, Purdue University, the University of Toronto/Ontario Institute for the Studies in Education, and the University of New Hampshire – second language writing specialists work closely with doctoral students, contributing to the development of the next generation of second language writing teachers, researchers, and teacher educators.

Another important sign of maturity for second language writing as a field is the existence of metadisciplinary discourse – or self-conscious inquiries into its nature and history (Matsuda, 1998). Metadisciplinary discourse may include, for example, the discussion of methodology (e.g., Goldstein, 2001; Polio, 2001, Chapter 2 this volume), history (e.g., Matsuda, 1999, 2001; Raimes, 1991; Silva, 1990), interdisciplinary relations (e.g., Atkinson & Ramanathan, 1995; Matsuda, 1998; Matsuda & Jablonski, 2000; Santos, 1992; Silva, Leki, & Carson, 1997), and ideological and political issues (e.g., Benesch, 1993, 2001; Santos, 1992, 2001), as well as personal reflections on professional growth (e.g., Belcher & Connor, 2001; Blanton & Kroll, 2002; Kroll, 2001), and the general discussion of the status of the field (e.g., Atkinson, 2000; Kaplan, 2000; Santos, Atkinson, Erickson, Matsuda, & Silva, 2000).

Thus far, the field has focused mostly on issues that are specific to the needs of international ESL students in U.S. higher education because of the historical circumstances surrounding the origin of second language writing; more recently, however, there has been an increasing attention to immigrant and refugee students in North America (e.g., Harklau, Losey, & Siegal, 1999).[9] This is not to say that research in contexts other than U.S. higher education or second languages other than English has not taken place. As Reichelt (1999) points out, there is a growing body of literature on foreign language writing in the United States that draws on both L1 and ESL composition research. An increasing number of studies have also examined L2 writing instruction outside the United States (e.g., Tarnopolsky, 2000), with many such studies coming out of Hong Kong and Japan. Unfortunately, these studies are often circulated locally and tend to remain unknown to researchers and teachers in other countries. The lack of interaction among scholars and teachers in various sites is problematic: just as theories of writing derived only from first language writers "can at best be extremely tentative and at worst totally invalid" (Silva, Leki, & Carson, 1997, p. 402), theories of second language writing derived only from one language or one context are also limited. For second language writing instruction to be most effective in various disciplinary and institutional contexts, it needs to reflect the findings of studies conducted in a wide variety of instructional contexts as well as disciplinary perspectives.

Directions for the future

The field of second language writing, which initially arose in reaction to immediate pedagogical concerns in U.S. higher education, has undergone a number of disciplinary and epistemological shifts to become an interdisciplinary field of inquiry with its own body of knowledge about the nature of second language writing and writing instruction. In addition, to facilitate and guide the development of knowledge, the field has developed its own disciplinary infrastructure and metadisciplinary discourse. Yet second language writing should not become completely independent from other fields that are also concerned with language and writing. Severing interdisciplinary ties would be counterproductive because the field does not have its own instructional domain; that is, L2 writing courses or programs are almost always situated in broader programs or departments, such as applied linguistics, composition studies, education, foreign languages, linguistics, and TESL. To maintain the field's ability to affect pedagogical decisions in a wide variety of institutional contexts, L2 writing teachers and researchers should continue to draw on and contribute to other domains of knowledge that may influence L2 writing instruction; in other words, the field of second language writing should be seen as a *symbiotic field* (Matsuda, 1998). As such, it can and should continue to provide an evolving discourse community in which specialists from various related fields can come together to discuss common issues and concerns – the nature of second language writing and writing instruction in various institutional contexts – and to negotiate differences in theoretical, ideological, and methodological perspectives.

Notes

1. Silva (1990) is an exception in that he begins his history from the 1940s.
2. For a personal perspective on the influence of the "Michigan approach" as it related to the teaching of writing in the 1960s, see Blanton (2002).
3. For a detailed discussion of ESL issues at CCCC and the creation of the disciplinary division of labor between L1 and L2 writing, see Matsuda (1999).
4. The interest in the teaching of ESL writing was not limited to the United States. While no other institutions placed so much emphasis on first-year composition courses as was found in U.S. higher education, growing skepticism about the audiolingual approach in the professional literature prompted second language teachers in other countries to explore different approaches to the teaching of writing.
5. For different perspectives on the development of pedagogical approaches or emphases, see Blanton (1995), Ferris and Hedgcock (1998), Leki (1992), Raimes (1991), Reid (1993), and Silva (1990).
6. For a succinct overview of L1 process pedagogy, see Tobin (2001).
7. The term "basic writing" first became popularized in the 1970s as an alternate for the term "remedial writing." Courses for L1 students with weak writing skills are also sometimes labeled "developmental writing." Such courses are considered below the level of freshman composition.
8. For an overview of placement options for ESL writers, see Silva (1994).
9. Kaplan (2000) contends that studies of issues related to L2 writing outside the United States have existed since the early part of the twentieth century, although, as Atkinson (2000) points out, they have not had a significant impact on the formation of the field of second language writing as "an organized academic field" (p. 318).

References

Allen, H. B. (1973). English as a second language. In T. A. Sebeok (Ed.), *Current trends in linguistics: Linguistics in North America* (Vol. 10, pp. 295–320). The Hague: Mouton.

Arapoff, N. (1967). Writing: A thinking process. *TESOL Quarterly, 1*(2), 33–39.

Archibald, A., & Jeffrey, G. (Eds.). (1997). *Second language acquisition and writing: A multidisciplinary approach*. Southampton, UK: The University of Southampton.

Atkinson, D. (2000). On Robert B. Kaplan's response to Terry Santos et al.'s "On the future of second language writing." *Journal of Second Language Writing, 9*, 317–320.

Atkinson, D., & Ramanathan, V. (1995). Cultures of writing: An ethnographic comparison of L1 and L2 university writing/language programs. *TESOL Quarterly, 29*, 539–568.

Belcher, D., & Braine, G. (Eds.). (1995). *Academic writing in a second language: Essays on research and pedagogy*. Norwood, NJ: Ablex.

Belcher, D., & Connor, U. (Eds.). (2001). *Reflections on multiliterate lives*. Clevedon, UK: Multilingual Matters.

Belcher, D., & Hirvela, A. (Eds.). (2001). *Linking literacies: Perspectives on L2 reading/writing connections*. Ann Arbor: University of Michigan Press.

Benesch, S. (1993). ESL, ideology, and the politics of pragmatism. *TESOL Quarterly, 27*, 705–717.

Benesch, S. (2001). Critical pragmatism: A politics of L2 composition. In T. Silva & P. K. Matsuda (Eds.), *On second language writing* (pp. 161–172). Mahwah, NJ: Lawrence Erlbaum.

Blanton, L. L. (1995). Elephants and paradigms: Conversations about teaching L2 writing. *College ESL, 5*(1), 1–21.

Blanton, L. L. (2002). As I was saying to Leonard Bloomfield: A personalized history of ESL/writing. In L. L. Blanton & B. Kroll et al., *ESL composition tales: Reflections on teaching* (pp. 135–162). Ann Arbor: University of Michigan Press.

Blanton, L. L., & Kroll, B., et al. (2002). *ESL composition tales: Reflections on teaching*. Ann Arbor: University of Michigan Press.

Bloomfield, L. (1942). *Outline guide for the practical study of foreign languages*. Special Publications of the Linguistic Society of America. Baltimore: Linguistic Society of America.

Brière, E. J. (1966). Quantity before quality in second language composition. *Language Learning, 16*, 141–151.

Campbell, C. (1998). *Teaching second-language writing: Interacting with text*. Boston: Heinle & Heinle.

CCCC Statement on Second Language Writing and Writers. (2001). *College Composition and Communication, 52*, 669–674.

Christensen, F. (1965). A generative rhetoric of the paragraph. *College Composition and Communication, 16*, 144–156.

Connor, U. (1996). *Contrastive rhetoric: Cross-cultural aspects of second-language writing*. New York: Cambridge University Press.

Connor U., & Johns, A. M. (Eds.). (1990). *Coherence in writing: Research and pedagogical perspectives*. Alexandria, VA: TESOL.

DeLuca, G., Fox, L., Johnson, M. A., & Kogen, M. (Eds.). (2002). *Dialogue on writing: Rethinking ESL, basic writing, and first-year composition*. Mahwah, NJ: Lawrence Erlbaum.

Emig, J. (1971). *The composing process of twelfth graders*. Urbana, IL: National Council of Teachers of English.

Erazmus, E. (1960). Second language composition teaching at the intermediate level. *Language Learning, 10*, 25–31.

Ferris, D. (1999). The case for grammar correction in L2 writing classes: A response to Truscott (1966). *Journal of Second Language Writing, 8*, 1–11.

Ferris, D., & Hedgcock, J. (1998). *Teaching ESL composition: Purpose, process, and practice*. Mahwah, NJ: Lawrence Erlbaum.

Flower, L., & Hayes, J. R. (1981). A cognitive process theory of writing. *College Composition and Communication, 22*, 365–387.

Fox, H. (1994). *Listening to the world: Cultural issues in academic writing*. Urbana, IL: National Council of Teachers of English.

Fries, C. C. (1945). *Teaching and learning English as a foreign language*. Ann Arbor: University of Michigan Press.

Garschick, E. (Ed.). (1998). *The directory of professional preparation programs in TESOL in the United States and Canada, 1999–2001*. Alexandria, VA: TESOL.

Goldstein, L. (2001). For Kyla: What does the research say about responding to ESL writers? In T. Silva & P. K. Matsuda (Eds.), *On second language writing* (pp. 73–89). Mahwah, NJ: Lawrence Erlbaum.

Grabe, W., & Kaplan, R. B. (1996). *Theory and practice of writing: An applied linguistic perspective*. London: Longman.

Hairston, M. (1982). The winds of change: Thomas Kuhn and the revolution in the teaching of writing. *College Composition and Communication, 33,* 76–88.

Harklau, L., Losey, K. M., & Siegal, M. (Eds.). (1999). *Generation 1.5 meets college composition*. Mahwah, NJ: Lawrence Erlbaum.

Horowitz, D. (1986). Process, not product: Less than meets the eye. *TESOL Quarterly, 20,* 141–144.

Hyland, K. (2002). *Teaching and researching writing*. Harlow, England: Longman.

Institute of International Education. (1961). *Handbook on international study: For foreign nationals*. New York: Institute of International Education.

Jespersen, O. (1904). *How to teach a foreign language*. (Sophia Yhlen-Olsen Bertelsen, Trans.). London: Allen and Unwin.

Johns, A. M. (1997). *Text, role, and context: Developing academic literacies*. New York: Cambridge University Press.

Johns, A. M., & Dudley-Evans, T. (1991). English for specific purposes: International in scope, specific in purpose. *TESOL Quarterly, 25,* 297–314.

Johnson, D., & Roen, D. H. (Eds.). (1989). *Richness in writing: Empowering ESL writers*. New York: Longman.

Jordan, R. R. (1997). *English for academic purposes. A guide and resource book for teachers*. New York: Cambridge University Press.

Kaplan, R. B. (1966). Cultural thought patterns in inter-cultural education. *Language Learning, 16,* 1–20.

Kaplan, R. B. (2000). Response to "On the future of second language writing," Terry Santos (Ed.) et al. *Journal of Second Language Writing, 9,* 317–320.

Krapels, A. R. (1990). An overview of second language writing process research. In B. Kroll (Ed.), *Second language writing: Research insights for the classroom* (pp. 37–56). New York: Cambridge University Press.

Kroll, B. (Ed.). (1990). *Second language writing: Research insights for the classroom*. New York: Cambridge University Press.

Kroll, B. (2001). The composition of a life in composition. In T. Silva & P. K. Matsuda (Eds.), *On second language writing* (pp. 1–16). Mahwah, NJ: Lawrence Erlbaum.

Kubota, R. (1998). An investigation of L1–L2 transfer in writing among Japanese university students: Implications for contrastive rhetoric. *Journal of Second Language Writing, 7,* 69–100.

Leeds, B. (Ed.). (1996). *Writing in a second language: Insights from first and second language teaching and research*. New York: Longman.

Leki, I. (1991). Twenty-five years of contrastive rhetoric. Text analyses and writing pedagogies. *TESOL Quarterly, 25,* 123–143.

Leki, I. (1992). *Understanding ESL writers: A guide for teachers.* Portsmouth, NH: Boynton/Cook.

Leki, I., & Silva, T. (1992). From the editors. *Journal of Second Language Writing, 1*(1), iii–iv.

Li, X. (1996). *"Good writing" in cross cultural context.* Albany: SUNY Press.

Matsuda, P. K. (1997). Contrastive rhetoric in context: A dynamic model of L2 writing. *Journal of Second Language Writing, 6,* 45–60.

Matsuda, P. K. (1998). Situating ESL writing in a cross-disciplinary context. *Written Communication, 15,* 99–121.

Matsuda, P. K. (1999). Composition studies and ESL writing: A disciplinary division of labor. *College Composition and Communication, 50,* 699–721.

Matsuda, P. K. (2001). Reexamining audiolingualism: On the genesis of reading and writing in L2 studies. In D. Belcher & A. Hirvela (Eds.), *Linking literacies: Perspectives on L2 reading/writing connections* (pp. 84–105). Ann Arbor: University of Michigan Press.

Matsuda, P. K., & Jablonski, J. (2000). Beyond the L2 metaphor: Towards a mutually transformative model of ESL/WAC collaboration. *Academic Writing, 1.* http://aw.colostate.edu/articles/matsuda_jablonski2000.htm.

North, S. M. (1987). *The making of knowledge in composition: Portrait of an emerging field.* Upper Montclair, NJ: Boynton/Cook.

Panetta, C. G. (Ed.). (2001). *Contrastive rhetoric theory revisited and redefined.* Mahwah, NJ: Lawrence Erlbaum.

Passy, P. (1929). *La phonétique et ses applications.* Cambridge, UK: International Phonetic Association.

Pennington, M. (1996). *The computer and the non-native writer: A natural partnership.* Cresskill, NJ: Hampton Press.

Pincas, A. (1962). Structural linguistics and systematic composition teaching to students of English as a foreign language. *Language Learning, 7,* 185–195.

Pincas, A. (1982). *Teaching English writing.* London: Macmillan.

Polio, C. (2001). Research methodology in second language writing research: The case of text-based studies. In T. Silva & P. K. Matsuda (Eds.), *On second language writing* (pp. 91–115). Mahwah, NJ: Lawrence Erlbaum.

Polio, C., & Mosele, P. (1998). *References on the teaching and learning of foreign language writing focusing on languages other than English.* Center for Language Education and Research, Michigan State University. http://polyglot.cal.msu.edu/clear/writing/.

Raimes, A. (1983a). *Techniques in teaching writing.* New York: Oxford University Press.

Raimes, A. (1983b). Tradition and revolution in ESL teaching. *TESOL Quarterly, 17,* 535–552.

Raimes, A. (1986). Teaching ESL writing: Fitting what we do to what we know. *The Writing Instructor, 5,* 153–166.

Raimes, A. (1991). Out of the woods: Emerging traditions in the teaching of writing. *TESOL Quarterly, 25,* 407–430.

Reichelt, M. (1999). Toward a more comprehensive view of L2 writing: Foreign language writing in the U.S. *Journal of Second Language Writing, 8,* 181–204.

Reid, J. M. (1993). *Teaching ESL writing.* Englewood Cliffs, NJ: Regents/Prentice Hall.

Rodby, J. (1992). *Appropriating literacy: Writing and reading in English as a second language*. Portsmouth, NH: Boynton/Cook.

Santos, T. (1992). Ideology in composition: L1 and ESL. *Journal of Second Language Writing, 1,* 1–15.

Santos, T. (2001). The place of politics in second language writing. In T. Silva & P. K. Matsuda (Eds.), *On second language writing* (pp. 173–190). Mahwah, NJ: Lawrence Erlbaum.

Santos, T., Atkinson, D., Erickson, M., Matsuda, P. K., & Silva, T. (2000). On the future of second language writing: A colloquium. *Journal of Second Language Writing, 9,* 1–20.

Sasaki, M. (2000). Toward an empirical model of EFL writing processes: An exploratory study. *Journal of Second Language Writing, 9,* 259–291.

Severino, C., Guerra, J. C., & Butler, J. E. (Eds.). (1997). *Writing in multicultural settings*. New York: Modern Language Association.

Shaughnessy, M. P. (1976). Basic writing. In G. Tate (Ed.), *Teaching composition: 10 bibliographical essays* (pp. 137–167). Fort Worth, TX: Texas Christian University Press.

Shaughnessy, M. P. (1977). *Errors and expectations: A guide for the teacher of basic writing*. New York: Oxford University Press.

Silva, T. (1990). Second language composition instruction: Developments, issues, and directions in ESL. In B. Kroll (Ed.), *Second language writing: Research insights for the classroom* (pp. 11–23). New York: Cambridge University Press.

Silva, T. (1993). Toward an understanding of the distinct nature of L2 writing: The ESL research and its implications. *TESOL Quarterly, 27,* 657–677.

Silva, T. (1994). An examination of writing program administrators' options for the placement of ESL students in first year writing classes. *WPA: Writing Program Administration, 18*(1–2), 37–43.

Silva, T., Brice, C., & Reichelt, M. (1999). *Annotated bibliography of scholarship in second language writing: 1993–1997*. Stamford, CT: Ablex.

Silva, T., Leki, I., & Carson, J. (1997). Broadening the perspective of mainstream composition studies: Some thoughts from the disciplinary margins. *Written Communication, 14,* 398–428.

Silva, T., & Matsuda, P. K. (Eds.). (2001a). *Landmark essays on English as a second language writing*. Mahwah, NJ: Lawrence Erlbaum.

Silva, T., & Matsuda, P. K. (Eds.). (2001b). *On second language writing*. Mahwah, NJ: Lawrence Erlbaum.

Slager, W. R. (1966). Controlling composition: Some practical classroom techniques. In R. B. Kaplan (Ed.), *Selected conference papers of the Association of Teachers of English as a Second Language* (pp. 77–85). Los Angeles: National Association for Foreign Student Affairs.

Spack, R. (1988). Initiating ESL students into the academic discourse community: How far should we go? *TESOL Quarterly, 22,* 29–51.

Susser, B. (1994). Process approaches in ESL/EFL writing instruction. *Journal of Second Language Writing, 3,* 31–47.

Swales, J. (1990). *Genre analysis: English in academic and research settings*. New York: Cambridge University Press.

Sweet, H. (1964). *The practical study of languages*. London: Oxford University Press. (Original work published 1899)

Tannacito, D. J. (1995). *A guide to writing English as a second or foreign language: An annotated bibliography of research and pedagogy.* Alexandria, VA: TESOL.

Tarnopolsky, O. (2000). Writing English as a foreign language: A report from Ukraine. *Journal of Second Language Writing, 9,* 209–226.

Tobin, L. (2001). Process pedagogy. In G. Tate, A. Rupiper, & K. Schick (Eds.), *A guide to composition pedagogies* (pp. 1–18). New York: Oxford University Press.

Truscott, J. (1996). The case against grammar correction in L2 writing classes. *Language Learning, 46,* 327–369.

Truscott, J. (1999). The case for "the case against grammar correction in L2 writing classes": A response to Ferris. *Journal of Second Language Writing, 8,* 111–122.

Tucker, A. (1995). *Decoding ESL: International students in the American college classroom.* Portsmouth, NH: Boynton/Cook.

Zamel, V. (1976). Teaching composition in the ESL classroom: What we can learn from research in the teaching of English. *TESOL Quarterly, 10,* 67–76.

Zamel, V., & Spack, R. (Eds.). (1998). *Negotiating academic literacies: Teaching and learning across languages and cultures.* Mahwah, NJ: Lawrence Erlbaum.

2 Research on second language writing: An overview of what we investigate and how

Charlene Polio

The main job for teachers of writing, whether their students be native speakers of the target language or second language learners, is to work with their students to help them achieve improved writing proficiency in accordance with student needs and course goals, advancing beyond their current skill level. How best to do this is, understandably, a concern that sits at the heart of the teaching enterprise. Many teachers are thus drawn into becoming researchers, wanting to investigate one or more of the many components that contribute to understanding writers and what is involved in promoting proficiency in writing.

Teachers who do not personally carry on their own research studies might additionally be drawn to research findings through interest in reading about the work of others whose questions under investigation help them better understand their own work as writing teachers. Even teachers who might claim that they are not researchers and are not research oriented nevertheless directly or indirectly tap into research findings as they choose textbooks, plan curricula and syllabi, work with student writers, and otherwise carry out their teaching lives. Thus, all writing teachers need to have a solid grounding in knowing what research investigations have already illuminated for us about the nature of writing, learning to write, and being a writer. Further, when they become knowledgeable enough about aspects of research design to be able to keep abreast of new developments, they are also able to reject claims that lack credibility, often as a direct result of flawed research design. This chapter should help novice teachers to become familiar with a range of research in second language (L2) writing and to consider some distinctions in different research designs – perhaps providing a foundation to help them become researchers as well.

As recently as twenty-five years ago, there was little published research on L2 writing. However, during the past twenty to twenty-five years, the amount of empirical research[1] on L2 writing has been increasing exponentially and shows no signs of diminishing. We only have to look at journals related to teaching English as a second language (ESL), most notably *TESOL Quarterly*, and foreign language teaching, most notably *Modern Language Journal*, to see a large increase in the number of research articles on writing. In addition, in 1992, a journal devoted solely to L2 writing, the *Journal of Second Language Writing,* began publication. Other journals once exclusively devoted to issues in first language composition, such as *Written Communication* and *Research in the Teaching of English,* have also relatively recently begun to publish research articles dealing with L2 writers and L2 writing.

Because L2 writing is a relatively new area of inquiry, an overview of the research should, on one hand, not be a daunting task. On the other hand, approaches to research on L2 writing are varied, thus making studies somewhat difficult to categorize and compare. One reason for this variation is the range of backgrounds of the researchers and the interdisciplinary nature of the field, as pointed out by Matsuda in Chapter 1 in this volume. Furthermore, the objects of inquiry are varied and may include writers' texts, writing processes, backgrounds, and attitudes, as well as their teachers, and the social context, both within and outside the writing classroom. These are exactly the sorts of topics that are addressed in most of the subsequent chapters in this volume.

This chapter is an overview of empirical research studies in second language writing, demonstrating that claims made about teaching and learning writing derive from the accumulated findings of numerous investigations in the field. The emphasis of this review is on the methodology and techniques used in the research as opposed to a summary of findings, and the chapter is organized according to the main object of inquiry, or the focus of the research. With such an overview, those new to the field will obtain an understanding of what L2 writing researchers study, what kinds of questions they ask, and how they go about finding the answers. For teachers, learning about the types of questions researchers ask will give them a better understanding of the complexity of L2 writing and identify for them the range of factors related to teaching L2 writers, issues that underpin the discussions presented on a topic-by-topic basis in later chapters of this volume. Furthermore, by reading about the research on areas of immediate concern to them in their own classrooms, teachers will be better able to examine their own practices critically.

Organization of chapter

Any discussion or review of research in the field of writing faces the challenge of determining how to present the material so as to group studies in a consistent and illuminating way without distorting the original goals of the researchers. The approach that has been selected for the discussion in this chapter is to focus on *what* the researchers were investigating, that is, to classify the studies under review according to the main focus of the research. The method for doing this, and a key organizational feature of this chapter, is the presentation of four tables, each listing studies that fall under the following categories:

1. Studies that focus on writers' *texts*, that is, the written products they compose (this focus relates to the discussion in Chapter 5 by Ferris, Chapter 6 by Frodesen and Holten, and Chapter 7 by Hamp-Lyons later in this volume)
2. Studies that focus on writers' *processes,* that is, *how* writers produce their texts (this is discussed by some second language writers in Chapter 4 by Silva et al. in this volume)
3. Studies that focus on *participants* in the learning and teaching process (this is the focus of Chapter 4 by Silva et al. and Chapter 3 by Cumming in the next section of this volume)
4. Studies that focus on the *context* of L2 writing both inside and outside the classroom (the focus of Chapter 8 by Johns, Chapter 9 by Connor, Chapter 10 by Grabe, and Chapter 13 by Leki in this volume)

Clearly, there is some overlap among categories. For example, studies that focus on the participants certainly do so within a social context. Thus, we can in some ways consider research on the participants as a subset of research on the social context, just as research on the writing process is a subset of research on the participants. Furthermore, much of the research cited here has more than one focus or more than one research question.[2] For example, some studies may ask questions about both the nature of teacher feedback and the writers' text, as opposed to simply being concerned with the effect of feedback on the text (issues that Ferris in Chapter 5 as well as Frodesen and Holten in Chapter 6 take up in greater detail in this volume).

In the discussions of specific research investigations into L2 writing, categorized according to the four areas or categories identified above, I shall review the foci, techniques, and methodological approaches used in the studies under review, try to provide a closer analysis of some of the key research questions that motivated the studies under discussion, and include some interpretive comments related to key aspects of the approaches and issues raised in the studies themselves, particularly pointing to potential methodological concerns. What unites all the studies identified in the tables are that they are undeniably examples of empirical research; they have been selected not only as examples of one (or more) of the four categories above, but also on the basis of their accessibility, that is, most of the works to be referred to are in print and in refereed journals. The tables include some works not discussed in the text and thus provide additional resources to direct readers to a wider range of empirical studies on the categories under focus.

Understanding empirical approaches

A key aspect in any research study is the approach that was used to set up the study and/or collect the data under investigation. For the purposes of this chapter, I have selected a set of five categories that have been used in a variety of educational research settings and are typical of approaches used in research on writing. A brief explanation of each of the categories follows.[3]

1. *Experimental*: In experimental (and quasi-experimental) research, the researcher actually manipulates an independent variable (which is some kind of treatment created for the purpose of the experiment) to study its effect. A key test for the rigor of experimental research is to provide results that can be replicated by other researchers conducting similar experiments at a later time (referred to as replicability). An example of experimental research in writing would be a study that has one group of students receive explicit instruction in certain grammatical features of English while another group (the control group) receives no explicit instruction. After the instruction (i.e., the treatment) is over, both groups are asked to write on the same topic and their level of grammatical accuracy is compared.

2. *Correlational*: In correlational research, the relationship between two or more variables (that is, the components of interest) is described with no causal relationship implied. An example would be a study that examines the relationship between reading scores on a multiple-choice comprehension test and writing scores on an essay test.

3. *Causal-comparative*: Causal-comparative research is somewhat similar to correlational research in that it also explores a relationship between variables; the difference is that subjects are divided into groups according to some categorical variable (e.g., gender, native language). An example would be a study that compares the nature of written peer feedback provided by male versus female students.

4. *Survey*: Survey research obtains answers from a large sample of the population in order to describe some characteristic of the population. An example would be a study of ESL students who frequent their campus learning resource center or writing lab to find out what aspects of writing they most frequently requested help with.

5. *Qualitative*. Generally, qualitative research attempts to explore individuals in their natural setting by using several different sources of data or methods of data collection. Qualitative research, perhaps because it does not begin from a predetermined set of questions for investigation, is the most problematic to define.[4] In general, the findings of qualitative research provide a more holistic picture of the phenomenon being

studied than the quantitative methods described previously. Within qualitative research, one may use a wide variety of techniques, including interviews, observation, or document analysis. An example of a qualitative study would be one in which a single novice writing teacher is observed and interviewed periodically for an entire term of teaching and various class documents are collected and analyzed. The research write-up then attempts to provide a rich portrait of the novice writing teacher's decision-making processes.

Structure of the tables

Each of the four tables classifying the studies under review offers a grid with six key pieces of information. First, the main focus of one or more key studies is identified, followed by a listing of the more specific focus found in each of the studies cited. These labels help to single out the types of concerns that published writing research has investigated. The third column in each table gives the authors and dates of studies that exemplify the particular focus. This is followed by an articulation of at least one specific research question of the given study. The next column identifies the specific measurement instrument or research technique used to analyze or investigate the research question as posed in the study. The final column categorizes the research approach of the study as a whole by assigning a label naming which of the five approaches identified in the previous section has been used.

The purpose of the discussions that follow is to use broad strokes to help teachers see what has been studied and how it has been researched. These discussions should help teachers identify the range of factors related to writing and understand why easy answers to questions regarding the teaching of L2 writing are not readily available. In subsequent chapters in this volume, most of the authors review empirical research within a more narrow perspective as they elaborate on a single component in the whole picture of teaching L2 writing.

Research on L2 writers' texts

Foci and techniques

The greatest number of studies described in this chapter fall under the first of the four categories identified, namely, research on L2 writers' text. Although the published studies presented here in Table 2.1 often examine characteristics of the writers, instruction, and the writing process, they are ultimately concerned with features of the text. This is arguably to be expected given that the majority of research has the goal of helping students produce better texts, definitions of quality aside.

TABLE 2.1. STUDIES FOCUSING ON WRITERS' TEXTS

Main focus	Specific focus	Study	Research question	Technique	Approach
Overall quality		Engber, 1995	How does overall writing quality correlate with other characteristics of a text?	Holistic scale	Correlational
		Tsang, 1996	How does a particular program of writing instruction affect overall writing quality?	Analytic scale	Experimental
Linguistic accuracy		Hamp-Lyons & Henning, 1991	How can various writing traits be reliably and validly measured?	Holistic scale	Correlational
		Robb et al., 1986	What is the effect of various types of feedback on linguistic accuracy?	Error-free T-units	Experimental
Syntactic complexity		Ishikawa, 1995	How do L2 writers' texts change over time?		Causal-comparative
		Bardovi-Harlig & Bofman, 1989	How do different groups of writers' texts differ?	Clauses/T-unit	Causal-comparative
		Coombs, 1986	What does a group of writers' writings look like with regard to syntactic complexity?	Document analysis	Qualitative
Lexicon	• Lexical sophistication	Laufer & Nation, 1995	What is a valid and reliable method of lexical quality?	Lexical frequency profile	Causal-comparative
	• Lexical variation	Engber, 1995	What measures of lexical quality correlate with overall quality?	Type/token	Correlational
	• Lexical errors	Kobayashi & Rinnert, 1992	How do writers' texts differ on different tasks?	Errors/words	Experimental

Category	Subcategory	Author	Research question	Measure	Design
Content	• Quality	Hedgcock & Lefkowitz, 1992	How do different types of feedback affect the content of an essay?	Holistic scale	Experimental
	• Higher-level propositions	Kepner, 1991	How do different types of feedback affect the content of an essay?	Number of propositions showing a variety of cognitive processes	Experimental
	• Topics	Valdes et al., 1992	How do students' writing differ at different levels of proficiency?	Document analysis	Qualitative
Mechanics		Tsang, 1996	How does a particular program of writing instruction affect overall writing quality?	Holistic scale	Experimental
Discourse features	• Quality	Devine et al., 1993	How do different groups of writers organize a text?	Holistic scale	Casual-comparative
	• Organization	Schneider & Connor, 1990	How do high- and low-rated essays differ?	Topic-structure analysis	Casual-comparative
	• Metadiscourse	Allison, 1995	What are some characteristics of NNSs' essays regarding assertions?	Document analysis	Qualitative
	• Cohesion	Reynolds, 1995	How do NS and NNS essays differ?	Analysis of lexical Repetition	Causal-comparative
	• Register	Shaw & Liu, 1998	How does L2 writing change over time?	Range of features	Causal-comparative

A variety of techniques or measures can be used to study either the overall quality of a text or a specific feature or construct within a text, such as linguistic accuracy or syntactic complexity. Some researchers look at an aspect of the lexicon, content, mechanics, or coherence and discourse features. Choosing the best measure is usually not straightforward. Researchers who want to quantify the *quality* of a complete text can choose from a range of holistic measures, which assign one overall score to an essay, such as the Test of Written English scale, used, for example, in the study by Engber (1995) on lexical proficiency. Another option is a composite score that is derived from the sum of scores assigned to various aspects of a text. This type of scale is called an analytic scale. One commonly used analytic scale, taken from Jacobs et al. (1981), gives scores in six areas resulting in a final score of up to 100. This scale is used, for example, by Tsang (1996) in a study involving reading and writing.

Studies that attempt to quantify linguistic accuracy or syntactic complexity have a range of measures as well. Measures of linguistic accuracy are reviewed in both Polio (1997) and Wolfe-Quintero, Inagaki, and Kim (1998). Constructs like lexical sophistication or lexical variation can pose identification and measurement challenges to researchers trying to select which of the potential measures best capture quality or development. Measures for these constructs are discussed by Engber (1995) and Laufer and Nation (1995).

Content, coherence, and discourse features are more difficult to operationalize. Content is generally a matter of quality, and thus researchers will often use a holistic scale that is part of an analytic scale assessing the entire piece of writing (e.g., Hedgcock & Lefkowitz, 1992). Other attempts to quantify content are infrequent, but one such example is the study by Kepner (1991), which tabulated the presence of higher-level propositions in her study on the effect of various types of feedback. Valdes, Haro, and Echevarriarza (1992) took another approach by looking qualitatively at the topics written by students at various levels of proficiency, thus making no attempt to assess or measure content but rather to describe it.

And finally, some researchers have examined writers' texts to look at coherence or discourse features not included in the categories discussed above. Although a few using holistic scales (e.g., Devine, Railey, & Boshoff, 1993) attempted to assess quality, most of the studies were really concerned with describing a range of discourse elements, such as metadiscourse features (Allison, 1995) or cohesion (Reynolds, 1995). The studies in this category vary more than those in other groupings as there is no common construct, such as grammatical accuracy or lexical sophistication, being measured. Hence the techniques used are not comparable, meaning we cannot say that any one is preferable to any other; they are examining different text features.

Research questions

Researchers examine writers' texts for a variety of reasons. One of the most common reasons is to study the effect of some intervention, such as kind of feedback (Hedgcock & Lefkowitz, 1992) or program of instruction (Tsang, 1996), on writing. Hence, these studies are ultimately concerned with a change in text quality. Some researchers, such as Kobayashi and Rinnert (1992), ask about writers' writing on different tasks. They are concerned with the cognitive processes involved in producing different kinds of writing or writing under different circumstances. And finally, some of the studies focus on development or change over time (Valdes, Haro, & Echevarriarza, 1992), including which measures best capture development (Ishikawa, 1995; Laufer & Nation, 1995).

Approaches and issues

Much of the research in the approaches and issues category is experimental; the researcher manipulates the independent variable (the intervention, as in Tsang, or the task, as in Kobayashi & Rinnert) to study its effect on the dependent variable (some feature of the text). Much of the research is also causal-comparative. Researchers compare groups of writers based on some characteristic such as their cognitive model (defined by Devine, Railey, & Boshoff, 1993, as what writers pay attention to when they write) or how high their essay was rated (Schneider & Connor, 1990). They study how the characteristics of the groups are related to some feature of the learners' writing. Correlational research is similar, but instead, two variables are correlated, as in Engber's study: she examined the relationship between overall quality and different measures related to the lexicon. This is different from a study such as Schneider and Connor's, which separated the essays into two groups (high and low rated), creating an additional variable, and then examined the texts' organization. And finally, a small set of studies in this category fall under the qualitative approach. Coombs (1986) examined the texts of L2 learners of German with regard to syntactic complexity, and Valdes, Haro, and Echevarriarza (1992) looked at how the topics of L2 learners of Spanish changed over time. Both these studies used document analysis, that is, they simply compared the features of essays from students at different proficiency levels. Neither, like much of the qualitative research mentioned in this chapter, drew from multiple sources of data, but they do share the characteristic of examining the data without predetermined hypotheses.

Because most of the research that focuses on writers' texts is experimental, correlational, or causal-comparative, the most important issue that researchers need to deal with is the reliability and validity of their measures. Hamp-Lyons (Chapter 7 this volume) also addresses the determination of reliability and validity, and I have discussed these issues more extensively in Polio (2001). To summarize, much research does not report interrater reliability, and this is problematic because a lack of reliability in the measure can mask significant findings. In addition, we do not know the extent to which the various measures that claim to measure the same characteristic really are doing so. In other words, are the various measures valid?[5] Furthermore, because much of the research in this area is experimental, researchers need to be concerned with replication. Much of the research is not fully or adequately reported, thus making it difficult for others to replicate the results in full or to use the measures in other studies.[6]

Research on the writing process

Foci and techniques

The studies included in this category are those that examine some part of the writing process, broadly defined, as opposed to the actual outcome (i.e., the text that the writer produces). Some of the studies described below do consider the writers' texts (e.g., McGroarty & Zhu, 1997), but at least one research question in the studies focuses on some point in the writing process. Some of the studies focus on what the writer does as he or she writes, and others examine how various kinds of feedback are given and/or used during the process.

The first set of studies in Table 2.2 examines the entire process. Other studies focus on some specific aspect of the process – for example, revision (i.e., how writers change what they have written), fluency (i.e., how quickly one writes), the prewriting process, or even how students use dictionaries while writing. In addition, some researchers look at a specific intervention within the writing process. For example, a study may examine how a student interprets and uses teacher feedback while revising. A study may also focus on what happens during a peer review or a conferencing session as part of the writing process.

The techniques for examining the writing process differ depending on what the main focus of the research is. For those who want a picture of the entire writing process, as much as one can attain this, five different techniques have been used: stimulated recall, interviews, text analysis, observation, and talk aloud protocols. In stimulated recall, the writer is videotaped while writing, as in Bosher (1998). Immediately after writing, the researcher sits down with the writer to discuss the writer's thought processes while they view the videotape together. One of the first to use this technique was Rose (1984) in a study of native language (L1) writing. (More about this technique can be found in Gass and Mackey,

TABLE 2.2. STUDIES FOCUSING ON THE WRITING PROCESS

Main focus	Specific focus	Study	Research question	Technique	Approach
General process		Bosher, 1998	Do two groups of writers have different writing processes?	Stimulated recall	Qualitative/ causal-comparative
		Zamel, 1983	How do advanced ESL writers write?	Interviews/doc. analysis observation	Qualitative
		Penningtion & So, 1993	Do writers have the same writing process in their L1 and L2?		Qualitative/ causal-comparative
		Whalen & Menard, 1995	What kinds of knowledge and information do writers use as they plan, revise, and evaluate in their L1 vs. their L2?	Talk aloud protocol	Causal-comparative
Revision	• Type of change	Hall, 1990	Do writers revise in the same way in their L1 and L2?	Coding of written text	Causal-comparative
		Phinney & Khouri, 1993	How does computer experience and writing proficiency affect revision on a computer?	Coding of written text	Causal-comparative
	• General process	Porte, 1997	What does a group of underachieving EFL students see as revision and why?	Interviews	Qualitative
	• Restructuring	Roca de Larios et al., 1999	What kinds of knowledge and information do writers process when they restructure their L2 written discourse production? (p. 18)	Talk aloud protocols	Qualitative
Fluency		Henry, 1996	How do L2 writers' texts change over time: can they produce more over time?	Counting of words in text	Causal-comparative

(continued)

TABLE 2.2. (*continued*)

Main focus	Specific focus	Study	Research question	Technique	Approach
Prewriting	• Choosing a topic	Intaraprawat & Steffensen, 1995	How do good and poor essays differ?	Counting of words in text	Causal-comparative
		Polio & Glew, 1996	How do students choose topics during a writing exam?	Interviews	Qualitative
			How much time do students spend choosing a topic on a writing exam?	Observation	Qualitative
Written feedback	• Use of feedback	Cohen & Cavalcanti, 1990	How do students handle the feedback they receive?	Multiple case study	Qualitative
		Hyland, 1998	How do students use and interpret written feedback?	Multiple case study	Qualitative
Peer review	• Strategies	Villamil & deGuerrero, 1996	What takes place during peer review?	Observation	Qualitative
	• Student comments	McGroarty & Zhu, 1997	What are the effects of training for peer review on students' ability to comment on classmates' writing?	Coding of comments/ observation	Experimental
Conferencing/ tutoring	• Use of feedback	Goldstein & Conrad, 1990	To what extent is meaning negotiated in ESL writing conferences? (p. 446)	Multiple case study	Qualitative/ causal-comparative
	• Discourse used in session	Cumming & So, 1996	How do two types of tutoring and language choice (L1/L2) affect the discourse used in an L2 writing tutoring session?	Coding oral data	Experimental
Dictionary use		Christianson, 1997	How do students use dictionaries while writing?	Interviews/doc. analysis	Qualitative

2000.) Talk aloud protocols, used by Whalen and Menard (1995), are perhaps a more controversial technique. Talk alouds were used earlier by psychologists in studies of problem solving (e.g., Newell & Simon, 1972) and in studies of L1 writing (e.g., Emig, 1971). This technique has the writer verbalize what he or she is doing while writing. This method has been criticized, in part, for the effect it may have on the writing process; that is, it may change how the writer writes.[7] Furthermore, using the talk aloud process may be more problematic with L2 writers whose L2 oral proficiency may be insufficient to verbalize complex thought processes. On the other hand, using the L1 to describe what one is doing in the L2 may be extremely difficult as well. Observations can also be used. Pennington and So (1993) developed an on-line coding scheme in which the observer can code a writer's behavior while the writer is writing. Interviews, such as those used by Zamel (1983), have also been used and can be supplemented by document analysis – that is, looking at the writers' notes and drafts. The benefit of such a technique is that the researchers look outside of a controlled setting and study the writer in real life.

For researchers who want to study a more specific point in the process, the technique will vary with what is being studied. To measure fluency, generally the number of words written in a given time is counted. (But see Wolfe-Quintero et al., 1998, for a discussion of other measures.) The studies listed in Table 2.2 that examine choosing a topic on a writing exam (Polio & Glew, 1996) and dictionary use (Christianson, 1997) both used interviews, supplemented by observation and analysis of students' texts, respectively. Revision can be studied with a variety of techniques, such as comparing a draft and revision, using talk aloud protocols while a writer revises, or interviewing writers about what they do.

Describing what takes place in peer review or conferencing sessions is generally done through observation and coding of the oral data. The studies that examined how students use written feedback are multiple case studies that used verbal reports, questionnaires, draft and revisions of assignments, and classroom observations. (Ferris, Chapter 5 this volume, discusses the contributions of feedback in greater detail.)

Research questions

Why do researchers want to know about the writing process? If we look at the various research questions, we can see three kinds of questions being asked. The first is a very general question, such as in Zamel (1983) or Roca de Larios, Murphy, and Manchon (1999) simply asking what the process is like. The question can be asked of a specific group, such as in Porte (1997), or about two different groups, such as in Bosher (1998) or Phinney and Khouri (1993). In addition, several studies have attempted to compare the writing process in students' L1 and L2 (Hall, 1990; Pennington & So, 1993; Whalen & Menard, 1995).

A second set of questions addresses interventions and may result in an answer that is descriptive, such as Villamil and deGuerrero (1996), who asked what takes place during peer review, or Hyland (1998), who studied how students use and interpret written feedback. Some of the questions regarding interventions seek to determine the effect of some treatment on the intervention itself, as opposed to on the final outcome, the written text. For example, McGroarty and Zhu (1997) looked at the effect of peer training on students' ability to comment on their classmates' writing. Cumming and So (1996) studied the effect of the kind of tutoring and the choice of language on the discourse used in the session.

And finally, a very limited number of studies have looked at change in writers over time. One cross-sectional study by Henry (1996) studied change in terms of how fluent the writers became – that is, whether they wrote any faster over time. Sasaki (2000) studied the writing process using both cross-sectional and longitudinal data to examine the differences in the writing process of novices and experts, and before and after instruction.

Approaches and issues

A few experimental studies (Cumming & So, 1996; McGroarty & Zhu, 1997) manipulate variables and measure the outcome of some intervention on the writing process. Unlike research that focuses ultimately on the product, however, most of the research that focuses on the process is qualitative. These studies seek to describe a particular phenomenon, such as the interpretation of feedback (Hyland, 1998) or restructuring within revision (Roca de Larios, Murphy, & Manchon, 1999). Some of the studies are causal-comparative in that they examined how some aspect of the writing process differs for two different groups of writers (Phinney & Khouri, 1993) or writers writing in their L1 rather than their L2 (Hall, 1990). Some of the researchers, such as Pennington and So (1993) and Bosher (1998), asked causal-comparative-type questions using a design appropriate for answering such questions. Because of the small sample sizes, however, they did not report statistics and simply described the data.

The most difficult problem regarding studies of the writing process itself is how to study something for which there is normally no tangible product (given that the process implies internal behaviors that may or may not coincide precisely with such external documents as notes or drafts). Specifically, how can researchers describe what L2 learners are doing and thinking as they write? Some of the difficulties involved are mentioned above, and Smagorinsky (1994) provides a coherent overview of the problems in his book on research methods used to study the writing process.

A logistic difficulty is the time-consuming nature of the data collection process in some of these studies. One session with one student doing a stimulated recall can take several hours, followed by the time it takes to transcribe the recall. Compare this to having 100 students produce a piece of writing in one sitting. Because collecting and analyzing data on the writing process take so much time, studies in this category often use very small sample sizes. Although qualitative research generally uses small sample sizes, it often produces several different data for the researcher to draw on; this allows for a process of triangulation, used to draw conclusions based on coming at the data from a variety of angles. Most of the research reviewed here, however, does not triangulate the data, an exception being Sasaki (2000) in his study of English as a foreign language (EFL) writing processes. Furthermore, although some of the research asks causal-comparative questions posed as hypotheses, because of low sample sizes, the researchers simply describe the data. Formulating conclusions about hypotheses without testing for statistical significance is problematic because one cannot know if the results obtained were simply due to chance.

Because of the time-consuming nature of research on the writing process, most of this research actually studies the writing process within an artificial setting so as to limit the time and location of the data collection procedure. Capturing the on-line process as writers write in real life is nearly impossible. Therefore, most of the research on the writing process, simply for logistical reasons, captures students writing short, timed essays. The results of these studies may not be generalizable to other writing tasks. Also, these studies do not, as qualitative research generally demands, capture participants in their natural setting.

Much of the research on the writing process includes some kind of coding of data – for example, type of revision, student comments during peer review, or what they focus on in talk aloud protocols. Categories for coding any of these data are not straightforward. The explicitness of the coding schemes vary; intercoder reliability is sporadically reported as well. Research that does not report reliability, as is often the case in qualitative research, should provide other sources of data for triangulation, such as Sasaki (2000), who in addition to triangulating data reports intercoder reliability. Both Sasaki and McGroarty and Zhu (1997) use multiple data sources and should be held up as examples for other L2 writing researchers.

A final issue related to studies of the writing process is whether they provide useful information. Those studies that focus on a specific issue, such as how students handle feedback or teachers' comments in a conference, are no doubt helpful to teachers who may want to improve their feedback techniques. Those studies that describe the writing process are quite different in that the results must be applied more cautiously. On one hand, finding out what good writers do and telling weak writers to do the same may not be appropriate; the same strategies may not work for two different individuals, let alone groups. On the other hand, if we see the process approach as an intervention (e.g., Susser, 1994), discovering problem points within the process and providing options to help students solve those problems should be useful and valuable for teachers.

Research on the participants

The next set of research focuses on the various participants involved in the teaching and learning of L2 writing. In this category I have included studies whose main research question addresses the attitudes, backgrounds, or behaviors of a specific group of people. The groups studied are divided into four categories, as shown in Table 2.3, including teachers, students, raters of exams, and content teachers (i.e., professors) in tandem with writing teachers of native English speakers. Because the majority of studies on the participants in this and the following section of this chapter on the social context are qualitative and seek to describe various phenomena, I discuss the specific focus, research questions, and techniques for each group in relation to the main focus of the study, as opposed to dealing with the research questions separately as was done in reviewing the two previous tables.

Teachers

The first set of studies, all done within a qualitative framework, focuses on the teachers. Some studies examine their views and practices regarding the teaching of writing, a key focus for the study reported on by Cumming (Chapter 3 this volume). Pennington et al. (1997) used questionnaires and interviews to find out how the views and practices of ESL and EFL teachers in the Pacific Rim were similar and different. Shi and Cumming's (1995) study is more specific and not only asked about teachers' views but also examined how they responded to a pedagogical innovation. This research used a multiple case study approach following five teachers through observations and interviews. Cumming (1992) also used multiple case studies to look at teachers' instructional routines. Winer (1992) sampled preservice teachers' attitudes toward teaching writing and asked how they changed over time. She did so by analyzing teaching journals and questionnaires. Rather than a multiple case study approach, in which a few participants are studied using more than one source of data, Winer looked at about 100 preservice teachers by analyzing only written

TABLE 2.3. STUDIES FOCUSING ON THE PARTICIPANTS

Main focus	Specific focus	Study	Research question	Technique	Approach
Teachers	• Instructional routines	Cumming, 1992	What instructional routines are common to experienced, skilled ESL teachers?	Multiple case study	Qualitative
	• Preservice attitudes toward teaching writing	Winer, 1992	How do preservice teachers' awareness of the writing process and attitudes toward teaching writing change during a practicum?	Analysis of journals and questionnaires	Qualitative
	• Views and practices	Pennington et al., 1997	How different or similar are the views and practices of ESL/EFL teachers in the Asia-Pacific region?	Questionnaire/ interviews	Qualitative
	• Views and practices	Shi & Cumming, 1995	What are ESL teachers' conceptions about L2 writing instruction, and how do they respond to a pedagogical innovation?	Multiple case study	Qualitative
Students/writers	• Attitudes toward peer response	McGroarty & Zhu, 1997	What are the effects of training on students' attitudes toward peer response?	Questionnaire	Experimental
	• Backgrounds/previous instruction	Liebman, 1992	What kind of rhetorical instruction did students receive in their L1?	Closed and open-ended survey	Survey
	• Text in students' L1	Kubota, 1997	What is the structure of Japanese expository prose?	Document analysis	Qualitative
	• Experience in a content course	Spack, 1997	Why is a student having difficulty in a particular content course?	Case study	Qualitative

(continued)

TABLE 2.3. (continued)

Main focus	Specific focus	Study	Research question	Technique	Approach
	• EAP and content experience	Leki & Carson, 1997	What are ESL students' experiences regarding three types of writing in their content and ESL classes?	Interviews	Qualitative
	• Perspective on plagiarism	Deckert, 1993	What are students' perspectives on plagiarism?	Closed-ended survey	Survey
	• Immigrants' experience in ESL class	Harklau, 1999	What are the experiences of long-term US residents in ESL composition courses?	Ethnography	Qualitative
	• Coping strategies	Leki, 1995	What strategies do ESL students use to get by in their content classes?	Ethnography	Qualitative
Raters	• Effects of experience	Weigle, 1994	How do experienced and inexperienced raters' scores differ before and after training?	Raters' scores and talk aloud protocols	Experimental/causal-comparative
	• Judgment on prompt difficulty	Hamp-Lyons & Mathias, 1994	Do raters agree with one another on prompt difficulty?	Raters' judgments and scores	Correlational
	• NS vs. NNS	Kobayashi, 1992	Do NS and NNS evaluate and correct ESL essays differently?	Raters' analytic scores and analysis of their corrections	Causal-comparative
Professors/NES teachers	• Error tolerance	Janopoulos,1992	How tolerant are faculty of different error types?	Raters' judgments of sentences	Survey
	• Judgments compared with ESL teachers	Song & Caruso, 1996	Do NES and ESL teachers rate essays the same?	Holistic and analytic evaluation of essays	Causal-comparative

comments. Two of the studies in this category focus on a specific group of teachers. Cumming limited his participants to experienced, skilled ESL teachers and Pennington et al. to teachers in various countries across the Pacific Rim. The other two studies focus on changing attitudes: Winer's study on teachers over the course of a practicum and Shi and Cumming on teachers' response to a pedagogical innovation.

Students

A larger percentage of the studies represented in Table 2.3 examines the students, and most, but not all, are qualitative. Some are general and study various features of students' educational experience, such as their experience in content courses (Spack, 1997) or English for academic purposes (EAP) and content courses (Leki & Carson, 1997). Spack's study is a longitudinal case study of one particular student. Spack interviewed the student, observed her, talked to her content professors, and looked at her writing over three years. Leki and Carson interviewed thirty-six students about their perceptions of and experiences with different types of writing required in ESL and in content courses.

Two other studies that focus on students, Harklau (1999) and Leki (1995), examined immigrant students in ESL courses and ESL students in content courses, respectively. Harklau documented four immigrants' experiences in ESL classes over their last semester of high school and first semester of college. She interviewed the students ten to thirteen times throughout the study. In addition, she observed their classes, interviewed their instructors, collected documents from the classes, and examined the students' written work. Leki wanted to understand how ESL students dealt with the writing demands in their content classes. She interviewed five students once a week for a semester. Like Harklau, she also observed classes, interviewed professors, and collected written documents. Leki also had the students keep a journal about their academic experiences. These last two studies I have assigned to the category of ethnography, and this is discussed further below.

Some studies have tried to describe students' attitudes or experiences through the use of surveys. Deckert (1993) asked what Hong Kong students' perspectives on plagiarism were. Liebman (1992) studied Arab and Japanese students' previous writing instruction in their native countries.

Another approach is to study L1 texts in various languages to help understand what the students may bring to the process of L2 writing. These studies fall under the area of contrastive rhetoric and assume that, or question whether, such texts will influence a writer's L2 texts (a topic discussed in greater detail in the chapter by Connor, Chapter 9 this volume). One such study, listed in Table 2.3, is Kubota (1997). She reviewed several studies as well as historical documents to argue that

Japanese expository prose should not necessarily be characterized as inductive or reader-responsible. There are many other techniques that can be used in describing texts in a writer's L1 and these are reviewed in Connor's (1996) survey of contrastive rhetoric. (Note that studies falling under the area of contrastive rhetoric may also examine native language texts that the L2 writers have as their goal. These studies are mentioned in the next section of this chapter.) And finally, one study of students (McGroarty & Zhu, 1997) was done in an experimental paradigm. The effect of an intervention, peer response training, was studied to discover how it affected students' attitude toward peer response.

Raters

The studies that examine raters are among those in this group that do not take a qualitative approach. Kobayashi's (1992) study asked whether native and nonnative speakers evaluated EFL essays and corrected their errors differently. His study took a causal-comparative approach and compared raters' scores and their corrections. Hamp-Lyons and Mathias (1994) asked a different question: did raters agree with one another on prompt difficulty and what was the correlation between their scores and prompt difficulty? Weigle (1994) took yet another approach and studied not only the differences between experienced and inexperienced raters but also how training affected both groups' scores and thoughts. In addition to using the raters' scores in her study, she supplemented her findings with qualitative data taken from the raters' talk aloud protocols.

Professors and NES teachers

The last set of studies focuses on professors and teachers of native English speakers. Janopoulos (1992) examined the tolerance of university faculty for different error types by conducting a survey asking for reactions to ungrammatical sentences taken from ESL students' essays. Song and Caruso (1996) had ESL and native English speakers (NES) teachers rate essays and looked at the difference between the two groups.

Approaches and issues

Most of the studies examining the participants are qualitative studies in that they describe a phenomenon without attempting to manipulate variables. A few studies, however, actually study how a particular treatment affects participants' attitudes or practice through an experimental study. For example, McGroarty and Zhu (1997) studied how peer training affected participants' attitudes toward peer response. Weigle (1994) looked at experienced and inexperienced raters and the effect of training on them. Her study was both experimental and causal-comparative in that she looked at a pre-existing variable (experience) and one that she manipulated (training).

To describe participants' views or practices, researchers have used different methods. The method used by Liebman (1992), Deckert (1993), and Janopoulos (1992) was surveys. The obvious benefit of using a survey is that a large number of participants can be studied. But even with open-ended questions, surveys can lack the depth of interviews. Other researchers (Pennington et al., 1997) have supplemented written survey research with interviews, allowing the researcher to probe more deeply into certain areas. Just as with other types of research, surveys involve many decisions to be made by the researcher, such as how to administer the survey, whether to use open-ended questions, and for L2 writing researchers, which language to conduct the survey in.[8] When writing up the research, the study should provide a full copy of the survey in the appendix.

Qualitative research in this category can involve analyzing certain documents. In Winer's (1992) study that used questionnaires, she also looked at preservice teachers' journals to find out more about their attitudes. Kubota (1997), who wanted to study texts in students' first language, simply analyzed Japanese writing without ever studying the students themselves. Researchers who use a case study or multiple case study approach within a qualitative framework often analyze certain documents in addition to interviewing and observing participants. (For more on case study research, see Yin, 1994.)

I have listed two of the studies in this category as examples of ethnography,[9] not because the authors use the term *ethnography* in their studies[10] but because they are holistic, trying to provide the reader with a wide-angle view of an issue; are longitudinal; use multiple data sources; and most important, provide an emic perspective – that is, they provide a picture of the phenomenon from the perspective of those being studied.

One last point is that quantitative and qualitative approaches can often be successfully combined. In Weigle's (1994) experimental study, she examined raters' scores before and after training, in addition to collecting verbal talk aloud data from the raters to find out the reasons behind their scores, something that she could not have discovered from the quantitative data alone. This combination of approaches was appropriate in Weigle's study, but sometimes there can be problems in combining the two approaches; these are discussed in the conclusion section.

Research on the social context

Studies that examine the social context of the learning and teaching of L2 writing are listed in Table 2.4. Of course, anyone learning how to

TABLE 2.4. STUDIES FOCUSING ON THE SOCIAL CONTEXT

Main focus	Specific focus	Study	Research question	Technique	Approach
Goals outside the class	• Structure of texts in the target language	Swales, 1990	What is the structure of introductions in English research articles?	Document analysis	Qualitative
		Posteguillo, 1999	What is the structure of computer science research articles?	Document analysis	Qualitative
	• Linguistic features of texts in the target language	Williams, 1996	What kind of lexical verbs are used in two kinds of medical research reports	Document analysis	Qualitative
	• Content class assigments and exams	Horowitz, 1986a; 1986b	What kind of writing tasks are required in academic courses?	Document analysis	Qualitative
	• Content class tasks	Currie, 1993	What kind of conceptual activities are required in a particular academic course?	Case study	Qualitative
		Benesch, 1996	How can teachers help students meet the demands of an academic course and create possibilities for change?	Critical theory	Qualitative
What happens in the classroom	• Speech moves	Weissberg, 1994	What kind of speech moves occur in writing classes, and who makes them?	Analysis of classroom discourse	Qualitative
Programs	• Program administration	Williams, 1995	Are NS and NNSs taught composition separately? Who are the instructors for the ESL courses?	Open- and closed-ended survey	Survey
	• Attitudes and behaviors toward teaching writing	Atkinson & Ramanathan, 1995	What are the program-level attitudes and behaviors toward teaching writing in an L1 and L2 program?	Ethnography	Qualitative

write learns in some social context and all education takes place in some context as well. The studies discussed here are those that do not attempt to isolate factors related only to the written text, the writing process, or the attitudes and behaviors of the participants. One set of studies focuses specifically on the students' goals outside the L2 writing class. The other studies focus on writing instruction at either the classroom or program level, without singling out one particular set of participants.

Goals outside the classroom

With regard to goals outside the classroom, one can focus on several factors. All the studies fall within the qualitative framework; they seek to describe a phenomenon, the goals.

The first set of studies simply describes the target texts – that is, texts in the second language that are similar to those the learner will have to write. One approach to this kind of research falls under what is often called genre analysis, an approach associated with John Swales, among others, and further discussed by Johns (Chapter 8 this volume). Swales and his colleagues have provided thorough descriptions of English academic research articles (Swales, 1990). An example of a specific area he has focused on is the structure of introductions in those academic articles. Another example of this type of study is Posteguillo (1999), who looked at the structure of research articles in the field of computer science. Another approach was taken in earlier studies in the area of English for specific purposes. These studies (e.g., Oster, 1981) described specific linguistic features of target texts. A more recent example of this type of study is Williams (1996), who examined lexical verbs in medical reports. The preliminary goal of these studies is to describe texts similar to those students may have to write, but they may be useful for those involved in writing (and reading) instruction in the field of language for specific purposes.

Other studies have looked at what students need to accomplish in content classes outside the language classroom. One approach is to analyze a large number of writing tasks given in a range of university courses, as exemplified in work by Horowitz (1986a, 1986b). Another approach is to do a case study of a particular content class, as in Currie (1993), who examined the assignments and writing tasks more closely and included observations and/or interviews with faculty and students.

In this section I have included also Benesch (1996), which although a qualitative case study, took a very different approach to needs analysis. She examined the needs of students in an EAP writing class paired with a large introductory psychology class. Benesch's study is an example of a critical needs analysis falling within the paradigm of critical pedagogy. This approach targets problem areas that may represent contradictions for the students and suggests possible actions for change. For example, students had to pass a university-wide argumentative essay exam yet took multiple-choice tests for course assessment. Her study, in fact, goes beyond looking at writing assignments, but I have given it as an example to portray the wide range of approaches used by researchers.

What happens in the classroom

Another focus of study is what actually transpires in L2 writing classrooms. Surprisingly little has been written on this topic; most of the classroom research focuses on the teachers themselves. One study that does focus on the L2 writing classroom context is Weissberg's (1994) study of speech moves in an ESL composition class. His study is an analysis of classroom discourse and examines both teachers' and students' speech without focusing on one group.

Composition programs

And finally, a few studies have looked at L2 composition programs. Williams (1995) surveyed several programs to study the structure of the programs and who the teachers were. Taking a very different approach, Atkinson and Ramanathan (1995) conducted an ethnography of an L1 and an L2 writing program and focused on the attitudes of those involved toward teaching writing and how those attitudes were reflected at the program level. They conducted interviews and observations and studied documents from the programs.

Approaches and issues

As would be expected, virtually all the research in this category is qualitative. Even the study classified as survey research (Williams, 1995) sought to describe something: writing programs. Studies such as the one by Williams (1996), which reported the results using numbers, still fall within the range of qualitative research in that it described a particular phenomenon.

What is most interesting in this category of research is the wide variation of techniques used to study similar things. For example, comparing Horowitz's (1986a) study of content class tasks with Currie's and Benesch's, we see three very different studies. Horowitz is able to provide data from several different content courses whereas Currie's study probes more deeply into one course. Benesch takes a different approach, putting the researcher in a very different role.

Similarly, Williams (1995) and Atkinson and Ramanathan (1995) also nicely complement one another in that Williams provides an overall picture that can be done only through surveys and Ramanathan and Atkinson provide an in-depth picture that only an ethnography can produce.

Weissberg's study examined what takes place in the classroom through an analysis of classroom discourse. It is surprising is that so little research actually studies what goes on in the classroom because this is where writing instruction takes place. Other studies mentioned in this chapter do classroom observations but more to focus on one set of participants (e.g., Cumming, 1992; Harklau, 1999).

Summary and conclusions

The most important point to be taken from this overview is the wide scope of L2 writing research. It has been my goal to at least touch on all the factors that go into writing instruction as well as the various ways to look at students' texts and what students go through as they produce their texts. For future researchers, I hope that this overview has provided a range of approaches and techniques as well as a picture of what has and has not been studied. For example, little research has been conducted on what actually happens in writing classes. Although many people have studied teachers' views about teaching writing and students' views about what they need, not much has been done regarding how they converge (or diverge) in the writing classroom. What techniques and materials are used? What do syllabi for these courses look like?

Another point to consider is the dearth of research on writing in a foreign language context, both on teaching English outside North America and on teaching languages other than English in North America. Several studies do exist that have not been discussed here, and for more on foreign language writing in the United States, see Reichelt (1999), and for references to L2 writing research on languages other than English, see an on-line bibliography established by the Center for Language Education and Research (CLEAR, 1980–1996). Nevertheless, such studies are few in number. This is not particularly surprising in that writing may not be an important goal, at least for foreign language students in the United States, and thus the needs are not so easily identified.

Just as multiple foci of L2 writing research are necessary, so are multiple approaches and techniques. We simply cannot study the same phenomena using exclusively experimental or exclusively qualitative methods. Although certainly not everyone would agree, what is important is not to privilege one approach over the other but to work carefully within the guidelines of that approach.[11] Similarly, different techniques – for example, the variety of those that probe the writing process – can each tell us different things, each provide a piece of the puzzle. What is important is that one understands and acknowledges the limitations of a technique.

Regardless of the approach or technique, careful reporting of methodology is essential. For quantitative research, others should be able to look at the methods section and replicate the study (Polio & Gass, 1998). For qualitative research, the guidelines are not necessarily as clear. For research involving interviews, for example, one can provide questions used at the starting point. Space, however, would prohibit providing transcripts, nor could they be provided on request because it could compromise the anonymity of the subjects. For ethnographic research, the problems are far more complex. (See Ramanathan & Atkinson, 1999, for further discussion of the specific concerns.)

And finally, whether one is reading empirical research or doing it, results need to be interpreted cautiously in several respects. For example, many of the quantitative studies use timed essays so that certain variables can be controlled. Generalizing results to non-timed essays can be problematic. Furthermore, nonsignificant results should also be interpreted cautiously. A wide range of factors can hide significant effects, including poor interrater reliability. Many studies, for example, have not shown significant long-term effects for various types of error correction in L2 writing. (See Truscott, 1996, for a review.) A poorly done experimental study can result in no significant findings but fail to prove that no effect exists. With regard to pedagogy, practitioners need to interpret results cautiously. For example, simply finding out what good writers do and teaching those strategies to weak writers may not be appropriate. An intervention that has been shown to result in more grammatically accurate writing may have negative effects not addressed in the research.

In conclusion, keeping abreast of the latest research can guide teachers in making curricular and pedagogical decisions. The literature, however, must be critically examined so that claims can be fully evaluated; the conclusions from empirical research do not always have directly applicable pedagogical implications. Nevertheless, I believe that learning about the many areas encompassed by L2 writing research leads to a fuller picture of L2 writing.

Notes

1. Empirical research refers to any type of research in which data are systematically collected and analyzed for the purpose of understanding or making claims about a specific phenomenon capable of being observed and/or measured in some way.
2. At times only part of a study will be discussed as an example of a particular kind of research. I will not discuss every research question or focus of every single study cited for discussion.

3. Categorization schemes are not without their controversies, but for the purposes of this chapter, I have relied primarily on categories that are frequently cited in the literature as common to educational research. The labels I have selected are specifically from Fraenkel and Wallen (1996).
4. Two useful books for those interested in reading more about qualitative research are Denzin and Lincoln (1994) and Patton (1990).
5. For readers wanting to learn more about validity, a useful book is Cumming and Berwick (1995). Although the book focuses more on testing than research, the introduction provides a thorough description of the various types of validity with specific reference to L2 learning.
6. This problem is discussed more thoroughly in Polio (2001), where a more detailed discussion of the various measures and analyses of L2 writers' texts is given as well as the various problems involved in using some of the measures.
7. See Stratman and Hamp-Lyons (1994) for a discussion of the so-called reactivity problem.
8. One reference for anyone planning to do survey research includes Fowler (1995).
9. Defining ethnography is far from straightforward, and thus I refer readers to a lucid article on ethnographic approaches in L2 writing research by Ramanathan and Atkinson (1999).
10. Leki (1995) never called her own study an ethnography. Rather, she said, "The extensive amount and the variety of data sources were intended to ensure triangulation of the information gathered to contribute to a more complex, richer, and thicker, as Geertz (1983) describes it, ethnographic description than might be possible through the examination of single data sources" (p. 239). Harklau (1999) said that she used "an ethnographic case study methodology" (p. 111).
11. *TESOL Quarterly*'s research guidelines, which provide guidance for both quantitative and qualitative researchers, is a particularly useful resource for novice researchers.

References

Allison, D. (1995). Assertions and alternatives: Helping ESL undergraduates extend their choice in academic writing. *Journal of Second Language Writing, 4,* 1–16.

Atkinson, D., & Ramanathan, V. (1995). Cultures of writing: An ethnographic comparison of L1 and L2 university writing/language programs. *TESOL Quarterly, 29,* 539–568.

Bardovi-Harlig, K., & Bofman, T. (1989). Attainment of syntactic and morphological accuracy by advanced language learners. *Studies in Second Language Acquisition, 11,* 17–34.

Benesch, S. (1996). Need analysis and curriculum development in EAP: An example of a critical approach. *TESOL Quarterly, 30,* 723–738.

Bosher, S. (1998). The composing process of three Southeast Asian writers at the post-secondary level: An exploratory study. *Journal of Second Language Writing, 7,* 205–242.

Christianson, K. (1997). Dictionary use by EFL writers: What really happens. *Journal of Second Language Writing, 6,* 23–44.

CLEAR (Center for Language Education and Research). Bibliography: References on the teaching and learning of foreign language writing focusing on languages other than English (1980–1996). www.polyglot.cal.msu.edu/clear/writing.

Cohen, A., & Cavalcanti, M. (1990). Feedback on compositions: Teacher and student verbal reports. In B. Kroll (Ed.), *Second language writing: Research insights for the classroom* (pp. 155–177). New York: Cambridge University Press.

Connor, U. (1996). *Contrastive rhetoric: Cross-cultural aspects of second-language writing.* New York: Cambridge University Press.

Coombs, V. (1986). Syntax and communicative strategies in intermediate German composition. *The Modern Language Journal, 70,* 114–124.

Cumming, A. (1992). Instructional routines in ESL composition teaching: A case study of three teachers. *Journal of Second Language Writing, 1,* 17–36.

Cumming, A., & Berwick, R. (Eds.). (1995). *Validation in language testing.* Clevedon, England: Multilingual Matters.

Cumming, A., & So, S. (1996). Tutoring second language text revision: Does approach to instruction or the language of communication make a difference? *Journal of Second Language Writing, 5,* 197–226.

Currie, P. (1993). Entering a disciplinary community: Conceptual activities required to write for one introductory university course. *Journal of Second Language Writing, 2,* 101–118.

Deckert, G. (1993). Perspectives on plagiarism from ESL students in Hong Kong. *Journal of Second Language Writing, 2,* 131–148.

Denzin, N., & Lincoln, Y. (Eds.). (1994). *Handbook of qualitative research.* Thousand Oaks, CA: Sage.

Devine, J., Railey, K., & Boshoff, P. (1993). The implications of cognitive models in L1 and L2 writing. *Journal of Second Language Writing, 2,* 203–225.

Emig, J. (1971). *The composing process of twelfth graders.* Urbana, IL: National Council of Teachers of English.

Engber, C. (1995) The relationship of lexical proficiency to the quality of ESL compositions. *Journal of Second Language Writing, 4,* 139–155.

Fowler, F. (1995). *Improving survey questions: Design and evaluation.* Thousand Oaks, CA: Sage.

Fraenkel, J., & Wallen, N. (1996). *How to design and evaluate research in education.* New York: McGraw-Hill.

Gass, S., & Mackey, A. (2000). *Stimulated recall methodology in second language research.* Hillsdale, NJ: Lawrence Erlbaum.

Goldstein, L., & Conrad, S. (1990). Student input and negotiation of meaning in ESL writing conferences. *TESOL Quarterly, 24,* 443–460.

Hall, C. (1990). Managing the complexity of revising across languages. *TESOL Quarterly, 24,* 43–60.

Hamp-Lyons, L., & Henning, G. (1991). Communicative writing profiles: An investigation of the transferability of a multiple-trait scoring instrument across ESL writing assessment contexts. *Language Learning, 41,* 337–373.

Hamp-Lyons, L., & Mathias, S. P. (1994). Examining expert judgments of task difficulty on essay tests. *Journal of Second Language Writing, 3,* 49–68.

Harklau, L. (1999). Representing culture in the ESL writing classroom. In E. Hinkel (Ed.), *Culture in language teaching and learning* (pp. 109–130). New York: Cambridge University Press.

Hedgcock, J., & Lefkowitz, N. (1992). Collaborative oral/aural revision in foreign language writing instruction. *Journal of Second Language Writing, 3,* 255–276.

Henry, K. (1996). Early L2 writing development: A study of autobiographical essays by university-level students of Russian. *The Modern Language Journal, 80,* 309–326.

Horowitz, D. (1986a). What professors actually require: Academic tasks for the ESL classroom. *TESOL Quarterly, 20,* 445–462.

Horowitz, D. (1986b). Essay examination prompts and the teaching of academic writing. *English for Specific Purposes, 5,* 107–120.

Hyland, F. (1998). The impact of teacher-written feedback on individual writers. *Journal of Second Language Writing, 7,* 255–286.

Intaraprawat, P., & Steffensen, M. (1995). The use of metadiscourse in good and poor ESL essays. *Journal of Second Language Writing, 4,* 253–272.

Ishikawa, S. (1995). Objective measurement of low-proficiency EFL narrative writing. *Journal of Second Language Writing, 4,* 51–69.

Jacobs, H., Zinkgraf, S., Wormuth, D., Hartfiel, V., & Hughey, J. (1981). *Testing ESL composition: A practical approach.* Rowley, MA: Newbury House.

Janopoulos, M. (1992). University faculty tolerance of NS and NNS writing errors: A comparison. *Journal of Second Language Writing, 2,* 109–122.

Kepner, C. (1991). An experiment in the relationship of types of written feedback to the development of second-language writing skills. *Modern Language Journal, 75,* 305–313.

Kobayashi, H., & Rinnert, C. (1992). Effects of first language on second language writing: Translation vs. direct composition. *Language Learning, 42,* 183–215.

Kobayashi, T. (1992). Native and nonnative reactions to ESL compositions. *TESOL Quarterly, 26,* 81–112.

Kubota, R. (1997). A reevaluation of the uniqueness of Japanese written discourse. *Written Communication, 14,* 460–480.

Laufer, B., & Nation, P. (1995).Vocabulary size and use: Lexical richness in L2 written production. *Applied Linguistics, 16,* 307–322.

Leki, I. (1995). Coping strategies of ESL students in writing tasks across the curriculum. *TESOL Quarterly, 29,* 235–260.

Leki, I., & Carson, J. (1997). "Completely different worlds": EAP and the writing experiences of ESL students in university courses. *TESOL Quarterly, 31,* 39–70.

Liebman, J. (1992). Toward a new contrastive rhetoric: Difference between Arabic and Japanese rhetorical instruction. *Journal of Second Language Writing, 1,* 141–166.

McGroarty, M., & Zhu, W. (1997). Triangulation in classroom research: A study of peer revision. *Language Learning, 47,* 1–43.

Newell, A., & Simon, H. (1972). *Human problem solving.* Englewood Cliffs, NJ: Prentice Hall.

Oster, J. (1981). The use of tense in "reporting past literature" in EST. In L. Selinker, E. Tarone, & V. Hanzeli (Eds.), *English for academic and technical purposes* (pp. 76–90). Rowley, MA: Newbury House.

Patton, M. (1990). *Qualitative evaluation and research methods.* Newbury Park, CA: Sage.

Pennington, M., Costa, V., So, S., Shing, J., Hirose, K., & Niedzielski, K. (1997). The teaching of English-as-a-second-language writing in the Asia-Pacific region: A cross-country comparison. *RELC Journal, 28,* 120–143.

Pennington, M., & So, S. (1993). Comparing writing process and product across two languages: A study of 6 Singaporean University student writers. *Journal of Second Language Writing, 2,* 41–63.

Phinney, M., & Khouri, S. (1993). Computers, revision, and ESL writers: The role of experience. *Journal of Second Language Writing, 2,* 257–277.

Polio, C. (1997). Measures of linguistic accuracy in second language writing research. *Language Learning, 47,* 101–143.

Polio, C. (2001). Research methodology in second language writing research: The case of text-based studies. In T. Silva & P. Matsuda (Eds.), *On second language writing* (pp. 91–116). Mahwah, NJ: Lawrence Erlbaum.

Polio, C., & Gass, S. (1997). Replication and reporting. *Studies in Second Language Acquisition, 19,* 499–508

Polio, C., & Glew, M. (1996). ESL writing assessment tasks: How students choose. *Journal of Second Language Writing, 5,* 35–50.

Porte, G. (1997). The etiology of poor second language writing: The influence of perceived teacher preferences on second language revision strategies. *Journal of Second Language Writing, 6,* 61–78.

Posteguillo, S. (1999). The schematic structure of computer science research articles. *English for Specific Purposes, 18,* 139–160.

Ramanathan, V., & Atkinson, D. (1999). Ethnographic approaches and methods in L2 writing research: A critical guide and review. *Applied Linguistics, 20,* 44–70.

Reichelt, M. (1999). Toward a more comprehensive view of L2 writing: Foreign language writing in the U.S. *Journal of Second Language Writing, 8,* 181–204.

Reynolds, D. (1995). Repetition in nonnative speaker writing: More than quantity. *Studies in Second Language Acquisition, 17,* 185–210.

Robb T., Ross, S., & Shortreed, I. (1986). Salience of feedback on error and its effect on EFL writing quality. *TESOL Quarterly, 20,* 83–95.

Roca de Larios, J., Murphy, L., & Manchon, R. (1999). The use of restructuring strategies in EFL writing: A study of Spanish learners of English as a foreign language. *Journal of Second Language Writing, 8,* 13–44.

Rose, M. (1984). *Writer's block: The cognitive dimension.* Carbondale: Southern Illinois University.

Sasaki, M. (2000). Toward an empirical model of EFL writing processes. *Journal of Second Language Writing, 9,* 259–292.

Schneider, M., & Connor, U. (1990). Analyzing topical structure in ESL essays: Not all topics are equal. *Studies in Second Language Acquisition, 12,* 411–427.

Shaw, P., & Liu, E. (1998). What develops in the development of second-language writing? *Applied Linguistics, 19,* 225–254.

Shi, L., & Cumming, A. (1995). Teachers' conceptions of second language writing instruction: Five case studies. *Journal of Second Language Writing, 4,* 87–112.

Smagorinsky, P. (1994). Think aloud protocol analysis: Beyond the black box. In P. Smagorinsky (Ed.), *Speaking about writing: Reflections on research methodology* (pp. 3–19). Thousand Oaks, CA: Sage.

Song, B., & Caruso, I. (1996). Do English and ESL faculty differ in evaluating the essays of native English-speaking and ESL students? *Journal of Second Language Writing, 5,* 163–182.

Spack, R. (1997). The acquisition of academic literacy in a second language: A longitudinal case study. *Written Communication, 14,* 3–62.

Stratman, J., & Hamp-Lyons, L. (1994). Reactivity in concurrent think-aloud protocols: Issues for research. In P. Smagorinsky (Ed.), *Speaking about writing* (pp. 89–112). Thousand Oaks, CA: Sage.

Susser, B. (1994). Process approaches in ESL/EFL writing instruction. *Journal of Second Language Writing, 3,* 31–48.

Swales, J. (1990). *Genre analysis: English in academic and research setting.* New York: Cambridge University Press.

Truscott, J. (1996). The case against grammar correction in L2 writing classes. *Language Learning, 46,* 327–369.

Tsang, W. K. (1996). Comparing the effects of reading and writing on writing performance. *Applied Linguistics, 17,* 210–233.

Valdes, G., Haro, P., & Echevarriarza, M. (1992). The development of writing abilities in a foreign language: Contributions toward a general theory of L2 writing. *The Modern Language Journal, 76,* 333–352.

Villamil, O., & deGuerrero, M. (1996). Peer revision in the L2 classroom: Social-cognitive activities, mediating strategies, and aspects of social behavior. *Journal of Second Language Writing, 5,* 51–75.

Weigle, S. (1994). Effects of training on raters of ESL compositions. *Language Testing, 11,* 197–223.

Weissberg, B. (1994). Speaking of writing: Some functions of talk in the ESL composition class. *Journal of Second Language Writing, 3,* 121–140.

Whalen, K., & Menard, N. (1995). L1 and L2 writers' strategic and linguistic knowledge: A model of multiple-level discourse processing. *Language Learning, 45,* 381–418.

Williams, I. (1996). A contextual study of lexical verbs in two types of medical research report: Clinical and experimental. *English for Specific Purposes, 15,* 175–197.

Williams, J. (1995). ESL composition program administration in the United States. *Journal of Second Language Writing, 4,* 157–180.

Winer, L. (1992). "Spinach to chocolate": Changing awareness and attitudes in ESL writing teachers. *TESOL Quarterly, 26,* 57–80.

Wolfe-Quintero, K., Inagaki, S., & Kim, H. Y. (1998). Second language development in writing: Measures of fluency, accuracy, and complexity (Technical Report #17). Honolulu: National Foreign Language Resource Center.

Yin, R. (1994). *Case study research: Design and methods.* Thousand Oaks, CA: Sage.

Zamel, V. (1983). The composing processes of advanced ESL students: Six case studies. *TESOL Quarterly, 17,* 165–190.

Zhang, S. (1987). Cognitive complexity and written production in English as a second language. *Language Learning, 37,* 469–481.

PART II:
EXPLORING THE VOICES OF KEY STAKEHOLDERS: TEACHERS AND STUDENTS

The desire to make sense of language teaching and language learning requires close study of both learners and teachers as well as the learning/ teaching situation itself. In a recent study of highly experienced English as a second language (ESL) teachers in Australia, for example, Breen et al. (2001) report on the relationships between teachers' actual classroom practices and the principles that they felt guided those practices. In a different type of study, Bailey et al. (1996) discuss how creating and reviewing the language learning autobiographies of future teachers provides positive outcomes toward teacher development.

These methodologies are particularly applicable to studying teachers and learners in the second language (L2) writing environment. After all, writing instruction takes place only as some kind of interaction involving students and a teacher, even though researchers can and do study learning and writing as abstract constructs. Teachers and students are definitively the key stakeholders in the field of second language writing. Settings clearly vary and individuals clearly vary, but it is important to try to learn whether there is a common core of beliefs, practices, and behaviors among members of the teacher class and members of the learner (student writer) class. These are the topics addressed in this section.

Do ESL/EFL writing courses as delivered in different locations and settings around the world share similarities or differ in their instructional approaches?

With the teaching of ESL and EFL (English as a foreign language) writing occurring in so many different geographic locations and situations, it is important for the profession to be able to determine the extent to which such courses derive from a common core of principles and practices or vary widely because of divergent situations. Chapter 3, by Alister Cumming, provides a broad-based study to address just such concerns. He reports on how experienced ESL/EFL writing instructors working in six different countries conceptualize their teaching. His research findings indicate a great deal of commonality in how writing is presented in several different settings, leading him to conclude that there appears to be a common body of pedagogical knowledge worthy of being acquired by any future teacher of writing. Although one can take many different approaches to provide writing instruction for students (and for more on this, see particularly Chapter 8 by Ann Johns and Chapter 11 by Stephanie Vandrick in this volume), certain components are common to all writing curricula. As I have suggested elsewhere, "the constants of any writing course [include] teacher-planned lessons, presentation of writing assignments, student-written texts, and feedback on writing," (Kroll, 2001, p. 219). Cumming's chapter identifies both these commonalities and indicates where the differences lie by using the actual voices of a number of teachers to provide insights into their thinking.

In what ways do second language writers themselves see their writing as uniquely different from the writing they do in their native languages?

In the past few years, writing teachers and language professionals who have achieved high levels of fluency in a second language have begun to share their personal stories by publishing reflective narratives describing their own journeys to finding a voice in a second language and coming to grips with cross-cultural communication in writing (e.g., Belcher & Connor, 2001; Chiang, 1998; Fox, 1998; Lvovich, 1997).

Following in this tradition, in Chapter 4, Tony Silva and Melinda Reichelt have turned to students themselves to provide the narratives that allow them to offer an insightful summary of the similarities and differences between native and second language writers – both their writing processes and their written products. They have invited five L2 writers to co-author this chapter by crafting narratives of their own individual writing autobiographies to give readers of this volume direct access to the voices of a highly articulate sample of the population whom teachers serve. The first languages of these authors are Chinese, Japanese, Spanish, and American Sign Language; their narratives describe their learning to write English as a second language. Also represented is a native speaker of English discussing her experiences in learning to write French. Silva and Reichelt are committed to allowing L2 writers to tell their own stories from their own perspectives. They follow the narratives with their own discussion, synthesis, and interpretation of the key ideas about learning and writing raised by the five L2 writers. This chapter will also be particularly informative for L1 teachers who often have L2 students in their classrooms and are conflicted about whether to treat them the same as or different from their L1 students.

References

Bailey, K. M., Bergthold, B., Braunstein, B., Fleischman, N. J., Holbrook, M. P., Tuman, J., Waissbluth, X., & Zambo, L. J. (1996). The language learner's autobiography: Examining the "apprenticeship of observation." In D. Freeman & J. C. Richards (Eds.), *Teacher learning in language teaching* (pp. 11–29). New York: Cambridge University Press.

Belcher, D., & Connor, U. (Eds.). (2001). *Reflections on multiliterate lives.* Clevedon, England: Multilingual Matters.

Breen, M. P., Hird, B., Milton, M., Oliver, R., & Thwaite, A. (2001). Making sense of language teaching: Teachers' principles and classroom practices. *Applied Linguistics, 22,* 470–501.

Chiang, Y-S. D. (1998). English – yours, mine, or ours: Language teaching and the needs of "nonnative" speakers of English. In E. Decker & K. Geissler (Eds.), *Situated stories: Valuing diversity in composition research* (pp. 128–141). Portsmouth, NH: Boynton/Cook Heinemann.

Fox, H. (1998). "Getting it": When what is *not* said is the most important data. In E. Decker & K. Geissler (Eds.), *Situated stories: Valuing diversity in composition research* (pp. 20–30). Portsmouth, NH: Boynton/Cook Heinemann.

Kroll, B. (2001). Considerations for teaching an ESL/EFL writing course. In M. Celce-Murcia (Ed.), *Teaching English as a second/foreign language* (3rd ed., pp. 219–232). Boston: Heinle & Heinle.

Lvovich, N. (1997). *The multilingual self: An inquiry into language learning.* Mahwah, NJ: Lawrence Erlbaum.

3 Experienced ESL/EFL writing instructors' conceptualizations of their teaching: Curriculum options and implications

Alister Cumming

Education for future language teachers, like the training to become any kind of teacher, involves a process in which novices must acquire both relevant content knowledge and training in pedagogical strategies to be able to create successful classroom experiences for their future students. This is undoubtedly true for English as a second or foreign language (ESL/EFL) writing instructors, who must develop the relevant professional expertise required for this field. Conceptualizing, planning, and delivering courses is the primary focus of the work that such instructors engage in. To help clarify some of the complexities of this practical, professional knowledge, the present chapter[1] identifies and analyzes the usual practices that a variety of experienced ESL/EFL writing instructors use to organize their courses. The descriptions of individual and general practices are based on data collected from personal interviews conducted in several different countries; a primary goal of these in-depth interviews was to gather specific information regarding the curriculum practices of highly experienced instructors offering classes in a range of settings.

One might expect that the scope of the variables that ESL/EFL writing instructors typically face when they plan and conduct their courses contributes to a range of curriculum practices. One can also anticipate that experienced instructors would be able to draw from a common pool of practices that reveal some commonality in their courses as well. Thus, identifying areas of commonality and difference in their stated curriculum practices should be of particular value in helping novice instructors to focus their thinking on key aspects of their courses, to reflect on their ongoing teaching experiences from a global perspective, and to anticipate curriculum alternatives that they may wish or be obliged to pursue. It should be noted that the close investigation of teaching practices follows from much recent inquiry into teachers' professional, practical knowledge, building on theories elaborated in educational research (e.g., Clark & Peterson, 1986; Connelly & Clandinin, 1988), including second-language education specifically (e.g., Freeman & Johnson, 1998; Freeman & Richards, 1996; Gebhard & Oprandy, 1999; Johnson, 1999; Woods, 1996).

In fairness, while this chapter is based on empirical evidence from practicing teachers, there are various other possible sources of information that exist to describe how experienced instructors organize their courses for ESL/EFL writing instruction, and these sources may also be valuable for informing novice instructors' professional knowledge. Still, these sources of information are limited in scope. For instance, numerous outlines of principles or general schemes exist that could usefully guide instructors to organize ESL/EFL writing courses (e.g., Feez, 1998; Ferris & Hedgcock, 1998, pp. 51–122; Reid, 1993, pp. 73–145; Shih, 1986). But these take the form of intuitive pedagogical advice rather than deriving from empirical analyses of what experienced writing instructors actually do. So we cannot be certain how closely their suggestions for curriculum organization correspond to what ESL/EFL writing instructors really have to do or what conditions may exist for teaching a particular course. At the other extreme, there are diverse case studies that detail the practices of ESL/EFL writing instructors engaged in curriculum planning and organization (e.g., Burns & Hood, 1995; Cumming, 1993; Franco, 1996; Frodesen, 1995; Jacoby, Leech, & Holten, 1995; Shi & Cumming, 1995; Trueba, 1987) or studies documenting, through direct observation, the researcher's own classroom teaching (Cumming, 1992; Riazi, Lessard-Clouston, & Cumming, 1996; Weissberg, 1994). But these studies are so few in number and so restricted to unique contexts that it is difficult to know whether the individual instructors studied could be representative of pedagogical practices more extensively or in locations other than where the case studies were done. Likewise, comparative reviews of policies for ESL/EFL education internationally (e.g., Dickson & Cumming, 1996; Eggington & Wren, 1997; Herriman & Burnaby, 1996) have taken such a broad, macro-perspective on educational programs that they convey little about what happens from the micro-perspective of actually teaching ESL/EFL, let alone of teaching writing in particular.[2]

Recognizing this lack of systematic information about ESL/EFL writing instruction as viewed by its practitioners, I undertook a study to document in detail how highly experienced instructors of ESL/EFL writing in six different countries conceptualized their teaching. I aimed for a small, purposive sample of instructors in each country, seeking people who were acknowledged by their peers for their expertise and knowledge about teaching writing to adults learning ESL/EFL. The six countries selected included three countries where English was the dominant language (Australia, New Zealand, and the province of Ontario in Canada) and where English was taught for both academic purposes (to visiting or immigrant students in universities) and settlement purposes (in federally sponsored programs for recent immigrants). Further, these three countries were chosen because their national ESL programs for adults are fundamentally similar (see Cumming, 1998a), making a comparison of teachers' classroom organizational strategies appropriate. For contrast, I selected four other countries or regions where English was taught at universities as an international or foreign language (i.e., not widely spoken in local communities but used in some institutions; cf. Dickson & Cumming, 1996; Stern, 1983, pp. 9–18): Hong Kong, Japan, Thailand, and the province of Quebec in Canada. In addition to surveying different sociocultural contexts, my intention was to see what commonalities or differences might emerge between situations where English writing was taught as either a foreign or second language, and either for academic purposes in universities or for settlement purposes in immigrant settlement programs.

In the analysis that follows, I focus primarily on what the instructors said about their curricula, since the specific ways in which their courses are organized and presented indicate which particular approaches to teaching writing and/or philosophies of teaching are favored by these highly experienced teachers. Throughout this chapter, there are numerous direct quotes where I share exactly what the teachers themselves had to say.

Approach to the study

To gather information about teaching practices in the six countries selected, I interviewed a total of 48 instructors; the breakdown of their teaching situations is shown in Table 3.1. I conducted 31 of the interviews in English-dominant countries; 17 were in contexts where English is an international language. In the English-dominant countries, 19 interviews were in academic programs at universities and 12 were in immigrant settlement programs (i.e., government-sponsored agencies or adult education programs at school boards). All the instructors were highly experienced at teaching ESL/EFL writing, all had relevant postgraduate degrees (most with doctorates), most had published articles or books on ESL writing, and about a third had distinctive international reputations for their research in this domain. They were a selective group of practicing experts in this field, rather than being representative of the general population of ESL/EFL writing instructors in these countries.

For the interviews I asked each person three open-ended questions:

1. How is the curriculum for ESL or EFL writing organized in your institution?
2. Could you describe a typical syllabus for an ESL or EFL writing course at your institution? Please select one course that you usually teach.
3. How are students typically assessed in their ESL or EFL writing?

TABLE 3.1. CONTEXTS OF THE 48 INTERVIEWS

English Is the Majority Language		English Is an International Language
Settlement Programs	*Academic Programs*	
New Zealand (6)	New Zealand (6)	Hong Kong (4)
Australia (3)	Australia (7)	Thailand (5)
Canada (Ont.) (3)	Canada (Ont.) (6)	Japan (6)
		Canada (Que.) (2)
Totals: 12 Interviews	19 Interviews	17 Interviews

I audio-recorded the interviews, took detailed notes during the interviews, and collected any course outlines and samples of instructional materials that the instructors provided.[3] In the interviews and analyses below, I have used the term *syllabus* to refer narrowly to a fixed plan for instruction (e.g., a course outline or program policy representing the basic elements of what is intended to be taught) and the term *curriculum* more broadly and comprehensively to describe the enactment of teaching, learning, and content that people performed and experienced in the context of a particular course (see Stern, Allen, & Harley, 1992, p. 20).

Options for curriculum organization

Concepts defining curricula

Five guiding concepts defined the instructors' conceptualizations of their curricula for ESL/EFL writing, though there was considerable overlap among these concepts for most of the courses described (so the percentages below for each of these concepts merely represent the *one* concept that individuals emphasized most). That is to say, any given instructor did not necessarily structure a course around a single one of the five concepts presented below, but one of these five concepts seemed to take preeminence in the description of practices as provided by each instructor. For this reason, one should consider these concepts as curriculum "options" in the manner described by Stern, Allen, and Harley (1992, pp. 103–273) – that is, as alternative means of defining multidimensional aspects of content possible for language study. These concepts of ESL/EFL writing curricula focused on the following:

1. Composing processes
2. Genres or text types

3. Text functions or structures
4. Topical themes
5. Personal, creative expression

Although each concept places a unique emphasis on a different aspect of writing (see Cumming, 1998b), these concepts are complementary and potentially compatible with one another; indeed, most instructors referred to several of them in conjunction while describing their courses. Taken as a whole, these concepts provide novice instructors an indication of the key options available to them to structure ESL/EFL writing courses.[4]

COMPOSING PROCESSES

A significant number of instructors (33%) described their courses as having the primary goal of prompting students to practice and develop their processes for composing in English. Many instructors described elaborate tasks for information gathering, writing and group cooperation in drafting or editing, and instructional feedback as the principal means of organizing their courses to achieve this end:

They do a single project, which they first design working in groups of about 4, they make a questionnaire, they collect and share data, make an oral presentation, then submit the written report. They divide the report into 3 sections and each person writes individually then shares it. I do just-in-time-tasks related to the needs of this project, for example, while they are proofreading. (Hong Kong)

For the first task, they have to write an essay from 3 library sources. We approach this as a process. We do workshops in groups, using checklists. Then I present referencing guidelines and how to do this. They write their first drafts along with a cover sheet that asks them to form goals. Peers respond to this. Then they hand in a self-assessment on the essay, aimed to develop their meta-cognitive awareness. They get feedback from the tutor and have to rewrite the first draft substantially in terms of content, organization, and language. After that, I provide feedback on the next draft and mark the quality of their revisions. (New Zealand)

GENRES OR TEXT TYPES

Other instructors (21% of the total) described particular types of texts or genres of writing as the principal concept guiding the organization of their writing courses (see Chapter 8 by Johns, this volume, for a full discussion of genre). From this orientation, selecting, designing, and sequencing the writing tasks that students were to complete formed the principal instructional decisions these instructors recounted:

In this course the writing is functionally oriented toward future employment. First, they fill in forms, second job applications, third resumes, fourth interviews, where they practice interviewing techniques, preparing scripts in groups of 3 to 5. They really enjoy the play aspect of this. Then they take notes from phone conversations, which involves listening and note-taking. (Thailand)

It is a text-based syllabus. The outcomes are generalized, using genre theory, in terms of whole texts and picking up salient language components. We use a scaffolded approach, based on cycles of learning, where the teacher gradually stands back as students begin to take control. Teachers design courses, based on assessments of students' needs and working toward particular outcomes. Specific genres are set out already, and the teacher customizes them to learners' needs. The teacher's job is to specify the register, usually with prototypical examples of text types. (Australia)

TEXT FUNCTIONS OR STRUCTURES

Other instructors (23% of the total) conceptualized their curricula for ESL/EFL instruction principally in terms of smaller, functional units of writing, such as formal text units, stylistic devices, or lexico-grammatical features of academic prose:

In the English for Academic Purposes course, students start with paragraphs then go through to a full essay. We are mainly concerned with academic conventions, such as quotations, bibliographies, not plagiarizing, etc. I have developed a manual that covers topic sentences, paragraph completion, proofreading, organizing ideas, and all the usual things. We stress the structure and content, assuming they have the basics of grammar. (New Zealand)

I present samples of writing, and we explore the internal structure of writing, functionally relating words to sentences to genres. In the first task, we look at technical, complex texts, particularly in their vocabulary and syntax, and contrast this with Gertrude Stein's texts. We critique these using [a] readability scale and the role of audience – if they share a common background or not. Then we do differences in spoken and written language, and I get them to notice what distinguishes them. Then we do micro-stuff: words, vocabulary choice, lexical cohesion, grammatical cohesion and function words. Then sentence grammar communicatively: SV, SVO, SVC, SVA patterns, basic clauses, subordination and coordination. Then nominal versus verbal style, its history in English, favoring certain styles, and what happens in the hands of bureaucrats. Students find especially valuable the discussion of thematic progression, given and new information. They say, "You've just turned the lights on. I understand what to do." (Australia)

TOPICAL THEMES

A fourth way of conceptualizing ESL/EFL writing courses (emphasized by 17% of the instructors) was in reference to substantive content. This was defined either in terms of themes that set a purpose and logical coherence for the course, as units of key ideas that students were to address in sequence, or as topics of interest selected by members of the classes themselves. This orientation also involved attention to processes of composing and cooperative exchanges of information, as indicated in these quotations from interviews:

This course is based on themes and issues. There are 4 units. First, relationships: Are they comfortable or not comfortable with them? Second, culture and change: This examines social life, comparing past and present. Here I introduce paragraph writing in academic style with specific topics. Third, social problems, for example, teenagers in the U.S. and Thailand to see if there are similarities and differences. They write a problem-solution essay. Fourth, media and images, for example how women are exploited in the mass media. We explore their likes and dislikes. (Thailand)

We don't really use the concept of syllabus here, as things are content-oriented or -based. The content defines the task. We emphasize the idea of autonomy. Students should become better language learners, identify problems and solve them. So we emphasize process-writing in writing workshops. These have theme or content units, which students work at on their own pace in the afternoons in an exploratory, discovery learning way. (New Zealand)

PERSONAL, CREATIVE EXPRESSION

A distinctly different conceptualization appeared among a few instructors (6% of the total, or just 3 instructors) who saw the primary goal of their writing courses to be the development of students' expressive capacities, based on their personal experiences and opinions:

All is based on the students' own experiences. We're sick of the *Norton Reader* [a text of canonical "great" essays]. Students write every week and do exercises within this context, paying attention to wordiness, cliches, pronouns, passive vs. active voice, parallelisms, and so forth. The textbook is a collection of past students' writing, and they can see models there. (Canada)

I try to challenge the students to be creative in expressing themselves. Students learn to express their feelings and opinions so that others can understand what they think and like to do. I've heard that prospective employers sometimes ask students what they have learned at the university, and that some students have showed them their poems. (Japan)

Independent courses versus integrated curricula

Organizationally, many instructors emphasized the importance of distinguishing whether the ESL/EFL writing courses they taught were delivered as independent, stand-alone courses or as integrated syllabus components combined with other aspects of ESL/EFL curricula. This would rarely be a curriculum option that an individual teacher could alter, but one must remember that a writing course may or may not be the only language course in which a given student is enrolled. Of the 48 instructors interviewed, 17 (or 35%) described courses in which they taught writing independently, whereas the other 31 (or 65%) taught writing in an integrated mode, either wholly or partially integrated with other curriculum components.

INDEPENDENT COURSES

The justification for ESL/EFL writing courses to be delivered independently (usually as a particular course for academic credit) was that writing represented a substantive area of need for students (see Chapter 13 by Leki, this volume). At one extreme (of students highly proficient in English), this perceived need was said to arise because student populations had mastered other, basic aspects of communication in English and now needed to hone their skills in the complexities and intricacies of writing:

This course focuses on writing because the advanced students can already read and communicate fluently. It gives students a variety of styles of writing as well as training in voice and audience. (Canada)

At the other extreme (of students with limited literacy in English), student populations (particularly those just starting university in certain countries) were perceived to need to study writing because they had not previously done so, either in English or (in some instances) in their mother tongues; therefore, they needed to acquire basic literacy skills:

Most students have not taken any writing classes previously in high schools, either in Japanese or English. In their freshman classes they don't in fact do much writing. So I want to do this. (Japan)

INTEGRATED COMPONENTS OF CURRICULA

Several rationales were given for writing to be integrated with other components in ESL/EFL curricula. Some instructors noted the holistic interdependence of writing and other modes of communication (such as reading, speaking, and listening); some stressed the potential for learning through writing to integrate knowledge gleaned from reading or talking; others saw the inherent utility of writing as a means of reporting on group tasks and expressing ideas from learning activities:

Writing is highly interactive here. It is really intertwined with their development of language, interacting with the 4 skills in thematic units. Writing out information aids their speaking. They understand more when they read. Their final products draw on their cultural and personal experiences. They use information from various sources that enriches their understanding. (Canada)

Writing grows out of topics in the class. Each week we look at newspapers. We select a topic. They work out the main ideas related to it, we discuss it, then they do some summary writing or note-taking, then they do report writing, finding out more information about it. We do close analytical reading to see the ways in which ideas are linked to grammar. (New Zealand)

PARTLY INTEGRATED COMPONENTS OF COURSES

A few instructors described intermediary situations between these extremes, wherein writing was combined, for example, with reading tasks to form a literate focus of instruction or with speaking tasks as alternative modes by which students could express their ideas or relay information they had researched. (See Chapter 10 by Grabe, this volume, for a fuller discussion of the value of connecting reading and writing tasks.)

We closely link reading and writing. You can't separate the two. People who read the most are invariably the best writers. But wide reading is not common among these students, even in their first languages. So we critically look at the structure of good writing, how it's done well, taking into account the structure and the content. (Australia)

Writing is not separate. The curriculum is designed for students' needs, and their faculty determine the content. For example, the Arts students do argumentative essays, emphasizing supporting details and conclusions. This is based on what the faculty say their needs are. The Nursing students write therapeutic reports on health-related survey projects. In the Social Sciences, they write research reports, for example, with literature reviews, explanation of methods, findings and conclusions. They do research. Each curriculum is very different for each faculty. (Hong Kong)

Specific versus general purposes

Another consistent difference that emerged among the instructors' conceptualizations of their curricula was whether they viewed their courses as serving specific purposes (as in the quotation immediately above from an instructor in Hong Kong) or general purposes (as in the quotation preceding that, from an instructor in Australia, who teaches courses to students from all faculties in the university together). As Swales (2000), among others, has explained, the logic of *specific-purposes* curriculum design is that language curricula are modeled on analyses (e.g., of discourse, vocabulary, speech functions) of situations in which students will have future needs for using the target language (e.g., Japanese for tour guides, English for waiters). This approach contrasts with more general purposes for language learning, as in courses that aim to develop students' communicative capacities in more broadly educational but less predictable terms (see Widdowson, 1983).

SPECIFIC PURPOSES

Among the 48 interviewees, 11 (or 23%) of the instructors described writing courses that distinctly had a specific-purpose orientation. For these ESL/EFL instructors, specific-purpose writing courses were defined in reference to students' current or future language needs. In academic settings, this usually meant the future writing needs – and associated genres or vocabulary – of professional faculties or academic disciplines. For example:

The courses are tailored to needs. They are mostly aimed at a particular faculty, for example, Engineering, Dentistry, or Law. The needs are assessed systematically through surveys and updated. (Hong Kong)

Specific purposes for ESL/EFL writing instruction were also defined in respect to features of academic texts that students were perceived to need to learn:

I teach a course that is just in its second year now, called New Academic Writing. It is based on a needs analysis for 3rd and 4th year university students, particularly to do research, cite sources, and so on, especially for thesis students, which is like an honors paper in a Canadian university at the end of their B.A. (Japan)

In immigrant settlement contexts, specific purposes tended to focus on writing for vocational purposes – for instance:

We are contracted by an employment center to train new migrants with good tertiary qualifications and professional experience but who lack English proficiency, are unfamiliar with the context, and don't know about the employment situation here. Writing is only part of the curriculum. It is largely workplace texts, such as recounts of an accident, workplace memos, letters of applications, or written reports. (New Zealand)

GENERAL PURPOSES

The 37 instructors (77% of the interviewees) who described ESL/EFL writing courses that had more-general purposes for learning mostly claimed they simply were teaching "academic writing" (meaning a kind of hybrid between specific and general purposes, suited to literate, university contexts; see Chapter 13 by Leki, this volume). But three additional rationales for general-purpose orientations to writing instruction appeared. One rationale was akin to the logic of independent writing courses described above: Students were perceived to have deficits or needs for learning to write that had not previously been addressed in their education. For instance:

English is not compulsory in school, but it is often required. Writing is not emphasized, or even taught at all. So some students at university have not written at all. So this is a major problem at the university level. And the entrance examination is reading, vocabulary and grammar – no writing, speaking or listening. So the universities have to do most of the work in teaching writing. A major difficulty is that no essay writing techniques are taught in Thai, so we have to teach these techniques and the language. (Thailand)

A second rationale for general-purpose orientations emphasized the diversity of students: Because student populations were so different in their abilities, backgrounds, and needs, only a very general approach to writing instruction appeared feasible to address all:

There is a huge spectrum of students. In the most basic courses, some students have been in Canada for a long time but have been laid off jobs, and who can't fill in job applications. There are discrepancies in their abilities too: for example, some Middle Eastern students speak better than they write, and some Hong Kong students write better than they speak. At the intermediate level, people are fairly well educated, but there are a number of Arabic speakers with limited literacy. In the advanced courses, people are hoping to go on to university or college, so they are already fairly well educated. We did have a basic literacy class until last year, but it was funded per student, and the numbers were low, so we canceled the class. But those were the people who needed it most. (Canada)

A third rationale for general-purpose orientations appeared among instructors who – either organizing their courses around topical themes or to promote individual students' expressive abilities – defined their curricula on the basis of interests voiced by their students. In these cases, as one instructor put it:

Writing emerges from topics of interest in class. The students are not looking for jobs or university entrance. They want to know about Canadian society, values, and current events. So the writing is organized around these interests. Writing is an extension of topics of relevance to students. (Canada)

Implications for achievement and assessment

As I suggested earlier, one can consider these pedagogical distinctions among curriculum conceptualizations, integrated/independent courses, and specific/general purposes as *options* that individual instructors may choose or interrelate according to their preferences or situations. That is what Stern, Allen, and Harley (1992) proposed for content elements (e.g., grammar, pronunciation, communication functions, culture) for language teaching in general. But a closer inspection of the interview data suggests that opting for one or another of these conceptualizations of ESL/EFL writing may not simply be a neutral decision: It may have important implications for instruction and consequences for students' learning. As Kroll (2002) claims, "Each choice made in the [writing] classroom speaks [not only] to a particular philosophy of teaching [but] works to shape the course as a whole" (p. 24).

Some potential implications appear in the indicators of student achievement that the instructors mentioned as well as the types of assessment they said they used for their courses. That is, each of these curriculum options implies a somewhat unique emphasis in teaching and in learning; these emphases in turn affect the kinds of achievements that instructors expect to see in their students and the types of assessment they use to evaluate what students have learned or can do in English writing. (But I must caution that the delicate and vital links among curricula, teaching, learning, and achievement could only be hinted at in the context of these interview data as opposed to more extensive methods of research, such as observation, achievement testing, and empirical modeling – see Cumming & Riazi, 2000).

Specific-purpose orientations

Conceptualizing ESL/EFL writing instruction as being for either specific or general purposes may be the most consequential of these options, as I have shown in a separate analysis of the present data (Cumming, 2001b). Choosing one or the other of these orientations seems to prompt instructors to adopt either narrow (i.e., specific purposes) or broad (i.e., general purposes) perspectives for organizing and assessing their students' learning. Instructors who conceived of their writing courses as being for specific purposes typically had straightforward, clear criteria and methods for establishing whether students had achieved the intended objectives of their syllabi. This was most obvious in competency-based curricula,[5] prevalent in Australia and New Zealand, in which core competencies were specified in the syllabus, and instruction, learning tasks, assessment, and reporting of students' achievement addressed these competencies directly through student writing performance. For example:

We do competency-based assessment. Analyses of register and appropriateness define the task and give the criteria. If the [students achieve] the task, then they are certified for having done it. If it is not achieved or only partly achieved, they resubmit it. The criteria for these really open up their eyes and broaden their perspectives on what makes for good writing. (New Zealand)

Similar principles obtained for specific-purpose courses in academic contexts, providing a framework for instructors and students alike to define explicit expectations for writing performance and to establish and know the criteria for how it will be assessed. For instance:

They do a simple project, first design it, second create a questionnaire, third collect data and analyze it, fourth make an oral presentation, then produce a written report. At the end of the course they present the final report, and it is marked when completed, which forces them to see it as a whole. I provide a list of criteria that are assigned holistically, not discretely. The university administration has added a level to this by asking us "to demonstrate gain." So we administer a pre-course test where they write in 1 hour the missing section of a report. Then we compare this with the final report they write, using a list of criteria, linked to the syllabus of the course, so we can score discrete achievement from 1 to 5 from start to end. (Hong Kong)

The students in their evaluations of the course said they learned new things. They find the content useful, for example, learning to fill in forms, prepare resumes, choose information, and make application letters. They build confidence. (Thailand)

General-purpose orientations

In contrast, the ESL/EFL writing courses that were defined more generally had a diverse array of assessment methods associated with them, and their instructors cited a wide variety of different types of achievement that they perceived their students making. As presented in Cumming (2001b), the ESL/EFL writing instructors who adopted general-purpose orientations in their courses described methods of assessment that ranged from proficiency tests, to rating scales, to university-type exams, to grading of assignments, to portfolios, as well as various combinations of all of these assessment methods. (See Chapter 7 by Hamp-Lyons, this volume, for descriptions of these assessment practices.) More consequentially, though, these instructors described their students as making qualitatively different types of achievements in their courses, including achievements in language and style, self-confidence and expressive abilities, composing processes, rhetorical abilities, and even acculturation (e.g., into academic or societal contexts) (cf. Katznelson, Perpignan, & Rubin, 2001). Viewed positively, the general-purpose orientation to ESL/EFL writing seems to allow for a wide range of possible achievements among students, suitable to the complexity of second-language writing itself (Cumming, 1998b; Cumming & Riazi, 2000), which might be assessed in a variety of ways. But if viewed more critically, one might wonder if the general-purpose orientation encompasses such a variety of possible learning outcomes, in ways that are diffusely defined and difficult to discern, that the opportunities to learn ESL/EFL writing may vary greatly from course to course and instructor to instructor.

For example, many instructors who taught general-purpose courses emphasized how their students learned aspects of English language and style:

It is rare in a 12 week course to see quantum leaps, but I am still surprised by the predictable pathways in development, for example, many students are able to write more coherent, satisfying conclusions, more aware of morphemes and tense and appropriate use of linking words, better at controlling sentence length and complexity, better paragraphs, referencing ideas. There are so many small things that go together to make good writing. (New Zealand)

Other instructors observed their students making gains in their unique expressive abilities and self-confidence:

At the advanced level, they show an expanded range of writing and are able to express themselves forcefully and coherently. They seem to be more unique in the way they write. They move away from a standard way of writing, for example, having to do an introduction and conclusion, and realize that the nature of the task defines this, not a pat formula. (Canada)

Other instructors observed improvements in students' composing processes:

Last year I examined how students' writing processes changed, based on interview and protocol pre-post data for 8 students. Students learned several good writing strategies, such as rereading and planning before writing, and they said they felt less anxiety and less resistance. (Japan)

Other instructors highlighted students' achievements in rhetoric and logical ordering of ideas:

They learn to express their thinking, lay it out, put it in logical order, and make it explicit, unraveling ideas and ordering them. So I see this as a great achievement. (Australia)

Still others described how their students, over the progress of ESL/EFL writing courses, socialized into academic or societal contexts:

People are noticeably more relaxed, they can approach people, make informal requests. They can better cope with the everyday demands of academic life. You can't separate writing out from this. It gives them confidence and the tools. And they feel they have got a place to discuss problems openly and comfortably. (New Zealand)

Presumably any and all of such student achievements are vital to ESL/EFL writing, though not all of them may be achievable or teachable in the same context.

Commonalities or differences?

A larger question that arises from this analysis goes beyond the students but focuses really on the writing course itself: Should we expect uniformity or diversity in ESL/EFL writing curricula? My sense is probably both. The instructors I interviewed displayed a range of common practices for organizing their courses. At the same time, the differences among their approaches to teaching writing did not relate in any consistent way to differences between English taught as a foreign or a second language and writing instruction in the academic or the immigrant settlement programs. This surprised me, because I had tried to design this research to reveal differences along these dimensions. Instead, I found the range of curriculum options described earlier, which seemed to be more or less universal in their realizations. This suggests that practices for ESL/EFL writing instruction may be more uniform internationally (and even within countries) than people might presume (though no previous research appears to have really investigated this issue). At least among highly experienced ESL/EFL writing instructors, there is considerable uniformity in their beliefs and claims about the teaching of writing, within the range of curriculum options described here. Such real distinctions as there are between foreign and second language contexts for learning and teaching or between writing instruction in academic or settlement programs may have less impact on ESL/EFL writing instruction than one might expect. Highly experienced instructors appear to do and think fundamentally similar things in these contexts. The contexts differ, but the principles for teaching seem consistent – for example, in respect to aspects of writing that form the focus of curricula – whether writing is taught as an independent ability or integrated with other aspects of language performance, or whether students are expected to learn to write in English for specific or for general purposes.

Indeed, many of the instructors' accounts of their teaching ESL/EFL writing were so similar that I felt any one of the instructors might have easily relocated from one teaching context to another – as in fact many of them had, having moved between countries either to further their careers or for post-graduate studies. Of course, some regionally oriented concepts appeared in the interviews, such as references to the influence of Systemic-Functional Linguistics or genre theory in Australia (schools of thought that focus on the interrelationship between the social contexts in which texts are produced and the purpose and language of texts[6]), a focus on learner autonomy in New Zealand, and concerns for functional bilingualism in Hong Kong. But such issues did not span the dimensions of second/foreign language contexts or academic/settlement programs in a sufficiently extensive or consistent way in the interview data as to indicate they are characteristic of differences in foreign/second sociolinguistic contexts or of educational program types internationally.

As with many political and economic activities, these findings may reflect the worldwide spread of English and of associated educational practices. As Pennington et al. (1997) concluded, "writing teachers in the Asia-Pacific region may be consolidating their practices around a common basis of theoretical and practical knowledge" (p. 138). As a consequence, opportunities for adults to learn English writing may, to some extent, be similar across these countries (though universities represent relatively affluent, specialized contexts, and of course different situations may prevail in other regions and parts of the world that I did not survey).

How might this sort of globalization have happened? One influence is professional networks, conferences, and publications to which the instructors were all readily attuned. One example is the adoption of style guides for writing in English that set common standards, emanating from the United States or Britain, for written formats and classroom expectations. For instance, according to one instructor from Japan: "I use the *MLA Style Guide*, which has been adopted officially by the Department." Similarly, commercially produced textbooks were observed to influence writing instruction on a regional and global scale, though focused on particular learners' needs and related to authentic situations:

We use commercial textbooks that have a strong realism about business writing and mix of thinking skills and emphasis on accuracy. These have changed to functional now; before it was situational. (Thailand)

We use a book [from the United States] with stories of immigrants to the U.S. This keeps it interesting for them and builds on their feelings as migrants. (New Zealand)

The influence of post-graduate education was also evident in the instructors' reflections on their teaching. For instance, while visiting a university in Thailand, where I was expecting to find a unique situation, I was surprised to encounter a native Thai instructor who explained, "I did my M.A. in [state in the U.S.] and got my TEFL degree in Australia." Within universities, research by faculty members was similarly said to exert an influence on writing instruction in ESL courses: "The research on vocabulary in the graduate program features explicitly in the English courses and in the tests" (New Zealand). Such influences from graduate studies extended to immigrant settlement programs as well; several instructors observed that books they had read as students had directly influenced their teaching practices.

Moreover, recent research and theory on second language writing seems to have instilled common terms and conceptualizations in the instructors' talk about their work. Some instructors observed, for instance, that their colleagues were familiar with ideas about processes of composing and communicative competence, adapting them to local circumstances for teaching:

The faculty are cognizant of writing theory and research, and can discuss this. But the university context makes it hard to implement. For example, we see students only infrequently, about 2 hours a week. The approach to instruction is broadly the communicative approach and process writing, but in practice this is widely interpreted, adapted to suit the circumstances, such as lots of students in class and a critical environment. (Canada)

In Australia, pedagogical orientations to language and literacy learning were observed to have considerable public currency, along with strong linkages between theory and practice:

> Debates about writing have been very intense here. For example, in Britain, educators have been compartmentalized. But in Australia that is not the case. Theoretical developments cross fields. There are close relations between researchers and teachers. This has produced very positive things. (Australia)

Similarly, instructors from Asian countries who had studied in North America saw themselves as representing, to their students, the worldwide potential to learn English effectively:

> One of my American colleagues suggests that students should resist English and the power of the U.S. But I have not experienced this, perhaps because I am Japanese. This is an advantage for me. Foreign teachers may bring the impression of American imperialism with them. But I think I represent a functional goal, that English gets you to the wider world. In fact many students are surprised at first that I speak Japanese. (Japan)

For novice instructors learning to teach in this domain, familiarity with these concepts is valuable pedagogical knowledge. Regardless of the situation in which one might teach ESL/EFL writing, one can expect to have to address issues related to composing processes, differing genres or text types, micro-functions or structures of written texts, topical themes, and personal, creative expression. Emphases on certain of these aspects may be prescribed in advance by a specific syllabus or institutional policy. Nonetheless, novice instructors can anticipate the value of honing their knowledge and expertise with these concepts – in the interests of becoming better able to design and provide instruction related to them as well as to select the orientations most appropriate for particular curriculum contexts, student groups, and individual teaching styles or preferences. Likewise, practicing instructors may find it valuable to know about commonalities in ESL/EFL writing instruction, as several participants in the research commented to me after reading a draft of this chapter: Because many instructors work in relative isolation, either within their classroom contexts or geographically or institutionally, even experienced instructors may not be aware of elements in their curriculum practices they share in common.

Where diversity does appear in ESL/EFL writing instruction is in the alternative conceptualizations of writing that instructors might emphasize as curriculum options; whether writing courses are conceived to be for specific or for general purposes; and whether writing instruction is delivered as an independent course or as a syllabus component integrated with other aspects of English study. Pursuing any one of these options may have implications for the achievements an instructor perceives or prompts students to make and for the types of assessment methods an instructor uses to discern what students have learned in

1. **Conceptualizations of Writing**: Writing is defined as

| Composing processes | Text types or genres | Text functions or structures | Topical themes | Personal expression |

2. **Curriculum Format**: The curriculum for ESL/EFL writing is

Independent   Partly integrated   Integrated

3. **Purposes for Writing Improvement**: Students are learning to write to develop

Specific competencies ←————————→ General capacities

4. **Achievements Expected**: Students are expected to improve their

| Language & style | Rhetoric & logic | Composing processes | Expression & confidence | Academic or cultural socialization |

Figure 3.1. Curriculum options in ESL/EFL writing instruction

their ESL/EFL writing courses. If we consider these elements together, construing each as a range of variable options that ESL/EFL writing instructors might adopt, we see the extent of realizations that ESL/EFL writing instruction might take. Figure 3.1 shows a relatively complex array of curriculum possibilities, within the relatively narrow domain of ESL/EFL writing instruction. But I think it is a realistic depiction of how ESL/EFL writing instruction is enacted, as indicated in the present empirical, interview data. To understand the relations between these curriculum elements more precisely would require further concerted, extensive research into the contexts of ESL/EFL instruction. A combination of comparative, ethnographic, and longitudinal research methods might help to illuminate these relations and their impacts on students' learning (see Polio, Chapter 2 this volume, for a description of such research methods).

For novice instructors, the fundamental nature of these differences in curriculum orientations is worth knowing about. These distinctions seem crucial to organizing ESL/EFL writing courses. Knowing which options are available or most suitable to certain student groups or prevalent in certain educational settings and purposes is a key step in planning a relevant, appropriate curriculum. Moreover, opting for any one of these orientations will impact the content of ESL/EFL writing that is emphasized in a course and the opportunities for learning that students may experience. Understanding these issues is a critical component in developing the professional expertise that is a vital part of an ESL/EFL writing teacher's education and training.

Notes

1. I thank Merrill Swain and 16 of the instructors who participated in interviews for useful comments on an earlier draft of this chapter. A version of this chapter was presented at the American Association of Applied Linguistics' Annual Meeting, March 14, 2000. In separate analyses, I report data selected from these same interviews that are focused on assessment practices of the instructors (Cumming, 2001b), and on the situation in Australia's Adult Migrant Education Program in particular (Cumming, 2001a).

2. The only previous, cross-national study of EFL / ESL writing that I am aware of is Pennington, Costa, So, Shing, Hirose, and Niedzielski (1997), which coincidentally involved instructors from many of the countries addressed in the present research. Pennington et al. (1997) found dichotomies between process versus product orientations to instruction as well as ideal versus actual situations for teaching. The present study extends these researchers' recommendations for more in-depth, comparative studies focused on ESL/EFL writing instructors' pedagogical practices and beliefs as well as the constraints they perceive in the educational circumstances of their work. The present analysis, however, was not designed to try to match what teachers said they did with what they actually did in their teaching, as Pennington et al. (1997) or Shi and Cumming (1995) had, though this would be useful to pursue in future research. Moreover, because I did not gather any evaluative data (e.g., on students' achievements) nor systematically observe any of the interviewees teaching, the present research cannot assess the effectiveness of the teaching practices described.

3. I promised the instructors full confidentiality, so no names of individuals or institutions are cited here. Most of the instructors were native speakers of English, though I also interviewed some non-native speakers of English in most of the countries. All of the instructors usually taught their courses in English, with the exception of two instructors in Japan who usually taught EFL composition in Japanese. Two of the instructors (1 in Australia and 1 in Canada) described English writing courses that were open to students from all backgrounds (including native speakers of English), though they tended to attract a fair number of ESL learners to them. For the present analyses, I selectively transcribed the 48 tape recordings of the interviews

and reviewed the transcripts, my notes, and course documents, attempting to identify prevalent themes that the instructors expressed about their teaching practices, using a constant-comparative method of grounded interpretation recommended by Miles and Huberman (1994) and other qualitative researchers. For verification, I conducted a member-check with the people I had interviewed by asking them to read a draft of the chapter and to evaluate, confirm, or query my interpretations. Sixteen participants responded to me (all by e-mail), mostly stating that they found my analyses interesting and appropriate; most people added refinements or, where needed, factual corrections to quotations I had extracted from their interviews.

4. It is not the purpose of this paper to discuss the actual *teaching* approaches associated with these curriculum options. For explicit discussions of classroom pedagogy in L2 writing, see, for example, Ferris and Hedgcock (1998); Grabe and Kaplan (1996); Leki (2001); and Tribble (1996).

5. Competency-based curricula define certain core competencies (e.g., to write a business letter seeking information) for students to attain as the explicit basis for their studies. Students know these in advance, so they work to achieve the competencies stipulated for their particular level of language study. Teachers also know these competencies and use them to organize their lessons and to assess their students' achievements. This is one type of outcomes-based curriculum, which focuses on the results that students and teachers should work toward in language study. See Brindley (1995, 1998) and Feez (1998) for discussion and examples.

6. Systemic-Functional Linguistics derives from the theoretical work of Halliday (1985) and is discussed in some detail by Johns, Chapter 8 this volume.

References

Brindley, B. (1995). Competency-based assessment in second language programs: Some issues and questions. In G. Brindley (Ed.), *Language assessment in action* (pp. 145–164). Sydney, Australia: National Centre for English Language Teaching and Research [NCELTR], Macquarie University.

Brindley, G. (1998). Outcomes-based assessment and reporting in second language learning programs: A review of the issues. *Language Testing, 15,* 45–85.

Burns, A., & Hood, S. (Eds.). (1995). *Teachers' voices: Exploring course design in a changing curriculum.* Sydney, Australia: NCELTR Publications, Macquarie University.

Clark, C., & Peterson, P. (1986). Teachers' thought processes. In M. Wittrock (Ed.), *Handbook of research on teaching* (pp. 255–296). New York: Macmillan.

Connelly, M., & Clandinin, J. (1988). *Teachers as curriculum planners: Narratives of experience.* New York: Teachers College Press.

Cumming, A. (1992). Instructional routines in ESL composition teaching. *Journal of Second Language Writing, 1,* 17–35.

Cumming, A. (1993). Teachers' curriculum planning and accommodations of innovation: Three case studies of adult ESL instruction. *TESL Canada Journal, 11,* 30–52.

Cumming, A. (1998a). Skill, service, or industry? The organization of settlement programs for adults learning English in Canada and Australia. *Prospect, 13,* 36–41.

Cumming, A. (1998b). Theoretical perspectives on writing. *Annual Review of Applied Linguistics, 18,* 61–78.

Cumming, A. (2001a). Curricula for ESL writing instruction: Options in the AMEP and internationally. *Prospect, 16*(2), 3–17.

Cumming, A. (2001b). ESL/EFL instructors' practices for writing assessment: Specific purposes or general purposes? *Language Testing, 18,* 207–224.

Cumming, A., & Riazi, A. (2000). Building models of second-language writing instruction and achievement. *Learning and Instruction, 10,* 55–71.

Dickson, P., & Cumming, A. (Eds.). (1996). *Profiles of language education in 25 countries.* Slough, UK: National Foundation for Educational Research in England and Wales.

Eggington, W., & Wren, H. (Eds.). (1997). *Language policy: Dominant English, pluralist challenges.* Amsterdam: John Benjamins.

Feez, S. (1998). *Text-based syllabus design.* Sydney, Australia: NCELTR Publications, Macquarie University.

Ferris, D., & Hedgcock, J. (1998). *Teaching ESL composition: Purpose, process, and practice.* Mahwah, NJ: Lawrence Erlbaum.

Franco, M. (1996). Designing a writing component for teen courses at a Brazilian language institute. In K. Graves (Ed.), *Teachers as course developers* (pp.119–150). New York: Cambridge University Press.

Freeman, D., & Johnson, K. (Eds.). (1998). Special-topic issue: Research and practice in English language teacher education. *TESOL Quarterly, 32,* 2.

Freeman, D., & Richards, J. (Eds.). (1996). *Teacher learning in language teaching.* Cambridge: Cambridge University Press.

Frodesen, J. (1995). Negotiating the syllabus: A learning-centered, interactive approach to ESL graduate writing course design. In D. Belcher & G. Braine (Eds.), *Academic writing in a second language: Essays on research and pedagogy* (pp. 331–350). Norwood, NJ: Ablex.

Gebhard, J. G., & Oprandy, R. (1999). *Language teaching awareness: A guide to exploring beliefs and practices.*New York: Cambridge University Press.

Grabe, W., & Kaplan, R. B. (1996). *Theory and practice of writing.* New York: Longman.

Halliday, M. A. K. (1985). *An introduction to functional grammar* (2nd ed.). London: Edward Arnold.

Herriman, M., & Burnaby, B. (Eds.). (1996). *Language policies in English-dominant countries.* Clevedon, UK: Multilingual Matters.

Jacoby, S., Leech, D., & Holten, C. (1995). A genre-based developmental writing course for undergraduate ESL science majors. In D. Belcher & G. Braine (Eds.), *Academic writing in a second language: Essays on research and pedagogy* (pp. 351–373). Norwood, NJ: Ablex.

Johnson, K. (1999). *Understanding language teaching: Reasoning in action.* Boston: Heinle & Heinle.

Katznelson, H., Perpignan, H., & Rubin, B. (2001). What develops *along with* the development of second language writing? Exploring the "by-products." *Journal of Second Language Writing, 10,* 141–159.

Kroll, B. (2002). What I certainly didn't know when I started. In L. Blanton & B. Kroll et al., *ESL composition tales: Reflections on teaching* (pp.16–36). Ann Arbor: University of Michigan Press.

Leki, I. (Ed.). (2001). *Academic writing programs.* Alexandria, VA: Teachers of English to Speakers of Other Languages.

Miles, M., & Huberman, A. (1994). *Qualitative data analysis: An expanded sourcebook* (2nd ed.). Thousand Oaks, CA: Sage.

Pennington, M., Costa, V., So, S., Shing, J., Hirose, K., & Niedzielski, K. (1997). The teaching of English-as-a-second-language writing in the Asia-Pacific region: A cross-country comparison. *RELC Journal, 28,* 120–143.

Reid, J. (1993). *Teaching ESL writing.* Englewood Cliffs, NJ: Regents/Prentice Hall.

Riazi, A., Lessard-Clouston, M., & Cumming, A. (1996). Observing ESL writing instruction: A case study of four teachers. *Journal of Intensive English Studies, 10,* 19–30.

Shi, L., & Cumming, A. (1995). Teachers' conceptions of second-language writing: Five case studies. *Journal of Second Language Writing, 4,* 87–111.

Shih, M. (1986). Content-based approaches to teaching academic writing. *TESOL Quarterly, 20,* 617–648.

Stern, H. H. (1983). *Fundamental concepts of language teaching.* Oxford: Oxford University Press.

Stern, H. H., Allen, P., & Harley, B. (Eds.). (1992). *Issues and options in language teaching.* Oxford: Oxford University Press.

Swales, J. (2000). Languages for specific purposes. *Annual Review of Applied Linguistics, 20,* 59–70.

Tribble, C. (1996). *Writing.* New York: Oxford University Press.

Trueba, H. (1987). Organizing classroom instruction in specific sociocultural contexts: Teaching Mexican youth to write in English. In S. Goldman & H. Trueba (Eds.), *Becoming literate in English as a second language* (pp. 235–252). Norwood, NJ: Ablex.

Weissberg, B. (1994). Speaking of writing: Some functions of talk in the ESL composition class. *Journal of Second Language Writing, 3,* 121–139.

Widdowson, H. (1983). *Learning purpose and language use.* Oxford: Oxford University Press.

Woods, D. (1996). *Teacher cognition in language teaching: Beliefs, decision-making, and classroom practice.* New York: Cambridge University Press.

4 Second language writing up close and personal: Some success stories

Tony Silva
Melinda Reichelt
Yoshiki Chikuma
Nathalie Duval-Couetil
Ruo-Ping J. Mo
Gloria Vélez-Rendón
Sandra Wood

"All of us who have tried to write something in a second language . . . sense that the process of writing in an L2 is startlingly different from writing in our L1." (Raimes, 1985)

Different indeed, but what is important for second language (L2) writing professionals is precisely how this difference manifests itself in second language writing. Questions about the distinct nature of L2 writing have driven a great deal of research in L2 writing studies (see Silva, 1993, for an overview and synthesis of some of this research). Researchers in second language writing have approached these questions in different (but all quite valid) ways with regard to who tells the story of this difference: in most such studies only the researcher speaks, reporting on and interpreting observations about L2 writers and/or L2 writing (for example, Hyland & Milton, 1997); others observe and interpret, too, but also use quotations from L2 writers to a greater or lesser extent to illustrate their (the researchers') points and warrant their claims (for example, Silva, 1992). However, only recently have L2 writers been given an opportunity to tell their own stories. (See Belcher and Connor, 2001, and Connor, 1999, who give voice to multiliterate writers; see also Belcher and Hirvela, 2001, who, in a related project, examine the notion of voice in L2 writing.) Such stories are told in a variety of research designs as well (see Polio, Chapter 2 this volume).

In this chapter, we (here and throughout referring to Silva & Reichelt) would like to add to the studies in the third category described above and to push the genre envelope a bit. We present and comment on (unfiltered and unedited) narratives solicited from five L2/bilingual writers addressing the development and the current state of their ability to write in a second language in terms of strategic, rhetorical, linguistic, and any other relevant issues.[1] We recognize that these individuals are accomplished and highly skilled L2 writers and thus not necessarily typical or representative of L2 student writers. We have chosen these writers, in part, to counterbalance accounts of L2 writers in the professional literature, which tend to portray L2 writers as "problems" or as producers of problematic prose.

The writers in this chapter represent native speakers of Chinese, Japanese, Spanish, and American Sign Language (ASL) discussing the acquisition of English writing skills, and a native speaker of English discussing the acquisition of French writing skills. These five narratives provide a firsthand longitudinal look at each writer's experience as an L2 writer and a look at different stages in the development of their L2 writing ability. A brief biographical statement appears before each narrative; our commentary follows the last narrative. We hope that these accounts accomplish two goals: we anticipate that these narratives will prove insightful for L2 writing teachers and researchers in ways that will promote richer understanding of the complexities of writing in a second language, and we hope the stories of these writers will encourage struggling L2 writers.[2]

L2 voice 1: Yoshiki Chikuma

...was born and grew up in Tokyo, Japan. He has a BA in Behavioral Science from Green Mountain College, an MEd in Teaching English to Speakers of Other Languages from Temple University, and a PhD in Foreign Language Education from Purdue University. He is currently an Assistant Professor of Japanese at the College of Charleston.

I started to write in English when I came to the States. When I came to the States, I didn't know anything about writing, period. In Japan, they don't teach you how to write, and although they give you essay assignments, students are left alone to come up with some kind of writing strategies. I did not like homework assignments for summer vacations where you had to write your impressions about books that you were assigned to read. These books were usually boring and even if they had been interesting, I would not have known how to present my thoughts in writing.

My English ability upon the arrival to the States was not so good. My TOEFL score was about 420–430 at that time. I did take a six-week ESL course before I entered an undergraduate college, but it didn't help much as there were so many Japanese students who were in that program and I didn't study much. So I learned to write in English in college by learning to write term papers. In the beginning, I had a very difficult time making myself understood in writing. My sentences tended to be short and direct translation of Japanese sentences. I didn't know that I was supposed to be logical or linear in thinking and choose a position in writing an opinion paper. So I often contradicted myself within a paragraph because I was not sure myself if I would support one position or the other. I was merely presenting the flow of my thoughts.

The sentences I wrote that seemed very explicit to me were not explicit enough for professors. I often got comments, "not clear" or question marks at various points in a paper. What bothered me most was having to write conclusions. What I had thought was a beautiful ending of a paper was not satisfactory for professors. They often wrote that I needed to write a conclusion. To me writing a conclusion was repeating what I had just written and it seemed redundant and unnecessary. But gradually, I started to conform to the norm. I was a behavioral science major so I was exposed to the APA Style and I learned the basic organization and logic of an academic paper from it. Spelling was never a problem for me and I learned punctuation rules in a freshman English course. By the end of my undergraduate years, I had begun to get the feel of what was expected in a paper written in English.

In addition to academic writing, by the second or third year in college, I had started to keep a diary and write poems in English or a mixture of English and Japanese. These writings had nothing to do with my academic life. I had had a habit of keeping diaries and writing poems before coming to the States, but I gradually started to mix the two languages in order to adequately express my feelings.

I went back to Japan after receiving a BA and enrolled in a master's program at an American institution in Japan. Professors there were all native speakers of English. I think my academic writing skills got mature while I was there. I really don't know why, but since then, professors keep giving me compliments about my writing. What is intriguing is that professors in Education at [name of school] tend to give me the greatest compliments about my writing skills in English. I assume that it's because they are not used to having second language writers of English in the classroom.

Currently I write in English most for informal e-mail and chat exchanges because I have always had English-speaking friends who live in a long distance. I am still not confident about writing formal letters. I had no idea what a cover letter was until I had to be on the job market last year. Basically what I did was to go to the online writing lab (OWL)[3] homepage [on the Web] and find a sample of a cover letter and change it to make it suit my situations. These templates help me a lot. I do not usually have a native speaker check my English for term papers, because s/he could make it worse (which I experienced in my undergraduate years). But for the cover letter, I had a friend help me revise it, which I am glad I did.

When I write, I usually use words that I already know and feel comfortable using. I hardly look up words unless I really lack the vocabulary for what I want to express. Choosing right prepositions is still hard for me, so I look up dictionaries when I am not confident about it. For writing, I use *Longman Dictionary of Contemporary English, Cambridge International Dictionary of English, Taishukan's Genius English-Japanese Dictionary*, and *the Kenkyusha Dictionary of English Collocations* (it's huge!). All of them have a lot of example sentences and I can apply them to coming up with my own sentences. I just do not trust Japanese-English dictionaries because I feel that they might give me wrong equivalents or make my English sound bookish.

When I write papers, I do not outline them. I think I have made an outline once in my freshman English class, but since then, I have not made an outline. I gradually organize my thoughts in my head and sometimes jot them down, but I do not make a nice, neat outline. I guess it's because I know I will change my mind as I write so I just start writing with vague ideas. I guess this is one of the reasons my sentences tend to be long with a lot of clauses. Also, I do not care much about my spelling mistakes while I'm writing. I care more about the choice of prepositions because that is not so easy to correct afterwards. In addition to prepositions, I am often not sure about whether a noun is countable or not, so I look that up while writing if I become aware of my uncertainty. And of course I will never completely understand the use of "the" and "a"! Generally, I just follow my hunch for these small grammatical difficulties and do not worry about them too much.

For me writing is a process of making my ideas accessible to readers. What I am concerned with most when I am writing is to be reader-friendly, which I would never have thought of if I had stayed in Japan. Having linking paragraphs and explaining what I would write about next and what I had just written about are a few examples of this idea. I'm not always successful though because I get lazy sometimes. I have also learned to let a draft sit for a while before revising it, and I believe that is part of the process of making the text reader-friendly too.

L2 voice 2: Nathalie Duval-Couetil

. . . was born in Paris, France, and grew up in Watertown, Massachusetts, in the United States. She has a BA in French from the University of Massachusetts at Amherst, an MBA from Babson College in Wellesley, Massachusetts, and an MS in Education from Purdue University. She is currently a PhD student in Education and English as a Second Language at Purdue University.

I grew up in the U.S. in a home where my parents spoke mainly French. Growing up I had few opportunities to write in French. Given that I could speak and understand the language, I chose not to take French in junior high or high school. I opted instead for Spanish from 7th through 12th grade and in high school, added two years each of Italian and Latin. I had little formal French instruction while growing up. My formal instruction consisted of grammar lessons that my mother gave me for a short period of time and a course or two that I took at the Alliance Française in Paris during summer vacations in France.

My first real opportunity to write in French was in college, where I took many French classes in an effort to get my knowledge of French grammar and writing to the level of my comprehension. I jumped right into intermediate and advanced courses where it was expected that I could write. It was in these classes that I realized how much I relied on my ear, as opposed to any grammatical rules that I had learned. One advanced French grammar course in particular truly humbled me. It was the first time that I had to work really hard at French.

During college and during a year abroad that I spent in Paris, I read an enormous amount of French literature, newspapers and magazines. This exposed me to written French and a language that was other than the relatively simple "household French" that I grew up hearing. The combination of academic courses, the reading I had done, and the fact that I was using French on a daily basis allowed my writing to catch up with my comprehension and speaking abilities within a relatively short period of time.

Most of my writing in French during college was related to course assignments. I enjoyed writing within an academic context very much. Since professors didn't expect perfection from students, I was free to take chances and writing was a pleasure. I also felt relatively confident about my writing in this context since my work was usually being compared to the work of native English speakers. Other writing I did during this time consisted of short notes to friends or cover letters for internships or jobs. These were much less fun, I was more self-conscious, took few risks, and always made sure I phrased things in a way that I was sure was grammatically correct.

After graduate school in business, I chose to take a job in the Paris office of an American company. In this context, where we conducted management and marketing studies, writing consisted of composing lengthy reports and exhibits for clients. When I was working on a project for a French client, these reports and all correspondence related to the project were in French. The freedom and confidence that I had associated with writing in French in college waned. In the workplace, I felt that I always needed to write "well." As a bilingual and dual-national, I felt that it was expected that I write well. The difficulty of the work itself, plus what I perceived as the extra burden of writing in French, extinguished any pleasure that I derived from writing in this context.

The nature of the writing was also different in a business setting. I find business French much more cumbersome than business English and writing business reports was quite frustrating at times. Linguistic structures and conventions didn't seem as simple and precise as they are in English. As a result, my French business phrases were probably a lot more direct than those composed by a native French writer. They probably closely resembled the structure of an equivalent English phrase. English vocabulary also seemed better suited for business. It was often difficult to translate what are simple, commonly used business terms in English into French. I distinctly remember a French colleague and I struggling to find the French equivalent for the word "issue" which had been used in many different ways in the training manual that we were translating. My use of American phrase structures or English terms wasn't always a negative. In certain European business contexts, an American style or use of American terms can pass quite well. Even if I made occasional mistakes, my American background may have given me some credibility in certain situations.

Luckily, I was rarely solely responsible for any written communication that would go to a French client. When I was working on such a project, there was usually a native French speaker on my team who would also be involved in the final writing stages of a report. I never really like having a peer read or review something that I have written. Way in the back of my mind is always the strange feeling that someone may "discover" that my writing doesn't live up to my ability to understand or speak French. This is not very rational.

I don't seem to use English as a crutch in my personal or non-business writing. This is probably because I was raised hearing and speaking non-business French and am accustomed to expressing myself in this register. Because "personal" French is familiar, I don't rely on English structures and conventions. I feel comfortable expressing my thoughts and have even been able to integrate word play and humor in my writing quite easily. Business French, which I learned later in life, doesn't come as naturally.

Overall, my composing processes in French and English are quite different. In terms of content, I am sure that my first draft of any writing in French is better than the equivalent first draft in English. In French, I choose my words more carefully and pay more attention to conveying a clear thought. In English, particularly since the invention of the word processor, I too often start with a stream-of-consciousness approach and edit, edit, edit until I get the concise document that I want.

Today, I have few opportunities to write in French except short correspondence and the occasional, short translation. As a result, I am increasingly insecure about my French writing and I use English whenever possible, even with friends and family in France. My insecurity doesn't really have much to do with my ability to compose a text, my ability to communicate my thoughts, or the ability to use proper vocabulary, sentence structure or spelling. Instead, I think I am fearful of making little, "stupid," mistakes such as adding an "s" or "t" to the end of a verb where it doesn't belong.

I probably write better in French than I give myself credit for. Over the years, I have had the opportunity to read things that I have written in the past and have been quite surprised to find what I was once capable of. In order to achieve the level of writing that I would feel comfortable with, I really would have to work at it everyday.

L2 voice 3: Ruo-ping J. Mo

. . . was born and grew up in Taipei, Taiwan. She has a BA in Foreign Languages and Literature from the National Taiwan University, two MAs in Linguistics (one from the Fu Jen Catholic University and one from the Ohio State University), and a PhD in English from Purdue University.

My first encounter with English was in junior high school. At that time, English, Mandarin and mathematics were the three main courses, and thus were offered daily. Because English was not regarded as a means of communication, but rather as a subject to be tested in the entrance exam, the content of the course was mostly exam-driven. A typical English class would include transcribing lexical items, listing the morphological properties of new vocabulary, and practicing various syntactic patterns. Memorizing fixed phrases and idioms was another big task. However, students paid more attention to the verb form after these phrases and idioms rather than how they were used in a given context. What's even more striking was that many students deemed the practice in school was not enough. They rushed to bookstores to get more grammar books and attended cram schools after class. The same practice continued through senior high school though in the school I attended students were encouraged to do some outside readings. It is believed that reading could enhance overall English proficiency. Most students chose the simplified version of western literature such as *Pride and Prejudice* and *A Tale of Two Cities*.

During the high school years, recitations, drills, and grammar exercises occupied most of the class time. Although sometimes we were asked to write English compositions, the main purpose was to practice English. In other words, English writing was not for students to develop their ideas or express themselves, but to provide them another opportunity to put together what they have learned in class, especially the grammar part. Hence, when I was asked to write English composition in class or at home, my first priority was to come up with grammatically sound sentences. The main idea and overall organization of the paper was formed in Mandarin in my head first, and then translated into English. Since there was no one-to-one correspondence between Mandarin and English, I had to rely on Chinese-English and English-Chinese dictionaries to help me complete the translation. However, because I used my native tongue to develop ideas and organize the paper, my English writing was contaminated by Chinese rhetoric. Moreover, because I learned my vocabulary through the word list in the textbook and English-Chinese dictionaries, which in many cases only provide Mandarin equivalents and no actual use, my word choice was also problematic. Yet as long as I did not make many grammatical mistakes and my composition was coherent, the English instructor was usually very generous.

After the university entrance exam, I was admitted to a prestigious Foreign Languages and Literature Department with an excellent reputation for its graduates' overall English proficiency. Students in this department were expected to make extra efforts to meet the higher standard set by it. Therefore, in addition to the heavily loaded literature courses, we had to take several English classes. Among them were freshman English, English conversation, English speech, listening comprehension, and two semesters of English composition. My first English composition teacher was a Hong Kongese who at that time was at the stage of finishing his dissertation. He taught us the basic rules of English rhetoric such as the three-part framing strategy of introduction-body-conclusion and the inclusion of a topic sentence at the beginning or the end of a paragraph. The textbook served as a model. We analyzed the organization of an article, discussed the strengths and weaknesses, and then incorporated the newly acquired strategy into our own writing. My second English composition teacher was a native speaker of English. He taught neither rhetoric nor grammar. He just let us write in class and answered our questions individually.

In addition to what has been taught in class, I also developed several ways to improve my English skills. First of all, I got rid of English-Chinese dictionaries. Knowing the Mandarin translation not only would not help me know how to use the corresponding English word or phrase, but would enforce my old habit of thinking in Mandarin and then translating into English. I added to my collection several English-English dictionaries and thesauruses. The latter helped me avoid using the same word over and over in the same paragraph or paper. Second, I forced myself to listen to English radio programs on a regular basis. Hopefully, my intuition would grow stronger because of this practice. The third one was related to my strategy in revision. After I finished the first draft, I would set it aside for a few days. And when I was ready to revise it, I would read it aloud. In this way, I could not only catch the sentences that did not sound right to my ears, but also check if the paper was coherent.

After coming to the United States, I was placed in an advanced ESL writing class. The instructor was a Greek majoring in linguistics. She used a textbook to discuss grammar issues and cohesive devices that could be incorporated in our paper. Following the brief lecture was the small group activity. Unlike the popular peer views in which students formed small groups to criticize each other's paper, the group work here was to provide us another opportunity to practice English. For example, we would interview our group members concerning a specific topic and then reported the result to the rest of the class. Generally speaking, I enjoyed the class because I could relax and socialize with my fellow countrymen. However, I did not think I learned a lot from the instructor or my peers.

As I continued to write, I gradually got a sense of what my weaknesses were in English composition. Most of them were surface problems such as articles, tense and aspect, and word choice. Since I knew what I needed, I could find help either through writing labs provided in schools, native English speakers, or by reading more papers and books.

L2 voice 4: Gloria Vélez-Rendón

... grew up in Medellín, Colombia. She holds a BA in Modern Languages from Universidad de Antioquia, Colombia, and an MS and a PhD in Foreign Language Education from Purdue University. Gloria is currently an Assistant Professor of Foreign Language Education and Spanish at Purdue University, Calumet.

I can still remember the sheer panic I experienced when faced with the task of my first writing assignment in English at the graduate level. I had no idea how to approach it and I felt that my previous experiences as a student had prepared me poorly for this challenging endeavor. It was in the process of writing it and through a very slow and painstaking labor that I think I truly started growing as a second language writer.

During my undergraduate years as an EFL major I had been required to take two English composition courses in the sixth and seventh semesters of the program. The courses pretty much followed a grammar based approach to teaching writing. It involved memorizing the basic patterns of the English language, producing sentences modeled after these patterns, and doing a lot of filling-in-the-blank exercises and expansion exercises. Very few opportunities for actual writing were provided and the assignments were rather short. Looking at samples of my writing at that time I think I was still at some kind of interlanguage stage. My compositions showed numerous errors in use and form, limited and inaccurate vocabulary, and disjointed and undeveloped ideas. Subsequent undergraduate courses I took in English did not require much in terms of research or writing either. They were evaluated mainly via written exams that relied on the memorization of content. Since the bulk of my courses at that time was in English and French, I did not have many opportunities to write at the academic level in my native language either. I had shown some promise as a writer through my high school years though. I had a way with words and writing came easily to me; I had even won a short story contest in the seventh grade. Growing [up] in a household that valued and encouraged reading and writing a great deal contributed to make me an avid reader with some inclination to writing.

Upon arriving to the USA I became immersed in an English speaking world for the first time in my life. This resulted in a much improved language proficiency. I took some ESL and continuing education courses involving short writing assignments. It was then, I believe when my writing started to sound more English like. Although I still made mistakes at the linguistic level, they were not the kind that would obscure meaning, my word choice was appropriate for the most part, and I was able to produce a short coherent text. Writing did not come easily to me however. Having never benefited from explicit instruction about the writing process made mine a rather intuitive and laborious task. It took long and frustrating moments in front of the blank page before I was able to come up with something worthy and it involved incessant revision and heavy use of bilingual and monolingual dictionaries and thesauruses. I usually received positive feedback from my instructors and their corrections helped me identify problems in my writing and learn from them. The written assignments at that time were rather short and never involved writing an essay paper per se. So when I was first faced with the task of producing a twenty-page graduate research paper I felt totally overwhelmed. I did not seem to have much difficulty representing in my mind what my instructor expected me to do in terms of the assignment. Identifying and researching a topic did not pose major challenges either. Even though I had very little experience with these processes, I was highly motivated and eager to start exploring all the numerous bibliographical resources available to me. I felt that reading not only provided me with the information necessary for developing my topic but also helped me gain awareness of acceptable academic written discourse features and conventions. However, when it came to actually writing the paper I was completely at a loss, my only pre-writing strategies included highlighting relevant information and jotting down domain specific terminology from my sources. It did not occur to me to summarize, let alone synthesize the information I had gathered. Not having a plan or an outline either, I just started by putting down rough ideas in the paper in a disorderly fashion and from there I composed an initial draft which I would improve through revising and rewriting. It was only after having some thoughts down in paper that I was able to gain some focus and to conceive a tentative rhetorical organization. When blocked, I would start working in a different section of the draft or I would go back to my bibliographical sources; rereading passages helped activate the content in my memory and provided good models for my writing. I also found that taking some distance from my writing always helped. I would return to it with a fresh perspective and better processed thoughts. Revising was a solitary and time-consuming process though; I relied only on manuals, dictionaries, and my own non-native speaker intuitions to achieve this task. Asking assistance from a native speaker for this purpose did not seem appropriate. In my mind this practice was as unacceptable as plagiarism for some obscure reason. It was only later that I would learn about the acceptability of such a practice and the availability of a writing lab to help you identify problems and improve your writing. After long hours of writing, detecting and correcting mistakes, deleting redundancies, detecting contradictions, developing and refining ideas, re-arranging text, improving style, and so on, I was finally able to craft what I perceived as an acceptable product. The positive feedback from my instructor was for me the definitive confirmation that I had done a good job. Although my writing process in the subsequent semesters continued being as demanding, I faced it with a newly gained confidence in my ability to produce a decent work.

After graduating from my masters, I returned to my country to live and work there for five years. During this period of time, I consciously sought opportunities to keep up with my English language skills such as interacting constantly with speakers of the language, reading mostly in English and watching cable television. However, I did very little in the way of writing – only letters. It was the time for writing in my native language. The process seemed similar to writing in English in terms of thought processing and strategic use, but it was considerably much easier. I did not have to struggle so much to give form to my thoughts and organize my ideas coherently and do a more polished job aesthetically speaking. I was also able to be creative.

Back in the USA to pursue my doctoral studies, I was again faced with the challenge of writing research projects in English. I felt that I had not grown as a second language writer in the five precedent years, yet I had gained expertise in my field through my readings and experiences and had a much clearer vision of a number of issues. I approached my first writing tasks pretty much in the same way I had done it before but with a broader knowledge base. As I advanced in my coursework, I started incorporating, though not consistently, more effective strategies. For example, through the readings and discussions in [a graduate seminar on second language writing], I gained insights about the writing process in general and mine in particular. So I started doing more in the way of summarizing and synthesizing my sources after reading. I found that this practice sped up my writing a great deal. Instead of trying the impossible task of committing to memory so much information, I got my processed reading down on paper and I was able to use it later in my writing. Similarly, through my research courses, I became a better-informed and more critical reader of research. This is reflected in a much improved ability when writing article critiques and literature reviews.

I feel that I still need to do a better job at the planning and revising stages of my writing. For example, I should be more consistent at doing summaries and synthesis of my readings. I also need to think harder as I approach my writing in order to better envision what I want to accomplish. When revising, I believe I should use more efficient strategies as well. I usually try to revise at all levels at the same time instead of just focusing on one. I can probably improve my approach to writing in other ways I am not aware of yet.

Regarding the present state of my writing, I feel that I have come a long way since my undergraduate years, but I still have a lot of path to cover. I am still at the stage in which the struggle for making meaning leaves no time for originality, depth of thought, and a better aesthetic form, which are my ideals as a writer.

L2 voice 5: Sandra Wood

...was born and grew up in Franklin, Indiana, in the United States. She has a BA in Psychology and Linguistics and an MA in Linguistics from Purdue University. She is currently a PhD student at the University of Connecticut. Her work focuses on the syntax and semantics of negation in American Sign Language.

Compared to most bilingual speakers, my situation is markedly different for learning English. I was born deaf to an American family who were all hearing. They were all monolingual users of English. My mother was not aware of the Deaf community and its language, American Sign Language (ASL), until I was approximately three years old. Consequently, it was assumed that I would learn English and my mother worked with me constantly from the time she realized I was deaf (eight weeks old). From her, I learned to speak in English and was able to put a sentence together when I was two and half years old. Interestingly enough, due to my mother's use of visual sentences and constant writing out of words, I was able to read English by the age of three years old. I was able to read a Walt Disney book, which had several short stories but consisted of 200 pages, in one day by the time I was four. Obviously, my reading level in English was very high when I was young. I was also able to write rather well, writing in cursive by the age of five years old.

Most Deaf people learn ASL through attending a residential school for the Deaf. Only ten percent of all Deaf people learn ASL from their parents, the rest learn from each other at school. Since I went to the Indiana School for the Deaf (ISD) from the age of three to six, I was fluent in ASL and English by the time I was six years old. My mother learned ASL when I was six years old, because she realized that I signed constantly with my friends. She wanted to be able to communicate with me on both levels, especially after enrolling me in a public school with no other Deaf students. This, I believe, made a crucial difference in my intellectual and academic development. I was able to gain access to more information through signed discussions with my mother who would explain much of the things I needed to know that most hearing students pick up on their own.

After realizing that I was rather advanced in my language skills and not challenged enough at ISD, my parents enrolled me in the local public schools. I remained in the public school system until I graduated from high school, with no interpreter or notetaker. At the time, that was the standard situation for any Deaf student in the public school system. Consequently, not many Deaf students were placed in the public schools. Nowadays, it is quite different with several resources available to the student such as interpreters, speech therapy, notetakers, and a resource teacher.

I was always the only Deaf child in the school so I never had any restrictions placed on me as to how well I was expected to do in academics. Most people assume that Deaf students have difficulty achieving academic success and often will treat them as such, which sometimes leads to a "self-fulfilling prophecy." As long as I sat in the front row and attempted to follow what was being said through lip reading and guesswork, I was considered to be doing "okay." To be fair, I did rather well in academics, being a member of the National Honor Society and receiving academic awards, so my teachers and my parents did not realize that I was still in need of an interpreter. I was unaware that I had the right to have an interpreter for my classes until I was a senior in high school.

My first exposure to writing a paper was in eighth grade in which I wrote a paper with twenty-five pages (longhand) on the roles of Black people in the Civil War. My teachers were quite impressed with my ability to write a research paper, using references and footnotes. They felt that my writing ability was on par with a college freshman. I was able to write with a particular perspective in mind and present my arguments to support this perspective in a structured and logical manner. This experience led me to realize that I enjoyed research writing and I would always look forward to a research assignment given by the teacher throughout high school.

In high school, I was given increasingly harder topics and I would often play around with different ways to write my papers. I noticed that my teacher seemed to like it when I would write as scholarly as possible with lots of "long words." I considered that kind of writing to be rather "pompous" but I would continue to write in that vein if it was what the teacher wanted. I never had any difficulty with spelling or grammar. My main difficulty was with the mechanics, particularly punctuation, of writing. My papers were always missing most of the commas and semi-colons that I needed. This may be due to the fact that hearing people pause in the places where one would put a comma if it were written out. I probably did not have that awareness as well developed as other hearing people did.

By the time I arrived in college, I had a confident attitude towards writing in English, which was reinforced by my professors. They often commented on my ability to structure my papers well with an introduction, body of arguments, and conclusion. I did have a very good English teacher in high school that insisted we learn how to structure our papers well. She would use a visual diagram of the introduction as an inverted triangle, the body of arguments as blocks, and the conclusion as a triangle. This illustrates that the introduction should be broad in the beginning and narrow down to my thesis statement. The conclusion should condense the previous discussion, beginning with a paraphrase of my thesis statement and broadening out to a final conclusion. This technique has served me well, even now as a graduate student. I often draw out my papers using this technique and writing in the main points of each section.

Another tool I use in writing my papers is ASL. I often sign my main thoughts and arguments to myself either out loud or mentally. When I am stymied by a mental block in presenting my analysis, I sign to myself until I arrive at the point where I can translate my thoughts into English. It is also helpful when I cannot quite find the right word for what I am trying to convey. I will sign it several different ways to see which interpretation best fits with my concept. If I still cannot think of an appropriate English translation of my ASL, I then consult with my colleagues who are experienced in interpreting ASL to English and vice versa.

Once I started graduate work, however, my whole perspective on English shifted radically. I started to question my ability in writing my research papers because my professors became much more demanding with me. They insisted I have everything perfect, down to the last jot and tittle. I realized that writing in an academic vein was completely different than any other writing I had ever done. I had to learn to write for a linguistic audience, using correct terminology and following standard conventions of linguistic writing. It was almost like learning a new language for me. My mechanics were pretty well developed so I did not have to worry about my punctuation as I did in high school. I had to worry more about making sure my words were chosen carefully because the choice of words could be so potentially misleading. For example, I could not use the word "specific" unless I was using it as in the semantics sense. I would have to use the word "certain" or "particular" instead. Therefore, I started using the thesaurus to help me avoid being redundant.

Also, my grammar had to be refined even further. I had to become more conscious of how I used "the" and "a" because the flow of the sentence would be quite different even if I could interchange them with no discernible difference in the semantics. Sometimes, it was not even necessary to use the determiner before the noun phrase. That was a new one for me. Furthermore, writing for a submission to a linguistic journal demanded that I use either the APA style or the *Linguistic Inquiry* style.[4] I then became aware of the difference between 'which' and 'that' for nonrestrictive clauses and restrictive clauses.

The verbosity of my previous papers that was so well received by my teachers was not appreciated by my professors. I had to learn not to ramble so excessively but to be direct and make sure that everything flowed from my thesis statement. I feel the reason for my rambling was due to my tentativeness in establishing my claim or argument. I felt I had to justify my argument before I even made the argument. Since then, I have improved my academic writing considerably but I still tend to rewrite my introduction several times before it really makes any sense.

One thing that really surprised me in my journey as a graduate student was how even the professors would give their own papers to a colleague for feedback. Once I realized that the feedback by my professors was not a reflection of my skill in English but a necessary check to ensure that my audience would understand my paper, I regained my confidence in my ability to write a good research paper. I also realized native speakers of English struggle with academic writing also, sometimes more than I do. My journey as a writer is not and never will be complete but I do feel that I can present myself well in either English or ASL.

Discussion

In this section of the chapter, we attempt to offer a useful summary/synthesis of these stories and from this generate some questions for research on and instruction in L2 writing.

Affect seemed to play a large role in the L2 writers' accounts of their experience. And while positive notes were sounded (enjoyment, pleasure, confidence, freedom), negative feelings were also voiced (self-consciousness, extinguished pleasure, aesthetic struggle, insecurity, a feeling of being overwhelmed or completely at a loss, sheer panic), reflecting, in our view, the rewarding, but long and difficult road to successful L2 writing taken by this small sample of writers. In addition, there seemed to be a point on that road after which the narrators became substantially more comfortable with and confident about writing. Regrettably, not every L2 writer reaches the point of comfort and confidence that these writers have. For Chikuma, the catalyst was his MA program; for Duval-Couetil, it was a combination of reading a great deal and taking coursework in her second language while functioning in her L2 on a daily basis; for Vélez-Rendón, producing her first L2 research paper in her MA program; and for Wood, the demands of her professors in graduate school.

In addition to affect, the L2 writers said quite a bit about composing strategies or processes. One aspect of this is the use of the native language (L1) and translation from L1 to L2 in second language writing. Chikuma notes that in his early L2 writing his sentences were mostly short and direct translations of Japanese. Mo talks about developing ideas and organization in Mandarin and then translating into English. Wood tells of signing her main thoughts, arguments, and specific words aloud or mentally until she is able to translate them into English. A related issue is the use of reference books – dictionaries, thesauruses, and manuals. Most of the L2 writers mention using (sometimes reluctantly) dictionaries and/or thesauruses to a greater or lesser extent. Chikuma reports using several dictionaries to look up words he is not comfortable using. Mo talks about needing reference books to help her translate from L1 to L2 and to achieve some lexical variety. Vélez-Rendón reports heavy use of dictionaries, thesauruses, and manuals to help her through the revision process and to avoid redundancy. However, misgivings about using dictionaries (especially L1–L2 dictionaries) are voiced, as are concerns about getting inaccurate equivalents, sounding bookish, and reinforcing the practice of translation from L1–L2.

The second language writers also took advantage of written models and writing guides in constructing their texts. Chikuma writes that he learned about the organization and logic of an English academic paper by using the APA style manual and that the templates from a writing center helped him develop formal cover letters. Mo indicates that she was well served by model texts in a textbook. Vélez-Rendón reports using passages from source materials as models for writing, and Wood indicates that her writing profited from her study of guidelines for submissions of manuscripts to scholarly journals in her field.

Additionally, the L2 writers seemed to see revision as both a necessity and a challenge, the most detailed account coming from Vélez-Rendón, who talks about long frustrating moments in front of a blank page and a solitary, time-consuming process requiring long hours of finding and correcting mistakes, deleting redundancies, detecting contradictions, developing and refining ideas, rearranging text, and improving style. Finally, Chikuma, Mo, and Vélez-Rendón all report profiting by getting some distance from their texts – that is, letting a draft sit for a while before attempting a revision.

The way in which these L2 writers talk about their texts reflects an explicit understanding of rhetorical features (e.g., coherence, creativity, depth, directness, disjointed ideas, explicitness, linearity, logic, organization, originality, redundancy, verbosity) and rhetorical elements (e.g., argument, conclusion, introduction, paragraph, thesis statement, topic sentence). Several of these elements are critical to an understanding of the properties that typify academic genres (see Johns, Chapter 8 this volume). In addition, Wood credits a high school English teacher for teaching her what is often referred to in the literature on writing as the five-paragraph essay, a textual construction technique that served her well from high school through graduate school. Furthermore, each of the L2 writers' narratives reflects an acute sense of audience.

It also seemed clear to us that the L2 writers were quite cognizant of but not overly concerned about making errors (grammatical, lexical, mechanical) and that their errors were primarily local rather than global. They reported problems with such things as articles, prepositions, and verb tense and difficulties due to limited lexical resources. The L2 writers were able to address errors by going to writing labs, consulting with native speakers (though this practice was sometimes problematic), and reading extensively in the second language. Several of their concerns with grammar are discussed in the chapter by Frodesen and Holten (Chapter 6 this volume).

The L2 writers talked a lot, typically in a positive way, about teacher response to their writing, a topic discussed more thoroughly by Ferris (Chapter 5 this volume). Chikuma seemed pleased that his graduate school professors complimented his skills in English, even though he modestly claims that they probably did so because they were not used to having second language writers of English in the classroom. Duval-Couetil seemed reassured when her undergraduate professors didn't expect perfection in her writing. Mo reported that her high school teacher was usually very generous as long as she had not made many grammatical mistakes and her composition was coherent. Vélez-Rendón saw feedback from instructors as confirmation that she had done a good job and felt that corrections from instructors helped her identify problems in her writing and learn from them. Wood noted that her undergraduate professors reinforced her confident attitude toward writing, often commenting favorably on her ability to structure her texts. She adds that her graduate school professors were much more demanding, noting, however, that she saw the value in this once she realized that their feedback was not a critique of her writing ability but an attempt to make her writing more reader friendly.

Interestingly, the L2 writers spoke relatively little about getting feedback from native English-speaking peers, and what they did say was primarily negative. Chikuma notes that heeding such advice sometimes made his papers worse. Duval-Couetil describes her feelings of discomfort with having a native French-speaking colleague check her writing. And Vélez-Rendón reports that she first saw asking a native English speaker for assistance with her revising as inappropriate, even plagiaristic. It was only later that she would learn about the acceptability of such a practice and the availability of a writing lab to help her identify problems and improve her writing.

For us, finding this variety in such a small sample of five L2 writers underscores how important it is for teachers to present a variety of perspectives, approaches, and strategies to their students so that eventually each writer can develop a process that works for her or him in a given writing situation (see Ferris & Hedgcock, 1998).

Conclusion

Questions

We recognize that these five narratives – as interesting, insightful, and enlightening as they are – and our observations about them do not constitute a basis for making general or specific claims about the nature of L2 writing, L2 writers, or L2 writing instruction. However, we believe that the foregoing does address some issues worthy of (re)consideration by L2 writing professionals. Therefore, in light of these narratives, we ask the following questions and offer some personal commentary.[5]

With regard to L2 writers:

- Is the notion that L2 writing is a long, slow, painstaking process that never really ends not diametrically opposed to the common situation in higher education of requiring students to take one or two writing classes in their first year in the hope that this will inoculate them once and for all against "bad writing"?
- Should affective considerations be given as large a role in instruction as the cognitive and social considerations?
- Could students be helped to get to the point at which they become substantially more comfortable and confident about L2 writing more quickly and less painfully?

With regard to L2 writing processes:

- In what contexts and at what stages of development are L1 use in L2 writing and L1 to L2 translation beneficial or harmful?
- Is explicit instruction in the use of dictionaries, thesauruses, and guidebooks warranted?
- What are the pros and cons of using bilingual and monolingual (L2) dictionaries in L2 writing?
- Should the use of models and guidelines (e.g., style manuals), which is currently out of favor, be reconsidered?
- Should the "optimal distance" between drafting and revising, that is, the amount of time a draft is left to sit before beginning to revise, be looked into further?

With regard to L2 texts:

- Should explicit instruction on rhetoric be part of L2 writing courses?
- Given that it seemed to serve one of the L2 writers well from high school through graduate school, should the value of teaching the so-called five-paragraph essay in academic contexts be reexamined?
- Should vocabulary instruction be given a (larger) role in the L2 writing classroom?

With regard to readers:

- Are L2 writing students wrong to see their teachers as their primary readers and to value teacher feedback over peer feedback?
- Are students wrong to see peer feedback as potentially bad advice or to feel uncomfortable about asking for such feedback?

Finally, as we found these and many other writing autobiographies quite interesting and enlightening, would such autobiographies be useful as data in L2 writing research and as assignments in L2 writing classes – to raise consciousness for both L2 writing students and their teachers?[6]

Commentary

In writing this chapter, we have come to feel that as L2 writing practitioners we need to be stronger advocates for our students in every way we can, especially in making our faculty colleagues and our administrators better understand the long, slow, painstaking process that is L2 writing. A primary need is to foster realistic expectations of L2 writers, to pursue a goal of progress rather than perfection, and to meet L2 writers where they are in terms of their L2 skills, not only in (L2 or L1) writing classes but across the curriculum as well. Additionally, in closely examining the various paths these L2 writers reported, we believe we have developed an increased sensitivity to affective factors in the development of L2 writing ability, one that has helped us create more supportive and comfortable classroom communities. Moreover, we think it has made us more open-minded in our (re)consideration of a number of issues: L1 use in L2 writing, the role of (bilingual and monolingual) dictionaries and other reference tools in composing, the importance of models and guidelines, incubation time between drafting and revising, explicit instruction in rhetoric, traditional patterns of textual organization, vocabulary instruction, the teacher as audience, and potential problems with peer response. We believe that all writing teachers would benefit from visiting these issues as they plan their own courses for L2 writers.

Notes

1. Silva sent the five writers the initial request to participate in this chapter. After stating that he and Reichelt were planning to write a chapter centered around firsthand accounts of what it is like to write in a second language from the perspectives of highly skilled second language writers, his invitation stated:

    We would very much like you to be a part of this project, that is, to produce a narrative account of your experience in writing in a second language. What we're interested in is a fairly brief (1000 words or so) text in which you address the development and the current state of your ability to write in a second language in terms of rhetorical, linguistic, strategic, and any other relevant issues.

2. Each of the narratives is presented using the exact wording of the writer. Rather than editing or polishing each writer's words, we have chosen to let each writer speak for himself or herself to demonstrate the writer's current (and admittedly highly sophisticated) skill level in English. On a few occasions, the L2 writer's original wording naming a specific school or course has been replaced with wording in brackets that provides a more generic reference; for example, in lieu of ENGL 630, as found in one original text, we substituted "[a graduate course on second language writing]."
3. Many universities provide online writing help through their campus writing resource centers. The original and oldest example of such online writing labs (OWLs) is the OWL at Purdue University, a service provided by the Department of English at Purdue University. Many of its features are accessible to the public via its Web site as well: http://owl.english.purdue.edu.
4. *Linguistic Inquiry* is the name of a journal that requires use of its own style sheet for articles submitted for publication in that journal.
5. Additional discussion of the issues mentioned in the questions can be found both in a number of book-length treatments of second language writing in general (Ferris & Hedgcock, 1998; Leki, 1992; Reid, 1993) and in recent work addressing specific issues like L2 composing processes (Krapels, 1990; Manchon, 2001), L1 use in L2 writing (Friedlander, 1990), dictionary use among L2 writers (Christianson, 1997), lexical issues in L2 writing

(Engber, 1995), and peer and teacher feedback to L2 writing (Zhang, 1995). Extensive inquiry into these and other L2 writing issues can be conducted through the use of annotated bibliographies by Tannacito (1995) and Silva, Brice, and Reichelt (1999) and the "Bibliography of recent scholarship in second language writing," which appears in every issue of the *Journal of Second Language Writing*.

6. In fact, we would like to mention that we have both used writers' biographies as initial assignments in our L2 writing classes and feel that this has served us well not only in getting to know our students better but also in helping us understand and more intelligently and tactfully deal with our students' perceptions and values with regard to their written work.

References

Belcher, D., & Connor, U. (Eds.). (2001). *Reflections on multiliterate lives.* Clevedon, England: Multilingual Matters.

Belcher, D., & Hirvela, A. (Eds.). (2001). *Voice in L2 writing* [Special issue]. *Journal of Second Language Writing, 10(1–2)*.

Christianson, K. (1997). Dictionary use by EFL writers: What really happens. *Journal of Second Language Writing, 6, 23–43.*

Connor, U. N. (1999). Learning to write academic prose in a second language: A literacy biography. In G. Braine (Ed.), *Non-native educators in English language teaching* (pp. 29–42). Mahwah, NJ: Lawrence Erlbaum.

Engber, C. (1995). The relationship of lexical proficiency to the quality of ESL compositions. *Journal of Second Language Writing, 4, 139–155.*

Ferris, D., & Hedgcock, J. S. (1998). *Teaching ESL composition: Purpose, process, and practice.* Mahwah, NJ: Lawrence Erlbaum.

Friedlander, A. (1990). Composing in English: Effects of a first language on writing in English as a second language. In B. Kroll (Ed.), *Second language writing: Research insights for the classroom* (pp. 109–125). New York: Cambridge University Press.

Hyland, K., & Milton, J. (1997). Qualification and certainty in L1 and L2 students' writing. *Journal of Second Language Writing, 6, 183–205.*

Journal of Second Language Writing. New York: Elsevier Science.

Krapels, A. (1990). An overview of second language writing process research. In B. Kroll (Ed.), *Second language writing: Research insights for the classroom* (pp. 37–56). New York: Cambridge University Press.

Leki, I. (1992). *Understanding ESL writers: A guide for teachers.* Portsmouth, NH: Boynton-Cook.

Manchon, R. M. (Ed.). (2001). Writing in the L2 classroom: Issues in research and pedagogy [Special issue]. *International Journal of English Studies, 1(2).*

Raimes, A. (1985). What unskilled ESL students do as they write: A classroom study of composing. *TESOL Quarterly, 19, 229–258.*

Reid, J. M. (1993). *Teaching ESL writing.* Englewood Cliffs, NJ: Regents/ Prentice Hall.

Silva, T. (1992). L1 vs L2 writing: ESL graduate students' perceptions. *TESL Canada Journal, 10, 27–47.*

Silva, T. (1993). Toward an understanding of the distinct nature of L2 writing: The ESL research and its implications, *TESOL Quarterly, 27, 657–677.*

Silva, T., Brice, C., & Reichelt, M. (1999). *Annotated bibliography of scholarship in second language writing: 1993–1997.* Stamford, CT: Ablex.

Tannacito, D. (1995). *A guide to writing English as a second or foreign language: An annotated bibliography of research and pedagogy.* Alexandria, VA: TESOL.

Zhang, S. (1995). Reexamining the affective advantage of peer feedback in the ESL writing class. *Journal of Second Language Writing, 4,* 209–222.

PART III:
EXPLORING WRITERS' FINISHED TEXTS

It is perhaps axiomatic to say that one learns to write by writing. And while no one disputes that many second language (L2) writers will grow into better writers simply by producing sufficient quantities of writing over an extended period (during which time their general language skills presumably improve as well), both native and second language writers often benefit most and make the most progress when teachers and peers contribute to this goal through a variety of intervention strategies available in classroom settings.

As long as they have been in existence, writing classes have tended to revolve around assignments that require students to produce various types of texts. What has changed in more recent methodologies in writing classes is the opportunity students are given to craft their writing – rather than being forced into a situation where all writing tasks are undertaken in a one-shot approach. Even in the era of so-called post-process approaches (Babin & Harrison, 1999, p. 223; McComiskey, 2000), most classes allow students to approach writing tasks through a series of stages in some kind of process framework. Regardless of other distinctions in their approaches to curriculum design and syllabus planning, many writing teachers would probably agree that extended work on a single piece of writing contributes most to students' ability to expand their writing skills.

Previous sections in this volume have examined issues in second language writing as a field of study, have given some insight into the way teachers conceptualize courses, and have shown how second language writers view their own learning. The three chapters in this section are focused on the actual writing that students produce. As teachers, how do we respond to it? How do we approach the student's language struggles and assess the writing in general?

What are the issues and options for teachers to consider as they structure feedback opportunities for their students?

For students, the most time-consuming of the tasks they are asked to undertake in writing courses is preparing texts, that is, written responses to the required writing assignments. Sometimes this process is extended when they are also asked to incorporate peer response; this serves as a way to hone their abilities to analyze their own and others' texts. Once student writing is submitted to the teacher, the most time-consuming of all teacher tasks is crafting responses to student output. Teacher response typically takes the form of written commentary but can also be delivered orally via conference (or potentially via audiotape as well). Because learning to write useful comments is not an easy task, a recurrent theme in teacher training has been helping teachers improve the effectiveness of their comments (Mathison-Fife & O'Neil, 2001; Qualley, 2002; Yates & Kenkel, 2002).

Chapter 5 by Dana Ferris provides a survey of current L2 research on written teacher responses, on teacher-student conferences, and on peer responses. Ferris organizes her discussion around nine generalizations from previous research that highlight key issues and findings from a wide range of studies. Attention is given throughout to research on student attitudes toward teacher and peer response, description of teacher and peer commentary, and effectiveness of response on students' subsequent writing. A large number of studies have investigated the area of teacher response, but not to the satisfaction of everyone. Ferris echoes some of the reservations raised by Goldstein (2001), citing the need for future studies on this topic to pay greater attention to the classroom and institutional context in studying teacher commentary and subsequent student revision. Polio's earlier chapter on research methods (Chapter 2) cautions that any given technique might have its limitations; both Ferris and Goldstein (2001) call for more rigor in research.

What role(s) should grammar play in writing courses for second language students?

Accuracy in the linguistic properties of sentences and discourse structures can certainly contribute to overall text excellence, but finding ways to incorporate attention to grammar in L2 writing courses can be problematic. In exploring the debates about combining language and ESL writing instruction, in Chapter 6 Jan Frodesen and Christine Holten acknowledge the controversy over whether overt grammar instruction and/or specific feedback on grammar errors is useful to an ESL writer's overall language and writing development (see particularly Truscott, 1996; Ferris, 1999; and Truscott, 1999). Their chapter explores three key questions of concern to both practitioners and researchers regarding (1) the usefulness of grammar instruction, (2) the role of grammar in drafting, and (3) the place of feedback on error. Frodesen and Holten present a thorough discussion of appropriate principles to adopt for incorporating grammar in writing instruction in manageable and optimal ways, offering specific guidance for understanding the dynamic interrelationship between learners, their texts, and their writing processes. They also address the ways that evolving work in text linguistics figures in the debate, especially with its concerns for identifying properties of various genres.

What is the role for writing assessment in understanding writers' texts?

Whereas teacher and peer feedback provide opportunities for students to have their writing assessed on an ongoing basis, academic life provides numerous occasions for writing assessment to occur outside an individual class. For example, Brindley and Ross (2001) suggest that in the English for Academic Purposes (EAP) environment, assessment data guide "selection [of students], curriculum monitoring and program accountability" (p. 148).

Chapter 7 by Liz Hamp-Lyons provides an overview of writing assessment by discussing such general concepts as reliability and validity as well as key developments in how writing assessment has been viewed past and present. Her chapter covers students' role in and perceptions of writing tests, processes in the development of writing assessment instruments, uncertainties in the evaluation of the writing by raters, and issues in notions of "correctness" and "appropriacy" of written texts, tying in with some of the concerns raised by Frodesen and Holten in Chapter 6 and anticipating issues raised by Connor in Chapter 9. Hamp-Lyons argues that while some teachers would prefer to leave assessment to "someone else," teachers are the right people (and the best people) to ensure that students are assessed meaningfully and fairly. Williamson and Huot (2000, p. 206) have suggested that "the main difference between teachers and testers is that assessment developers are primarily interested in observing the differences between people, while most teachers are primarily interested in helping individuals to develop." Hamp-Lyons wants to ensure that such a gap is bridged.

References

Babin, E., & Harrison, K. (1999). *Contemporary composition studies: A guide to theorists and terms.* Westport, CT: Greenwood Press.

Brindley, G., & Ross, S. (2001). EAP assessment: Issues, models and outcomes. In J. Flowerdew & M. Peacock (Eds.), *Research perspectives on English for academic purposes* (pp. 148–166). New York: Cambridge University Press.

Ferris, D. (1999). The case for grammar correction in L2 writing classes: A response to Truscott. *Journal of Second Language Writing, 8,* 1–11.

Goldstein, L. (2001). For Kyla: What does the research say about responding to ESL writers. In T. Silva & P. K. Matsuda (Eds.), *On second language writing* (pp. 73–89). Mahwah, NJ: Lawrence Erlbaum.

Mathison-Fife, J., & O'Neil, P. (2001). Moving beyond the written comment: Narrowing the gap between response practice and research. *College Composition and Communication, 53,* 300–321.

McComisky, B. (2000). The post-process movement in composition studies. In R. Wallace, A. Jackson, & S. L. Wallace (Eds.), *Reforming college composition: Writing the wrongs* (pp. 37–53). Westport, CT: Greenwood.

Qualley, D. (2002). Learning to evaluate and grade student writing: An ongoing conversation. In B. Pytlik & S. Liggett (Eds.), *Preparing college teachers of writing* (pp. 278–291). New York: Oxford University Press.

Truscott, J. (1996). The case against grammar correction in L2 writing classes. *Language Learning, 46,* 327–369.

Truscott, J. (1999). The case for "The case against grammar correction in L2 writing classes." A response to Ferris. *Journal of Second Language Writing, 8,* 111–122.

Williamson, M., & Huot, B. (2000). Literacy, equality, and competence: Ethics in writing assessment. In M. A. Pemberton (Ed.), *The ethics of writing instruction: Issues in theory and practice* (pp. 191–209). Stamford, CT: Ablex.

Yates, R., & Kenkel, J. (2002). Responding to sentence-level errors in writing. *Journal of Second Language Writing, 11,* 29–47.

5 *Responding to writing*

Dana Ferris

Response to student writing and its effects on writers is a vitally important topic for second language (L2) writing teachers and researchers. For many teachers, the act of responding (whether orally or in writing) represents the largest investment of time they make as writing instructors. For students, the feedback they receive from both instructors and peers may be the most significant component in their successful development as writers. The potential value of teacher feedback has been highlighted by the widespread adoption over the past fifteen years of a process approach in North American English as a second language (ESL) writing classrooms (see Matsuda, Chapter 1 this volume), meaning that students have the opportunity to receive and review teacher feedback and then to submit revised versions of their papers. Further, the increased emphasis on other forms of response in both native language (L1) and second language (L2) composition teaching, such as teacher-student conferences and peer feedback, may also be attributed to the popularity of the process approach with its cycles of multiple drafts.

The nature and effects of teacher commentary and peer feedback in L2 writing classes have both been widely investigated over the past decade. This chapter looks first at historical perspectives on response to student writing and then moves to a discussion of key issues (and their pedagogical implications) in teacher and peer response to L2 writing that have been identified by previous research. Finally, it highlights questions and strategies for future studies on this vitally important area of L2 composition research.[1]

Perspectives on response to student writing

As noted by Leki (1990a), initial L1 research concerning written teacher commentary on student writing revealed a discouraging picture, with teachers finding that regardless of their comments, students' writing did not improve in subsequent writing tasks. A frequently cited early L1 review asserts, "We have scarcely a shred of empirical evidence to show that students typically even comprehend our responses to their writing, let alone use them purposefully to modify their practice" (Knoblauch & Brannon, 1981, p. 1). Reviews by Hillocks (1986) and Knoblauch and Brannon (1981) concluded that regardless of how written teacher feedback was delivered (in the margins or at the end of the paper, in red or black pen, through correction symbols or verbal commentary, etc.), it appeared to be unsuccessful in helping students to improve their writing; worse, students seemed either to resent or ignore teacher feedback. To the "composition slaves" of the world – teachers toiling away late into the night to provide comments or corrections on student papers (Hairston, 1986) – the conclusions of these research reviews were discouraging indeed. The resulting widespread view that teacher feedback was ineffective and unappreciated by students undoubtedly contributed to the corresponding rise in the use of peer feedback and teacher-student conferencing in writing classes, classroom concepts that later came to be termed collaborative approaches.[2]

The next phase in the history of response to student writing thus focused on strategies considered less "appropriative" (i.e., directly or indirectly forcing onto the author of a paper the teacher's views of what student writing should achieve). As chronicled by Zhang (1995), in native language composition, peer feedback was widely adopted because it was seen as more appealing and less threatening and disempowering than teacher commentary. When teachers did give feedback, they were encouraged to do so in face-to-face teacher-student writing conferences, again seen as preferable to written teacher feedback because conferences offered students opportunity for on-the-spot negotiation and clarification.

As time went on, other researchers began to point out that the response-and-revision dynamic was far more complex than previous studies and reviews had considered. Most early studies had been conducted in contexts in which students wrote only one draft of a paper, submitted it to the teacher for correction and evaluation, and then moved onto the next writing assignment. As students and teachers increasingly adopted multiple-draft approaches to writing instruction, it became important for researchers to consider carefully the effects of feedback on student writing given prior to asking students to revise their papers. In addition, scholars argued that earlier teacher feedback studies were too decontextualized, looking at the student paper and written teacher comments in isolation without considering anything else about the writing class or the relationships between teachers and students (see Ferris, Pezone, Tade, & Tinti, 1997; Leki, 1990a; Mathison-Fife & O'Neill, 1997; Reid, 1994; Silva, 1988, for discussions of these contextual issues). Given the differing contexts in which research was conducted, it should not be surprising that results of studies and researchers' interpretations of their findings in the area of responding to writing have been somewhat inconclusive and even contradictory (not unlike the findings in other areas of L2 research). In a recent review of numerous studies on teacher commentary in the English as a second language (ESL) or English as a foreign language (EFL) context, Goldstein (2001) calls on future researchers to remember that "[b]ecause teacher commentary, student reactions to commentary, and student revisions interact with each other, research needs to look at all three simultaneously" (p. 86).

Reid (1994) reports on an example from her own teaching that illustrates how teacher commentary taken out of context can be seen to misrepresent the dynamics of the classroom. In a unit in which her students were drafting persuasive essays late in the semester, she informed them that she would review their drafts and highlight any logical fallacies by using labels such as "hasty" or "oversimplification" in the margins. She notes:

An outside examiner viewing those remarks might conclude that I am being obtuse, negative, and appropriative. Instead, my students view it as a game: They fully understand the shorthand of the response, which reminds them of our classroom discussion and activates their background knowledge about logical fallacies. (p. 281, emphasis added)

As researchers and theorists continue looking at all types of response to student writing, it has become clear that such examinations need to take place within multiple-draft, longitudinal, and carefully contextualized research designs. It is encouraging to note that researchers examining response to student writing have recently begun to take seriously the need for triangulated, longitudinal research designs examining this issue and that some valuable insights have emerged as a result (e.g., Conrad & Goldstein, 1999; Ferris, 2001; Ferris, Chaney, Komura, Roberts, & McKee, 2000; McGroarty & Zhu, 1997; Polio, Fleck, & Leder, 1998).

Further, while teacher-student conferences and peer feedback are certainly appealing alternatives to written teacher feedback on student writing, they will not and should not completely replace written teacher commentary. Not all writing teachers have the time and space to hold regular one-to-one conferences with their students (due to heavy student loads and/or lack of office space). Some students may be uncomfortable with face-to-face interactions with their teachers; others may process and utilize feedback better in written than oral forms. Furthermore, peer feedback clearly represents a different response dynamic from teacher-student feedback because of varying levels of expertise and competence on the part of student writers as well as ascribed respect and authority. Teacher and peer response ideally should co-exist peacefully within a writing class, but there is no evidence, nor have any compelling arguments been advanced, that one should completely replace the other. It is thus assumed in this discussion that all three types of feedback – written teacher commentary, oral teacher-student conferences, and peer feedback – are

1. Feedback is most effective when it is delivered at intermediate stages of the writing process.

2. Teachers should provide feedback on all aspects of student texts, including content, rhetorical structure, grammar, and mechanics.

3. Teacher feedback should be clear and concrete to assist students with revision. At the same time, teachers need to be careful not to appropriate student texts.

4. Teacher feedback must take individual and contextual variables into account.

5. ESL writers attend to teacher feedback and attempt to utilize it in their revisions.

6. Teacher-student writing conferences may be more complex with L2 writers.

7. There is a great deal of variation in what students talk about during peer feedback and how they interact with one another – which may be related to how the teacher models feedback and structures peer response sessions.

8. Research evidence is conflicting about the degree to which students utilize peer feedback in their revisions.

9. Students appear to enjoy peer feedback and find it helpful.

Figure 5.1.   Response to student writing: Generalizations from previous research

qualitatively and practically different from one another and that all three forms have their legitimate roles within L2 writing instruction.[3]

Teacher response to L2 writing: Research approaches and findings

Examinations of teacher commentary on student writing have included text analytic studies, quasi-experimental approaches, and survey research on student attitudes toward teacher commentary. (See Polio, Chapter 2 this volume, for a discussion of these research types.) These studies have highlighted a number of specific issues and implications for L2 writing instructors. Figure 5.1 summarizes these issues; each is discussed in succeeding sections of the chapter.

FEEDBACK IS MOST EFFECTIVE WHEN IT IS DELIVERED AT INTERMEDIATE STAGES OF THE WRITING PROCESS

Most L2 composition instructors, researchers, and theorists now agree that teacher feedback is most effective when it is delivered at intermediate stages of the writing process, when students can respond to feedback in subsequent revisions and may thus be more motivated to attend to teacher suggestions (Ferris, 1995; Krashen, 1984; Leki, 1990a; Zamel, 1985). Thus many North American ESL writing instructors now encourage or even require students to write multiple drafts of their papers, providing opportunities for feedback (written teacher commentary, teacher-student conferences, peer feedback) during and between the writing of various drafts. With numerous opportunities for students to receive feedback and revise, teachers can choose to focus on different issues (content, organization, grammar, style) at different stages of the writing cycle. While some scholars have urged teachers to give feedback only on content and organization in early drafts, saving sentence-level issues for the end of the process (e.g., Zamel, 1985), others have noted that ESL writers are capable of dealing effectively with more than one type of feedback on the same draft (Fathman & Whalley, 1990; Ferris, 1997).

TEACHERS SHOULD PROVIDE FEEDBACK ON ALL ASPECTS OF STUDENT TEXTS, INCLUDING CONTENT, RHETORICAL STRUCTURE, GRAMMAR, AND MECHANICS

Influenced by process approach advocates and social constructionists (see Ferris & Hedgcock, 1998; Johns, 1990; Silva, 1990, for summaries), writing instruction and assessment have increasingly focused on students' ideas, mastery of rhetorical strategies and forms, and awareness of audience. As teachers' priorities for student writing have changed, the types of feedback they have given students about their writing have changed as well. Though early L2 studies of teacher feedback reported that ESL writing teachers focused almost exclusively on sentence-level errors (Cumming, 1985; Kassen, 1988; Zamel, 1985), later investigations, including both student survey research and text analytic examinations of teacher commentary, indicated that teachers (perhaps influenced by the process paradigm) provided feedback that responded to students' ideas and organization as well as their errors in grammar and mechanics (Cohen & Cavalcanti, 1990; Dessner, 1991; Ferris, 1995, 1997; Ferris et al., 1997; Hedgcock & Lefkowitz, 1994; Lam, 1992). Further, as teachers modeled these priorities, student writers indicated that they paid attention to and valued feedback on all aspects of their writing (Ferris, 1995; Hedgcock & Lefkowitz, 1994).

The above generalizations would suggest that teachers should focus their feedback efforts primarily on intermediate drafts of student texts, perhaps limiting final draft feedback to some affirmation of what the writer has done well and to a summative suggestion or two about problems or issues the writer should consider for future assignments (and/or for future iterations of the paper in question if portfolio assessment is being utilized). It also seems clear that teachers should give feedback about a variety of writing issues, including ideas, organization, grammar, mechanics, vocabulary, and style, depending upon the needs of the individual student, the developmental stage of the text, the specifications of the particular assignment, and the overall expectations of the writing course.

TEACHER FEEDBACK SHOULD BE CLEAR AND CONCRETE TO ASSIST STUDENTS WITH REVISION. AT THE SAME TIME, TEACHERS NEED TO BE CAREFUL NOT TO APPROPRIATE STUDENT TEXTS

Both L1 and L2 survey studies on student reactions to teacher feedback have reported consistent findings that students appreciate clear, concrete, specific feedback (see, for instance, Ferris, 1995, and Straub, 1997). A text analytic study linking various types of teacher comments to the effectiveness of student revisions reported that teacher questions asking for specific information or giving concrete suggestions led to more-effective student revisions than feedback that was more general or abstract (Ferris, 1997, 2001). In a recent case study of three student writers' revisions after receiving teacher feedback, Conrad and Goldstein (1999) found that teacher comments that challenged students' logic or argumentation were most likely to be problematic for the student writers.

Such findings would indicate that ESL writing instructors should be straightforward, concrete, and fairly directive in their feedback to L2 writers. On the other hand, both L1 and L2 composition scholars have warned teachers against "appropriating" (taking over) students' texts by being too authoritative and direct in their feedback (see, e.g., Brannon & Knoblauch, 1982; Elbow, 1973; Krashen, 1984; Sommers, 1982; Zamel, 1985). When teachers cross out portions of student texts and substitute other words or ideas, make directive suggestions, or use the imperative mood, these behaviors communicate to student writers that the teacher's priorities are more important than what the writer wants to say in his or her own text. Such appropriative behavior can frustrate, demotivate, and otherwise disempower student writers. To avoid appropriation, teachers have been advised and even trained to ask questions rather than to use statements or imperatives, to avoid the use of "I" and "you" (as in "you should . . ."), to use hedges to soften criticism or suggestions, and to communicate that any revisions are left solely to the discretion of the text's author.

A number of L2 researchers and teachers have questioned whether a "nonappropriative" approach to feedback is optimal for L2 writers. Leki (1990a), commenting on this issue, notes that

while Knoblauch and Brannon's interesting perspective on improvement may well be pertinent for L1 writers, the peculiar situation of L2 writers makes adoption of their attitudes somewhat more problematic for the L2 writing teacher. *An element of prescription appears necessary in responses to L2 student papers* because L2 students have a smaller backlog of experience with English grammatical and rhetorical structure to fall back on, not having had the same exposure to those structures as native speakers have had. (p. 59, emphasis added)

Other researchers have highlighted the unique status of L2 writers and resulting implications for instruction and specifically teacher feedback (Ferris, 1999; Ferris & Hedgcock, 1998; Patthey-Chavez & Ferris, 1997; Silva, 1993, 1997). Reid (1994) spoke out strongly against what she termed "the myths of appropriation," arguing that composition teachers, out of fear of being appropriative, were failing to distinguish between appropriation and necessary intervention. Other researchers have pointed out that L2 writers may have linguistic, cultural, and rhetorical differences that could cause them to misinterpret teacher indirectness in either written comments or face-to-face conferences (Ferris, 1999; Ferris & Hedgcock, 1998; Goldstein & Conrad, 1990; Patthey-Chavez & Ferris, 1997). Second language writing teachers concerned with clarity and helpfulness on the one hand and appropriative behavior on the other must strive for a balance between the two concerns with which both they and their students feel comfortable.

TEACHER FEEDBACK MUST TAKE INDIVIDUAL AND CONTEXTUAL VARIABLES INTO ACCOUNT

The needs, desires, and abilities of individual student writers with regard to feedback are often overlooked by researchers and theorists. Teachers, in their efforts to be nonappropriative and consistent, may forget that "one size does not fit all" and that different students may require different types of feedback. In the United States, several authors have observed that there are differences in background between international student writers and long-term U.S. residents (i.e., immigrants) that may have specific implications for teacher feedback (Ferris, 1999; Leki, 1992; Reid, 1998; see also Harklau, Losey, & Siegal, 1999). For instance, international students may never have experienced "composing" or "revision" in their English classes in their home countries and may fail to see the need or purpose for multiple drafting, revision, or teacher feedback (except to explain their grade and tell them what they did "wrong"). While immigrant students may have already experienced multiple drafting and teacher feedback as characteristics of the American composition classroom, they may be unfamiliar with technical jargon related to either rhetorical issues ("thesis," "transition") or grammatical points ("subject-verb agreement," "sentence fragment"), terms they are likely to find written by teachers on their papers.

It is important for writing instructors to assess their particular students' prior experiences, knowledge, and expectations at the beginning of a course and to explain their own responding strategies to their students (see also Leki, 1992; Reid, 1998). Teachers also need to be aware of student motivations. Students and instructors in foreign language (FL) classes (e.g., students studying Spanish in the United States or English in FL contexts) tend to see writing as language practice or as a way to demonstrate comprehension of literature. Foreign language students may not be as motivated to revise and edit their writing as students who understand that their academic and future career success may depend to some degree on their ability to master the conventions of English writing (Hedgcock & Lefkowitz, 1994). In sum, not all L2 writers are identical in their experience, knowledge, and motivations simply because they are writing in a second language (see Silva and Reichelt, Chapter 4 this volume, for some student voices speaking out on this topic.)

Teachers also need to be aware that different types of assignments may lend themselves to diverse forms of feedback (Ferris et al., 1997). For instance, a teacher suggestion to "add more detail" might be very helpful if the student is working on a narrative description but counterproductive if the student is working on a persuasive text, in which extraneous detail could actually distract the reader and weaken the argument. Finally, as teachers analyze studies of teacher feedback and consider their own response strategies, they should be aware of institutional and course constraints on the effects of feedback. For instance, student journal entries are typically designed to build students' fluency and reflective thinking abilities and are almost never revised by students; feedback or correction on these is not likely to have much effect on student writing. Similarly, extensive feedback on an in-class graded midterm, while it might help the student know how to approach such a task the next time, will not have the same immediate and observable effects as comments on an intermediate draft of an essay to be revised for a grade or to be submitted in a portfolio. Teachers, therefore, should consciously vary their feedback to match the goals of the writing task: responding as a reader to the content of journal entries, giving test-taking strategy tips in feedback on in-class essay exams, and giving specific text-based suggestions on papers that students will revise again.

ESL WRITERS ATTEND TO TEACHER FEEDBACK AND
ATTEMPT TO UTILIZE IT IN THEIR REVISIONS

As previously noted, early L1 reviews reported discouraging findings about students' attention to and utilization of teacher feedback. However, it is important to remember that these reviews were written in the 1970s and early 1980s and were primarily studies of classes and teachers following the "current-traditional" paradigm: teachers gave feedback, along with a grade, on the ONLY draft, which was never expected to be revised. More recent L1 studies (e.g., Beason, 1993; Sperling, 1994; Straub, 1997, 2000) have indicated that although student writers may have strong feelings about the types of feedback they prefer, they nonetheless appreciate and take seriously the comments and suggestions made by their teachers.

Early ESL studies focused only on the effects of error correction on student writing, reporting similarly discouraging results (see Leki, 1990a; Truscott, 1996, for reviews). Again, however, when researchers began to look at the effects of feedback in multiple-draft settings, they quickly saw that L2 writers were just as inclined (maybe more so) as their L1 peers to attend to and address their teachers' feedback. Such evidence comes from some of the research paradigms discussed by Polio (Chapter 2 this volume), including student survey research, text analysis, and quasi-experimental studies (e.g., Cohen & Cavalcanti, 1990; Fathman & Whalley, 1990; Ferris, 1995, 1997, 2001; Hedgcock & Lefkowitz, 1994; Kepner, 1991; Patthey-Chavez & Ferris, 1997). However, because ESL writers are likely to at least attempt to follow their teachers' suggestions in revision does not always mean they will be successful in doing so (Conrad & Goldstein, 1999; Ferris, 1997, 2001). As already noted, research on the effects of teacher feedback indicates that ESL writers may be more capable of dealing successfully with some types of comments than others (e.g., statements rather than indirect requests or suggestions). Though this body of research is still too small and preliminary for definitive pronouncements, it is fair to say that since ESL writers will likely take teacher feedback very seriously, teachers need to be thoughtful in providing feedback, helpful in showing students how to revise their texts successfully (with or without feedback), and determined to hold students accountable for at least considering feedback they have received (see Ferris, 1997, 2001).

Student survey research on reactions to teacher commentary has also been helpful in highlighting the types of comments ESL writers appreciate and feedback that is (at least occasionally) problematic for them. For instance, students indicate that they appreciate praise but not at the expense of constructive criticism, that they struggle with understanding correction symbols and codes, that teacher questions may either be too specific or too general and therefore confusing, and that they value feedback on all aspects of their writing, although they feel the most strongly about receiving feedback on their grammar problems (Cohen & Cavalcanti, 1990; Ferris, 1995; Hedgcock & Lefkowitz, 1994; Leki, 1991). Finally, if asked to choose, most students prefer teacher feedback to peer- or self-evaluation (Hedgcock & Lefkowitz, 1994; Zhang, 1995).

TEACHER-STUDENT WRITING CONFERENCES MAY BE MORE COMPLEX WITH L2 WRITERS

As previously noted, teacher-student conferences have become a popular pedagogical tool, especially in L1 composition classes. Suggestions are plentiful on ways to implement such conferences successfully, with "success" usually defined as amount of student engagement in the discussion, particularly in books by Murray (1985) and Harris (1986). Some L1 scholars are so enthusiastic about the potential of the face-to-face writing conference that they suggest doing away with most other writing class activities so that time can be allotted for conferences (Carnicelli, 1980; Garrison, 1974). Though L2 writing specialists are also favorably disposed toward writing conferences (see Ferris & Hedgcock, 1998; Zamel, 1985), almost no research has been done on the nature and effects of teacher-student conferences with ESL writers.

The best-known study on writing conferences with ESL students is a case study by Goldstein and Conrad (1990). They examined the writing conferences and subsequent revisions of three university ESL writers, finding qualitative and quantitative differences in the nature of the conferences themselves and in their influence on students' later writing. Goldstein and Conrad point out that "ESL students bring with them diverse cultures and languages...that potentially affect how students conference and how their teachers respond to them" (1990, p. 459). A related study by Patthey-Chavez and Ferris (1997) examined the first drafts, conference transcripts, revisions, and first drafts of the next assignment written by eight university composition students – half native English speakers and the other half international students. The researchers found differences in the conferences and revisions between high- and low-achieving students; however, they also found that even weaker writers attempted to utilize their teachers' suggestions when revising and that all eight students improved their essays after conferences with their teachers. These two studies, covering only seven ESL writers in total, can hardly be considered conclusive.

Further, both L1 and L2 researchers have warned that "in empowering students to retain ownership of their writing, we force them into roles for which they are not prepared and with which they are not comfortable" (Ferris & Hedgcock, 1998, p. 142). Some students may have aural comprehension problems that may limit the effectiveness of conferences; others may feel inhibited from questioning or arguing with a teacher under any circumstances and may thus not understand teachers' attempts to "empower" them, instead incorporating instructors' suggestions verbatim into their papers because of teachers' perceived superior knowledge (Delpit, 1988; Goldstein & Conrad, 1990; Newkirk, 1995; Patthey-Chavez & Ferris, 1997). Ferris and Hedgcock (1998) suggest that teacher-student writing conferences may be implemented successfully if teachers explain the purpose, nature, and dynamics of conferences and if students take notes and/or audiotape conferences to augment their memory and place less of a burden on their aural comprehension abilities. If students are uncomfortable for cultural or personal reasons with meeting privately with an instructor, conferences can be conducted in threes (two students, one teacher), during class with peers otherwise engaged, or online via e-mail (see Pennington, Chapter 12 this volume, for further discussion of online possibilities).

Peer response in L2 writing classes: An overview

Potential benefits and drawbacks of peer feedback

Second language writing teachers and researchers appear to hold attitudes toward peer feedback that are almost exactly opposite their views on teacher response. Although few practitioners muster much enthusiasm about the work involved in giving feedback to their student writers (mainly because it is so labor-intensive), most nonetheless would acknowledge the necessity for teacher feedback, and all would agree that their students seem to expect it. In contrast, a great deal of excitement – mostly coming from L1 research and pedagogy – has been generated by the notion of peers giving each other feedback. However, as research and practice have intersected, L2 writing teachers and theorists have begun increasingly to question the appropriateness of peer response activities for ESL writers.

Ferris and Hedgcock (1998, pp. 170–171) summarize various potential benefits claimed by advocates of peer response:

- Students can take active roles in their own learning (Mendonca & Johnson, 1994).

- Students can "reconceptualize their ideas in light of their peers' reactions" (Mendonca & Johnson, 1994, p. 746).
- Students can engage in unrehearsed, low-risk, exploratory talk, which is less feasible in whole-class or teacher-student interactions.
- Students receive "reactions, questions, and responses from authentic readers" (Mittan, 1989, p. 209, but see Leki, 1990b, and Newkirk, 1984 for counterarguments to this assertion).
- Students receive feedback from multiple sources (Chaudron, 1983; Mittan, 1989).
- Students gain a clearer understanding of audience (readers') needs by receiving feedback on what they have done well and on what remains unclear (Mittan, 1989; Moore, 1986; Witbeck, 1976).
- Responding to peers' writing builds the critical skills needed to analyze and revise one's own writing (Leki, 1990b; Mittan, 1989).
- Students gain confidence (or reduce apprehension) by seeing peers' strengths and weaknesses in writing (Leki, 1990b; Mittan, 1989).

However, a number of scholars, researchers, and teachers have also raised various concerns and objections about peer response:

- Students misunderstand the purposes for peer feedback and are uncomfortable with it (Leki, 1990b; Nelson & Carson, 1998; Zhang, 1995).
- Peer feedback activities can be especially uncomfortable for students from "collectivist" cultures, who are more interested in group solidarity than individual achievement (Allaei & Connor, 1990; Carson, 1992; Carson & Nelson, 1994, 1996).
- Students, due to their limitations as both developing writers and L2 learners, are simply not very good at giving one another helpful feedback, thus calling into question the time and effort needed to implement peer response (Connor & Asenavage, 1994; Leki, 1990b; Nelson & Carson, 1998).

Research on peer feedback

Research on written teacher commentary and teacher-student conferences has been relatively sparse, but there has been a proliferation of studies on peer response in L2 writing classes over the past ten years.[4] This body of research has examined the nature of interaction in peer feedback dyads or groups (including analysis of the substance of comments made in addition to participation dynamics and stances taken by peers), the effects of peer response on student writing, and student attitudes toward peer response. From these studies emerge three generalizations about the content of peer feedback, its effects on revision, and student reactions to peer response. Next, these generalizations are presented and discussed briefly.

THERE IS A GREAT DEAL OF VARIATION IN WHAT STUDENTS TALK ABOUT DURING PEER FEEDBACK AND HOW THEY INTERACT WITH ONE ANOTHER – WHICH MAY BE RELATED TO HOW THE TEACHER MODELS FEEDBACK AND STRUCTURES PEER RESPONSE SESSIONS

Several researchers have looked at the nature of commentary peers give about other students' papers (Lockhart & Ng, 1995; Mangelsdorf & Schlumberger, 1992; Mendonca & Johnson, 1994; Villamil & deGuerrero, 1996). Though terminology and methodology have varied from one study to another, these researchers have examined issues such as the aspect of the texts students focused on (e.g., thesis, support, mechanical issues, organization), whether they asked questions or offered critical evaluations or suggestions, and what personae or "stances" they assumed (e.g., prescriptive, interpretive, or collaborative). It is difficult, because of the differences across these studies, to offer generalizations about their findings, but it is fair to say that all four sets of researchers found peer feedback to be a complex process affected by a wide variety of interpersonal and contextual factors and that a wide variety of feedback types and stances appeared to benefit a range of student writers in various ways. Further, both L1 and L2 researchers (e.g., Connor & Asenavage, 1994; Howard, 2001) have suggested that peer feedback, for better or for worse, can be influenced by the priorities modeled by the teacher in giving feedback and in structuring the class in general and peer response sessions in particular. For instance, if the teacher functions primarily as proofreader, marking grammar, spelling, and punctuation without ever giving substantive comments on content, students giving each other feedback may follow the teacher's lead and focus on the same issues. In addition, a key to successful peer feedback sessions is prior training of students to be effective responders (Berg, 1999; Ferris & Hedgcock, 1998; Mittan, 1989; Stanley, 1992).

One specific pedagogical issue that arises is the degree to which instructors should structure peer response sessions by providing specific questions or tasks on a "feedback form" to which peers respond, either orally or in writing, in conjunction with peer feedback activities. Some writers, concerned again with issues of teacher appropriation, have advocated leaving peer response largely unstructured and allowing students to set their own agendas (see Elbow, 1973; Lockhart & Ng, 1995; Nelson & Murphy, 1992/93). Others have argued that novice student writers (especially L2 writers) lack necessary schemata to assess each other's writing, to give helpful feedback, and to frame such feedback in appropriate terms (e.g., Mittan, 1989; Reid, 1994). This latter view would support peer feedback sessions that are "teacher-choreographed" – including careful modeling and training of students prior to beginning peer feedback activities, providing specific tasks and questions for peer feedback sessions, and building in accountability mechanisms so that both responder and receiver would take the feedback process seriously (see Ferris & Hedgcock, 1998).

RESEARCH EVIDENCE IS CONFLICTING ABOUT THE DEGREE TO WHICH STUDENTS UTILIZE PEER FEEDBACK IN THEIR REVISIONS

Studies of the effects of peer response on students' subsequent revisions have focused on one or more of the following issues: (1) Do students utilize their peers' comments when they revise (Connor & Asenavage, 1994; Mendonca & Johnson, 1994; Nelson & Murphy, 1993)? (2) What sorts of revisions do students make after receiving peer feedback (Berger, 1990; Connor & Asenavage, 1994; Huang, 1994; Resh, 1994)? (3) Does peer feedback help students to improve their papers (Hedgcock & Lefkowitz, 1992; Resh, 1994)? Results of these studies have been mixed. Connor and Asenavage (1994) report that only 5 percent of student revisions were attributable to comments made by their peers, while Mendonca and Johnson (1994) found that their participants utilized peer feedback in 53 percent of their revisions. Berger (1990) found that the majority of her subjects made only surface changes, while Connor and Asenavage noted that at least some of their subjects made more text-based (global) changes after receiving peer feedback. As already noted, subjects and research methodologies varied widely in these studies, so it is difficult to draw conclusions about the effects of peer response in all contexts. For instance, Connor and Asenavage's eight subjects were freshmen who also received teacher feedback prior to undertaking revision; Mendonca and Johnson's subjects, however, were graduate students, most of whom were paired with peers in the same academic discipline. Further, the graduate students were writing papers about their own academic fields, but the freshmen were writing on more general composition class topics. Under such circumstances, it stands to reason that this latter group of students would hold their peers' feedback in higher regard than the freshmen writers would, especially when students knew that they would also receive feedback from the teacher on the same draft.

To consider the overall "effects" of peer feedback, a number of issues need to be looked at more extensively by researchers:

- Were students trained or prepared for peer feedback, and did this preparation affect the substance of their peer feedback sessions and how they subsequently approached revision?

- Do students give more-effective feedback and take the process more seriously when teachers structure the process for them, or when students themselves have the responsibility to choose the direction, tone, and focus of the peer response sessions?
- Is peer response implemented regularly in the writing class, and are students placed in consistent pairings or groupings?
- Are teacher expectations for peer response clear and reasonable?

When such questions have been examined systematically in a body of research, then we can more accurately assess the nature and effects of peer response and determine whether it is beneficial for L2 writers (or at least for some of them). Because at least some studies have suggested that students *do* utilize peer suggestions in revision, it is premature to suggest, as some have done (e.g., Nelson & Carson, 1998; Zhang, 1995), that peer feedback is not appropriate for ESL writers.

STUDENTS APPEAR TO ENJOY PEER FEEDBACK AND TO FIND IT HELPFUL

In general, researchers have found that peer response is well received by student writers and that they enjoy the process (Leki, 1990b; Mangelsdorf, 1992; Mendonca & Johnson, 1994). On the other hand, students sometimes question the efficacy of peer feedback, express concern about either their peers' competency to evaluate their work or their ability to give critical feedback constructively and not hurtfully, and clearly prefer teacher feedback over peer feedback when asked to choose (Berger, 1990; Leki, 1990b; Zhang, 1995). To this point, the available evidence does not suggest that ESL student writers have strongly negative feelings toward peer feedback or feel that it is harmful to them.

Summary of previous research

As previously noted, the scarcity of research on some aspects of response to student writing and the lack of comparability of studies that do exist make it difficult, and perhaps even inappropriate, to draw hard-and-fast conclusions about how teachers should approach their own commentary and peer response activities. Still, several generalizations do emerge:

- Students appear to appreciate and value both teacher and peer feedback and to feel that feedback helps them to improve their writing.
- Teachers and peers, in providing commentary, take a wide variety of stances and cover a range of issues about student texts. Though it may have been accurate in the past to claim that teachers and peers respond only to sentence-level issues, this no longer appears to be true.

- There is considerable variation across teachers and peers giving feedback and student writers processing it as to the nature of feedback given and the ways in which the commentary is utilized by writers. This variation occurs across text types, students' linguistic and cultural backgrounds, and their L2 proficiency and writing ability.
- Students, at least under some circumstances, consider and utilize teacher and peer feedback in constructing revisions of their texts. These revisions occur on both global and surface levels.

Implications for teaching

These generalizations lend themselves to several practical conclusions for responding to student writing. First, teachers should not abandon either providing feedback themselves or facilitating peer response. Though there are some caveats to this – for instance, students at lower levels of language and writing proficiency are probably less capable of processing copious teacher feedback or engaging in peer response – there is enough positive evidence that both sources of feedback are valuable to (and valued by) students to continue these practices until such time as there is overwhelming evidence to the contrary. Second, teachers should examine their own responding practices to see whether their feedback is clear and responsive to the needs of individual students and/or texts. They should also be diligent in preparing students for peer feedback, particularly in modeling the types of feedback that are most helpful and appropriate. Finally, teachers should be intentional in helping students to revise, seeing that they understand and can utilize feedback they have received, and creating accountability mechanisms to make sure that students are taking the response-and-revision process seriously.

Limitations of previous research

The review of research on written and oral teacher feedback and on peer response has shown that many questions about response to student writing have not been adequately considered by previous researchers. First, because of the time- and labor-intensive nature of discourse analytic research, sample sizes in many studies have been quite small. It is necessary therefore to add data and observations from more teachers and students. In addition, it is important to consider the student population being studied and how the characteristics of that audience may affect the response-and-revision dynamic. For instance, newly arrived international students in the United States may have limited experience with either teacher feedback during the writing process or with peer response

(Ferris, 1999). If they either react negatively to feedback or do not utilize it effectively in revision, this may be due more to student characteristics than to flaws in the feedback they have received. Similarly, the effects of age, maturity, educational experience, and expertise about the topic under discussion may all impact the results of the studies of response and revision. To summarize, we must be careful not to prematurely embrace or dismiss various response strategies unless adequate numbers of subjects and contexts have been examined using consistent methodologies and research paradigms. (See Goldstein, 2001, and Polio, Chapter 2 this volume, for a discussion of various ways to conduct rigorous research on L2 writing response.) We might, once such studies have been conducted, decide (for instance) that peer feedback is more appropriate for some student audiences than for others, or that some students could succeed with less teacher intervention. At this point, however, we have too little data to make such pronouncements.

Second, there has been, for the most part, a disconnect between the suggestions of practitioners about response to student writing and research that has been conducted on various aspects of response. As a result, many crucial pedagogical questions remain unexamined by researchers. For example, with regard to peer feedback, a number of concrete suggestions have been offered about how to make peer response activities more effective (e.g., Ferris & Hedgcock, 1998; Mittan, 1989). These include issues such as carefully grouping students into permanent response pairs, providing structured peer response forms, and implementing mechanisms to hold peer feedback givers and receivers accountable for taking the process seriously. Yet none of the previous studies have investigated whether such practical ideas make a difference in the nature and effects of peer response.

As for teacher response, various suggestions have also been made: that teachers carefully explain their responding strategies to their students, that they give students options about the types of feedback that they would like to receive, and that teachers hold students accountable for explaining how they have (or have not) utilized the feedback they have received. It has also been suggested that teachers avoid rhetorical and grammatical jargon and indirectness and that they selectively prioritize their feedback rather than overwhelming the student with too many criticisms and suggestions. Again, however, we have little evidence as to whether any of these ideas ultimately makes a difference in the effects of teacher commentary on student writing.

Most crucially, we have almost no longitudinal evidence about the extent to which feedback helps students to improve their writing over the long term. Studies of teacher and peer feedback typically consider only how the effects can be observed in revisions of the same paper. There are few attempts to trace these effects any further. Though it would be challenging and time-consuming to address this issue, various types of text-analytic and ethnographic approaches could be used to investigate it, to the great potential benefit of students and teachers alike.

There is no doubt that "coaching from the margins" (Leki, 1990a) is a challenging and time-consuming task, whether it is undertaken through teachers' written commentary, teacher-student conferences, or peer feedback. However, there also appears to be little doubt among teachers or their students about the importance of feedback to students' development as writers. We have made great strides in the past fifteen years in understanding the nature and effects of feedback, but we still have a long way to go. Most important, teachers and researchers need to identify and execute a research agenda that addresses the most critical questions still surrounding the processes of feedback, revision, and student development.

Notes

1. This chapter focuses on research and implications regarding response to student writing that emphasizes students' ideas and rhetorical structure. For a discussion of grammar issues in L2 writing, see Frodesen and Holten, Chapter 6 this volume.
2. For a recent discussion on the history and use of such collaborative pedagogies as conferencing and peer review in the L1 setting, see Howard (2001).
3. Other types of feedback that are discussed in the literature include audio-taped teacher feedback and teacher or peer response delivered electronically (via e-mail or specialized software). However, because research on these forms of feedback is as of this writing relatively rare, these options are not explored further in this chapter.
4. For a review and analysis of many of these studies on peer review in greater depth than space permits in this chapter, see Liu and Hansen (2002).

References

Allaei, S., & Connor, U. (1990). Exploring the dynamics of cross-cultural collaboration. *The Writing Instructor, 10,* 19–28.

Beason, L. (1993). Feedback and revision in writing across the curriculum classes. *Research in the Teaching of English, 27,* 395–421.

Berg, E. C. (1999). The effects of trained peer response on ESL students' revision types and writing quality. *Journal of Second Language Writing, 8,* 215–241.

Berger, V. (1990). The effects of peer and self-feedback. *CATESOL Journal, 3,* 21–35.

Brannon, L., & Knoblauch, C. H. (1982). On students' rights to their own texts: A model of teacher response. *College Composition and Communication, 33,* 157–166.

Carnicelli, T. A. (1980). The writing conference: A one-to-one conversation. In T. Donovan & B. McClelland (Eds.), *Eight approaches to teaching writing* (pp. 101–131). Urbana, IL: NCTE.

Carson, J. G. (1992). Becoming biliterate: First language influences. *Journal of Second Language Writing, 1,* 37–60.

Carson, J. G., & Nelson, G. L. (1994). Writing groups: Cross-cultural issues. *Journal of Second Language Writing, 3,* 17–30.

Carson, J. G., & Nelson, G. L. (1996). Chinese students' perceptions of ESL peer response group interaction. *Journal of Second Language Writing, 5,* 1–19.

Chaudron, C. (1983). *Evaluating writing: Effects of feedback on revision.* Paper presented at the 17th Annual TESOL Convention, Toronto. (EDRS No. ED 227 706).

Cohen, A. D., & Cavalcanti, M. C. (1990). Feedback on compositions: Teacher and student verbal reports. In B. Kroll (Ed.), *Second language writing: Research insights for the classroom* (pp. 155–177). New York: Cambridge University Press.

Connor, U., & Asenavage, K. (1994). Peer response groups in ESL writing classes: How much impact on revision? *Journal of Second Language Writing, 3,* 257–276.

Conrad, S., & Goldstein, L. (1999). ESL student revision after teacher written comments: Text, contexts, and individuals. *Journal of Second Language Writing, 8,* 147–180.

Cumming, A. (1985). Responding to the writing of ESL students. *Highway One, 8,* 58–78.

Delpit, L. (1988). The silenced dialogue: Power and pedagogy in educating other people's children. *Harvard Educational Review, 58,* 280–298.

Dessner, L. E. (1991). English as a second language writers' revision responses to teacher-written comments. *Dissertation Abstracts International, 52*(3), 827A.

Elbow, P. (1973). *Writing without teachers.* New York: Oxford University Press.

Fathman, A., & Whalley, E. (1990). Teacher response to student writing: Focus on form versus content. In B. Kroll (Ed.), *Second language writing: Research insights for the classroom* (pp. 178–190). New York: Cambridge University Press.

Ferris, D. R. (1995). Student reactions to teacher response in multiple-draft composition classrooms. *TESOL Quarterly, 29,* 33–53.

Ferris, D. R. (1997). The influence of teacher commentary on student revision. *TESOL Quarterly, 31,* 315–339.

Ferris, D. R. (1999). One size does not fit all: Response and revision issues for immigrant student writers. In L. Harklau, K. Losey, & M. Siegal (Eds.), *Generation 1.5 meets college composition* (pp. 143–157). Mahwah, NJ: Lawrence Erlbaum.

Ferris, D. R. (2001). Teaching writing for academic purposes. In J. Flowerdew & M. Peacock (Eds.), *Research perspectives on English for academic purposes* (pp. 298–314). Cambridge; England: Cambridge University Press.

Ferris, D., & Hedgcock, J. (1998). *Teaching ESL composition: Purpose, process, and practice.* Mahwah, NJ: Lawrence Erlbaum.

Ferris, D., Chaney, S., Komura, K., Roberts, B., & McKee, S. (2000, March). *Perspectives, problems, and practices in treating written error.* Colloquium presented at the International TESOL Convention, Vancouver, B.C.

Ferris, D., Pezone, S., Tade, C., & Tinti, S. (1997). Teacher commentary on student writing: Descriptions and implications. *Journal of Second Language Writing, 6,* 155–182.

Garrison, R. (1974). One-to-one: Tutorial instruction in freshman composition. *New Directions for Community Colleges, 2,* 55–83.

Goldstein, L. (2001). For Kyla: What does the research say about responding to student writers. In T. Silva & P. K. Matsuda (Eds.), *On second language writing* (pp. 73–89). Mahwah, NJ: Lawrence Erlbaum.

Goldstein, L., & Conrad, S. (1990). Student input and the negotiation of meaning in ESL writing conferences. *TESOL Quarterly, 24,* 443–460.

Hairston, M. (1986). On not being a composition slave. In Charles W. Bridges (Ed.), *Training the new teacher of college composition* (pp. 117–124). Urbana, IL: NCTE.

Harklau, L., Losey, K., & Siegal, M. (Eds.). (1999). *Generation 1.5 meets college composition.* Mahwah, NJ: Lawrence Erlbaum.

Harris, M. (1986). *Teaching one-to-one: The writing conference.* Urbana, IL: NCTE.

Hedgcock, J., & Lefkowitz, N. (1992). Collaborative oral/aural revision in foreign language writing. *Journal of Second Language Writing, 1,* 255–276.

Hedgcock, J., & Lefkowitz, N. (1994). Feedback on feedback: Assessing learner receptivity to teacher response in L2 composing. *Journal of Second Language Writing, 3,* 141–163.

Hillocks, G., Jr. (1986). *Research on written composition: New directions for teaching.* Urbana, IL: ERIC Clearinghouse on Reading and Communication Skills and the National Conference on Research in English.

Howard, R. M. (2001). Collaborative pedagogy. In G. Tate, A. Rupiper, & K. Schick (Eds.), *A guide to composition pedagogies* (pp. 54–70). New York: Oxford University Press.

Huang, S. (1994). Learning to critique and revise in an English-as-a-foreign-language university writing class. *Dissertation Abstracts International, 55(10),* 3120A.

Johns, A. M. (1990). L1 composition theories: Implications for developing theories of L2 composition. In B. Kroll (Ed.), *Second language writing: Research insights for the classroom* (pp. 24–36). New York: Cambridge University Press.

Kassen, M. A. (1988). Native and non-native speaker teacher response to foreign language learner writing: A study of intermediate-level French. *Texas Papers in Foreign Language Education, 1(1),* 1–15.

Kepner, C. (1991). An experiment in the relationship of types of written feedback to the development of second-language writing skills. *Modern Language Journal, 75,* 305–313.

Knoblauch, C., & Brannon, L. (1981). Teacher commentary on student writing: The state of the art. *Freshman English News, 10,* 1–4.

Krashen, S. (1984). *Writing: Research, theory, and application.* Oxford: Pergamon Press.

Lam, C. Y. P. (1992). Revision processes of college ESL students: How teacher comments, discourse types, and writing tools shape revision. *Dissertation Abstracts International, 52(12),* 4248A.

Leki, I. (1990a). Coaching from the margins: Issues in written response. In B. Kroll (Ed.), *Second language writing: Research insights for the classroom* (pp. 57–68). New York: Cambridge University Press.

Leki, I. (1990b). Potential problems with peer responding in ESL writing classes. *CATESOL Journal, 3*, 5–19.

Leki, I. (1991). The preferences of ESL students for error correction in college-level writing classes. *Foreign Language Annals, 24*, 203–218.

Leki, I. (1992). *Understanding ESL writers*. Portsmouth, NH: Heinemann.

Liu, J., & Hansen, J. (2002). *Peer response in second language writing classrooms*. Ann Arbor: University of Michigan Press.

Lockhart, C., & Ng, P. (1995). Analyzing talk in peer response groups: Stances, functions, and content. *Language Learning, 45*, 605–655.

Mangelsdorf, K. (1992). Peer reviews in the ESL composition classroom: What do the students think? *ELT Journal, 46*, 274–284.

Mangelsdorf, K., & Schlumberger, A. L. (1992). ESL student response stances in a peer-review task. *Journal of Second Language Writing, 1*, 235–254.

Mathison-Fife, J., & O'Neill, P. (1997). Re-seeing research on response. *College Composition and Communication, 48*, 274–277.

McGroarty, M. E., & Zhu, W. (1997). Triangulation in classroom research: A study of peer revision. *Language Learning, 47*(1), 1–43.

Mendonca, C. O., & Johnson, K. E. (1994). Peer review negotiations: Revision activities in ESL writing instruction. *TESOL Quarterly, 28*, 745–769.

Mittan, R. (1989). The peer review process: Harnessing students' communicative power. In D. M. Johnson & D. H. Roen (Eds.), *Richness in writing: Empowering ESL students* (pp. 207–219). New York: Longman.

Moore, L. (1986). Teaching students how to evaluate writing. *TESOL Newsletter, 20*(5), 23–24.

Murray, D. M. (1985). *A writer teaches writing* (2nd ed.). Boston: Houghton Mifflin.

Nelson, G. L., & Carson, J. G. (1998). ESL students' perceptions of effectiveness in peer response groups. *Journal of Second Language Writing, 7*, 113–132.

Nelson, G. L., & Murphy, J. M. (1992/93). Writing groups and the less proficient ESL student. *TESOL Journal, 2*(2), 23–26.

Nelson, G. L., & Murphy, J. M. (1993). Peer response groups: Do L2 writers use peer comments in revising their drafts? *TESOL Quarterly, 27*, 135–142.

Newkirk, T. (1984). Direction and misdirection in peer response. *College Composition and Communication, 35*, 301–311.

Newkirk, T. (1995). The writing conference as performance. *Research in the Teaching of English, 29*, 193–215.

Patthey-Chavez, G. G., & Ferris, D. R. (1997). Writing conferences and the weaving of multi-voiced texts in college composition. *Research in the Teaching of English, 31*, 51–90.

Polio, C., Fleck, C., & Leder, N. (1998). "If only I had more time": ESL learners' changes in linguistic accuracy on essay revisions. *Journal of Second Language Writing, 7*, 43–68.

Reid, J. (1994). Responding to ESL students' texts: The myths of appropriation. *TESOL Quarterly, 28*, 273–292.

Reid, J. (1998). "Eye" learners and "Ear" learners: Identifying the language needs of international student and U.S. resident writers. In P. Byrd &

J. M. Reid, *Grammar in the composition classroom: Essays on teaching ESL for college-bound students* (pp. 3–17). Boston: Heinle & Heinle.

Resh, C. A. (1994). A study of the effects of peer responding on the responder as writer-reviser. *Dissertation Abstracts International, 55*(12), 377 1A-3772A.

Silva, T. (1988). Comments on Vivian Zamel's "recent research on writing pedagogy": A reader reacts... *TESOL Quarterly, 22,* 517–520.

Silva, T. (1990). Second language composition instruction: Developments, issues, and directions in ESL. In B. Kroll (Ed.), *Second language writing: Research insights for the classroom* (pp. 11–23). New York: Cambridge University Press.

Silva, T. (1993). Toward an understanding of the distinct nature of L2 writing: The ESL research and its implications. *TESOL Quarterly, 27,* 657–671.

Silva, T. (1997). On the ethical treatment of ESL writers. *TESOL Quarterly, 31,* 359–363.

Sommers, N. (1982). Responding to student writing. *College Composition and Communication, 33,* 148–156.

Sperling, M. (1994). Constructing the perspective of teacher-as-reader: A framework for studying response to student writing. *Research in the Teaching of English, 28,* 175–207.

Stanley, J. (1992). Coaching student writers to be effective peer evaluators. *Journal of Second Language Writing, 1,* 217–233.

Straub, R. (1997). Students' reactions to teacher comments: An exploratory study. *Research in the Teaching of English, 31,* 91–119.

Straub, R. (2000). The student, the text, and the classroom context: A case study of teacher response. *Assessing Writing, 7,* 23–55.

Truscott, J. (1996). The case against grammar correction in L2 writing classes. *Language Learning, 46,* 327–369.

Villamil, O. S., & deGuerrero, M. C. M. (1996). Peer revision in the L2 classroom: Social-cognitive activities, mediating strategies, and aspects of social behavior. *Journal of Second Language Writing, 5,* 51–76.

Witbeck, M. C. (1976). Peer correction procedures for intermediate and advanced ESL composition lessons. *TESOL Quarterly, 10,* 321–326.

Zamel, V. (1985). Responding to student writing. *TESOL Quarterly, 19,* 79–102.

Zhang, S. (1995). Reexamining the affective advantage of peer feedback in the ESL writing class. *Journal of Second Language Writing, 4,* 209–222.

6 Grammar and the ESL writing class

Jan Frodesen and Christine Holten

Good writing is indeed an elusive concept, one that varies according to the entire rhetorical situation in which it is produced. It is clear, however, that certain properties of good writing can be identified. Most would concur that for writing to be deemed "successful" to its overall purpose, it must conform to the conventions of English syntax and usage, generally referred to as *grammar*.[1] Grammar is indisputably an essential element of second language writing instruction, but the ways in which it is integrated with other components of writing courses have varied.

Until the introduction in the 1980s of communicative language teaching, grammar was often the main curricular focus in English as a second language (ESL) writing instruction: Courses concentrated on having students manipulate and master grammatical forms with little attention to the content or organization of the texts they were producing.[2] More recently, grammar instruction has been assigned a less prominent role in second language writing classrooms. For example, in classrooms that follow a process model, the writer, the content and purpose, and multiple drafts are central and grammar is often reserved until the final editing phase. In genre-based classrooms, the central focus is on the type of text (e.g., research report, summary, problem-solution text) as well as the content, organization, and audience considerations that it entails. Here grammar instruction derives from an analysis of the dominant grammatical features of a given text type (e.g., past tense in the methods section of a research report).

Regardless of instructional approach, integrating grammar into ESL composition teaching is a complex task (cf. Brinton & Holten, 2001). After all, there are only so many instructional hours in a term. Problems arise because university-level ESL writers need so many skills – the ability to think and read critically, to understand difficult texts, to synthesize information and perspectives from multiple sources, to develop and organize arguments and analyses adequately and logically, and the list could go on. If students are not able to produce well-organized texts or have difficulty grasping ideas in the readings they will draw on when writing their papers, how can teachers take precious time to focus on subject-verb agreement, relative clauses, or subordinate sentence structures?

141

A second obstacle to successful integration of grammar and writing instruction arises because many ESL writing courses have students with diverse levels of language proficiency. Grammar instruction in these classes is difficult because students vary widely in several ways: (1) overall language proficiency and command of English syntax and grammar; (2) familiarity with structures and vocabulary commonly used in academic writing; and (3) background in formal grammar instruction needed to successfully revise and edit written products. In such instructional contexts, the task of finding a grammatical focus useful for all students seems daunting. In addition, the "return" on grammar instruction is often disappointing. Teachers find that even when a grammatical feature has been covered and practiced, students may not use it accurately in their own writing. This has led many teachers to question the value of formal grammar instruction in ESL writing classes.

In this chapter, we explore the role of grammar in second language (L2) writing instruction, focusing on three questions that have been of central concern to researchers and practitioners: (1) Is formal grammar instruction useful for L2 writers? (2) What is the role of grammar in the drafting process? (3) Is individualized feedback on errors in student writing an effective strategy? We then extend this discussion by considering other factors that can inform language-focused instruction in second language writing courses.

Questions about grammar in second language writing instruction

Question 1: Is formal grammar instruction useful for L2 writers?

How to – or even whether to – incorporate grammar instruction into the teaching of writing has been hotly debated in first language (L1) composition circles and later among experts in second language writing. Experts in first language composition began disputing the issue in the early 1960s, dividing into what Hartwell (1985) termed the pro- and anti-grammar instruction camps. An early challenge to the prevailing practice of focusing on rules of grammar and punctuation in writing instruction came in the 1963 seminal book *Research in Written Composition* by Braddock, Lloyd-Jones, and Schoer. They wrote, "Formal grammar instruction has negligible or...even harmful effects on improvement in writing" (pp. 37–38). By the mid-1980s, this view began to gain wide acceptance, supported by the powerful arguments and evidence against the usefulness of teaching formal grammar advanced by such L1 composition experts as Emig (1981) and Bartholomae (1980). The seminal case was made by Hartwell (1985) in "Grammar, Grammars, and the Teaching of Grammar." He presents the misconceptions that grammar proponents have about their students' lack of grammatical knowledge and about the way that language is best learned and used. The central and most compelling premise of his argument is that grammar is an internalized system of rules. This means that native-speaking writers already know language rules intuitively, if not overtly, and therefore, any attempts to teach them are redundant. He then turns his attention to how language is best used and learned. Language cannot be learned in isolation but only by manipulating it in meaningful contexts. Given this, Hartwell argues that grammar rules can have little connection to productive control of the language and, quoting personal communication from James Britton, he likens the teaching of rules to "forcing starving people to master the use of a knife and fork before they can eat" (p. 380).

The controversy about the role of grammar in L1 writing instruction in some sense forced researchers and practitioners to reconsider the relationship between grammar instruction and language accuracy in student writing. This is most evident and helpful in the publication of Mina Shaughnessy's groundbreaking work, *Errors and Expectations* (1977), in which she redefined the notion of error. In her research and teaching, she found that native-speaking student writers reading their compositions aloud could actually correct (most) errors without realizing they had made them. She concluded that contrary to teachers' assumptions, students don't make errors because of an incomplete grasp of the rules of English grammar; in fact, they have an intuitive grasp of many grammar conventions. When they do make errors, these are often performance errors or ones based on "rules" about written language that they have erroneously intuited. Shaughnessy's work and that of subsequent researchers in the field of basic writing have encouraged writing teachers, who may have been prone to prescriptivism, to view error as a window on students' development as writers.[3]

Following suit with the L1 composition world, ESL composition researchers and writing teachers began to re-evaluate the tendency in ESL writing instruction to "over focus" on language form (Zamel, 1983). Like Hartwell and other L1 composition researchers, L2 composition experts drew on the work of Stephen Krashen to make their case. Krashen's monitor model (1978, 1982) held that second language learners' ability to consciously use the formal grammar rules they have learned in classroom settings is limited. In other words, learning about grammar rules does not necessarily translate into correct production of those forms in actual language use.[4]

There are, however, problems posed by this crossover from L1 to L2 composition pedagogy in practice and thinking about grammar instruction. It is first of all problematic that second language writing experts have accepted a view based largely on native-speaking writers' intuition about language. This intuition is, of course, something that comes to L2 writers only gradually (or not) through long exposure to and/or study of the second language. Even ESL writers who have spent many years in U.S. schools complain that they lack the "feel" for written language that native speakers have. Equally problematic is the L1 interpretation of Krashen's monitor model that has been adopted by both L1 and L2 writing instructors. In adopting Krashen's *noninterventionist* position, as Long and Robinson (1998) have termed it, both L1 and L2 compositionists have underemphasized an important aspect of the monitor model: namely, that the monitor can be used effectively when there is enough time for learners to apply a rule to their language output. That is, if a learner has time to recall and apply formal rules, these rules can aid in accurate language use. Such conditions do not hold in speaking, but can and do obtain in writing.

The noninterventionist position has been challenged by a growing body of L2 research and pedagogy concerning the importance of attention to form in L2 learning. In recent years, some L2 acquisition researchers who formerly supported the noninterventionist position have, on the basis of classroom research, stressed the need for focus on form, not in the "old" or traditional sense of decontextualized lessons on grammar, but as a component of instruction that starts with a focus on meaning. Lightbown (1998), for example, now believes that "focused attention to language features is often beneficial and sometimes necessary" (p. 180).

In light of both new research findings and the inherent differences in L1 and L2 writers' literacy development, it is clear that ESL writing instructors have a role to play in making writers aware of language form. Overt and systematic grammar instruction can help students access the grammar rules that they know and use their intuitions about the language judiciously.

Question 2: What is the role of grammar in the drafting process?

The 1970s and 1980s saw much research about the nature of the writing process. Both L1 research and practicing writers portrayed writing as recursive and cyclical in nature, requiring multiple and interconnected phases of planning, writing, and rewriting. This new understanding inevitably led to profound changes in how composition was taught. Rather than teaching writing as a series of carefully sequenced skills, the new model of writing instruction emphasized the primacy of content planning and idea generation. It encouraged learners to write multiple drafts and learn about their own preferred writing process so as to exploit and guide it. This radical shift in understanding the activity of writing itself also spurred the re-evaluation of the role of grammar instruction in the composition classroom. Studies on the writing process (Perl, 1979; Sommers, 1980) have drawn distinctions between effective and ineffective writers. This research portrays effective writers as waiting until the final stages of the drafting process to edit their work and ineffective writers as focusing on form early in the process rather than looking at content and organization. Flower and Hayes (1980, 1981) and other writing process researchers have also found that editing for language is a relatively "low level" concern for writers when this focus competes with activities like idea generation and planning.

Second language composition researchers have also investigated the writing processes of ESL writers, finding similarities between the processes of L1 writers and those of ESL writers. Studying the writing processes of six advanced ESL students, Zamel (1983) observed that the subjects she categorized as "better writers" waited to deal with language issues until the end of the process while those seen as "poorer writers" revised words and phrases all during composing. Raimes (1985) draws similar conclusions about the role of language for ESL writers. In a study of eight students, she found that "the students did not, as a group, seem preoccupied with error or with editing" (p. 247).

These findings have had direct pedagogical implications in L2 writing classrooms. Some ESL writing teachers take it as an article of faith that the drafting process itself will take care of many language problems. Believing that students' grammatical and lexical errors will gradually disappear as they review their written output and clarify their thoughts on a topic, teachers frequently encourage writers to delay attending to language until the final draft. Such a practice is grounded in the idea that students cannot attend to multiple concerns at one time. However, in a study of teacher feedback, Fathman and Whalley (1990) found that students who received feedback on grammar and content simultaneously improved their written texts in both areas, while students who received feedback on content only actually made more errors in subsequent drafts. In a later study of the editing practices of ESL writers, Shih (1998) found that adopting a hands-off approach to grammar editing often leaves students, especially those with the weakest overall language proficiency, with texts replete with language errors, errors they often lack the editing strategies or grammar knowledge to tackle.

Research that has examined the place of grammar in an individual's writing process suggests that it is in the best interest of L2 writers to attend to language issues consistently throughout the drafting process. While teachers obviously do not want to drown student papers in a sea of red ink on early drafts, the end result of putting off attention to lexical and grammatical issues in student writing may be counterproductive. By this, we are not suggesting that teachers mark errors on every draft. There are many other types of grammar instruction beyond feedback and error marking that can be useful in developing students' academic literacy skills.[5]

Question 3: Is individualized feedback on errors in student writing an effective strategy for improving accuracy and developing overall language proficiency?

One instructional option commonly adopted by L2 composition teachers for dealing with grammar is to give feedback on the actual grammatical and lexical choices that student writers make in their compositions when such choices violate conventions or rules. This negative feedback can have several forms. Some teachers take an indirect approach that requires students to figure out what the nature of the error is and edit it independently. Some instructors indicate the presence of an error by underlining or circling; others use a more elaborate system of symbols that represent categories of common grammar errors. More-direct methods include marking and correcting lexical or grammatical errors. While grammar correction of student drafts is often individualized, some teachers spend a portion of whole-class instruction considering and correcting error-filled sentences that they have culled from a number of their students' texts.

Although it has been widely endorsed and adopted, individualizing feedback on grammatical and lexical choices is by no means uncontroversial. Truscott (1996) started a debate that generated much heat and light in the field when he wrote, "Grammar correction has no place in writing classes and should be abandoned" (p. 361). This sentence concludes a carefully argued case against grammar correction. Truscott bases part of his case on evidence from several studies (Kepner, 1991; Semke, 1984; Robb, Ross, & Shortreed, 1986, among others) that seems to suggest that error correction, regardless of how it is implemented, does not improve the accuracy of a student's written text. He then provides theoretical explanations for why this method might not work. First, the notion that marking errors will show students the gap between their production and correct forms of written English fails to acknowledge the complexity and idiosyncratic nature of language development. In addition, he maintains that the structures noted by the instructor may not be ones that the student is developmentally ready to acquire. Finally, he notes that teachers often lack the training, ability, consistency, or time to notice errors, and even if they do, they may not be able to explain what is wrong. Students, on the other hand, sometimes find the teachers' marks or explanations difficult to understand or demoralizing, or they are not motivated to use the feedback they are given. (See Chapter 5 by Ferris in this volume for more on this topic.)

Ferris (1999) has effectively responded to Truscott, finding his conclusions about the efficacy of error feedback too "gloomy." She cites evidence from her own research (Ferris, 1995, 1997) and that of others who have investigated the effects of error correction (Fathman & Whalley, 1990; Lalande, 1982) to show that many students do benefit from feedback aimed at helping them become independent self-editors. These findings were corroborated in a later empirical study by Ferris and Roberts (2001) that indicated students who received no feedback were less able to self-edit their own texts than those who received either explicit or general feedback on their errors.

In addition to Ferris's reservations as presented in her published response to his claims (Ferris, 1999), Truscott's position has other problems. While he advocates abolishing grammar correction in L2 writing classrooms, he suggests nothing to put in its place. Readers are left imagining a classroom in which students write and receive feedback on the content and organization in their papers, but not on the accuracy of the language they use to convey their ideas. There are two problems with his ideal classroom. First, much has been written about the benefit of instruction that focuses on grammatical form. Spada (1997), among others, has stated that learners need instruction and practice that focuses both on form and meaning in language development. Truscott's approach (at least the one we can imagine in the face of his silence on the matter) would provide students with lots of meaning-focused practice but no opportunity for practice with forms that self-editing provides. Other researchers (Rutherford, 1987) have pointed to the importance of classroom activities that raise students' consciousness about the language. These tasks help students notice grammatical forms, focus explicitly on the gap between their output and what native speakers would write, and expose them to language forms that they may not be ready to acquire immediately, but will be at some point in their acquisition trajectory.

Taking Truscott's claim seriously would mean that the L2 composition classroom should not or cannot be a place where the seeds of later language acquisition can be planted. This is emphatically not the case. As research and teacher experience indicates, error feedback can have several important functions, helping ESL writers to (1) gain awareness of where their written texts do not follow conventions of standard written English and (2) develop self-editing skills by focusing their attention on the patterned nature of their errors. Most important, when teachers provide careful feedback on the language features in a student draft, they are sending a powerful message that clarity and appropriateness of language forms is a key to effective written communication.

Principles for incorporating grammar in writing instruction

The review of the central questions related to the role of grammar in L2 writing suggests that form-focused instruction remains an essential component in ESL writing curricula. Issues of language are inseparable from content, organization, and audience considerations, and they should all be given equal weight in ESL composition classes. Furthermore, attention to language is a non-negotiable part of L2 writing instruction, given L2 writers' backgrounds and needs. Nonetheless, the themes that the literature has tended to focus on reflect a limited notion of the role that grammar can play in ESL composition, claiming that editing and error feedback *are* grammar instruction. A more comprehensive perspective would view grammar instruction as an opportunity to build writers' linguistic resources for academic literacy and to create understanding of the relationships between language form and written message. In the remainder of this chapter, we would like to outline a principled approach to incorporating grammar in L2 writing classes, one that expands the role grammar plays in writing classrooms beyond a focus on error.

L2 writing classroom variables: Learners, texts, processes

Recent L2 composition research and pedagogy, as well as second language acquisition studies, have identified several variables in the writing equation that are useful in formulating a principled approach to grammar instruction. These variables include learners (students), stages of writing processes, and written discourse texts and contexts, schematized in Figure 6.1. Attention to these three areas helps in determining when to direct learners' attention to form, what grammatical forms merit attention, and how best to engage different kinds of L2 writers in grammar activities that promote writing development.

The three areas of focus are not isolated components but rather, as illustrated, interact dynamically. For purposes of our discussion, however, we will consider how attention to and reflection on each of these L2 writing classroom components can help inform our teaching.

Learners

One of the most critical choices in course design for language teaching is whether the starting point should be *the learner* or *the language to be taught*. Long and Robinson (1998) note that in most classrooms throughout the world, language constitutes this starting point. In the United States, however, a primary focus of current composition pedagogy is the

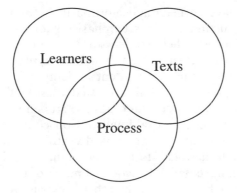

Figure 6.1. Classroom variables

learner and his or her language learning processes. Byrd and Reid (1998) support this current trend, stating that "planning for the grammar in ESL curricula needs to begin not with the structures but with students" (p. 1).

More and more ESL composition classrooms around the world typically comprise heterogeneous student populations. These students exhibit differences in linguistic, ethnic, and cultural backgrounds as well as in language proficiency, academic skills, and cognitive and metacognitive strategy use, among others. They also vary in their motivations and attitudes toward language learning and the acquisition of academic skills (Ferris & Hedgcock, 1998).

These variables are clearly important in decisions about grammar instruction. Some student variables, however, deserve greater attention as they impact curricular models for incorporating language into the teaching of writing. The L2 composition literature has emphasized that teachers need to distinguish the different types of L2 writers who often get lumped under the label "ESL" (including English as a foreign language [EFL] students). One of the most significant is the distinction between international students, who have completed secondary school in their native countries, and permanent resident, or immigrant, students in English-speaking countries such as the United States (Byrd & Reid, 1998; Leki, 1992). Individual students who fall into these two broad categories obviously differ in many of the complex ways already noted, but more significant to teachers are several important distinctions between the two populations that can inform instructional choices.

In decades past, international (EFL) students made up the majority of learners in L2 postsecondary writing classes; they are still a sizeable population in many colleges and certainly in most graduate schools and intensive English programs on university campuses throughout North America (as well as in other English-dominant countries). International students have typically developed strong literacy skills in their native languages. They have learned English primarily in foreign language class-rooms, with instruction that has emphasized formal study of English grammar. Consequently, these students are generally able to access and explain grammar rules even though their writing may be more "nonna-tivelike" than that of permanent resident students. Because their speaking and listening comprehension skills are usually less well developed (Leki, 1992), the linguistic resources international students access tend to de-rive from written rather than oral English. Consequently, they tend to be familiar with the conventions of standard written English.

In contrast to international students, permanent resident ESL students in North America have typically acquired much of their English outside the classroom, often by ear rather than through print media (Reid, 1998). Consequently, they are generally very familiar with the grammar and vocabulary of informal spoken English and often import these into aca-demic writing contexts. In addition, much of their intuition about English grammar and syntax may derive from their knowledge of oral English. Whereas an international student may access a language rule to identify and explain an ungrammatical form, an immigrant ESL student intuits that the form "sounds wrong" much as a native English speaker might. In other cases, resident ESL students may identify some formal language structures as incorrect (e.g., possessive gerund phrases such as "their objecting to the amendment") because they have not encountered these forms in oral English.

Further complicating the profile of permanent resident ESL students is that many who enter postsecondary institutions may be bicultural and biliterate, and some have had formal English grammar instruction in their native countries. However, an increasing population of L2 learners is more literate in English than in the L1 and, in some cases, may be lit-erate only in English. Recent research has focused on the language needs of this growing population of U.S.-educated L2 learners, referred to as "Generation 1.5," a term first used by Rumbaut and Ima (1988) to char-acterize students whose traits and experience "lie somewhere between the first and second generation" (Harklau, Losey, & Siegal, 1999, p. vii).

These students' problems with the conventions of written English do not result from a lack of exposure to English. As Scarcella (1996) has pointed out, their difficulties arise in some part because K–12 language education has neglected attention to linguistic form and de-emphasized corrective feedback; as a result, these learners enter postsecondary writ-ing classrooms without awareness of their very real language difficulties in academic English. Given the complex roots of their language prob-lems, grammar instruction designed for inexperienced users of English will fail to meet their literacy development needs (Frodesen & Starna, 1999; Harklau, 2000).

To summarize, an awareness of learner variables and the distinctions between different types of L2 writers is important for teachers if they are to avoid the simplistic and erroneous conception of ESL writers as simply "writers with language errors." While ESL writing instructors cannot be expected to consider at all times the entire complex of student variables when designing and implementing language instruction, knowledge of these variables may often provide valuable insights at different stages of writing instruction and in different learning contexts.

Bear in mind that there may be a disconnect between what a teacher teaches and what a student learns. The degree to which students take away the knowledge of a structure or form as intended by the instructor and their ability to subsequently use that structure productively in their own writing may depend on one or more of the variables outlined in this section. In the end, as Long and Robinson (1998) point out, it is not a matter of the *lesson* per se – or the teacher's intention – that constitutes "focus on form" but rather whether the instruction successfully encourages the *learners' focus* on language and leads to language development – in this case the language of written English.

Writing processes

THE PLACE OF GRAMMAR IN COMPOSING

Most postsecondary L2 composition courses in the United States now incorporate some form of a process-based model of composing into their writing courses. As L2 writers work through sequences of pre-writing (invention and organization tasks), drafting, revising, and editing, many opportunities occur for instructors to help students draw on their implicit knowledge of English structures and the ways in which these forms realize meanings. Through grammar-based instruction, teachers can model appropriate forms for students to use not only in their papers but to accomplish classroom discourse tasks, such as brainstorming ideas, responding to a peer's paper, and conferencing with their teacher. The forms writers acquire should prove useful throughout their university studies and perhaps beyond.

In addition, opportunities arise to draw on and develop explicit knowledge of less familiar (and often complex) structures and form-function relationships. During these activities, teachers can raise consciousness about language, such as differences between spoken and written English or the use of certain verb tenses in particular types of texts (e.g., the use of past tense in describing experiments). Focused instruction at various stages of composing processes allows L2 writers to imitate the types of language-based choices that native speakers make in creating written texts. As Little (1994) has noted, effective communication in written discourse typically requires a high level of correctness, and native speakers often use explicit knowledge, "whether [they] take it from memory or reference books, when [they] plan, monitor and edit more formal kinds of written and spoken discourse" (p. 104).

ERROR FEEDBACK AND CORRECTION

Feedback on errors has generally been a staple of ESL writing instruction. Influenced largely by the process approach to writing, this activity is now generally reserved for the end stage of students' drafting after they have worked through their ideas and organizational issues. Some instructors, in fact, use error feedback as the predominant method of grammar instruction. Perhaps this instructional strategy enjoys such popularity because it satisfies the many practical and theoretical imperatives related to grammar instruction that we have previously outlined. First, it allows teachers to individualize grammar instruction, thereby acknowledging that language learning is complex and varies from individual to individual. It also appeases the fear that other types of grammar instruction may seem irrelevant to student writers or fail to transfer into student production. In addition, error feedback allows teachers to put editing in its proper place in the writing process – after students have done pre-writing, planning, and drafting and while they are revising their texts. Finally, such an approach is pragmatic because it allows teachers to integrate attention to grammar while not detracting from the primary aim of the course: teaching students writing skills appropriate for academic contexts.

Error feedback is indeed a useful way to incorporate attention to language into L2 writing courses, especially when it is done selectively and strategically (Ferris, 1999). Thanks to considerable research on this aspect of L2 writing instruction, ESL teachers now have excellent resources to guide them in creating feedback methods that will best meet the specific needs of their students and the constraints of their teaching contexts (e.g., Bates, Lane, & Lange, 1993; Byrd & Reid, 1998; Ferris & Hedgcock, 1998; Shih, 1998) as well as full descriptions of course curricula in this area (e.g., Camhi, 2000; Shih, 2001). In general, these discussions advocate the following: (1) limiting error feedback to certain types of errors, based on considerations such as attention to global – or more serious – errors, error frequency, or errors that may stigmatize writers (e.g., nonstandard forms of English considered to be "uneducated"); (2) providing indirect rather than direct corrections through such methods as underlining, checking, or coding errors; (3) considering individual writers' learning styles, metalinguistic knowledge, and overall proficiency level in deciding when and how to provide feedback. In sum, these generalizations direct teachers to focus on "aspects of grammar that can be explained, understood, and generalized to students' particular writing needs" (Ferris & Hedgcock, 1998, p. 205).

Two issues remain relative to the widespread use of error feedback. One is that some teachers of L2 writers lack sufficient knowledge of English structure and pedagogical grammar to accurately, consistently, and appropriately deal with learner errors (Truscott, 1996). This is a significant concern, since responding to students' errors, especially at advanced levels, is a complicated task, even for experienced and knowledgeable instructors. Clearly, effective error feedback requires that teachers possess thorough knowledge of English structure and pedagogical grammar. (See Kroll, 1993, for a discussion of other pitfalls of inadequate ESL teacher preparation.)

Another and somewhat broader issue concerns the reality that many teachers have come to rely on error correction as "the" way to address the grammar needs of second language writers. Assigning grammar instruction such a restricted role not only fosters a narrow conception of L2 writers as "error producers" and the L2 writing classroom as an "error repair shop" but also ignores much of the current research and theoretical discussion on pedagogical grammar. A richer and more comprehensive treatment of language in L2 writing classrooms should combine error feedback with lessons on the essential relationship between language and discourse structure (e.g., the use of modal verbs to hedge in argumentation). It would also, as Johns (1994) suggests, make second language learners co-researchers, discovering how grammar functions in academic texts and eventually transferring these discoveries into their own writing.

Written texts and genre

In addition to considering learners and the writing process, teachers should consider written texts themselves as key in making decisions about grammar instruction in L2 writing. Research and pedagogy in a number of areas – discourse and genre analysis, functional linguistics, L1 and L2 composition, and second language acquisition (SLA) – offer insight and inspiration for instructors in using written texts to enhance students' understanding of how grammatical systems function in communication, to illustrate the co-occurrence patterns of grammatical structures and vocabulary (or *lexis*, as the latter is often termed), and to identify the grammatical features that typically cluster in different genres of written discourse.

For teachers who are attentive to grammatical patterns in written discourse, the readings they assign in class can serve as a source of authentic and interesting examples of features of English grammar, examples that can make students sensitive to the choices that writers make to convey meaning. In the English for academic purposes (EAP) classroom, written texts representing the genres that students are expected to write offer models not only for rhetorical structures but for the language used to create them. For L2 writers, instruction focused on how language is used in different genres – such as a problem-solution text, the literature review in a research paper, or the short essay required in exam contexts – should be an essential part of an academic writing class. (See Johns, Chapter 8 this volume, for further discussion on this topic.)

Expository texts are not the only ones that can be mined for rich grammatical input. As Holten (1997) discusses, ESL writing instructors typically use only "academic" expository prose as a context for grammar instruction and tend to regard literature as a "break" from language-focused activities. But short stories or excerpts from novels offer excellent opportunities for students to look at language features, partly because these texts treat topics that are often more accessible to students than those in expository or "textbook" selections. Thus, students may be more willing to examine language in these texts than ones they find difficult to relate to. (See Vandrick, Chapter 11 this volume, for a fuller discussion of this topic.)

From the preceding discussion, it might sound as if L2 composition instructors must become experts in text linguistics. There is, in fact, a wide variety of resources for them to draw on. As Hyland (2002) points out, however, all of the approaches used to investigate the discourse of texts "have sought to discover how writers use patterns of language options to accomplish coherent, purposeful prose" (p. 10). Developments in computer-based text analysis have enabled researchers to analyze large corpora of spoken and written English, identifying grammatical features that typically cluster together in particular discourse contexts (Biber, 1988; Conrad, 1996, among others). In *Variation across Speech and Writing* (1988), Biber has identified a number of dimensions along which speaking and writing vary and the ways in which grammatical features cluster in these dimensions. While Biber's dimensions and features do not identify genres per se, they are often associated with particular genres. For example, narrative communication often characterizes historical writing. Thus, the grammatical features can be exploited in helping writers select appropriate forms to meet particular rhetorical demands.

Computer analyses of written texts can also provide L2 writing teachers with authentic examples of the ways in which grammar and vocabulary interact. These analyses, referred to as concordance data, can be found in reference texts such as *Collins COBUILD English Language Dictionary* (1987) and the *Longman Grammar of Spoken and Written English* (Biber et al., 1999) or can be created using software programs. In these kinds of written text data, key words (e.g., *therefore*, *thus*, and *hence*; definite article *the*) or syntactic structures (e.g., all verbs followed by *that* clauses) are extracted from large collections of texts and appear in lists of sentences or parts of sentences that teachers can use to focus on particular language forms and choices writers make. Johns (1994) describes a variety of lessons created for advanced L2 writers based on concordance information, noting that when students and teachers work together on data, "they discover things unobserved and unsuspected by the teacher when the materials were prepared" (p. 299).

Bringing texts and learners together

While genre analysis and corpus linguistics have much to offer ESL composition instructors in their choices about grammar instruction, this body of knowledge must be applied in a principled way, taking into account the central purpose of the composition class: the development of learners' writing proficiency. As Tribble (2002) points out, "Content and writing process knowledge will [always] remain an area for . . . teachers and students to address, however much contextual and linguistic investigation" (p. 145) students might engage in. A primary concern, then, is what kinds of text-based instruction may best allow students to attend to, or notice, relevant forms and to provide them practice in using these forms. Several considerations may assist teachers in reflecting on what forms to choose and how to structure lessons for learners.

The first consideration in creating lessons is the types of activities in which students will engage: text analysis or text production. Text analysis activities ask writers to describe or notice how certain structures are used in extended discourse. For example, they might identify contexts in which writers use passive verbs or notice how embedded noun clauses are created from previously mentioned information expressed as sentences (e.g., *the results may not be valid* → *whether or not the results are valid*). These "noticing" exercises heighten students' awareness of language features for later productive tasks, assuming that they are appropriate for students' proficiency levels. In addition to analyzing published writing, students can analyze language features in their own texts and those of their classmates in peer response activities.

If we expect students to access and use the explicit knowledge they have discovered through written text analysis, they must go beyond simply noticing grammatical relationships or contrasts in grammatical forms. They must practice these structures productively. Productive practice may range from controlled work, such as revising instructor-underlined sentences, to guided work, such as a dictogloss, in which learners reconstruct an extended text that has been dictated to them (Wajnryb, 1988), to communicative writing practice, such as summarizing a published persuasive text using reporting verbs. All of these tasks require learners to draw on their grammatical knowledge. Productive activities following text analysis tasks are important not only to provide opportunities for students to transfer their newly gained knowledge in language output but to help instructors evaluate the effectiveness of text analysis exercises in helping students develop writing fluency and accuracy.

These two types of literacy development activities – text analysis and productive activities – can and should be used in tandem in L2 writing classrooms. Ideas on how to integrate text analysis and student production tasks can be gleaned from comparative studies of L2 writers' attempts to meet the linguistic demands inherent in certain genres. Schleppegrell's (2000) study, for example, identifies language required for expressing assumptions in a science lab report. She outlines the different ways in which *assume* was used in a model report – as passive verb (*is assumed*), nonfinite verb (X, *assuming* Y), noun (this *assumption*), and so on – illustrating the linguistic resources used to convey meaning and create lexical cohesion. Using similar genre-based authentic materials, teachers could create a text analysis lesson that focuses students' attention on these word class variations of a key concept, followed by a production task in which writers construct a cohesive text using various forms of a particular vocabulary item. Analysis and production tasks can address other language needs common across text types, such as summary and paraphrase. These skills require students to make connections between their texts and those of others and, in the process, to manipulate language forms such as complex clauses or idiomatic language.

A second consideration involves the intersection between written texts, learner production and the ways in which learners will best profit from focus on form. SLA literature provides a helpful distinction here between *proactive and reactive focus*. As Doughty and Williams (1998) explain, teachers "can plan in advance to ensure that a focus on form will occur, or they can wait for a pressing learner need to arise and develop an 'on-the-spot' ... lesson in response" (p. 205). Process-based models of instruction have tended to favor a reactive rather than a proactive approach. Language-focused instruction in the ESL writing class could, and generally should, include both types of focus. For example, in planning the syllabus, the instructor may proactively include lessons focused on particular verb tenses that she predicts her students will need to work on. As part of a reading assignment, she may include a lesson on the ways in which writers employ different reference words and phrases, such as demonstrative pronouns and adjectives, definite article *the* + noun, and personal pronouns *it* and *they* to create cohesion and avoid ambiguous reference. As the class progresses, *reactive* lessons may surface in answer to students' questions, in response to observed patterns of error in students' drafts, or during individual conferences. Reactive lessons may thus respond to needs of the class as a whole or to individual learners. By combining proactive and reactive lessons, teachers can help students expand their existing linguistic resources while at the same time capitalizing on the learning opportunities that student errors provide.

Revisiting the role of grammar in ESL writing

Can clear answers be found to the questions surrounding the role of explicit grammar-based instruction in the second language writing classroom? It appears that the answers – and new questions – lie in considering the relationship of second language literacy acquisition to second language learning in general and in clarifying our perspective on grammar's role in written communication of all kinds. If, as a great deal of current research has indicated, some degree of focus on form is not only beneficial for learners but necessary in second language learning (Lightbown, 1998), then it seems the question is not *whether* we should "teach" grammar but *how best* to do it. Instructors need to pay careful attention to the many learner variables that may affect students' abilities and motivations in developing language-based knowledge. They need to consider the stages of writing process and the role that grammar plays in generating ideas, drafting, and revising. They need to identify genre-based demands of writing tasks, academic and otherwise. And if we view grammar as an essential component of all communication – as a set of linguistic resources from which native and nonnative speakers alike select forms based on appropriateness for meaning, for audience, and for textual demands – then grammar and writing are inseparable. We simply cannot convey meaning properly without grammar, and it stands to reason that the richer our students' grammatical resources are and the better their knowledge of form-function relationships are, the better they will be able to communicate. Grammar in ESL writing is not just about error, and this aspect should not be the sole focus of grammar instruction in second language writing pedagogy.[6]

Perhaps ESL writing teachers can best integrate the teaching of grammar with the teaching of writing by drawing not only on their knowledge of the issues discussed thus far but also on their classroom experience and intuition. Ellis (1994) recommends this combination of research and teacher experience in all language teaching contexts. In L2 writing classrooms, such a combination will allow instructors to create meaningful ways for students to access and develop the linguistic resources they will need to communicate effectively in a wide range of writing tasks.

Notes

1. These conventions, of course, differ across genres and from country to country where English is a primary language for written communication in academic, professional, or governmental settings. Nevertheless, the concept of conventions is relevant no matter what the genre or form of world English because readers expect and need the language of a text to communicate its

ideas clearly and appropriately. A more comprehensive discussion of world Englishes, however, is beyond the scope of this chapter.
2. In Blanton and Kroll et al. (2002), several veteran L2 writing teachers reflect on their use of these grammar-focused approaches in teaching their own ESL/EFL writing classes in the 1960s and 1970s.
3. We thank one of the anonymous reviewers of this manuscript for this insightful comment.
4. Thornbury (1999, pp. 14–28) provides a more extensive review of these arguments in a highly readable format.
5. For some specific suggestions about classroom activities to promote improved proficiency, see Frodesen (2001).
6. There are helpful resources for teaching the intersection between grammar and style, for example, including Joseph Williams's *Style: Ten Lessons in Clarity and Grace* (1999) and Martha Kolln's *Rhetorical Grammar: Grammatical Choice, Rhetorical Effects* (1999).

References

Bartholomae, D. (1980). The study of error. *College Composition and Communication, 31*, 253–269.

Bates, L., Lane, J., & Lange, E. (1993). *Writing clearly: Responding to ESL compositions.* Boston: Heinle & Heinle.

Biber, D. (1988). *Variation across speech and writing.* Cambridge, England: Cambridge University Press.

Biber, D., Johannson, S., Leech, G., Conrad, S., & Finegan, E. (1999). *The Longman grammar of spoken and written English.* Harlow, England: Pearson Education Limited.

Blanton, L., & Kroll, B., et al. (2002). *ESL composition tales: Reflections on teaching.* Ann Arbor: University of Michigan Press.

Braddock, R., Lloyd-Jones, R., & Schoer, L. (1963). *Research in written composition.* Urbana, IL: National Council of Teachers of English.

Brinton, D. M., & Holten, C. A. (2001). Does the emperor have no clothes? A reexamination of grammar in content-based instruction. In J. Flowerdew & M. Peacock (Eds.), *Research perspectives on English for academic purposes* (pp. 239–251). New York: Cambridge University Press.

Byrd, P., & Reid, J. (1998). *Grammar in the composition classroom: Essays on teaching ESL for college-bound students.* Boston: Heinle & Heinle.

Camhi, P. J. (2000). Well-formedness principles on syntactic structures. In M. Pally (Ed.), *Sustained content teaching in academic ESL/EFL* (pp. 117–131). Boston: Houghton Mifflin.

Collins COBUILD English Language Dictionary. (1987). London: Collins.

Conrad, S. (1996). Investigating academic texts with corpus-based techniques: An example from biology. *Linguistics and Education, 8,* 299–326.

Doughty, C., & Williams, J. (1998). Pedagogical choices in focus on form. In C. Doughty & J. Williams (Eds.), *Focus on form in classroom second language acquisition* (pp. 197–261). New York: Cambridge University Press.

Ellis, R. (1994). Implicit/explicit knowledge and language pedagogy. *TESOL Quarterly, 28,* 166–172.

Emig, J. (1981). Non-magical thinking: Presenting writing developmentally in schools. In C. H. Frederiksen & J. F. Dominic (Eds.), *Writing: The nature, development and teaching of written communication* (Vol. 2, pp. 21–30). Hillsdale, NJ: Lawrence Erlbaum.

Fathman, A., & Whalley, E. (1990). Teacher response to student writing: Focus on form versus content. In B. Kroll (Ed.), *Second language writing: Research insights for the classroom* (pp. 178–190). New York: Cambridge University Press.

Ferris, D. (1995). Can advanced ESL students be taught to correct their most serious and frequent errors? *CATESOL Journal, 8,* 41–62.

Ferris, D. (1997). The influence of teacher commentary on student revision. *TESOL Quarterly, 31,* 315–339.

Ferris, D. (1999). The case for grammar correction in L2 writing classes: A response to Truscott. *Journal of Second Language Writing, 8,* 1–11.

Ferris, D., & Hedgcock, J. (1998). *Teaching ESL composition: Purpose, process and practice.* Mahwah, NJ: Lawrence Erlbaum.

Ferris, D., & Roberts, B. (2001). Error feedback in L2 writing classes: How explicit does it need to be? *Journal of Second Language Writing, 10,* 161–184.

Flower, L., & Hayes, J. A. (1980). The cognition of discovery: Defining a rhetorical problem. *College Composition and Communication 31,* 21–32.

Flower, L., & Hayes, J. A. (1981). The pregnant pause: An inquiry into the nature of planning. *Research in the Teaching of English, 15,* 229–243.

Frodesen, J. (2001). Grammar in writing. In M. Celce-Murcia (Ed.), *Teaching English as a second or foreign language* (3rd ed., pp. 233–248). Boston: Heinle & Heinle.

Frodesen, J., & Starna, N. (1999). Distinguishing incipient and functional bilingual writers: Assessment and instructional insights gained through second-language writer profiles. In L. Harklau, K. Losey, & M. Siegal (Eds.), *Generation 1.5 meets college composition: Issues in the teaching of writing to U.S.-educated learners of ESL* (pp. 61–79). Mahwah, NJ: Lawrence Erlbaum.

Harklau, L. (2000). From the "good kids" to the "worst": Representations of English language learners across educational settings. *TESOL Quarterly 34,* 35–67.

Harklau, L., Losey, K., & Siegal, M. (1999). *Generation 1.5 meets college composition: Issues in the teaching of writing to U.S.-educated learners of ESL.* Mahwah, NJ: Lawrence Erlbaum.

Hartwell, P. (1985). Grammar, grammars, and the teaching of grammar. *College English, 47,* 105–127.

Holten, C. (1997). Literature: A quintessential content. In M. Snow & D. Brinton (Eds.), *The content-based classroom: Perspectives on integrating language and content* (pp. 377–387). White Plains, NY: Longman.

Hyland, K. (2002). *Teaching and researching writing.* Harlow, UK: Longman.

Johns, T. (1994). From printout to handout: Grammar and vocabulary teaching in the context of data-driven learning. In T. Odlin (Ed.), *Perspectives on pedagogical grammar* (pp. 292–313). New York: Cambridge University Press.

Kepner, C. G. (1991). An experiment in the relationship of written feedback to the development of second-language writing skills. *Modern Language Journal, 75,* 305–313.

Kolln, M. (1999). *Rhetorical grammar: Grammatical choices, rhetorical effects.* Boston: Allyn and Bacon.

Krashen, S. (1978). Individual variation in the use of the monitor. In W. Ritchie (Ed.), *Second language acquisition research* (pp. 175–185). New York: Academic Press.

Krashen, S. (1982). *Principles and practice in second language acquisition.* Oxford: Pergamon Press.

Kroll, B. (1993). Teaching writing IS teaching reading: Training the new teacher of ESL composition. In J. Carson & I. Leki (Eds.), *Reading in the composition classroom: Second language perspectives* (pp. 61–81). Boston: Heinle & Heinle.

Lalande, J. F., II (1982). Reducing composition errors: An experiment. *Modern Language Journal, 66,* 140–149.

Leki, L. (1992). *Understanding ESL writers.* Portsmouth, NH: Boynton/Cook Publishers.

Lightbown, P. (1998). The importance of timing in focus on form. In C. Doughty & J. Williams (Eds.), *Focus on form in classroom second language acquisition* (pp. 177–196). New York: Cambridge University Press.

Little, D. (1994). Words and their properties: Arguments for a lexical approach to pedagogical grammar. In T. Odlin (Ed.), *Perspectives on pedagogical grammar* (pp. 99–122). New York: Cambridge University Press.

Long, M., & Robinson, P. (1998). Focus on form: Theory, research, and practice. In C. Doughty & J. Williams (Eds.), *Focus on form in classroom second language acquisition* (pp. 15–41). New York: Cambridge University Press.

Perl, S. (1979). The composing processes of unskilled college writers. *Research in the Teaching of English, 13,* 317–336.

Raimes, A. (1985). What unskilled ESL students do when they write: A classroom study of composing. *TESOL Quarterly, 19,* 229–255.

Reid, J. (1998). Learning styles and grammar teaching in the composition classroom. In P. Byrd & J. Reid, *Grammar in the composition classroom: Essays on teaching ESL for college-bound students* (pp. 18–30). Boston: Heinle & Heinle.

Robb, T., Ross, S., & Shortreed, I. (1986). Salience of feedback on error and its effect on EFL writing quality. *TESOL Quarterly, 20,* 83–95.

Rumbaut, R. G., & Ima, K. (1988). *The adaptation of Southeast Asian refugee youth: A comparative study* (Final report to the Office of Resettlement). San Diego, CA: San Diego State University. (ERIC Document Reproduction Services No. ED 299 372)

Rutherford, W. E. (1987). *Second language grammar: Learning and teaching.* New York: Longman.

Scarcella, R. (1996). Secondary education in California and second language research: Instructing ESL students in the 1990s. *CATESOL Journal, 9 (1),* 129–151.

Schleppegrell, M. (2000, February). *Challenges of the science register for ESL students: Interpersonal and intertextual meanings.* Presented at the Conference on Advanced Literacy, University of California, Davis.

Semke, H. D. (1984). Effects of the red pen. *Foreign Language Annals, 17*, 195–202.

Shaughnessy, M. (1977). *Errors and expectations: A guide for the teacher of basic writing* (Chapter 3: Syntax, pp. 44–89). New York: Oxford University Press.

Shih, M. (1998). ESL writers' grammar editing strategies. *College ESL, 8*, 64–86.

Shih, M. (2001). A course in grammar editing for ESL writers. In J. Murphy & P. Byrd (Eds.), *Understanding the courses we teach: Local perspectives on English language teaching* (pp. 346–366). Ann Arbor: University of Michigan Press.

Sommers, N. (1980). Revision strategies of student writers and experienced adult writers. *College Composition and Communication, 31*, 378–388.

Spada, N. (1997). Form-focused instruction and second language acquisition: A review of classroom and laboratory research. *Language Teaching, 30*, 73–85.

Thornbury, S. (1999). *How to teach grammar.* Harlow, UK: Longman.

Tribble, C. (2002). Corpora and corpus analysis: New windows on academic writing. In J. Flowerdew (Ed.), *Academic discourse* (pp. 131–149). Harlow, UK: Longman.

Truscott, J. (1996). The case against grammar correction in L2 writing classes. *Language Learning, 46*, 327–369.

Wajnryb, R. (1988, July). The Dictogloss method of language teaching: A text-based, communicative approach to grammar. *English Teaching Forum*, 60–63.

Williams, J. M. (1999). *Style: Ten lessons in clarity and grace* (5th ed.). New York: Addison-Wesley.

Zamel, V. (1983). The composing processes of advanced ESL students: Six case studies. *TESOL Quarterly 17*, 165–187.

7 Writing teachers as assessors of *writing*

Liz Hamp-Lyons

Many teachers feel that assessment is not their concern, that their job is to teach well, and that assessment is something to be taken care of by someone else – by a special person within their school who is responsible for testing or by external, invisible means (often through large-scale tests devised and administered by an agency outside of their own institution). But if teachers accept responsibility for the progress of the people they teach, and if they want to ensure that those they teach will be judged fairly (and all teachers do!), they must have some involvement with evaluation. Teachers must know enough about assessment practices to be able to look at the assessments being brought into their programs, or being taken externally by their students, and evaluate them. From this perspective, assessment is *every* teacher's job.

In this chapter, I first provide a short overview of some key aspects of assessment in general and follow with a focused discussion of the most critical issues that writing teachers need to be aware of in a variety of situations they are likely to face – when they plan writing tests for their own students, take part in a school-wide writing assessment, participate in decisions about what writing test to use for a specific purpose, or talk to parents about the meaning and implications of tests their children are taking. Without such information, it is very difficult for teachers to make informed and knowledgeable decisions about a very critical component in the full picture of teaching writing.

Among the many changes that have occurred in the field of writing assessment, especially in the past twenty years, a particularly significant one relates to the changing relationship between direct and indirect measures of writing. Nowadays, when systems do use indirect measures of "writing" (including multiple-choice, grammar completion, cloze, etc.), they are likely to do so with some apology and appeal to expediency. Such indirect tests tend to be used as only one component of the assessment of "writing ability," and they are administered in tandem with direct writing assessments that have become a common part of large-scale tests. For example, the Test of Written English (TWE) was introduced in 1986 as an optional component in addition to the three compulsory, multiple-choice sections of the widely used Test of English as a

Foreign Language (TOEFL), and the new TOEFL computer-based test includes a direct writing assessment.

As this chapter shows, direct tests have become common, and the importance of authenticity and validity has been generally accepted. We still have much to learn about the assessment of writing, however, and much progress must be made before we can feel that this assessment is fully able to measure literacy education in the modern world.

Expectations of writing assessments

Two key terms that factor into any assessment discussion are "reliability" and "validity." After briefly reviewing the general interpretation of these terms, I discuss validity from the current perspective, in which construct validity is seen as the overarching and encompassing validity, and I identify some *other* expectations of (writing) assessments that used to receive less attention than they do now. These new expectations of writing assessments reflect changes in our understanding of the goals of education and the roles of teachers, learners, and assessors in the educational enterprise.

Reliability

In general terms, reliability refers to the ability of the test scores to be replicable – for example, from one test occasion to another, or from one essay prompt to another. Writing tests cannot be 100%, and are rarely more than 80%, reliable. This realization made the statisticians unhappy, and in the United States of the 1950s and 1960s the statisticians ruled educational assessment (see Lemann's 1999 history of the Scholastic Aptitude Test [SAT]). The solution proposed was to replace the assessment of actual pieces of real writing with multiple-choice, standardized, so-called objective tests, and that solution was implemented in many contexts. This was a period that coincided with a behavioral approach to language teaching and its concomitant focus on rules and the importance of accuracy. However, direct testing (or the elicitation of writing samples) lends itself to a type of reliability in terms of rating procedures. In the United States and many other countries, we are now at a stage in which reliability above 75% is consistently achieved when measured as agreement between two or more raters on the score assigned to a given sample of writing, and this, coupled with strong validity, is accepted in most educational contexts.

However, because writing is a very complex activity involving thinking, planning, organizing, and linking as well as several levels of language manipulation (sentence and clause levels as well as word and phrase level, plus spelling, punctuation, etc.), there are inherent problems with the expectation of reliability when viewed from the perspective of the *writing* rather than the perspective of the *rating*. The same person does not necessarily write equally well on different days or about different subject matter. Differences in the same person's scores might not, then, mean the scores are not reliable: in fact, the scores might be reliably reflecting differences in that person's performances. Considerably more complexity is added because writing is judged by human beings – teachers and/or raters – and these human beings are likely to vary from day to day, from subject to subject; they are likely to have preferences for certain kinds of ideas or structures, or dislike for some choices of words or arguments.

In Britain and its former colonies, direct assessment of writing continued, as did written examinations in almost every subject, even when multiple-choice testing was introduced as part of examinations in many content areas. Wiseman (1949) proposed the "Devon method," a system of multiple marking of writing to improve reliability, and because this kept writing assessment "respectable" the essay test never fell out of favor as it did in the United States. However, some British English as a foreign language (EFL) tests still do not use multiple marking for reasons of cost and instead use a system of "moderation" to check on the accuracy of raters by sampling their scoring; therefore, it is not possible to accurately evaluate the reliability of these tests. This approach is not considered satisfactory by writing assessment specialists and represents a battle still to be won with the British test agencies.

Traditional validities

Coupled with concern for reliability, assessment is also concerned with validity. In writing assessment, as with most assessment contexts, it has been traditional to consider four kinds of validity: face validity, content validity, criterion validity, and construct validity (see Hamp-Lyons, 1990). The simplest validity is face validity, or what looks to an intelligent outsider as if it is valid. Content validity is related to face validity but is grounded in some actual evidence. It is often claimed, for example, that if the students are history majors, we should give them a writing test that asks them to write about history. The problem with content validity is the difficulty of defining what it is that writers do when they write, for example, a history assignment, and of finding ways to test that without depending on any specific content.

Another kind of validity is criterion validity. This refers to the measurable relationship, usually correlational, between a particular test of writing and various other measures ("criterial" measures). Criterion validity includes concurrent validity, in which the criterion performance is compared against another performance measured at the same or close time, and predictive validity, in which the criterion performance will be compared with another performance at a future time. As with all such studies, the key problem when we try to look at the criterion validity of a writing test is identifying a reasonable criterion measure against which the writing test is to be compared. Studies over the years have shown that writing tests often correlate highly with concurrent "objective" measures, and this was the argument used by ETS (Educational Testing Service) for many years as the reason for not testing writing directly. But few ESL professionals these days are prepared to believe that we can test writing by any means other than having students actually write. The arguments for including direct performances in any assessment relate to construct validity and to washback and impact, which are discussed later. But it is worth noting that the new computer-based TOEFL, administered by ETS, accepts such arguments and includes a writing sample.

Construct validity and the "new" validities

Attitudes and priorities in language testing have changed significantly since 1990. Reliability and the traditional validities still have importance, but it is better understood that a good test demands more than this. Traditionally, if a test has construct validity it appropriately represents or reflects the reality of behavior in the area being tested. A construct-valid test is designed to measure certain human responses. The actual "constructs" themselves are rather abstract things, like "ability to write." Constructs cannot be seen but have to be measured by capturing some examples of behavior that tap that construct. However reliable a test is, it cannot be valid if it isn't capturing information about the right construct. The example often used to explain the difference between a reliable test and a construct valid one is as follows: Imagine a target. If you shoot three arrows and they all hit the same spot, your aim is very reliable. But suppose those three arrows hit the edge of the target? Your aim is reliable, but not effective. Suppose one arrow hits the bullseye and the other two go in different directions? You have some effectiveness but no reliability. Now suppose all three arrows hit the bullseye? Your aim is both effective and reliable. Construct validity demands that you not only hit the same spot most of the time, but that it's the right spot.

The new, integrated view of validity includes content validity, quality assurance over test development, the traditional construct validity described above, test usefulness, the ability of the test to have meaning and re-levance in more than one context ("validity generalization"), and one that appeals most to writing teachers and researchers: consequential va-lidity. This current sense of validity is drawn mainly from the work of Messick, especially his seminal 1989 paper (Messick, 1989) and his rein-terpretation of his ideas for a specific second language (L2) testing audience (Messick, 1996). Whereas many of these elements, such as content and construct validity, are not new, a less familiar component is "validity generalization" (Messick, 1994), which is essentially a commonsense quality: the scores generated by a test should make sense to people likely to look at them without too much explanatory information being provided. Not only is this economical, but it also helps ensure that the meaning of a test score is not misinterpreted to the disadvantage of test-takers. The key requirement of test validity is in the interpretation and use of scores, so if test scores are misinterpreted and therefore wrongly used, the test will be invalid. This is a particular issue in specific purpose testing (Douglas, 2000), such as a test of English for medical doctors in which there was no speaking component: test scores could *not* be interpreted as information about whether the doctor could communicate effectively with staff or patients.

Consequential validity addresses concerns that tests should not be used in ways that are biased, are unfair, or encourage the unjust treatment of certain individuals or groups of people. The first "new" expectation subsumed within consequential validity is that the assessment should as a minimum do no harm to instruction or to learning (Hamp-Lyons, 1989a). This expectation is found in discussions of test "washback" (e.g., Wall & Alderson, 1993).[1] Claims about negative consequences of tests are very familiar to writing teachers who have worked hard to teach students to write with confidence and enjoyment and to do so sufficiently well to succeed in academic assignments, only to have their students' "writing ability" judged by a standardized multiple-choice test (Erickson, 1992).

Teachers' instinctive distrust of what are usually called "indirect" tests of writing is theoretically supported by Messick (1996). He stresses the importance of tests having the two characteristics of "construct representation" and "construct relevance." Construct representation means that the test should be as like the real ability as is possible, and this is usually judged by the test's authenticity and directness. Construct relevance means that the test should test only skills that are part of the construct: there should be no difficulties in the test that are not part of the ability/skill itself. We can easily see that multiple-choice tests do not meet the construct representation requirement of either authenticity or directness. Multiple-choice tests also might introduce some construct irrelevant difficulty since students would have to learn the skills of standardized test-taking, which are not part of a writing curriculum.

All of these aspects that contribute to optimal writing assessment procedures are of direct importance to teachers who have long understood, without necessarily being aware of the vocabulary of testing, that tests failing to meet expectations of construct representation and construct relevance are likely to have negative washback into teaching and learning.

But even when the test is authentic, direct, and designed very well, there are other concerns we must all be very aware of. Messick (1996) reminds us that it is not the test itself that might do good or harm to people and institutions, but the ways that tests, especially test scores, are *used*. For example, it is fairly common for TOEFL "practice tests" to be used repeatedly and for changes in individuals' scores on TOEFL practice tests or institutional TOEFLs to be the basis for their placement into a course level, or for pre- and post-"TOEFL" scores to be used to prove or disprove learning.[2] The fact that ETS states that TOEFL cannot be validly used in those ways does not prevent it from happening. Worse still, test scores are sometimes used to judge the teaching competence of teachers as well as the abilities of learners. Not only is this not the purpose of the test, and therefore is construct invalid, but it can also be deeply harmful to those teachers, their students, and the wider society. This concern with uses of tests and their scores beyond the classroom and the understanding of the power for good or bad that test scores carry is known to language testers as "impact" (Wall, 1998a). Because tests, especially large-scale tests run by international agencies, hold such power, those who run the agencies and those who choose to be employed in those agencies must take their power and the responsibility it carries very seriously (Hamp Lyons, 2000). Messick (1981) made this point over twenty years ago, but it has taken this long for his view to become widely accepted: that testing agencies (by which I mean *whoever* holds the moral responsibility for the existence and use of the test) must take responsibility for "the critical value contexts in which (their tests) are embedded and ... a provisional reckoning of the potential social consequences of alternative uses" (Messick, 1981, p. 19).

Seeing construct validity as an integrative and demanding way of evaluating the quality of a test instrument, its appropriacy for its intended purpose, and the potential for misuse of the test means that we can bring together all our questions and concerns about any test, or any kind of testing – such as the assessment of writing – within a construct validation approach, and this is what I do in the rest of this chapter.

Assessing the constructs of writing ability

In earlier work (Hamp-Lyons, 1990) I said that it is convenient to think of four components of a direct test of writing for which validity must be established: the task, the writer, the scoring procedure, and the reader(s). As our perceptions of the task of assessing writing and our expectations of excellence and accountability in assessment have expanded, those four components have remained relevant. However, in the next section of this chapter, I discuss each of these components in turn but in a different order. Here I put the writer first, recognizing that in the present critical humanist orientation of applied linguistics and language teaching, greater attention is on the people at the heart of assessments. Additionally, I have added a fifth component that focuses specifically on the text, recognizing the growth of research into text structure and text characteristics. I then argue for an approach to writing assessment that takes account of who the learner is, the context the learner has come from, and the context in which the learner must work toward educational success. The chapter closes with a consideration of writing assessment, an activity necessarily concerned with written products, in the light of current thinking about composing processes.

The writer

In writing assessment research the writer has too often been forgotten, probably because researchers are more distant from actual writing classrooms than they should be. Classroom teachers, when they prepare essay tests or other kinds of writing tests and assignments for their students, do not forget the human beings they work with and who will be taking the test. Their consciousness of the people being tested shapes teachers' responses to choices of topics and of reading material (if any) to be used for content input; it gives them clear views on the amount of time writers will need to carry out a task and the criteria by which the writing should be judged. For a long time, writing assessment researchers, most of whom are university professors or employees of large-scale test agencies such as ETS and ACT (American College Testing), have lost themselves in the obscurities of different ways of judging test reliability, in the debate about construct validity versus reliability, and in the difficulties and controversies surrounding such issues as topic choice. Research focusing on students who take writing tests, including students' responses and preferences, has been lacking.

This lack is regrettable and problematic in all contexts. Of primary significance, lack of student-focused research means that we cannot with any confidence (other than by a quantitative comparison of actual score patterns) advise teachers or education authorities on whether L2 students' writing should be assessed separately from that of first language (L1) writers. Yet this is a major question for school districts in English-speaking countries with large non-native-speaking immigrant populations such as the United States, Australia, Canada, and the United Kingdom. Opinions on this vary; in Britain, all school students are tested together; in Australia, practice varies, and in some states special, complex L2 assessments exist. In the United States, the current trend is toward no "special treatment" for L2 students; in Canada, the trend seems to be the opposite. Clearly, we need to understand whether L2 writers are really disadvantaged by generic assessments and then consider the sociopolitical implications of any disadvantage.

What we already know is that L2 learners are tremendously varied in language background and degree of cultural integration as well as socioeconomic status, personality, learning style, and all the other factors that apply equally to L1 learners. If a writing assessment is to be humanistically as well as psychometrically defensible, all of these factors should be accounted for. As Basham and Kwachka (1991) showed in their work with the Athabaskan people of Alaska, and Ballard and Clanchy (1991) with Asian learners in Australia, we do not yet possess sufficient knowledge of culturally determined writing behaviors to be able to teach students what to change in their writing in order to conform to expectations, should they wish to do so. Although it is now fairly well accepted that written text production is in part culturally determined (e.g., see Connor, 1996; Connor & Kaplan, 1987; Hamp-Lyons, 1989b), there is still far too little research to make assertions about the "usual" cultural patterns and/or problems of writers from any particular background (Hamp-Lyons & Zhang, 2001).

However, for the classroom teacher/assessor of writing, the details of research on differences is unimportant. What matters is the understanding that *all* writers are influenced by who they are and how they became this person: race, gender, ethnicity, culture, language background, level of education in L1 and in L2, stage of cognitive development, learning style, motivation, degree of support in the home background – all these contribute to individuality. Because of the complexity and the intimacy of writing, even writing on tests and exams, each writer brings the whole of himself or herself to the writing. In classroom assessment it is difficult to forget this, because the teacher knows the writers personally. If, in large-scale testing, test developers forget this, readers (raters) do not. The essay reader, bringing his or her own expectations, is coming in on a dialogue of sorts between the test setter and the writer.

But writers bring expectations to this dialogue too, born of the education they have up to this point as well as their life experiences. Those responsible for conducting writing assessments, whether at the classroom, school, district, national, or international level, must ensure that there is as close a fit as possible between the expectations and understanding of the writers and those of the testers. This means that it is essential to provide writers with full information about the test they are taking. Examples of satisfactorily detailed candidate information include that for the Test of Written English (TWE 1985–1999) and the GSLPA (Graduating Students' Language Proficiency Assessment – Hong Kong Polytechnic University, 1999). Candidate information should include test format, including number of tasks, possible task types, length of time for each task, specific parameters, such as minimum or maximum amount that must be written, and the criteria that will be used in scoring the writing. These seem like simple requirements, but many testing programs do not meet them. If we are serious about respecting the rights of writers and ensuring that our assessments do no harm and allow writers to show the best they are capable of, these standards of informativeness must be met.

An additional writer issue is that in interpreting a task and creating a response to it, each writer must create a "fit" between his or her world and the world of the essay test topic. Very little work has been done in this area, but Weaver (1973) suggests that each writer needs to take the other-initiated test task and transform it into a "self-initiated" topic – that is, make it his or her own. In order to match her or his response to the tester's expectations, the writer must follow the steps of attending to, understanding, and valuing the task (and must hope that the task is well designed!). If this process breaks down, the writer will replace the task with a related or a different one but will not respond to the topic intended. The problem here is that it may not be clear to the rater whether the writer has done this deliberately (creating what I previously [Hamp-Lyons, 1988] called a "challenge") or accidentally through lack of topic knowledge or linguistic incompetence. In observing and recording a number of second-language writers reading a prompt on a large-scale essay test (Hamp-Lyons, 1997), I reported four cases as examples of the ways in which individual writers "read" a prompt. Of the four writers, only one "read" in the expected way and wrote an essay that wholly "fit" the test setter's and the reader's expectations. Not surprisingly, this writer was rewarded, while the other three suffered to various degrees for their inability to match the test setter's expectations.

Additionally, the other four elements (discussed in the next sections) significantly influence the writer, either through the task the writer has to perform or through the judgment and the consequences of that judgment. Thus, even when I am not discussing the writer directly in discussing other key constructs in writing assessments, the writer should never be perceived as a forgotten element.

The task

The number of variables that have been found to measurably affect writers' performance is lengthy and includes those that relate to the nature of the writing task itself. Research into issues of prompt development undertaken in the past decade indicates no additional insights than were available ten years earlier (Wolcott & Legg, 1998); if anything, further research has raised rather than answered questions. For instance, we are more aware that since an essay question requires something to write *about*, the subject matter of the prompt is critical. When students are asked to write about unfamiliar content, they may be at a disadvantage. Some of the difficulties that surface from various studies include the following:

- Haviland and Clark (1992) found that it was difficult to determine what students from a wide range of cultures would know.
- Hale et al. (1996), looking at a large number of actual writing tasks assigned at a number of North American universities, found that the assignments were quite unlike the TWE test prompts in various ways.
- Lewis and Starks (1997) found that expected genres and formats as well as content vary from discipline to discipline, so that students are differently prepared to write in different genres. (For more on the issue of genre, see Johns, Chapter 8 this volume.)

Exhaustive guidelines for writing prompts that try to take account of some of the many task variables and to provide a basis for writing equivalent prompts can be found in Ruth and Murphy (1988); in writing about the L1 situation, they take the view that difficulty resides almost wholly in the writer as opposed to the task.

Research into the effect of the task is difficult because we can never be sure how much we are separating the writer's writing ability from the other influences on a score, such as the test method, the scoring categories, and the raters' backgrounds, knowledge, and skills. This confusion makes it difficult to answer one of the most frequently asked questions about writing assessment: whether writers should have a choice of prompts to write on. (See Polio & Glew, 1996, for an excellent overview of this issue; see also Brossell & Hoetker Ash, 1984; Freedman & Calfee, 1983; Pollitt et al., 1985; Wolcott & Legg, 1998).

Goldberg, Roswell, and Michaels (1998) found a choice of writing task valid and fair, but this was in a low-stakes context (no major educational decisions were based on it), and they recommended much fuller work on scoring instrument development and rater training if choices are to be given; thus, they see difficulty as at least partly residing in the rater. Such a study was carried out by Spaan (1993), who chose two MELAB (Michigan English Language Battery) prompts of the same task type: her study also showed no significant effect for the prompt. On balance, a choice of prompts is likely to help students, as long as the prompts are very carefully developed to be as parallel as possible in difficulty and accessibility.

In an earlier study, Reid (1990) analyzed a corpus of TWE essays using the computer series Writer's Workbench. Because she found significant quantitative variations on several features of student texts written across topic types, Reid raised important questions about whether lack of score differences across topics and topic types is a feature of the topics themselves or of some aspect of the scoring procedure. A study by Weigle

(1994), with a focus on essay raters, found that raters do score writing on different prompts differently. I argued (Hamp-Lyons, 1991) that the scoring procedure and, indeed, the raters themselves, do in fact account for the lack of differences in scores across prompts, a view partly supported by this writer's empirical work with Mathias (Hamp-Lyons & Mathias, 1994).

New validities emphasize, among other things, the importance of learners' and test-takers' views of instruction and assessment, and the impact that variations in these things have on them. Looking at the tasks/topics on writing tests from the writer's point of view, we may see writing tests quite differently, as Hamp-Lyons (1996) did. Jennings, Fox, Graves, and Shohamy (1999) found that a choice of topic affected neither scores nor text characteristics; they also found that low-proficiency writers made different choices from those made by high-proficiency writers. But they also found that test-takers were very anxious to have a choice of topics, and point out that alleviating students' anxiety may itself have a positive effect on scores (a finding similar to that in a study by Polio & Glew, 1996). From the available evidence, it would seem that a choice of topics to write on should be given in any classroom or other low-stakes assessment. This will ensure that students feel comfortable in the testing situation, and the majority will have a better chance to show what they are best capable of. In large-scale, high-stakes testing situations the decision is more difficult.

Kroll and Reid (1994) provide very practical guidance on prompt development following a step-by-step approach based on their experience with the TWE. But what they and all writing test developers have been unable to do is to devise writing test prompts that are "authentic." The very situation of a test makes the writing inauthentic, even if the task is based closely on real-life situations. What writers themselves feel is "authentic" is to create their own "prompt" and write about something that interests them and they know about. This is increasingly common in writing courses; but it meets with tremendous resistance in writing assessment. Tedick (1989) looked at the writing of university graduate students who, in a classroom assessment, were given a very broad prompt, within which all were able to write about their own interest and experience, and she recommended this approach. This could work in classroom assessment, but in a formal, large-scale test it could not because the task itself would be very easy to remember and after one administration any student could prepare a "stock answer." Very soon the results would have no meaning. There is increasing experimentation with "reading to write" prompts, which carry at least the semblance of "authenticity"; there are some indications that such elaborated prompts are helpful – but also, that they bring their own scoring problems.

We have seen in this section that deciding what test-takers should write about on an essay test is no easy task. We have also seen some indications that it is not an isolated or independent issue: questions of task choice and task difficulty are closely bound up with decisions about how a test should be scored, and who should read and judge the writing, topics to be addressed later in this chapter.

The text

Probably the aspect of writing assessment that has changed least in the past fifty years is the text itself (with the exception of the portfolio assessment, as discussed later). The texts produced in most writing assessments are written products that were planned and composed in no more than one hour and that were written on a more or less expository topic. And the text-related issues that have caused the most debate and therefore have received the most research attention are (1) the nature and significance of "error"; (2) the notion of appropriate genre or register; and (3) the influence of cross-cultural rhetoric. These three are, of course, interconnected, relating at least as much to what aspects/characteristics of texts readers respond to as to any notion of "real" error.

I. THE NATURE AND SIGNIFICANCE OF "ERROR"

The role of error, specifically error identified by raters as being "second-language error," is complex[3] and difficult to separate out of the many other aspects of the writing and reading of assessment texts. Among many studies in this area, Carlisle and McKenna (1991) found that even ESL-trained essay scorers could not reliably identify ESL essays by their error pattern. Janopoulos (1993) conducted a reader-recall study of ESL essays judged to be at different score levels and found that readers recalled more from higher-scored essays, showing, he claims, that scores were influenced more by content than lower-level attributes such as mechanics. Sweedler-Brown (1993) also looked at the influences of "ESL errors" on the scores given by English composition raters and found that these raters were able to look beyond them at higher-order qualities of writing. Kobayashi (1992) considered whether ESL and English college teachers rate writing by ESL and native-speaker students differently; he found that while the groups of raters gave similar scores to both student groups, the ESL writers tended to be scored lower on syntax and mechanics and higher on content. This is a finding that will sound familiar to many college ESL teachers. On the other hand, Vann, Lorenz, and Meyer (1991) looked at error from the point of view of faculty members' responses to it and found that faculty in non-English subjects were more tolerant of some forms of error than were English faculty, but less tolerant of "error" at high levels, such as in content accuracy and formal conventions.

2. APPROPRIATE GENRE OR REGISTER

Formal assessments inevitably carry with them a weight of expectations, not only for excellence, but also for excellence of certain kinds.

Even in so-called general test contexts, the types of tasks set have broad genre/register patterns associated with them, and test-takers are often penalized if they do not write within those expectations. For example, on the Cambridge FCE (First Certificate in English) a letter is often set; test-takers are marked down if they do not follow the conventions of a letter, even though the hypothesized context/audience is informal. When the assessment context lies within a college setting or is used to assess college readiness, the conventions are more stringent.

Shaw and Liu (1998) report a study that looked at Elbow's (1991) descriptions of "academic writing" and Biber's (1988) corpus-based characterization of academic prose to see whether change in student writing could be found over the period of a summer (less than three-month) writing course. Shaw and Liu (1998) report in detail on finding writing that demonstrated increasing impersonality, increasing formality, increasing explicitness, increased hedging, and more-complex syntax and rich, varied, and subtle modification. However, they did *not* find improvement in the proportion of error-free T-units (a measure of syntactic complexity); they hypothesize that this is because the writers were "advancing into new territory" (Shaw & Liu, 1998, p. 246) while perfecting their knowledge of certain academic conventions. As we shall see later, this is important because raters on writing tests in academic contexts vary considerably in their tolerance of unconventional genre/register as well as of sentence and morphological level error. It would seem from this detailed study, as well as from others (e.g., Rifkin & Roberts, 1995), that increasing control over genre and register is not necessarily related to reducing error frequencies.

3. THE INFLUENCE OF CROSS-CULTURAL RHETORIC

Another area that has frequently been related to measures of quality in second-language writing is cross-cultural or "contrastive" rhetoric (introduced by Kaplan, 1966, 1987; and reviewed by Connor, Chapter 9 this volume). Contrastive rhetoric theory claims that rhetorical conventions vary across language in predictable and noticeable ways. Proponents of contrastive rhetoric in writing assessment claim that these contrasts of rhetoric influence readers to make judgments of writing that are less – or more – favorable than they perhaps should be, because of their personal preferences for some rhetorical forms and conventions over others. Contrastive rhetoric studies have been carried out on test essays written by Japanese students (Connor-Linton, 1995; Hinds, 1983, 1987, 1990; Kobayashi & Rinnert, 1996; Sasaki & Hirose, 1996), Chinese students (Hinds, 1990; Shi, 2001; Tsao, 1983; Zhang, 1999), Korean students (Chang, 1983; Eggington, 1987; Hinds, 1990), Spanish-speaking students (Chelala, 1981; Edelsky, 1982; Lux, 1991), and students speaking a number of other languages. Although this work is extremely interesting, to date it has not been able to explain the kinds of variations we see in text quality or overall writing proficiency among L2 writers, or development (or lack of it) within a single writer – or indeed, among raters' reactions to texts.

The scoring procedure

The last thirty years have produced a great many developments in scoring procedures for writing assessments. Most, however, can be placed into one of the following three categories: (1) holistic scoring, (2) multiple trait or analytic scoring, and (3) primary trait scoring.

I. HOLISTIC SCORING

A true holistic reading of an essay involves reading for an individual impression of the quality of the writing, by comparison with all other writing the reader sees on that occasion. Holistic scoring is based on the view that the construct of writing is a single entity that can be captured by a single scale that integrates the inherent qualities of the writing, and that this quality can be recognized only by carefully selected and experienced readers using their skilled impressions, not by any objectifiable means (White, 1985). And yet study after study, the earliest and best known of which is Diederich, French, and Carlton (1961), has found that the judgments made by essay readers under these conditions are unreliable, and that considerable effort must be expended to establish and maintain reliable judgment. Indeed, Diederich (1974) claimed that until holistic scoring procedures were codified and refined, the score an essay received could depend more on who the rater was than on any qualities inherent in the text itself. But an equally serious problem with holistic assessments is that the context in which they are carried out – where the average time to score a single two-page handwritten essay of about 500 words may be less than one minute – means that it is not possible to capture performance data from raters as they are doing the rating task, and therefore it is impossible to get far enough into that performance to be able to understand fully what is going on. Without research that enables us to understand the processes actually used by individual raters, we shall never be able to find ways to make judgments more reliable and at the same time more valid (i.e., the "new validities" described above). We turn to raters in the final section of this part of the chapter.

2. PRIMARY TRAIT SCORING

Primary trait scoring (Lloyd-Jones, 1977; Mullen, 1980) involves deciding which *one* aspect of writing is key to success on this task, developing a highly detailed set of descriptors for performance on that aspect ("trait"), and training teachers/raters in its use. Primary trait scoring has not been often used because its key element, the development of a single scale on a single feature of writing seen to be most salient for a very specific task, makes it very resource intensive. Primary trait scoring scales have to be developed afresh for every context. However, the primary trait approach was the source for Hamp-Lyons's (1986, 1991) development of multiple trait scoring, discussed next.

3. MULTIPLE TRAIT SCORING

In striking contrast to holistic assessment, multiple trait assessment of writing defines a procedure that is context sensitive at all stages and in all dimensions of the test development, implementation, scoring, and score reporting. As its name implies, multiple trait scoring[4] treats the construct of writing as complex and multifaceted, it allows teachers or test developers to identify the qualities or traits of writing that are important in a particular context or task type and to evaluate writing according to the salient traits in a specific context. Multiple trait scoring also allows raters to pay attention to the relative strengths and weaknesses in an individual writer's text and score some traits higher than others. There may be some arguments in favor of holistic scoring of the writing of fairly advanced native users of a language – cost and practicality being the main ones – but when we turn to the specific problems and needs of assessing *second language* writing, those arguments are much weaker than the arguments in favor of multiple trait assessment. Furthermore, multiple trait scoring is a useful tool for researching what is going on inside a writing assessment because of the detailed way it opens up the process; it is also a vital tool for teachers of L2 writers because it provides teachers, placement officers, and admission program personnel with rich information that will facilitate decisions about remedial courses, selection of course types, and other choices.

Since the work of Jacobs et al. (1981) on the ESL Composition Profile and of myself (Hamp-Lyons, 1986, 1987, 1991) on the English Language Testing Service (ELTS) and then International English Language Testing System (IELTS) writing assessment scales, it has become increasingly common for test developers designing new L2 writing assessments to use multiple trait scoring. This approach has become the dominant one in the United Kingdom (Fulcher, 1997; Weir 1993), Canada (Cumming & Mellow, 1996), and Australia (Lumley, 2000), whereas in the United States holistic scoring is still quite common.

Scale length

The most common practice, in such major U.S. postsecondary institutions as the City University of New York system, the University of Michigan, and the University of California system, and in many other parts of the world, is to have a scale with six scale steps seen as having equal distances between them. However, the IELTS writing test has a nine-step scale, and the MELAB scale has ten steps. Many writing assessments that have developed from specific practices in schools have longer "scales" – even up to 100 – but there is no statistical evidence to prove that raters can reliably distinguish more than ten levels of writing quality. In fact, I would discourage any teacher or test developer from using a scale longer than nine steps.

The complexities of scoring

In the past ten years or so, research has certainly helped to identify ways in which the scoring of writing can be made more reliable and more valid; but it has also uncovered many new complexities. As specialists in writing assessment have increasingly turned their attention to scoring, to what qualities of writing are judged, how they are judged, who the judges are, and many other issues (Connor-Linton, 1995; Lumley, 2000; Shohamy, Gordon, & Kraemer, 1992; Weigle, 1994; Zhang, 1999), it has become more and more evident that scoring is a far more complex process than was ever imagined. In the research of the last decade the strength and complexity of the link between the scoring procedure and the human beings who apply the procedure (or seem to) has become strikingly clear.

The reader

A large body of research investigating the work of readers' practices in writing assessment led to the emphasis on reader training that became so common in writing assessment programs from the early 1980s on. Over forty years ago, Diederich, French, and Carlton (1961) had shown that different readers responded to different facets of writing, and did so with some internal consistency. Hake (1973), looking at raters' responses to native speakers' essays, showed that where raters deviated from their own typical response patterns, these deviations could be explained by affective interactions between the rater and the text. Newcomb (1977), also looking at raters' responses to native speakers' essays, found that raters' behaviors varied and could to some degree be predicted by background characteristics of the rater, such as sex, race, and geographic origin within the United States. Similar findings from a variety of studies resulted in a concern to create training procedures to counteract the possibility that readers would bring different agendas to the reading and assessing of the same text.

In the L2 context, Vaughan (1991), using ethnographic methods, found results that were similar to Diederich et al.'s (1961) findings related to individual reader agendas. I found (Hamp-Lyons, 1989b) found that readers of ESL essays responded to cultural differences in them, and did so differentially in ways that appeared to be partially attributable to their experiential backgrounds and to their response to the students' linguistic/rhetorical backgrounds. Cumming (1990) looked at the decision-making behaviors of expert and novice raters rating ESL writing and found that the expert raters spent more of their attention on higher-order aspects of the writing and were more reflective about their own processes, whereas novice raters focused more on lower-order aspects of the writing, and practiced on-line editing of the texts as a way to help themselves make sense of the texts and reach judgments of quality. Vann, Lorenz, and Meyer (1991) found that faculty's responses to error in L2 writing could be partially attributed to their discipline and sex as well as to the amount of exposure they had to the writing of nonnative users of English.

Among the surprisingly few controlled studies of rater training effects are Freedman (1977), Newcomb (1977), and Stalnaker (1936), and in the ESL context, Lumley (2000) and Weigle (1994). The work of Robinson (1985) and Vaughan (1991) questions the commonly heard claim that training is effective in bringing readers' responses together, although Weigle's study is more encouraging in this regard. This question may be of lesser interest to large-scale testing agencies, who will be satisfied that *scores* are brought together even if the bases for the scores are not. But teachers will find this of significance because in judging writing in the classroom context, each teacher acts as the sole judge and arbiter of grades and therefore of consequences, and wants to feel reasonably confident that students' work would receive similar responses from other teachers.

By the early 1980s, White (1985, p. 32), writing about L1 settings, felt able to celebrate the effectiveness of holistic assessments of writing and to assert not only the reliability of the holistically derived scores but also the validity of holistic reading processes. In the L2 context, we have learned a great deal more in the past ten years about the behavior of readers through quantitative scoring comparisons (Brown, 1991; Janopoulos, 1989) and detailed ethnographic studies of essay raters (Lumley, 2000; O'Loughlin, 1993; Shi, 2001; Weigle, 1994; Zhang, 1999). The evidence from such studies suggests that, left to their own judgments, raters cannot agree on the absolute quality or the relative quality of essays, nor can they agree on the specific qualities in essays that make them good, worse, or worst. But more interestingly, these rich studies have shown the complexity of the rating process that White (1985) asserted, and have taken it further. Zhang (1999) shows that raters are influenced by their own cultural contexts and learning/teaching experiences perhaps as much as by the variation in quality of student essays; Lumley (2000) shows that even the most experienced and skilled raters act as individuals, using their own values, even in situations with good and extensive rater training and well-defined criteria. Clearly, we are a long way yet from being able to characterize what raters do and explain when, how, and why they are able to do it consistently.

Alternative ways of assessing writing

The alternative assessment movement has been largely driven by, and certainly powerfully guided by, developments in writing assessment. As long ago as 1987, Bizzell was able to say:

> Locally developed, holistically scored writing tests enable participating academic communities to define standards of "good" writing that can be responsive to the particular strengths of their own student population, rather than crushing such particularities and the creative spirits of the students who express them under the yoke of nationally imposed standards of correctness. (Bizzell, 1987, p. 579)

Since then we have increasingly come to realize that local development and implementation, when done well, is a powerful force for positive educational change. This is one benefit of portfolios that has made them so popular in L1 literacy assessment, and there are strong reasons that the argument would be equally or more relevant in ESL/EFL contexts. But as we shall see in the following sections, when we move into alternative ways of assessing writing, it becomes even more important to be explicit to ourselves, our students, the readers, and the people who receive and use the scores or other forms of judgments that come out of these assessments.

Portfolios

Portfolio assessment is the best-known and now most popular form of alternative writing assessment (Belanoff & Dickson, 1991; Hamp-Lyons & Condon, 2000; Yancey & Weiser, 1997). A portfolio is a collection of the writer's own work over a period of time, usually a semester or school year. The writers, perhaps aided by classmates or the teacher, make selections from their collected work through a process of reflection on what they have done and what it shows about what they have learned. These three elements – collection, selection, and reflection – are the core of a portfolio, but if a portfolio assessment is to be authentic it must involve more than a representation of the writer's own work. It must use criteria and a means of arriving at scores or grades that make ecological sense – that is, that make sense in the eyes of the writers and their teachers, and in the context for which an assessment is required. Early portfolio assessment programs did not demonstrate that the requirements of good assessment practice apply to performance assessments also, and a number of studies uncovered problems with portfolio assessments in practice (e.g., Callahan, 1995; Despain & Hilgers, 1992; Hamp-Lyons, 1996; Hamp-Lyons & Condon, 1993) while others proposed means of remedying or reconciling the difficulties (e.g., Calfee & Perfumo, 1996; Elbow & Belanoff, 1997; Herman, Gearhart, & Aschbacher, 1996). But all commentators on portfolio assessment agree that it is an excellent, if not the best, form of professional development activity for teachers. Smith and Murphy (1992) make this point strongly in the case of school-level staff development programs within the United States; in Hong Kong, in a professional development program on portfolios, working with mainly non-native writing teachers and focusing on college prep and college freshman EFL students, I have found the same benefits and the same enthusiasm (Hamp-Lyons, 1999).

However, as Smith and Murphy (1992, p. 14) caution, portfolios "do not lend themselves to a drive-through workshop." Developing a writing course based on the students building up a portfolio of their work is a skilled teaching activity, but one that teachers find extremely rewarding because it brings them so close to their students and the best aspects of the teacher role. But building a portfolio *assessment* is an equally skilled activity. Making the transfer from portfolios for teaching to portfolios for assessment requires, for most teachers, good professional development support (one option for which is peer support). Taking responsibility for assessment makes some teachers uncomfortable, because it puts assessment at the heart of their teaching, whereas many teachers would like to put assessment as far away as possible. But learners can't escape assessments; why should teachers? Portfolios let students show what they can do by showing what they have done. A portfolio often also shows the weak points in a student's mastery, but this is an opportunity for the teacher or the program to *use* the information to provide the right kind of teaching, the right kind of environment, for the learner. This is particularly important for writers using a language that is not their own, as I have argued elsewhere (Hamp-Lyons, 1996), because the opportunities for improvement are often much greater, and the skills they have already mastered may not be well balanced. A well-planned portfolio can show the teacher *and* the learner where the high and low points of the skills are.

Computer-based writing tests

A very new development, brought about through new ways in which computers contribute to the teaching of writing (see Pennington, Chapter 12 this volume) is the possibility of assessing writing on-line. At least in theory, on-line writing assessment allows the development of tests that fit the levels, purposes, and needs of test-takers, as well as of future employers, admissions officers, and others. It allows the design of writing tasks that can be built out of multiple elements previously identified, ensuring authenticity and task variety. A really "smart" computer-based writing assessment system would enable each writer to build a portfolio of writing and select from it according to a particular purpose. A computer-based writing assessment would enable multiple pathways for writers through the many pitfalls of tests; but this flexibility to choose pathways, like all advanced options, will benefit skilled writers and thinkers more than their less-developed counterparts. In considering the possibilities for computer-based writing assessment directed specifically toward ESL writers, it would be possible not only to offer spelling and grammar checkers but to query unclear content references, suggest synonyms for learners with limited vocabularies, and so on through multiple dialogue possibilities. The problems and limitations here are not in the computer software but in what "the system" will allow.

Usually, when assessment specialists think about the possibilities of computer applications they think about the scoring of writing. Because human scoring is very time-consuming and therefore expensive, it is tempting to look for ways to take the scoring away from humans and give it to machines, as was done in the 1930s with multiple-choice testing. Of the several such essay scoring systems that have been designed, the most advanced is probably Page's Project Essay Grader (Page & Petersen, 1995; Shermis, Koch, Page, Keith, & Harrington, 1999). PEG (Project Essay Grader) claims to simulate human ratings through counts of text features related to content; it does this by recording the content frequency in actual student essays and building its scoring around that. This is a promising beginning, but there are many other characteristics that contribute to the strength and weakness of any essay that have not been captured by the program. Computerized scoring is not yet mature enough to satisfy the expectations of writing teachers, but it will deserve our serious attention over the next decade.

Enduring questions

In the brief closing chapter of an edited collection on writing assessment from over a decade ago (Hamp-Lyons, 1991), I considered issues for the future, and it seems appropriate to look at those questions again here. The first issue was the acknowledgment that those who plan and conduct writing assessments know too little about the writers who are the test-takers, and I do not see that this has changed much in the past ten years or so. While there *has* been a fair amount of further research on prompts, it remains contradictory and serves to caution us that prompt equivalency may be unobtainable. We are also more aware that assessment prompts do poorly in terms of authenticity than was claimed in the 1980s. Work on texts continues, but apart from some developments in contrastive analysis, it seems that such work has little to contribute in writing assessment, partly or even primarily because of the greater awareness we have of the role of reader/raters in judgments of writing. Indeed, the area where the most research on L2 writing assessment has been done in the last decade or so is probably this one: as a result of the studies of Lumley (2000), Vaughan (1991), Weigle (1994), and others, we are increasingly aware of what readers do and why, and that readers are truly in charge of the rating process. Even in writing assessment programs with very draconian rater training and monitoring systems, such as those run by ETS, the reader factor is stronger than the prompt factor and may be almost as strong as the writer factor.

But the areas attracting most of our attention these days concern the effects of assessments and the relationship between assessment and power.

One of the most important lessons that people who work in the field of educational assessment/measurement have learned in the past decade is that no assessment is value-free. Nor is any assessment free of effects that reach beyond the narrow confines of the assessment event itself. This is true of multiple-choice tests and of national and state tests; but it is equally true of "good" tests like direct writing tests, and even of classroom assessments. We call the effects that a test or assessment has on instruction and learning "washback." There is now plenty of evidence that the existence of tests changes the curriculum and the ways that teachers behave (Cheng, 1997; Smith, 1991; Wall, 1998b). But increasingly we realize that the effects of tests extend well beyond the classroom: tests affect students' lives, sometimes critically, opening or closing the opportunities on which their entire futures depend – in "exam cultures" like Hong Kong, Singapore, and Japan, testing pressures have led to suicides. When a society values test results more than abilities and potentials, and when tests/assessments become the only or primary route to higher education, careers, status, and wealth, inevitably there is a great impact on families' lives and there is danger that information resulting from these assessments will be liable to educational, administrative, and political abuses (Shohamy, 1999). The individual teacher and the individual testing specialist cannot prevent such pressures or abuses. However, both can work within their own context to make sure that the assessments they are involved in are the best possible, developed and administered with the best interests of the test-takers in mind. Each can help students, parents, and teachers' groups to understand the limitations of test-based information and to encourage decision-making based on a *range* of information, not just assessment information.

In the final chapter of an early but influential collection on (primarily L1) writing assessment, Brossell (1986) emphasized that writing assessments should

reflect our best knowledge of how writing occurs and how it is best taught. That is, it ought to proceed from an understanding of writing as a complex process of discovering and conveying meaning, a process that involves rhetorical, structural and mechanical choices.... [It] ought to reinforce and even extend our instructional programs. (p. 180)

He continued:

At the heart of the relationship between the assessment of writing and its teaching is the question of how to create the conditions of assessment that approximate the conditions under which good writing occurs. (Brossell, 1986, p. 180)

As many chapters in this volume show, we have learned a great deal about the development of writing skill in the past fifteen years – and perhaps more within L2 than L1 contexts. We have also learned a great deal about how to assess writing in meaningful ways. Yet there is still a gap between best practice in teaching and responding to writing (see Ferris, 2002; Chapter 5 this volume), and best practice in writing assessment, which are related topics. Furthermore, there are few contexts worldwide where best practice in either teaching or assessment of writing is actually taking place.

Researchers play their part in uncovering the elements that lead to good practice; teacher education programs play their part in building models of curriculum that can help implement good instructional practice. But the burden of effective teaching is on the teacher, as it has always been. In the rising demand for "accountability" that marks the turn of the millennium, the burden on teachers in many countries is heavier than ever before. A firm understanding of how assessment works, what it can do, and what it *cannot* do, is an essential tool for today's teachers.

Notes

1. "Washback" is the effect a test or assessment instrument has on the teaching and learning that precede it; washback can be either beneficial or detrimental.
2. In a related discussion, Silva (1997) argues for the ethical treatment of ESL writers. He reports on the potential for negative impact when programs fail to take the specific situations of L2 writers into account in both classroom and testing situations.
3. For more about error, see the chapter by Frodesen and Holten, Chapter 6 this volume.

4. In fact, the term "analytic" was used for a similar approach to scoring in the 1970s by those who argued against it and in favor of holistic scoring. However, I have argued that the term carries a behaviorist baggage with it that the more fully developed and construct-relevant multiple trait procedures do not deserve (see Hamp-Lyons, 1986, 1991, 1995).

References

Ballard, B., & Clanchy, J. (1991). Assessment by misconception: Cultural influences and intellectual traditions. In L. Hamp-Lyons (Ed.), *Assessing second language writing in academic contexts* (pp. 19–35). Norwood, NJ: Ablex.

Basham, C., & Kwachka, P. (1991). Reading the world differently: A cross-cultural approach to writing assessment. In L. Hamp-Lyons (Ed.), *Assessing second language writing in academic contexts* (pp. 37–49). Norwood, NJ: Ablex.

Belanoff, P., & Dickson, M. (Eds.). (1991). *Portfolios: Process and product*. Portsmouth, NH: Boynton/Cook.

Biber, D. (1988). *Variation across speech and writing*. New York: Cambridge University Press.

Bizzell, P. (1987). What can we know, what must we do, what may we hope? Writing assessment. *College English, 49*, 575–584.

Brossell, G. (1986). Current research and unanswered questions in writing assessment. In K. Greenberg, H. Wiener, & R. Donovan (Eds.), *Writing assessment: Issues and strategies* (pp. 168–182). New York: Longman.

Brossell, G., & Hoetker Ash, B. (1984). An experiment with the wording of essay topics. *College Composition and Communication, 35*, 423–425.

Brown, J. D. (1991). Do ESL and English faculties rate writing samples differently? *TESOL Quarterly, 25*, 587–603.

Calfee, R., & Perfumo, P. (1996). *Writing portfolios in the classroom: Policy and practice, promise and peril*. Hillsdale, NJ: Lawrence Erlbaum.

Callahan, S. (1995). Portfolio expectations: Possibilities and limits. *Assessing Writing, 2*, 117–151.

Carlisle, R., & McKenna, E. (1991). Placement of ESL/EFL undergraduate writers in college-level writing programs. In L. Hamp-Lyons (Ed.), *Assessing second language writing in academic contexts* (pp. 197–211). Norwood, NJ: Ablex.

Chang, S. J. (1983). English and Korean. In R. B. Kaplan (Ed.), *Annual review of applied linguistics* (pp. 85–98). Rowley, MA: Newbury House.

Chelala, S. (1981). *The composing process of two Spanish speakers and the coherence of their texts*. Unpublished doctoral dissertation, New York University.

Cheng, L-y. (1997). How does washback influence teaching? Implications for Hong Kong. *Language and Education, 11*, 38–54.

Connor, U. (1996). *Contrastive rhetoric*. New York: Cambridge University Press.

Connor, U., & Kaplan, R. B. (Eds.). (1987). *Writing across languages: Analysis of L2 text*. Reading, MA: Addison-Wesley.

Connor-Linton, J. (1995). Cross-cultural comparisons of writing standards: American ESL and Japanese EFL. *World Englishes, 14*, 99–115.

Cumming, A. (1990). Expertise in evaluating second language compositions. *Language Testing, 7,* 31–51.

Cumming, A., & Mellow, D. (1996). An investigation into the validity of written indicators of second language proficiency. In A. Cumming & R. Berwick (Eds.), *Validation in language testing* (pp. 72–93). Clevedon, England: Multilingual Matters.

Despain, L., & Hilgers, T. L. (1992). Readers' responses to the rating of non-uniform portfolios: Are there limits on portfolios' utility? Validity and reliability issues in the direct assessment of writing. *WPA: Writing Program Administration, 16,* 24–37.

Diederich, P. B. (1974). *Measuring growth in English.* Urbana, IL: NCTE.

Diederich, P. B., French, J., & Carlton, S. (1961). *Factors in judgments of writing ability.* ETS Research Bulletin 61-15. Princeton, NJ: Educational Testing Service.

Douglas, D. (2000). *Assessing languages for specific purposes.* New York: Cambridge University Press.

Edelsky, C. (1982). Writing in a bilingual program: The relation of L1 and L2 texts. *TESOL Quarterly, 16,* 211–228.

Eggington, W. G. (1987). Written academic discourse in Korean: Implications for effective communication. In U. Connor & R. B. Kaplan (Eds.), *Writing across cultures: Analysis of L2 text* (pp. 153–168). Reading, MA: Addison-Wesley.

Elbow, P. (1991). Reflections on academic discourse: How it relates to freshmen and our colleagues. *College English, 53,* 135–155.

Elbow, P., & Belanoff, P. (1997). Reflections on an explosion: Portfolios in the '90s and beyond. In K. B. Yancey & I. Weiser (Eds.), *Situating portfolios: Four perspectives* (pp. 19–33). Logan: Utah State University Press.

Erickson, M. (1992). Developing student confidence to evaluate writing. *The Quarterly of the National Writing Project and the Center for the Study of Writing and Literacy, 14*(1), 7–9.

Ferris, D. (2002). *Responding to L2 student writing: Research and applications.* Mahwah, NJ: Lawrence Erlbaum.

Freedman, S. W. (1977). *Influences on the evaluators of student writing.* Unpublished doctoral dissertation, Stanford University.

Freedman, S.W., & Calfee, R. (1983). Holistic assessment of writing: Experimental design and cognitive theory. In P. Mosenthal, L. Tamor, & S. Walmsley (Eds.), *Research in writing: Principles and methods* (pp. 75–98). New York: Longman.

Fulcher, G. (1997). *Writing in the English language classroom.* Hemel Hemstead, England: Prentice Hall Europe ELT.

Goldberg, G. L., Roswell, B. S., & Michaels, H. (1998). A question of choice: The implications of assessing expressive writing in multiple genres. *Assessing Writing, 5,* 39–70.

Hake, R. (1973). *Composition theory in identifying and evaluating essay writing.* Unpublished doctoral dissertation, University of Chicago.

Hale, G., Taylor, C., Bridgeman, B., Carson, J., Kroll, B., & Kantor, R. (1996). *A study of writing tasks assigned in academic degree programs,* TOEFL Research Report #54. Princeton, NJ: Educational Testing Service.

Hamp-Lyons, L. (1986). *Testing second language writing in academic settings.* Unpublished doctoral dissertation, University of Edinburgh.

Hamp-Lyons, L. (1987). Performance profiles for academic writing. In K. Bailey, R. Clifford, & E. Dale (Eds.), *Papers from the ninth annual Language Testing Research Colloquium* (pp. 78–92). Monterey, CA: Defense Language Institute.

Hamp-Lyons, L. (1988). The product before: Task-related influences on the writer. In P. Robinson (Ed.), *Academic writing: Process and product* (pp. 35–46). London: Macmillan/British Council.

Hamp-Lyons, L. (1989a). Language testing and ethics. *Prospect, 5*, 7–15.

Hamp-Lyons, L. (1989b). Raters respond to rhetoric in writing. In H. Dechert & C. Raupach (Eds.), *Interlingual processes* (pp. 229–244). Tubingen, Germany: Gunter Narr Verlag.

Hamp-Lyons, L. (1990). Second language writing: Assessment issues. In B. Kroll (Ed.), *Second language writing: Research insights for the classroom* (pp. 69–87). New York: Cambridge University Press.

Hamp-Lyons, L. (Ed.). (1991). *Assessing second language writing in academic contexts*. Norwood, NJ: Ablex.

Hamp-Lyons, L. (1995). Rating nonnative writing: The trouble with holistic scoring. *TESOL Quarterly, 29*, 759–762.

Hamp-Lyons, L. (1996). Applying ethical standards to portfolio assessment of writing in English as second language. In M. Milanovich & N. Saville (Eds.), *Performance testing and assessment: Selected papers from the 15th Language Testing Research Colloquium* (pp. 151–164). New York: Cambridge University Press.

Hamp-Lyons, L. (1997). Exploring bias in essay tests through student interviews. In C. Severino, J. Guerra, & J. Butler (Eds.), *Writing in multicultural settings* (pp. 51–66). New York: Modern Language Association.

Hamp-Lyons, L. (1999). *Efficacy and ethical issues of portfolios as assessments of nonnative students' writing*. Research Project Report June 1999. Hong Kong: Hong Kong Polytechnic University: Research and Postgraduate Studies Office.

Hamp-Lyons, L. (2000). Social, professional, and individual responsibility in language testing. *System, 28*, 579–591.

Hamp-Lyons, L., & Condon, W. (1993). Questioning assumptions about portfolio-based writing assessment. *College Composition and Communication, 44*, 176–190.

Hamp-Lyons, L., & Condon, W. (2000). *Assessing the portfolio: Practice, theory and research*. Cresskill, NJ: Hampton Press.

Hamp-Lyons, L., & Mathias, S. P. (1994). Examining expert judgments of task difficulty on essay tests. *Journal of Second Language Writing, 3*, 49–68.

Hamp-Lyons, L., & Zhang, B. (2001). World Englishes: Issues in and from academic writing assessment. In J. Flowerdew & M. Peacock (Eds.), *Research perspectives on English for academic purposes* (pp. 101–116). New York: Cambridge University Press.

Haviland, C. P., & Clark, J. M. (1992). What can our students tell us about essay examination designs and practices? *Journal of Basic Writing, 11*(2), 47–60.

Herman, J. L., Gearhart, M., & Aschbacher, P. R. (1996). Portfolios for classroom assessment: Design and implementation issues. In R. Calfee & P. Perfumo (Eds.), *Writing portfolios in the classroom: Policy and practice, promise and peril* (pp. 27–59). Mahwah, NJ: Lawrence Erlbaum.

Hinds, J. (1983). English and Japanese. In R. B. Kaplan (Ed.), *Annual review of applied linguistics* (pp. 78–84). Rowley, MA: Newbury House.

Hinds, J. (1987). Reader vs. writer responsibility: A new typology. In U. Connor & R. B. Kaplan (Eds.), *Writing across languages: Analysis of L2 text* (pp. 141–152). Reading, MA: Addison-Wesley.

Hinds, J. (1990). Inductive, deductive, quasi-inductive: Expository writing in Japanese, Korean, Chinese and Thai. In U. Connor & A. M. Johns (Eds.), *Coherence in writing* (pp. 87–109). Alexandria, VA: TESOL.

Jacobs, H., Zinkgraf, A., Wormuth, D., Hartfiel, V., & Hughey, J. (1981). *Testing ESL composition.* Rowley, MA: Newbury House.

Janopoulos, M. (1989). Reader comprehension and holistic assessment of second language writing proficiency. *Written Communication, 6,* 218–237.

Janopoulos, M. (1993). Comprehension, communicative competence, and construct validity. In M. A. Williamson & B. Huot (Eds.), *Validating holistic scoring for writing assessment* (pp. 303–325). Cresskill, NJ: Hampton Press.

Jennings, M., Fox, J., Graves, B., & Shohamy, E. (1999). The test-takers' choice: An investigation of the effect of topic on language test performance. *Language Testing, 16,* 426–456.

Kaplan, R. B. (1966). Cultural thought patterns in intercultural education. *Language Learning, 16,* 1–20.

Kaplan, R. B. (1987). Cultural thought patterns revisited. In U. Connor & R. B. Kaplan (Eds.), *Writing across languages: Analysis of L2 text* (pp. 9–21). Reading, MA: Addison-Wesley.

Kobayashi, H., & Rinnert, C. (1996). Factors affecting composition evaluation in an EFL context: Cultural rhetorical patterns and readers' background. *Language Learning, 46,* 397–437.

Kobayashi, T. (1992). Native and nonnative reactions to ESL compositions. *TESOL Quarterly, 26,* 81–110.

Kroll, B., & Reid, J. (1994). Guidelines for designing writing prompts: Clarifications, caveats and cautions. *Journal of Second Language Writing, 3,* 231–255.

Lemann, N. (1999). *The big test: The secret history of the American meritocracy.* New York: Farrar, Straus & Giroux.

Lewis, M., & Starks, D. (1997). Revisiting examination questions in tertiary academic writing. *English for Specific Purposes, 16,* 197–210.

Lloyd-Jones, R. (1977). Primary trait scoring. In C. Cooper & L. Odell (Eds.), *Evaluating writing: Describing, measuring, judging* (pp. 33–66). Urbana, IL: NCTE.

Lumley, T. (2000). *The process of the assessment of writing performance: The rater's perspective.* Unpublished doctoral dissertation, University of Melbourne.

Lux, P. (1991). *Discourse styles of Anglo and Latin American college student writers.* Unpublished doctoral dissertation, Arizona State University.

Messick, S. (1981). Evidence and ethics in the evaluation of tests. *Educational Researcher, 10,* 9–20.

Messick, S. (1989). Validity. In R. L. Linn (Ed.), *Educational measurement* (3rd ed., pp. 13–103). New York: Macmillan.

Messick, S. (1994). The interplay of evidence and consequences in the validation of performance assessments. *Educational Researcher, 23*(2), 13–23.

Messick, S. (1996). Validity and washback in language testing. *Language Testing,* *13,* 241–256.

Mullen, K. (1980). Evaluating writing proficiency in ESL. In J. Oller & K. Perkins (Eds.), *Research in language testing* (pp. 91–101). Rowley, MA: Newbury House.

Newcomb, J. S. (1977). *The influence of readers on the holistic grading of essays.* Unpublished doctoral dissertation, University of Michigan.

O'Loughlin, K. (1993, August). *The assessment of writing by English and ESL teachers.* Paper presented at the International Language Testing Colloquium, Cambridge, England.

Page, E. B., & Petersen, N. S. (1995). The computer moves into essay grading: Updating the ancient test. *Phi Delta Kappan, 76,* 561–565.

Polio, C., & Glew, M. (1996). ESL writing assessment tasks: How students choose. *Journal of Second Language Writing, 5,* 35–49.

Pollitt, A., Hutchinson, C., Entwhistle, N., & DeLuca, C. (1985). *What makes exam questions difficult? An analysis of 'O' grade questions and answers.* Research Report for Teachers No. 2. Edinburgh: Scottish Academic Press.

Reid, J. (1990). Responding to different topic types: A quantitative analysis from a contrastive rhetoric perspective. In B. Kroll (Ed.), *Second language writing: Research insights for the classroom* (pp. 191–210). New York: Cambridge University Press.

Rifkin, B., & Roberts, F. D. (1995). Error gravity: A critical review of research design. *Language Learning, 45,* 511–537.

Robinson, F. (1985). *Evaluating foreign students' compositions: The effects of rater background and of handwriting, spelling and grammar.* Unpublished doctoral dissertation, University of Texas at Austin.

Ruth, L., & Murphy, S. (1988). *Designing writing tasks for the assessment of writing.* Norwood, NJ: Ablex.

Sasaki, M., & Hirose, K. (1996). Explanatory variables for EFL students' expository writing. *Language Learning, 46,* 137–174.

Shaw, P., & Liu, E. T-k. (1998). What develops in the development of second-language writing? *Applied Linguistics, 19,* 225–254.

Shermis, M. D., Kock, C. M., Page, E. B., Keith, T. Z., & Harrington, S. (1999). *Trait ratings for automated essay scoring.* Unpublished manuscript. Indiana University-Purdue University, Indianapolis.

Shi, L. (2001). Native and nonnative-speaking EFL teachers' evaluation of Chinese students' English writing. *Language Testing, 18,* 303–325.

Shohamy, E. (1999, April). *Critical language testing, responsibilities of testers and rights of testtakers.* Paper presented at the Annual Meeting of American Educational Research Association.

Shohamy, E., Gordon, C., & Kraemer, R. (1992). The effect of raters' background and training on the reliability of direct writing tests. *Modern Language Journal, 76,* 27–33.

Silva, T. (1997). On the ethical treatment of ESL writers. *TESOL Quarterly, 31,* 359–363.

Smith, M. A., & Murphy, S. (1992). "Could you please come and do portfolio assessment for us?" *The Quarterly of the National Writing Project and the Center for the Study of Writing and Literacy, 14*(1), 14–17.

Smith, M. L. (1991). Put to the test: The effects of external testing on teachers. *Educational Researcher, 20*(5), 8–11.

Spaan, M. (1993). The effect of prompt in essay examinations. In D. Douglas & C. Chapelle (Eds.), *A new decade of language testing research: Selected papers from the twelfth annual Language Testing Research Colloquium* (pp. 98–122). Washington, DC: Teachers of English to Speakers of Other Languages.

Stalnaker, J. M. (1936). The measurement of the ability to write. In W. S. Gray (Ed.), *Tests and measurement in higher education* (pp. 203–215). Chicago: University of Chicago Press.

Sweedler-Brown, C. O. (1993). ESL essay evaluation: The influence of sentence-level and rhetorical features. *Journal of Second Language Writing, 2*, 3–17.

Tedick, D. (1989). *The effect of topic familiarity on the writing performance of nonnative writers of English at the graduate level.* Unpublished doctoral dissertation, Ohio State University.

Tsao, F-f. (1983). English and Mandarin. In R. B. Kaplan (Ed.), *Annual review of applied linguistics* (pp. 99–117). Rowley, MA: Newbury House.

Vann, R. J., Lorenz, F. O., & Meyer, D. M. (1991). Error gravity: Faculty response to errors in the written discourse of nonnative speakers of English. In L. Hamp-Lyons (Ed.), *Assessing second language writing in academic contexts* (pp. 181–195). Norwood, NJ: Ablex.

Vaughan, C. (1991). Holistic assessment: What goes on in the raters' minds? In L. Hamp-Lyons (Ed.), *Assessing second language writing in academic contexts* (pp. 111–125). Norwood, NJ: Ablex.

Wall, D. (1998a). Impact and washback in language testing. In C. Clapham (Ed.), *The Kluwer encyclopedia of language in education, Vol. 7: Testing and assessment* (pp. 334–343). Dordrecht, Germany: Kluwer.

Wall, D. (1998b). Introducing new tests into traditional systems: Insights from general education and innovation theory. *Language Testing, 13*, 334–354.

Wall, D., & Alderson, J. C. (1993). Examining washback: The Sri Lankan impact study. *Language Testing, 10*, 41–70.

Weaver, F. (1973). *The composing processes of English teacher candidates: Responding to freedom and constraint.* Unpublished doctoral dissertation, University of Illinois.

Weigle, S. C. (1994). *Effects of training on raters of English as a second language compositions: Quantitative and qualitative approaches.* Unpublished doctoral dissertation, University of California at Los Angeles.

Weir, C. (1993). *Understanding and developing language tests.* Hemel Hempstead, England: Prentice Hall Europe.

White, E. M. (1985). *Teaching and assessing writing.* San Francisco: Jossey-Bass.

Wiseman, S. (1949). The marking of English compositions in grammar school selection. *British Journal of Educational Psychology, 19*(3), 200–209.

Wolcott, W., & Legg, S. (1998). *An overview of writing assessment theory, research and practice.* Urbana, IL: NCTE.

Yancey, K. B., & Weiser, I. (Eds.). (1997). *Situating portfolios: Four perspectives.* Logan, UT: Utah State University Press.

Zhang, W-x. (1999). *The rhetorical patterns found in Chinese EFL student writers' examination essays in English and the influence of these patterns on rater response.* Unpublished doctoral dissertation, Hong Kong Polytechnic University.

PART IV:
EXPLORING CONTEXTUALITIES
OF TEXTS

As mentioned previously in this volume, writing courses are situated in specific places and contexts, accounting for some of the variation in how they are structured and what students are expected to learn or accomplish during their period of study. Having considered the voices of teachers and students in Part II of this volume and addressed issues surrounding student texts in Part III, we now, in Part IV, take up several additional factors that teachers and researchers must investigate in order to expand their understanding of what it means to teach second language writing.

Moving beyond an exploration of students, teachers, and texts, many writing theorists in both native language (L1) and second language (L2) studies call attention to the critical notion of "disciplinary communities," recognizing that it is necessary to identify the ways writing is used to create knowledge in potentially different ways in different disciplines (see, for example, Berkenkotter & Huckin, 1995; Lea & Street, 1999; Prior, 1998; Swales, 1990). A key challenge for learners is that as they "move from one discipline to another... they are faced with the problem of reconciling differences and even contradictions associated with varying disciplinary practices" (Bhatia, 2002, p. 38). From this perspective, it becomes critical for writing teachers to understand genre, the topic of Chapter 8.

The extent to which discourse and rhetorical styles are culturally situated is another contextual factor that is specifically applicable in talking about L2 writing (as opposed to L1 writing). This is the focus of contrastive rhetoric, explored in Chapter 9. Understanding how "to write the U.S. way" (Angelova & Riazantseva, 1999) or any other culturally specific way is important not just for students but also for many people in academia, business, industry, and politics.

Another context that both illuminates and complicates explorations into L2 writing is a full consideration of reading and writing connections, the topic of Chapter 10. It is hard to imagine a setting in which academic writing could be seen as divorced from source texts (reading), though in the late 1960s and early 1970s, popular L1 pedagogy promoted a writing-only class in which the only "reading" was to be the texts generated by student writers, exemplified in the expressionist movement (Burnham, 2001).

The final context addressed in this section is the use of one very particular kind of reading material of potential value in structuring L2 writing courses, namely literature, the topic of Chapter 11.

What exactly is "genre" and how does it relate to the L2 writing course?

"Genre" is a word that does not easily lend itself to simple definition as its meaning seems to vary enormously by context. As it has come to be used in composition studies, however, it typically refers to textual properties that can be identified to distinguish one text type from another. Furthermore, L2 writing teachers, as Freedman (1999) points out, "must attend *not only* to the texts but to the ways in which texts respond to the complex discursive, ideological, social, cultural, institutional context within which they are set" (p. 766; emphasis mine). Given the importance for students of understanding the role(s) that genre plays in the academy, "[h]eightening genre awareness among L2 writing instructors is one way of ensuring that...genre sensitivity gets passed down the line...to their students" (Ramanathan & Kaplan, 2000, p. 185).

Chapter 8 by Ann Johns reviews the history of the term, provides a thorough discussion of research studies on genre, and then discusses three prominent genre-based approaches to teaching composition, comparing and contrasting the ways each approach translates into rather different views of how to help student writers learn to improve. While Johns acknowledges that genre-based pedagogies are perhaps more complex than some other (earlier) approaches to teaching composition, genre is an area that cannot be ignored, especially in programs oriented toward English for academic purposes (EAP) (Jordan, 1997).

What are some implications for the role of culture in how writing gets created and valued?

It's been over 35 years since Robert Kaplan (1966) first introduced the idea of "contrastive rhetoric" to discussions of L2 writing, and its basic concept that specific cultures favor particular ways to structure texts remains compelling though not without controversy. Examining discourse from a contrastive rhetoric perspective provides specific insights into the complex relationships between language, national culture, and genre in L2 writing (see also Ostler, 2002).

Chapter 9 by Ulla Connor presents highlights of the field to novices and shows the evolving nature of what we mean when we talk about the potential interference or transfer of cultural rhetoric from one language to another. Her chapter takes an especially close look at work in Europe, reviewing the impact of the growing internationalization of English, and provides some detailed examples from Africa and Japan as well. Connor also specifically addresses some of the criticisms of contrastive rhetoric and offers cogent arguments as to how we can reconcile concerns for individualism with broad-based notions derived from studying the impact of cultural notions on writing.

How can understanding the connections between reading and writing serve to promote improved mastery of writing?

Although the texts that are central to a writing course should be the ones that student writers produce, it is not completely possible nor is it appropriate to separate reading from writing. Readings are not only able to serve as exemplars of well-constructed texts (a role beyond the mere notion of models), but they also serve as input that contributes to the acquisition of writing skills. The interactions between these two skills are multidirectional and complex. Chapter 10 by William Grabe investigates these numerous relationships by providing a thorough discussion of a large body of research on the topic in both L1 and L2 settings. He points out ways in which the relationships between reading and writing can work together to promote the development of literacy skills, particularly in EAP settings. The development of L2 writing skills and the development of L2 language skills can be and have been studied apart from each other, but looking at them together provides teachers with a more thorough grounding for meeting the needs of their students. Throughout the review and interpretation of research, Grabe explores its implications for instructional practices, and he concludes with some suggested future directions for both research and instruction.

Is there a role for literature in the L2 writing course?

For decades, the standard approach for teaching L1 composition was for students to read and write about works of literature. In foreign language settings, language study typically was oriented toward providing learners with enough knowledge of grammar and vocabulary to be able to read (and appreciate) literary works in the target language. With changing philosophies of teaching composition in both L1 and L2 settings, literature was often cast aside as an outdated if not to say inappropriate methodology for achieving course goals. In more recent times, the discussion of the possible uses of literature in teaching both L1 and L2 writing has become a vibrant and controversial debate topic in the field (Belcher & Hirvela, 2000). Chapter 11 by Stephanie Vandrick details the claims in this debate, providing a rich discussion of the arguments that have been marshaled on both sides. In settings where L2 writing courses have no fixed "content" that instructors are required to cover in the service of helping students gain increased proficiency in writing, Vandrick offers a cogent and compelling case for the use of literature, discussing in some detail the possible use of multicultural texts. Her chapter provides numerous specific suggestions for how to choose and use literary texts as the reading material for the L2 writing course.

References

Angelova, M., & Riazantseva, A. (1999). "If you don't tell me, how can I know?" A case study of four international students learning to write the U.S. way. *Written Communication, 16,* 491–525.

Belcher, D., & Hirvela, A. (2000). Literature and L2 composition: Revisiting the debate. *Journal of Second Language Writing, 9,* 21–39.

Berkenkotter, C., & Huckin, T. (1995). *Genre knowledge in disciplinary communication.* Hillsdale, NJ: Lawrence Erlbaum.

Bhatia, V. K. (2002). A generic view of academic discourse. In J. Flowerdew (Ed.), *Academic discourse* (pp. 21–39). Harlow, UK: Pearson Education.

Burnham, C. (2001). Expressive pedagogy: Practice/theory, theory/practice. In G. Tate, A. Rupiper, & K. Schick (Eds.), *A guide to composition pedagogies* (pp. 19–35). New York: Oxford University Press.

Freedman, A. (1999). Beyond the text: Towards understanding the teaching and learning of genres. *TESOL Quarterly, 33,* 763–767.

Jordan, R. R. (1997). *English for academic purposes.* New York and Cambridge: Cambridge University Press.

Kaplan, R. B. (1966). Cultural thought patterns in intercultural education. *Language Learning, 16,* 1–20.

Lea, M. R., & Street, B. (1999). Writing as academic literacies: Understanding textual practices in higher education. In C. N. Candlin & K. Hyland (Eds.), *Writing: Texts, processes and practices* (pp. 62–81). New York: Addison Wesley Longman.

Ostler, S. (2002). Contrastive rhetoric: An expanding paradigm. In J. Flowerdew (Ed.), *Academic discourse* (pp. 167–181). Harlow, UK: Pearson Education.

Prior, P. (1998). *Writing/disciplinarity: A sociohistoric account of literate activity in the academy.* Mahwah, NJ: Lawrence Erlbaum.

Ramanathan, V., & Kaplan, R. B. (2000). Genres, authors, discourse communities: Theory and application for (L1 and) L2 writing instructors. *Journal of Second Language Writing, 9,* 171–191.

Swales, J. (1990). *Genre analysis.* New York: Cambridge University Press.

8 Genre and ESL/EFL composition instruction

Ann M. Johns

In everyday life, the word "genre" is used for many forms of expression in many contexts. Movie critics refer to certain types of films as "genres"; music fans talk about "rock and roll" and "rap" as "genres." There are parodies of genres in a variety of art forms, and there are artists of all types who defy the established generic rules. In literacy studies throughout the world, "genre" has also become an increasingly popular term. In this chapter, I discuss how the term "genre" is currently used in composition studies, and how the various theories of genre influence approaches to classroom teaching, particularly as applicable in English as a second language/English as a foreign language (ESL/EFL) contexts.

History and definition of the term

With its many applications within our cultures, "genre" has a variety of historical roots. In academic settings, "genre studies" has traditionally referred to analyses of works of literature, such as different types of poetry, novels, and literary essays. In these analyses, conventions of form, style, characterization, plot structure, and other features that distinguish a particular genre are analyzed, as are variations in conventions within a single genre across time.[1] Today, many literature departments still organize their courses around this concept and all that it implies.

Recently, the term "genre" has been used to capture the *social* nature of oral and written discourse by various theorists and practitioners from applied linguistics, especially those working in Systemic Functional Linguistics, English for Specific Purposes, and, in North America, the New Rhetoric, drawing from rich theoretical discussions (e.g., Bakhtin, 1986; Halliday, 1985; Miller, 1984; Swales, 1990). They note that most important non-literary texts, in school, in the workplace, and at home,

Material in this chapter quoted from F. Christie (1990), "The Changing Face of Literacy," in F. Christie (Ed.), *Literacy for a Changing World: A Fresh Look at the Basics*, is reprinted with permission from ACER Press. Material in this chapter quoted from P. Brett (1994), "A Genre Analysis of the Results Section of Sociology Articles," *English for Specific Purposes, 13*, is reprinted with permission from Elsevier Science.

are produced and negotiated in social contexts and thus result, at least in part, from social practices. In the case of written discourses, many factors, including the purposes or functions of a text, the roles and relationships of readers and writers, the context in which the text is produced and processed, the formal text features, the use of content, and even what the text is called are determined in and by the culture or community in which these texts are produced or processed. Thus, the term "genre" has been expanded in literacy studies to "refer to a distinctive category of discourse of any type ... with or without literary aspirations" (Swales, 1990, p. 33).

One of the most interesting aspects of current literacy studies is that all types of genres are the subjects of research and discussion – "vernacular" (Barton & Hamilton, 1998) discourses as well as high-culture texts. An example of a "vernacular" genre that appears in newspapers throughout the world is the "obituary," a very interesting object for cross-cultural study. One semester, my diverse graduate students studied obituaries from their hometown newspapers. They found several conventions in the genre – the purpose (to report the death of an individual) and context (a special section of a newspaper) – but the variations in the texts themselves depended very much on cultural norms. Thus, though the genre name "obituary" brings to readers' minds prior knowledge or schemata, particular purposes and situations, the realizations of this genre in specific texts are very much shaped by local circumstances and cultural norms. (For more detail and multiple examples, see Johns, 1997, pp. 41–45.)

Experts argue that we must think of "genre" as a concept that is both cultural and cognitive (see Berkenkotter & Huckin, 1995) because, in fact, it is an abstraction developed from experiences with our own cultures and their texts. Elsewhere, I described an individual's genre knowledge as composed of many elements:

It is, at the same time, cognitive (integral to schemata, or prior knowledge) and social (shared with readers and writers who have experienced the same genre). It is "repeated" (Miller, 1984) in that it evokes previous, analogous contexts in which similar texts appeared; yet it is evolving ... because few, if any, rhetorical situations are exactly the same. Genre knowledge is systematic ... and conventional in that features of form and style may be repeated in texts. Yet a person's knowledge of conventions ... must be open to change ... , constantly subject to revision as situations are transformed. (Johns, 1997, pp. 21–22)

Genres are particularly useful to individuals and to teachers of composition because those who become familiar with common genres develop shortcuts to the successful processing and production of written texts. If we have already written a *memo, a letter to the editor, a political brief,* or *an invitation* within our culture, we are able to draw from that prior knowledge to produce a second, socially accepted text from the same genre. Thus, teaching within a framework that draws explicit attention to genres provides students a concrete opportunity to acquire knowledge that they can use in undertaking writing tasks beyond the course in which such teaching occurs.

Genre theory and research

Genre pedagogies are solidly grounded in theory and research, so it is important to examine what has been studied before proceeding to a discussion of classroom approaches. All theories, and the research that results from them, must begin somewhere; they must have a basic focus or core, though the applications may differ given that researchers begin at different places and with different foci (cf. Polio, Chapter 2 this volume). Candlin and Hyland (1999, p. 1) speak of approaching genre studies on one of three bases: "as *text*, as *process*, or as *social practice*." Many applied linguists and English for Specific Purposes researchers focus their interest primarily on the *texts* themselves, analyzing written discourses from a given genre to draw conclusions about the functions of language as well as the conventions and sometimes the values of a community or culture. They ask questions such as the following:

1. What types of genres are valued, or "elemental," within a community and thus are part of its "cultural capital," and what are the features of these genres? (Feez, 2002)
2. What basic features give a specific genre its "integrity," that is, what conventions seem to be relatively stable, or highly valued, across texts within a genre? (Bhatia, 1999)
3. How are valued genres organized, and what does this organizational structure tell us about a community's cultures and belief systems? (Martin, 1984; Swales, 1990, 1998)
4. How is metadiscourse[2] used in academic genres from various cultures and disciplinary communities? (Hyland, 1999; Mauranen, 1993)
5. What language (register) points to the relationships between readers and writers and their roles? For example, how do scientists use "hedging" in their research articles? (Hyland, 1998)
6. What features of texts indicate the immediate rhetorical context, such as the specific classroom? What features may reflect the values of the discipline, or profession, as a whole? (Samraj, 2002)
7. How are texts in one situation (e.g., the classroom) influenced by texts in another (e.g., the workplace)? (Samraj, 2002)
8. How does one genre – for example, the ubiquitous North American five-paragraph essay – influence the nature of teaching and testing in schools? (Coe, 1987)

9. How do genres blur and interact? How do writers incorporate other texts, through intertextuality, by citation or other means? (Flowerdew, 2002)

The more *text-driven* researchers and theorists, then, "locate the various norms, standards and conventions [in texts]...which may show community ownership" (Myers, 1999, p. 46). From close text analyses, they draw conclusions about the complex features of the communities and contexts in which the texts are valued. The pedagogical implications of this approach are major: in many classrooms throughout the world, students are encouraged to analyze text features and to use this knowledge to develop hypotheses about textual functions, communities, and their genres.

When genre theorists and researchers refer to the ways in which genres are *processed,* the second Candlin and Hyland focus, they are not referring to some idealized process over which the writer can develop considerable, or absolute, control as has been often assumed in the pedagogical realizations of the Process Movement (see Johns, 1997; Matsuda, Chapter 1 this volume). Acknowledging that discourses are situated and social, genre theorists view writers' processes as varied, dependent on their past writing experiences, the demands of the context, writers' roles vis-à-vis the readers, and the socially determined constraints of the genre itself. Thus, there is no one "process" for writing, but many, as writers juggle the various responsibilities they have to the genre, to the situation, to their roles, to the language, or to themselves as thinking, negotiating participants in the production and revision of texts. Of course, this complex view of process has major pedagogical implications: students must be provided with a variety of rhetorical situations (genres, audiences, roles, and contexts) in which to write and with opportunities to reflect on the various processes that are employed to produce texts within differing contexts.

Those genre theorists who focus on *writing processes,* while mindful of social practices, ask questions such as the following:

1. How do writers from one language group (e.g., Spanish) write texts in a second language (e.g., English)? Do their second language processes differ from their first language ones? (Bosher, 1998; Chenoweth & Hayes, 2001; Silva et al., Chapter 4 this volume; St. John, 1987)
2. What particular aspects of a rhetorical situation are foregrounded when a person is writing for identified audiences or communities? (Wright, 1999)
3. How do processes differ depending on the timing and pressures involved in the task? Do individuals process texts differently

when they have sufficient time to revise, for example? (Horowitz, 1986)

4. How do writers' cultures and past experiences influence the ways in which they approach a writing task? (Connor, Chapter 9 this volume; Leki, 1995)
5. How can students successfully process assigned texts while continuing to value the oral and writing practices in their first cultures? (Malcolm, 1999)
6. How do students vary, or fail to vary, their writing processes when enrolled in classes from different disciplines? (Leki & Carson, 1994)
7. What theories about texts and processes do students bring to writing tasks, and how can these theories be expanded or become more flexible? (Johns, 2002)
8. What social and contextual elements of tasks do novice and advanced students consider in their initial planning as they prepare to write a text? (Coe, 1994)

Thus, for practitioners working from this perspective, research questions about writing processes are dependent on a number of social factors: the values of cultures and the constraints of specific rhetorical situations as well as individual writer purposes and proclivities.

Finally, there are those theorists and researchers, especially in the New Rhetoric School in North America, whose principal interests revolve around *social practice – and the contexts in which social practices take place.* The first questions these researchers pose relate to the social forces that impinge on text production and the ways writers negotiate these forces. Their concern is not so much with text features[3] but with contextual elements that influence genres, especially in the workplace and professional world. Another strong interest of this group is in textual hegemony, i.e., the dominance of particular genres over the lives of individuals within a culture (see, e.g., Fairclough, 1992). These researchers ask questions such as the following:

1. What historical events within a community influence changes in genres over time? (Bazerman, 1998, 1999)
2. What factors engender conflict among genres, and what conflicts and negotiations influence texts? (Bhatia, 1999; Schryer, 1994)
3. How are writing tasks in a classroom revised and negotiated over time, and what influences these changes? (Prior, 1994)
4. How are "our perceptions [of genres] shaped by habitual, culture-specific uses of language, with its semantic categories and grammatical role systems?" (Lemke, 1995, p. 96)
5. What situational factors motivate, or demotivate, students to revise or otherwise improve their writing? (Rodby, 1999)

6. In what ways do literacies of home communities influence professional and academic literacies? Where do these literacies interact or come into conflict? What happens when hegemonic genres overwhelm home culture literacies? (Barton & Hamilton, 1998)

The pedagogical applications of this third theoretical focus, social practice, are less concretely stated in the literature except by a few critical pedagogues (see especially Benesch, 2001); however, these practitioners would agree that we should enable students to consider the rich environments in which texts are produced and encourage them to analyze and critique texts and institutions as part of their engagement in literacy studies.

Three approaches to the teaching of composition

Not surprisingly, the foci in theory and research discussed above are reflected in a variety of approaches to composition. In this section, I discuss the three most prominent genre-based approaches, classified according to theory, practice, and in some cases, geography. (For a more thorough discussion, see Hyon, 1996.)

The Sydney School

Undoubtedly the most sophisticated and mature genre pedagogies have been designed for three populations in Australia: primary and secondary school children (Macken, Martin, Kress, Kalantzis, Rothery, & Cope, 1989) and adult migrant second language learners (Feez, 2002). These pedagogies are based on the theoretical work of M. A. K. Halliday and Systemic Functional Linguistics (SFL)[4] and additional work by other, local genre theorists. This statement by Christie (1990) provides a theoretical overview of the "Sydney School" and SFL:

A text is understood as functioning in a context, where a context is said to operate at two levels: at the level of *register*, where *field* (social activity), *tenor* (the interpersonal relationships among people using language), and *mode* (the part played by language in building communication) all have consequences for the choices made in the linguistic system; and at the level of *genre*, where social purpose in using language also has consequences for linguistic choices made. For any given instance of language use, a genre is selected (be that a report, a narrative, a trade encounter, etc.) and particular choices are made with respect to field, tenor, and mode, all of which are realized in language choices. (p. 2)

Thus, the purposes of research and pedagogy stemming from SFL are to show "how the organization of language is related to its use since . . . language construes, is construed by, and (over time) reconstrues social context" (Martin, 1997, p. 2). Systemic Functional Linguists, like most genre theorists, envision perpetual interaction between the culture and social context, and the purposes, organization, and language of texts.

How, then, is language organized within a culture? The Sydney School linguists and practitioners have devoted more than two decades to identifying and analyzing the common, "elemental" genres of the general Australian culture and of the government-supported schools; and they have amassed a large body of research literature, most of which has implications for the teaching of composition (see, e.g., Cope, Kalantzis, Kress, & Martin, 1993). Theirs is a principled effort, for they believe that understanding the public, "elemental" genres of the culture will enable "disadvantaged" students, in particular, to enter academic life and develop textual "cultural capital" with some confidence.

Sydney School research and pedagogies have been designed, at least initially, for younger students and for ESL/EFL immigrants whose cultural norms and valued genres are most distant from the norms of the mainstream culture. These populations benefit from a pedagogical focus that provides explicit instruction in developing "cultural capital." Sydney School pedagogies include clearly outlined, straightforward elemental genre descriptions for teachers at a number of levels and in a variety of academic content areas. They also have guides and textbooks derived from research and theory in SFL. What do these pedagogical descriptions of elemental genres look like? Figure 8.1 shows a typical description, taken from a secondary school curriculum (Macken-Horarik, 2002).[5]

In Figure 8.1, the first column lists the names of elemental genres, identified by researchers as common across various educational and workplace cultures.[6] The second column describes the genres' social purposes – the principal function of a text within schools and the general culture. The third column, "social location," identifies contexts in which the genre is found. The next column outlines the text macro-structure, the organizational overview of the genre. Finally, the various moves, or stages, of the text are outlined.

An important element of curriculum design and implementation in the Sydney School is needs assessment. Teachers are encouraged to survey student needs in order to select the specific genres that are most relevant; then they are given considerable pedagogical guidance for working with the selected genres (Feez, 2002). In addition, teachers consider contexts of use and the particular language and other features that are typical of the situations in which students need literacy. Common to almost all Sydney School curricula is the "genre-based cycle of teaching and learning" based on the work of Vygotsky (1934/1978). The cycle supports, or "scaffolds," the learner through an interactive process of analysis, discussion, and

Genre	Social Purpose	Social Location	Schematic Structure	Description of Stages
Discussion	Discusses an issue in the light of some kind of "frame" or position. Provides more than one point of view on an issue.	Discussions are found in essays, editorials, and public forums, which canvass a range of views on issues. They also occur in panel discussions and research summaries.	[Issue ^ Arguments for and against ^ Conclusion]	*Issue:* gives information about the issue and how it is to be framed. *Arguments for and against:* canvasses points of view on the issue (similarities and differences or advantages and disadvantages). *Conclusion:* recommends a final position on the issue.
Procedure	Instructs in how to do something through a sequence of steps.	Procedures can be found in science experiments and in instructional manuals such as gardening books, cookbooks, and technical instruction sheets.	[Goal ^ Steps 1-n ^ (Results)]	*Goal:* gives information about the purpose of the activity (might be in the title or in the opening paragraphs). *Steps 1-n:* presents the activities needed to achieve the goal. They need to be put in right order. *Results:* optional stage describing the final state or "look" of activity.
Narrative	Entertains and instructs via reflection on experience. Deals with problematic events that individuals have to resolve for better or worse.	Narratives are found across all aspects of cultural life, in novels, short stories, movies, sit-coms, and radio dramas. They are important in subjects such as English.	[Orientation ^ (Complication, Evaluation) ^ Resolution]	*Orientation:* provides relevant information about the characters' situation. *Complication:* introduces one or more problems for characters to solve. *Evaluation:* highlights the significance of the events for characters. *Resolution:* sorts out the problems for better or worse.

Figure 8.1. Elemental genres and their features (Macken-Horarik, 2002). Note: ^ = *followed by. Reprinted with permission from Lawrence Erlbaum Associates and the author.*

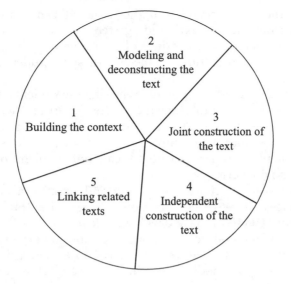

Figure 8.2. The cycle of teaching and learning (Feez, 2002, p. 65). Reprinted with permission from Lawrence Erlbaum Associates and NSW AMES Publications.

joint and individual construction of texts (Feez, 2002). It consists of the steps shown in Figure 8.2.

The first step involves assisting students in understanding the context for writing. For example, if students in the sciences were to prepare a *procedure*, they might visit a laboratory and view a video in which an expert works through this genre orally. Students are supported ("scaffolded") during this step by teacher questioning, direct instruction, vocabulary building exercises, role-plays, and jigsaw or other reading exercises. In the second step of the cycle, "modeling and deconstructing the text," students make use of various textual models of the chosen genre written by their contemporaries. The models are labeled according to stages (see Figure 8.1), ensuring that students can understand and appreciate how stages, purposes, and language interact. With the assistance of the teacher, the students study and analyze these models, using the genre descriptions. If the students are young, new to a discipline or profession, or less proficient in English (as are many ESL/EFL students), considerable care is given to discussion and practice of syntax, grammar, and lexicon found in the model texts. However, these features are always considered as functionally related to the genre and its purposes; no grammar or lexicon is practiced in isolation.

The next step, again consistent with Vygotsky (1934/78), is the joint construction of texts. Students work together or with their teacher to produce their own texts from the assigned genre, using data or experiences from the context-building step or from other sources. In this way, students learn to write collaboratively, an important skill within the Australian culture. In the fourth step, students write texts independently.

The final pedagogical move involves linking the students' written texts to other texts – that is, establishing the intertextuality and acknowledging the blurred nature of genres. Students may read other texts and cite them in their own; they may also compare their texts with others of the same genre. They may ask other students to read and comment on their texts and then write up a critique.

Thus, the Sydney School researchers and practitioners, using theoretical stances of Systemic Functional Linguistics (Halliday, 1985) and Vygotsky (1934/78), have developed clear, principled sets of genre descriptions and methods for analyzing linguistic and organizational features as functionally derived from genre purposes. Practitioners are encouraged to use, and modify, the learning and teaching cycle that organizes classroom activities. Two of the most important aspects of this approach are the study of language as functional within texts and social contexts and the presentation of a variety of elemental genre descriptions from the culture. There is no place for dull repetition of the classic, autonomous, North American Five–Paragraph Essay in the Sydney School!

These curricula, like all others, can be misused, of course. Novice or untrained teachers might portray the genre descriptions in Figure 8.1 as rigid text templates rather than as ways to begin the discussion of how texts, language, form, and social forces interact, thus returning to the "traditional" theories that were common more than 30 years ago (see Johns, 1990, 1997). These teachers might forget the first important step in the teaching-learning cycle: initial immersion into and discussion of social context. Another possible problem is that individual or culturally driven hegemonies might not be recognized and discussed by students and teachers, thus precluding critique and student negotiation of generic conventions. (See comments in Benesch, 2001, on the importance of critique.) Another possibility for misusing the Sydney School curricula comes from the apparent emphasis on text product. Martin (1985) argues, quite convincingly, that the Process Approach to writing, which encourages students to make their own meaning and find their own text forms, is "insidiously benevolent" in that it favors those students whose first culture and language are similar to those of the cultures in power. Nonetheless, process writing practices – peer editing, revising, and other strategies – should not be forgotten in the effort to encourage second language students to understand and produce texts from various genres.

English for specific purposes

A second genre "school" identified by Hyon (1996) is English for Specific Purposes (ESP), an international movement that has, since the early 1960s, been considerably more popular in English as a foreign language contexts than in English as a second language ones. Though based on considerable applied linguistics research, ESP, like the Sydney School, has always been proud of its practical bent (Swales, 1988), with a perpetual interest in course design and pedagogies. The basic principles of ESP are needs assessment, situational analysis, and discourse analysis (Johns & Dudley-Evans, 1991); thus the movement has long been positioned to move toward genre analysis through the interest in contexts of use and written discourses.

Undoubtedly the most famous research in ESP genre analysis has been conducted by John Swales. His analyses of "moves," or functional sections, in academic research articles, which began in the 1980s (summarized in Swales, 1990), have engendered a remarkable collection of publications and curricula throughout the world.[7] In fact, for some ESP scholars (see, e.g., Brett, 1994), moves analyses are synonymous with genre analysis. Swales's argument, consistent with Systemic Functional Linguistics, is that texts are conventionally divided into elements (or "stages," in the Sydney School model) that serve functions for both writer and community. Here is one incarnation of his model for moves in research article introductions (shown below in italics), with the examples taken from Brett (1994, p. 47), an article based on Swales's work:

Move 1: *Establishing the research field (introducing the topic, discussing its importance).* "Genre analysis has been of growing interest to applied linguists (Hopkins & Dudley-Evans, 1988; Swales, 1990). It offers a system of analysis that allows observations to be made on the repeated communicative functions found in genres and the linguistic exponents of these functions. This type of discourse analysis readily lends itself to the pedagogic concerns of those involved in the communicative ESP and EAP classroom."

Move 2: *Briefly summarizing the previous research.* "Genre analysts have largely concentrated their investigations on texts for the 'hard' or 'applied' sciences, for example, neuroscience (Belanger, 1982), electronics (Cooper, 1985), and biology (Swales, 1990)."

Move 3: *Preparing for present research (in many cases, showing the gap between the research reported in this article and previous research).* "Swales (1990), in an overview of moves analysis, says that 'it is easy to see that some fields are much less well

represented than others; for example, there is very little on disciplines such as economics or sociology' (p. 132)."

Move 4: *Introducing the present research.* "The purpose of this investigation was to examine 20 sociology research articles, using
genre analysis, to be able to provide a pedagogically useful description of the writing of this discourse community." (Brett,
1994, p. 47.)

What makes ESP different from the Sydney School, then? One difference, certainly, is found in the ways in which genres are identified. There
seems to be considerably less overlap in ESP between what Kiniry and
Rose (1993) call strategies for achieving particular goals ("definition,
narration, exemplification, comparison/contrast") and the genre names
themselves than there is overlap in the Sydney School. ESP analysts identify genres with discourse communities, such as academic disciplines or
particular professions, and use the nomenclature of these communities,
such as "research article," "court order," or "lab report," to identify
valued genres.

Rather than identify elemental genres of the general culture
(Candlin & Hyland, 1999) or the broad genres of schooling, ESP researchers tend to relate texts to more specific communities that use genres
to promote their ends. Rafoth (1990) says this about the relations among
discourse communities, language, and texts:

If there is one thing that most of [the discourse community definitions] have in
common, it is an idea of language [and genres] as a basis for sharing and
holding in common: shared expectations, shared participation, commonly (or
communicably) held ways of expressing. Like audience, discourse community
entails assumptions about conformity and convention. (p. 144)

Another important difference between the Sydney School and ESP relates to the populations for whom curricula are written. For the most
part, ESP curricula have been designed for adults, people who are motivated to learn quickly about specific language registers and discourse
communities so that they can progress rapidly in their work and study.
The fastest growing ESP population in the world is in the area of business (St. John, 1996), but there is also considerable need for ESP courses
in science and technology (see Swales & Feak, 1994) and for courses in
other academic disciplines, especially at the graduate level. A final important difference is that ESP is becoming increasingly context-driven,
and the overlap between the New Rhetoric, discussed below, and ESP
research and theory, becomes greater every year.

The fact that ESP course curricula are designed for specific populations
with specific needs, often in EFL contexts, influences the types of courses
that result. For advanced students in business, for example, one obvious

curricular approach is case studies, with the genres of business, resumes, different types of letters, and memoranda as the focus for writing practice (see, e.g., Rogers, 1995). Law students, on the other hand, might study legal cases and briefs (Bhatia, 1993). Graduate students benefit from studying the specific genres of their graduate work, generally the values and language that drive research articles or grant proposals (Swales & Feak, 1994), as well as theses, dissertations, and professional presentations (Swales & Feak, 2000). Thus, although practitioners, researchers, and theorists from both ESP and the Sydney School are concerned with the language, structures, and contexts of texts, there are considerable differences in their views of culture, in specificity in genre names, age and interest of student populations, the influences of other theories, and in curricula.

English for Specific Purposes, and its related field, English for Academic Purposes (EAP) become remarkably fuzzy and controversial in their literacy curricula for undergraduate students, in programs for students enrolled in general-purpose composition classes so common to universities, and some secondary schools, in North America. EAP students, below what Geisler (1994) calls "the Great Divide," are not yet considered initiates into disciplinary communities or professions. Instead, they are involved in their "general education" or breadth courses designed to give them a disciplinary overview or to prepare them for life in the university and in modern society. The controversies about what purposes these classes should serve and how they should be structured provide some of the major foci in articles and presentations at various professional conferences (and see also Leki, Chapter 13 this volume). Here are some of the controversial questions posed in EAP discussions:

1. Is there a general academic English?
2. Can teachers teach to certain general concepts, skills, or understandings that can be introduced in composition classes for novice students?

Numerous scholars argue that although academic writing is not monolithic, there definitely *are* conventions in all forms of this writing that we should be introducing to students at the undergraduate level. For example, Linton, Madigan, and Johnson (1994, p. 66) claim that three discourse categories are found in all academic genres: conventions of structure that control the flow of argument, conventions of reference that establish standard ways of addressing the work of other scholars, and conventions of language that reflect characteristic choices of syntax and diction.

Combining comments by Elbow (1991), Geertz (1983), and Purves (1991), and my own research, I also argue that most expository academic texts have some features in common:

1. Academic texts must be explicit in both argumentation and vocabulary use.
2. Topic and argument should be prerevealed in the introduction or as the genre requires.
3. Writers should provide "maps" or "signposts" for the readers throughout the texts, telling them where they have been and where they are going.
4. The language of texts should create a distance between the writer and topic to give the appearance of objectivity.
5. Writers should maintain a "rubber-gloved" quality of voice and register; "I" should be used sparingly and only in certain sections serving particular functions.
6. Writers should hedge (see Hyland, 1998), taking a guarded stance, especially when presenting their research work.
7. Texts should display an understanding of the reality shared by the reader or by members of the discourse community to which the text is addressed.
8. Texts should display an understanding of social and authority relationships, such as the roles of readers and writers.
9. Texts should acknowledge the complex and important influence of intertextuality, the exploitation of texts and data to promote argumentation and discussion.
10. Texts should comply with the genre requirements of a community or classroom. (Johns, 1997, pp. 58–64)

Most critics of ESP approaches focus on the undergraduate English for Academic Purposes dilemma discussed above. Benesch (1995, 2001) refers to much EAP curricula as "assimilative," requiring students to take on the genres and values of disciplinary communities without questioning the hegemonic nature of these powerful texts. Instead, she favors a "critical pedagogy," in which the focus is on "sociocultural awareness," stressing the "political, historical and economic factors that shape discourses" (1995, p. 192). Spack, another EAP critic, favors EAP approaches that draw from the composition instructor's own expertise and student motivations rather than from the genres and values of the students' chosen disciplines – which composition teachers may not understand themselves. This is one of her claims about academic writing and student engagement:

Academic writing is not detached and impersonal, as some of its products suggest. Rather, it is an engaging and personal – sometimes exuberant – process of seeking knowledge and understanding. Academic writing presupposes concern, curiosity, commitment, a need to know, and a need to tell. (1993, p. 185)

Spack outlines an EAP class that draws from students' own experiences and encourages writing about these experiences before reading. When they read, students annotate texts with their own comments and keep reading journals. Whereas other EAP courses tend to emphasize a variety of genres and rhetorical experiences, Spack devotes most of her class to student responses and student-generated texts. (See also Spack, 1988.)

The New Rhetoric

A third group of genre theorists and researchers, concentrated principally in North America, are the New Rhetoricians (NR). As the name indicates, this group consists of rhetoricians and composition theorists who have been educated in rhetorical theory and composition studies (drawn principally from the perspective of English as L1), a background that generally does not include studies in linguistics or second language acquisition. The New Rhetoricians' values, concepts, arguments, and conclusions stem from rhetorical, social, and ideological stances rather than from detailed analyses of language and text organization. Most of the rich, and very interesting, NR research involves studies of "specific genres as social actions within particular social and historical contexts" (Freedman & Medway, 1994a, p. 3). Research is devoted to investigating the ideological, social, and physical surroundings in which genres are produced and also to studying the ways in which genres evolve, are negotiated, and fall out of favor. In the New Rhetoric, genres are, most importantly, "inherently dynamic rhetorical structures that can be manipulated according to conditions of use" (Berkenkotter & Huckin, 1995, p. 3).

What NR genre theorists have discovered, not surprisingly, is that genre knowledge among experts in a discipline or profession is tacit, that even many who are full members of a discourse community and use a genre successfully cannot discuss the schematic/social knowledge they have that enables them to recognize, situate, understand, and produce a text in a genre. This tacit knowledge involves uses of content as well as a variety of other abilities to exploit prior knowledge and negotiate rhetorical situations (Johns, 1997, pp. 20–37; Purves, 1991).

Thus, the NR theoreticians argue that texts used in classroom study are no longer authentic when removed from their original contexts and purposes. What can teachers do then to expose students to issues that genre theory raises? How can students become sensitive to the variety of texts from a variety of ever-evolving rhetorical contexts? Freedman (1994) argues that the amount of explicit teaching of genres should be severely limited to "overall features of format or organization...and a limited set of rules regarding usage and punctuation" (p. 200). She also suggests that instead of explicitly teaching texts as genre exemplars, teachers need to "set up facilitative environments" for genre acquisition (p. 200), contexts that more closely approximate genuine, and varied, rhetorical situations. However, she does concede that under some circumstances additional explicit teaching might be appropriate:

> If learners are developmentally ready and involved in authentic tasks, explicit teaching *may* result in acquisition in very specific instances.... [When] learners are immersed in meaningful, authentic reading and writing tasks, explicit teaching which focuses on linguistic features of the discourse... being read... *may* raise the consciousness of some learners... [so] that they will be sensitized to, and notice the occurrence of such features at a subsidiary, attentional level, thereby acquiring that rule as part of their implicit knowledge so that it can be activated in future output. (Freedman, 1994, p. 205)[8]

One of my favorite NR theorists, Richard Coe, has provided some of the most sensible comments on the relationship between NR theory and pedagogy. In two useful and convincing essays he relates issues of genre and process, showing that considering a particular genre will provide a heuristic for student writing (Coe, 1987, 1994, 2002). As students represent a writing task, they might say, "This is a business letter, so I should begin by stating my reason for writing." Or "This is an essay, so I should state my thesis" (1994, p. 159). A second way in which a writer can exploit genre during the writing process is by considering reader expectations. Because genres are situated, the reader may be known or understood, and expectations may influence form, content, and register of the writer's text. The student writers must know that genres are social and not autonomous. All elements of a particular context have to be considered while writing and revising. Students might ask questions such as, "What purposes does this genre serve? How do its particular generic structures serve those purposes?[9] How is it adapted to its particular readers for this rhetorical situation?" "How is it appropriate to its context or situation?" (Coe, 1994, p. 160).

Though Coe, Freedman, and a few others in the New Rhetoric group work with issues of pedagogy, NR studies are not generally directed to the classroom. Instead, the focus is on issues of negotiation, or evolution of genres in the workplace or disciplines (see Bazerman, 1988; Schryer, 1994). Most NR theorists view the composition classroom as inauthentic; the authentic genres are produced in situations in which there is complex negotiation and often multiple audiences.

Certainly ESL/EFL composition instructors should acquaint themselves with the literature in the New Rhetoric, if for no other reason than to provide cautions against reductionist pedagogies that portray text descriptions as fixed templates instead of opportunities for studying evolving, negotiated, situated discourses. For "genres are not just text types; they imply/invoke/create/(re)construct situations (and contexts), communities, writers and readers" (Coe, 2002).

Conclusion

In this chapter, I have discussed issues of research and theory in genre-based composition instruction, and I have outlined the theoretical and pedagogical stances of the three "schools" described in Hyon (1996). There are considerable differences among the schools; however, the agreement on significant core principles can provide guidance for the ESL/EFL composition instructor as well. On what do genre theorists and practitioners seem to agree?

1. Non-literary texts are socially constructed. The influence of community or culture, however these are defined, is considerable – not only on text product but also on reading and writing processes.
2. Texts are purposeful; the functions of texts are often determined by the community long before the writer (or reader) begins to process them. Texts are written to get things done within a community and context.
3. Some texts, and registers, are valued more than others within a community. Some are dominant and hegemonic; others, like some student texts, have little effect. This is a reality that can be accepted or critiqued by teachers, researchers, and students.
4. Text organization, or macrostructure, is often not original with the writer. Form, as well as other text features, is often strongly influenced by the conventions of a genre and the immediate situation in which the text is being produced.
5. The grammar of texts, including its metadiscourse, is functional; it serves community and writer purposes within a genre and context.
6. What is present, or absent, in texts – such as content and argumentation – is often defined by the community or the particular situation in which the text is found.
7. Genres are ideologically driven; even in schools, there are no texts that are free from the values and beliefs of those involved in producing and processing them.
8. And finally, the language of texts, whether it be vocabulary, grammar, metadiscourse, or other features, should never be taught separately from rhetorical function. Language is purposeful, as are the texts themselves, though the purposes may sometimes be many – or hidden.

Certainly, genre-based pedagogies are complex, much more so than some of the earlier approaches to teaching composition. However, they have proved to be quite successful in several types of pedagogical situations throughout the world. For example, for the past 15 years or so, my colleagues and I have been teaching in an adjunct (linked) program for diverse, first-year university students who are enrolled in both a breadth class (biology, sociology, anthropology, etc.) and composition classes. In the composition classes, students become researchers into, and critics of, the rhetorical and generic situations of the breadth classes. They interview the breadth class teacher and analyze texts; they explore ways to negotiate their assignments to make them more personal or manageable; they view language and texts as integral to communities, but evolving and subject to negotiation. And perhaps fully as important, they expand their repertoire of text understandings and reflect on their varied processes as they attempt texts in a number of genres (see, e.g., Johns, 2001). They know that texts are not autonomous and that there are many literacies, even if their professors do not (see Johns, 1997, pp. 72–73), and they are grateful for the assistance their composition instructors give in enabling them to compete with others within academic contexts. Benesch (2001) also teaches literacy classes of this type (i.e., linked); however, she emphasizes the political nature of pedagogical efforts, helping students to organize to change their classroom conditions (p. 141), taking students a step farther in recognizing and opposing the hegemony of texts and contexts.

Teachers of genre-based curricula cannot forget what came before, as Coe (1987, 1994) and others have noted. The Process Movement changed everything in composition teaching, and its tremendous benefits should continue to be exploited. However, process instruction alone may not provide enough direction or situational focus for the ESL/EFL student who needs models, who needs to discuss cultures and cultural conflicts, and who needs practice in writing under a variety of conditions and in a variety of genres.

Notes

1. Multiple other potential roles for literature are discussed in Vandrick (Chapter 11 this volume), especially as they apply to teaching ESL/EFL students.
2. Metadiscourse refers to

   writing about reading and writing. When we communicate, we use metadiscourse to name rhetorical actions: *explain, show, argue, claim, deny, suggest, add, expand, summarize;* to name a part of our discourse, *first, second . . . in conclusion;* to reveal logical connections, *therefore, for example;* and to guide our readers, *Now we will move to the issue of. . . .* (Williams, 1989, p. 28)

   See also Hyland, 1999.
3. In fact, in some New Rhetoric research, the textual features are ignored.

4. Because of the influence of Chomsky, SFL may be a mystery to some North American readers. For an excellent introduction, see Butt, Fahey, Feez, Spinks, and Yallop (2000).
5. For a much more complete description of elemental genres and explanations for teaching, see *Teaching about Texts, English K-6* (1999).
6. Genre naming is a controversial topic in research, theory, and pedagogy. Are some of these terms referring to "text types" as discussed by Paltridge (2002)? Are they "strategies" for producing texts, as Kiniry and Rose (1993) argue? What they appear to be in this context is pedagogic names – that is, convenient ways for teachers and students to understand the purposes, organization, and language of texts.
7. Though Swales has moved on to other things (see Swales, 1998), the research on "moves" continues. In the summer of 1999, I attended a conference at the Hong Kong University of Science and Technology at which a graduate student reported her research on moves in scientific articles.
8. Is this a concession to the applied linguists in ESP and the Sydney School? Perhaps.
9. Does this sound like the Sydney School so far? There *is* overlap among "schools," certainly.

References

Bahktin, M. M. (1986). *Speech genres and other late essays* (V. W. McGee, Trans.; C. Emerson & M. Holquist, Eds.). Austin: University of Texas Press.

Barton, D., & Hamilton, M. (1998). *Local literacies: Reading & writing in one community*. London: Routledge.

Bazerman, C. (1988). *Shaping written knowledge: The genre and activity of the experimental article in science*. Madison: University of Wisconsin Press.

Bazerman, C. (1998). *The languages of Edison's light*. Chicago: University of Chicago Press.

Bazerman, C. (1999). Letters and the social grounding of differentiated genres. In D. Barton & N. Hall (Eds.), *Letter writing as social practice* (pp. 15–30). Amsterdam/Philadelphia: John Benjamins.

Belanger, M. (1982). A preliminary analysis of the structure of the discussion in ten neuroscience journal articles. (mimeo).

Benesch, S. (1995). Genres and processes in sociocultural contexts. *Journal of Second Language Writing, 4*, 191–96.

Benesch, S. (2001). *Critical English for academic purposes: Theory, politics, and practice*. Mahwah, NJ: Lawrence Erlbaum.

Berkenkotter, C., & Huckin, T. N. (1995). *Genre knowledge in disciplinary communities*. Hillsdale, NJ: Lawrence Erlbaum.

Bhatia, V. (1993). *Analyzing genre: Language use in professional settings*. London: Longman.

Bhatia, V. K. (1999). Integrating products, processes, purposes, and participants in professional writing. In C. N. Candlin & K. Hyland (Eds.), *Writing: Texts, processes, and practices* (pp. 21–39). London: Longman.

Bosher, S. (1998). The composing processes of Southeast Asian writers at the post-secondary level: An exploratory study. *Journal of Second Language Writing, 7*, 205–240.

Brett, P. (1994). A genre analysis of the results section of sociology articles. *English for Specific Purposes, 13,* 47–59.

Butt, D., Faye, R., Feez, S., Spinks, S., & Yallop, C. (2000). *Using functional grammar: An explorer's guide* (2nd ed.). Sydney, NSW: Macquarie University, National Centre for English Language Teaching and Research.

Candlin, C., & Hyland, K. (Eds.). (1999). *Writing: Texts, processes and practices.* London: Longman.

Chenoweth, N. A., & Hayes, J. R. (2001). Fluency in writing: Generating text in L1 and L2. *Written Communication, 18,* 80–98.

Christie, F. (1990). The changing face of literacy. In F. Christie (Ed.), *Literacy for a changing world: A fresh look at the basics* (pp. 1–25.). Hawthorne, Victoria: The Australian Council for Educational Research.

Coe, R. M. (1987). An apology for form, or who took the form out of process? *College English, 49,* 13–28.

Coe, R. M. (1994). Teaching genre as process. In A. Freedman & P. Medway (Eds.), *Learning and teaching genre* (pp. 157–169). Portsmouth, NH: Heinemann/Boynton-Cook.

Coe, R. M. (2002). The New Rhetoric of genre: Writing political briefs. In A. Johns (Ed.), *Genre in the classroom: Multiple perspectives* (pp. 195–206). Mahwah, NJ: Lawrence Erlbaum.

Cooper, C. (1985). *Aspects of article introductions in IEEE publications.* Unpublished M.Sc. dissertation, University of Aston, UK.

Cope, B., Kalantzis, M., Kress, G., & Martin, J. (1993). Bibliographical essay: Developing the theory and practice of genre-based literacy. In B. Cope & M. Kalantzis (Eds.), *The powers of literacy: A genre approach to the teaching of writing* (pp. 231–247). London: Falmer Press.

Elbow, P. (1991). Reflections on academic discourse. *College English, 53,* 135–155.

Fairclough, N. (1992). *Discourse and social change.* Cambridge, UK: Polity Press.

Feez, S. (2002). Heritage and innovation in second language education. In A. Johns (Ed.), *Genre in the classroom: Multiple perspectives* (pp. 47–68). Mahwah, NJ: Lawrence Erlbaum.

Flowerdew, J. (2002). Genre in the classroom: A linguistic approach. In A. Johns (Ed.), *Genre in the classroom: Multiple perspectives* (pp. 89–100). Mahwah, NJ: Lawrence Erlbaum.

Freedman, A. (1994). "Do as I say": The relationship between teaching and learning new genres. In A. Freedman & P. Medway (Eds.), *Genre and the new rhetoric* (pp. 191–210). London: Taylor & Francis.

Freedman, A., & Medway, P. (Eds.). (1994). *Learning and teaching genre.* Portsmouth, NH: Heinemann.

Geertz, C. (1983). *Local knowledge: Further essays in interpretive anthropology.* New York: Basic Books.

Geisler, C. (1994). Literacy and expertise in the academy. *Language and Learning Across the Disciplines, 1,* 35–57.

Halliday, M. A. K. (1985). *An introduction to functional grammar* (2nd ed.). London: Edward Arnold.

Hopkins, A., & Dudley-Evans, T. (1988). A genre-based investigation of the discussion sections in articles and dissertations. *English for Specific Purposes, 7,* 113–121.

Horowitz, D. M. (1986). Essay examination prompts and the teaching of academic writing. *English for Specific Purposes, 5,* 107–120.

Hyland, K. (1998). *Hedging in scientific research articles.* Erdenheim, PA: John Benjamins.

Hyland, K. (1999). Talking to students: Metadiscourse in introductory coursebooks. *English for Specific Purposes, 18,* 3–26.

Hyon, S. (1996). Genre in three traditions: Implications for ESL. *TESOL Quarterly, 30,* 693–722.

Johns, A. M. (1990). L1 composition theories: Implications for developing theories of L2 composition. In B. Kroll (Ed.), *Second language writing: Research insights for the classroom* (pp. 24–36). New York: Cambridge University Press.

Johns, A. M. (1997). *Text, role, and context: Developing academic literacies.* New York: Cambridge University Press.

Johns, A. M. (2001). An interdisciplinary, interinstitutional learning communities program: Student involvement and student success. In I. Leki (Ed.), *Academic writing programs* (Case Studies in TESOL Practice Series, pp. 61–72). Alexandria, VA: Teachers of English to Speakers of Other Languages (TESOL).

Johns, A. M. (2002). Destabilizing and enriching novice students' genre theories. In A. M. Johns (Ed.), *Genre in the classroom: Multiple perspectives* (pp. 237–246). Mahwah, NJ: Lawrence Erlbaum.

Johns, A. M., & Dudley-Evans, T. (1991). English for Specific Purposes: International in scope, specific in purpose. *TESOL Quarterly, 25,* 297–314.

Kiniry, M., & Rose, M. (1993). *Critical strategies for academic thinking and writing.* Boston: Bedford Books/St. Martin's Press.

Leki, I. (1995) Coping strategies of ESL students in writing tasks across the curriculum. *TESOL Quarterly, 29,* 235–260.

Leki, I., & Carson, J. G. (1994). Students' perceptions of EAP writing instruction and writing needs across the disciplines. *TESOL Quarterly, 28,* 81–101.

Lemke, J. (1995). *Textual politics: Discourse and social dynamics.* London: Taylor & Francis.

Linton, P., Madigan, R., & Johnson, S. (1994). Introducing students to disciplinary genres: The role of the general composition course. *Language and Learning Across the Disciplines, 1*(2), 63–78.

Macken, M., Martin, J. R., Kress, G., Kalantzis, M., Rothery, J., & Cope, B. (1989). *An approach to writing, K-12: The theory and practice of genre-based writing, years 3–6.* Sydney: Literacy and Education Research Network of the N.S.W. Department of Education, Directorate of Studies.

Macken-Horarik, M. (2002). "Something to shoot for": A systemic functional approach to teaching genre in secondary school science. In A. Johns (Ed.), *Genre in the classroom: Multiple perspectives* (pp. 17–46). Mahwah, NJ: Lawrence Erlbaum.

Malcolm, I. (1999). Writing as an intercultural process. In C. N. & K. Hyland (Eds.), *Writing: Texts, processes, and practices* (pp. 122–142). London: Longman.

Martin, J. R. (1984). Language, register, and genre. In F. Christie (Ed.), *Language studies: Children writing* (pp. 21–30). Geelong, Victoria: Deakin University Press.

Martin, J. R. (1985). *Factual writing: Exploring and challenging social reality.* Oxford: Oxford University Press.

Martin, J. R. (1997). Analyzing genres: Functional parameters. In F. Christie & J. R. Martin (Eds.), *Genres and institutions: Social processes in the workplace and school* (pp. 1–40). Herndon, VA: Cassell Academic.

Mauranen, A. (1993). Contrastive ESP rhetoric: Metatext in Finnish-English economics texts. *English for Specific Purposes, 12,* 3–22.

Miller, C. (1984). Genre as social action. *Quarterly Journal of Speech, 70,* 151–167.

Myers, G. (1999). Interaction in writing: Principles and problems. In C. N. & K. Hyland (Eds.), *Writing: Texts, processes, and practices.* (pp. 40–61). London: Longman.

Paltridge, B. (2002). Genre, text type, and English for Academic Purposes. In A. Johns (Ed.), *Genre in the classroom: Multiple perspectives* (pp. 71–88). Mahwah, NJ: Lawrence Erlbaum.

Prior, P. (1994). Response, revision, disciplinarily: A microhistory of a dissertation prospectus in sociology. *Written Communication, 11,* 483–533.

Purves, A. C. (1991). The textual contract: Literacy as common knowledge and conventional wisdom. In E. M. Jennings & A. C. Purves (Eds.), *Literate systems and individual lives: Perspectives on literacy and schooling* (pp. 51–72). Albany: State University of New York.

Rafoth, B. A. (1990). The concept of discourse community: Descriptive and explanatory adequacy. In G. Kirsch & D. H. Roen (Eds.), *A sense of audience in written communication* (pp. 140–152). *Written Communication Annual,* Vol. 5. Newbury Park, CA: Sage.

Rodby, J. (1999). Contingent literacy: The social construction of writing for nonnative English-speaking college freshmen. In L. Harklau, K. M. Losey, & M. Siegal (Eds.), *Generation 1.5 meets college composition: Issues in the teaching of writing to U.S.-educated learners of ESL* (pp. 45–60). Mahwah, NJ: Lawrence Erlbaum.

Rogers, D. (1995). *Business communications: International case studies in English.* New York: St. Martin's Press.

St. John, M. J. (1987). Writing processes of Spanish scientists publishing in English. *English for Specific Purposes, 6,* 113–120.

St. John, M. J. (1996). Business is booming: Business English in the 1990s. *English for Specific Purposes, 15,* 3–18.

Samraj, B. (2002). Texts and multiple contexts: Academic writing in content classes. In A. Johns (Ed.), *Genre in the classroom: Multiple perspectives* (pp. 161–174). Mahwah, NJ: Lawrence Erlbaum.

Schryer, C. (1994). Records as genre. *Written Communication, 10,* 200–234.

Spack, R. (1988). Initiating ESL students into academic discourse communities: How far should we go? *TESOL Quarterly, 22,* 29–52.

Spack, R. (1993). Student meets text, text meets student: Finding a way into academic discourse. In J. G. Carson & I. Leki (Eds.), *Reading in the composition classroom: Second language perspectives* (pp. 183–196). Boston: Heinle & Heinle.

Swales, J. M. (1988). *Episodes in ESP: A source and reference book on the development of English for science and technology.* New York: Prentice Hall.

Swales, J. M. (1990). *Genre analysis: English in academic and research settings.* Cambridge: Cambridge University Press.

Swales, J. M. (1998). *Other floors, other voices: A textography of a small university building.* Mahwah, NJ: Lawrence Erlbaum.

Swales, J. M., & Feak, C. B. (1994). *Academic writing for graduate students: Essential tasks and skills.* Ann Arbor: University of Michigan Press.

Swales, J. M., & Feak, C. B. (2000). *English in today's research world: A writing guide.* Ann Arbor: University of Michigan Press.

Teaching about texts: English K-6. (2001). Sydney: Board of Studies, Sydney, NSW.

Vygotsky, L. (1934/78). *Mind in society: The development of higher psychological processes.* Cambridge: Cambridge University Press.

Williams, J. (1989). *Style: Ten lessons in clarity and grace.* Glenview, IL: Scott, Foresman.

Wright, P. (1999). Writing and information design of healthcare materials. In C. N. Candlin & K. Hyland (Eds.), *Writing: Texts, processes, and practices* (pp. 85–98). London: Longman.

9 Changing currents in contrastive rhetoric: Implications for teaching and research

Ulla Connor

Broadly considered, contrastive rhetoric examines differences and similarities in writing across cultures. The underlying premise of the field is that any given language is likely to have written texts that are constructed using identifiable discourse features, and these features may differ across languages or be coded using different linguistic configurations. Contrastive rhetoric dates back to the seminal work of Robert Kaplan, whose early work within an applied linguistics framework (Kaplan, 1966) suggested that to the degree that language and writing are cultural phenomena, different cultures have different rhetorical tendencies. Furthermore, Kaplan's early work, arising out of an extensive examination of writing produced by university students of English as a second language (ESL), focused on the claim that the linguistic patterns and rhetorical conventions of a first (or native) language (L1) often transfer to writing in ESL and thus cause interference. Although mainly concerned in its first 20 years with student essay writing, today contrastive rhetoric contributes to knowledge about preferred patterns of writing with the goal of helping teachers and students (and writers) around the world in many situations, especially as regards English for specific purposes.

Undeniably, in its first decades, contrastive rhetoric has had an appreciable impact on our understanding of cultural differences in writing, and it continues to spawn interest internationally with such venues as the biennial International Conference on Contrastive Rhetoric at the American University of Cairo and a roundtable seminar on contrastive rhetoric, titled "Contrastive Rhetoric in the 21st Century," organized by Paul Kei Matsuda and me, following Purdue University's third international conference on second-language (L2) writing in October 2002.

In a volume of selected conference papers published subsequent to the first Cairo conference (Ibrahim, Kassabgy, & Aydelott, 2000), 13 chapters discuss studies that dealt with distinctive features of Arabic, Arabic and English contrasts, and contrastive rhetorical studies of Arabic native students' writing in English. The second Cairo conference, held in March 2001, attracted presenters in contrastive rhetoric from Europe and Asia as well as from Arabic-speaking countries.[1] As part of the program, a teleconference was held with Professor Kaplan, who spoke about

218

the evolution of contrastive rhetoric from his retirement in Port Angeles, Washington (U.S.A). In addition to special conferences organized around the topic of contrastive rhetoric like the ones mentioned above, the appeal of contrastive rhetoric as a topic of inquiry by graduate students and practicing teachers in English as a foreign language (EFL) situations is demonstrated by the large number of dissertations being written in various parts of the world on topics in the field of contrastive rhetoric. Recent dissertations by Aymerou Mbaye (2001), a Senegalese EFL teacher, and Toshiko Yoshimura (2001), a teacher in Japan, are described later in this chapter. These teacher/researchers have found contrastive rhetoric a powerful research tool and a useful theory for teaching.

Contrastive rhetoric has had and will continue to have an effect on teaching. In addition to being useful for raising teachers' awareness about L1 influence in their L2 students' English writing, contrastive rhetoric can offer specific activities for the ESL teacher of writing. Several recent treatments have discussed ways contrastive rhetoric can be used in the classroom. Johnson and Duver (1996) provide a number of classroom activities to help students understand contrastive rhetoric, including using model essays to contrast organizational patterns and encouraging journal writing to help students explore cultural differences in L2 writing. Panetta (2001a) contains several chapters dealing with specific implications of contrastive rhetoric for teachers. For example, Panetta's (2001b) own chapter in the volume addresses the importance of making L2 writing conventions explicit to L2 learners. Scoggins's (2001) chapter shows how ESL students in computer classes can use their L1 rhetorics to their advantage by suspending rather than excluding them from rhetorical choices. And Woolever's (2001) chapter provides an important discussion of the use of contrastive rhetoric theory to the teaching of business and technical writing and shows how translation, the use of illustrations and numbers, the development of Web sites, and oral presentations will benefit from the insights of contrastive rhetoric.

I begin the chapter by providing some examples to illustrate how a contrastive rhetoric perspective can illuminate distinctions in the features of texts produced by writers who come from different languages and cultures. Then I briefly review the goals and accomplishments of research in contrastive rhetoric during the past 30 years. In a book on this subject (Connor, 1996), I showed how the discipline expanded from its early beginnings as the study of paragraph organization in ESL student essay writing (Kaplan, 1966) to an interdisciplinary domain of second-language acquisition with rich theoretical underpinnings in both linguistics and rhetoric; this is briefly revisited here. Second, I discuss how contrastive rhetoric has been pursued with varying aims and methods within different types of institutions outside of and in addition to its initial applications in the field of composition studies. Examples are given from research conducted in EFL situations in Europe and elsewhere. Finally, I discuss recent criticisms of contrastive rhetoric and their effects on changing currents in contrastive rhetoric. The new currents deal with culture, literacy, and critical pedagogy and their influence on contrastive rhetoric.

Text analysis using a contrastive rhetoric perspective

To orient new teachers to the type of writing addressed by this field, it may be helpful to look first at some concrete examples of what contrastive rhetoric has actually examined before discussing how the field has evolved and grown.

Examples abound of differences in writing across cultures; however, the following examples come from just two different genres in professional writing: job application letters and grant proposals. The first set consists of (1) a job application letter written in English for a simulated job by a Flemish-speaking college student and (2) a letter written by a U.S. college student in the same simulated job application process (Figure 9.1). (See Connor, Davis, & DeRycker, 1995, for a description of the study.)

The Flemish applicant's letter is shorter, more to the point. The first sentence performs the speech act of application using few words; the next sentence mentions the student's university status and states that the applicant's credentials are listed on an attached résumé; and the last sentence expresses a desire for an interview. The U.S. applicant's letter, on the other hand, uses a large number of words to perform the same functions; the most noteworthy part is the lengthy discussion of the candidate's credentials applicable to the job even though a résumé is enclosed with this application as well. Furthermore, the applicant adds various types of information not seen in the Flemish letter: thus, in the first paragraph the applicant describes how he or she is especially suited for the position and how his or her background would benefit the job; this line of reasoning is expanded in the third paragraph of the letter. Finally, the U.S. applicant includes information on how to be contacted for an interview. Also noteworthy is the polite expression of thanks at the end of the letter.

The second example of cross-cultural differences in writing comes from European Union grant proposals written by Finnish and Swedish scientists (Figure 9.2). Instead of focusing on the scientific content of the proposals, this example highlights another section in the proposals, namely, the personnel section, in which the competence of the researchers is emphasized. The first example is a short autobiographical statement written by a Finnish scientist in the third person. Here, the scientist lists his appointments as well as the numbers of theses and dissertations

[Flemish applicant]

Dear Dr. Davis

In reply to your advertisement in wich [sic] you offer a business education Internship at your Indiana University, I would like to apply for the job.

I am doing my second year the Antwerp University of Economics and you will find a full account of my qualifications on the attached personal record sheet.

If you feel that my qualifications meet with your requirements, I shall be pleased to be called for an interview.

Sincerely yours

[U.S. applicant]

Dear Sirs:

Dr. Ken Davis, Professor of English W-331 at Indiana University-Purdue University at Indianapolis, has provided me with your job description for the position of Assistant to the Tourist Information Manager for the City of Antwerp, Belgium. This position greatly interests me because in [sic] encompasses both my work experience and my interest in international culture, as indicated on the attached resume.

I have had over twelve years experience in the public relations/marketing field. During that time, I have served as the Marketing Director for a major Indianapolis chiropractic clinic with responsibilities for developing marketing plans and public relations venues for four clinics. I also assisted with, produced and directed a local radio talk show for the clinic. My employment duties have included a variety of coordination duties for clients and dignitaries, including travel and hotel accommodations. As an assistant to the Practice Development Director at a major Indianapolis law firm, my duties included organization of client receptions, travel arrangements for attorneys and clients, and intercommunication with attorneys and clients, some of whom have been in foreign countries.

I have a special personal interest in European culture, based upon my experience as a host parent for Youth for Understanding international youth exchange program. During my involvement with this group, I have hosted children from Denmark, Finland and Germany, as well as Chile and Japan.

I will be available for interviews at any time. I may be reached at my place of business at (317) XXX-XXXX from 8:00 a.m. (USA time) until 5:30 p.m., Monday through Friday, or at home at (317) XXX-XXXX at any time.

Thank you for your review of this application.

Sincerely,

Figure 9.1. Sample letters

1. Prof. N. N. joined the Department of . . . in 19xx. He has been involved in X in Finland and abroad since 19xx. During 19xx–19xx he acted as the head of . . . On joining U University, N. N. initiated a research and teaching program focused mainly on the effects of E on the quality of Y. He has recently been appointed Assisting Co-leader of the UNESCO-sponsored project, which is aimed at . . . At present two Ph.D. theses and five Mse thesis projects are being carried. A number of abstracts have been published, some of which are mentioned in the list of publications below and the manuscripts of some of these are being in different stages of preparation for publication in international journals.

2. Professor N. N. has a very distinguished academic record with over 150 publications in scientific journals, books, and conference proceedings since 19xx including 80 publications in the last eight years. He has made over 65 presentations (oral and posters) at international meetings and over 20 at national scientific symposia, conferences and workshops, including several invited and plenary lectures since 19xx. He has led over 20 research grants and contracts as principal investigator and is a member of over 12 boards and scientific and technical committees. He has also undertaken consulting activities in relation to industrial problems of P. His teaching activities include courses in chemistry, processes in P and population control since 19xx. He has supervised 20 graduate students (Phd) since 19xx. The Department has excellent facilities for experimental studies of environmental systems, presently focused on . . . 25 theses have been submitted in the last x years. Additional members of the proposer's team will include Dr. A. A., Professor B. B., Dr. C. C., and Polish and German Contacts.

Figure 9.2. Sample competence claims in European Union grant proposals

supervised and papers published. No evaluation of the candidate's background and experience relative to the project is apparent.

In contrast, the second illustration in Figure 9.2 is a biography of a Swedish researcher. The statement is not a mere list; instead, two strong positive appraisals are included: "a very distinguished academic record," "the department has excellent facilities."

These examples illustrate differences in the content as well as in the style of writing of these genres in their respective cultures, and numerous other examples have been published to demonstrate differences in writing across cultures (e.g., see Brauer, 2000, among many such publications). Although its primary goal was not to advance contrastive rhetoric, a recent collection of literacy autobiographies of accomplished EFL writers (Belcher & Connor, 2001) provides convincing evidence of differences in writing norms among cultures. One of the authors, Soter (2001), writes:

> Nevertheless, my early encounters with writing American Academic discourse revealed that a natural form of expression that I had taken for granted as acceptable and indeed, had been a vehicle for success in Australian educational contexts, was suddenly a "problem" and that in order to continue to be successful, I would have to "clean up" my discourse, get rid of the embedding, become direct, get to the point, bare my thoughts and assert my views. (p. 69)

The examples in this section have shown differences in English writing by learners from varying cultural and linguistic backgrounds, writing for a number of different purposes.

Contrastive rhetoric in the United States during the past 30 years

As can be seen from the examples discussed in the previous section, contrastive rhetoric is an area of research in second-language acquisition that identifies problems in composition encountered by second-language writers, explaining these problems by referring to the rhetorical strategies of the first language (Connor, 1996, p. 5). It's important to distinguish this concern from issues of translation and potential interference at the level of grammar.[2] In contrastive rhetoric, the interference manifests itself – as we have seen in the earlier examples – in the choice of rhetorical strategies, including content.

Kaplan's (1966) study was the first serious attempt by a U.S. applied linguist to explain the written styles of ESL students, as opposed to patterns of L2 speech. His pioneering work analyzed the organization of paragraphs in ESL student essays and identified five types of paragraph development, each of which he characterized with a graphic symbol that he himself later referred to as "doodles" (Kaplan, 1987). He claimed that Anglo-European expository essays follow a linear development; Semitic languages use parallel coordinate clauses; Oriental languages prefer an indirect approach and come to the point at the end; in Romance languages and in Russian, essays employ a degree of digressiveness and extraneous material that would seem excessive to a writer of English.

As is well known, Kaplan's contrastive rhetoric has been criticized as being too ethnocentric and as privileging the writing of native English speakers, as well as for dismissing linguistic and cultural differences in writing among different languages, e.g., lumping Chinese, Thai, and Korean speakers in one Oriental group. It has also been criticized for drawing conclusions on the basis of writing samples written by developmental writers (Noor, 2001). Kaplan (1987) modified his earlier position himself, moving away from what could be described as a Whorfian interpretation, namely, that rhetorical patterns reflect patterns of thinking in L1. Instead, he holds that cross-cultural differences in writing can be explained by different conventions of writing, which are learned, rather than acquired (cf. Krashen, 1982).

At a Teachers of English to Speakers of Other Languages (TESOL) colloquium in honor of Kaplan's work in 1996, I proposed new diagrams to supplement Kaplan's 1966 "doodles." Those playfully drawn "squiggles," here presented in Figure 9.3, show that the writing of native English speakers, such as article introductions, does not follow a straight line. Letters of job application vary greatly in their linearity among U.S., Belgian, and Asian samples. Finally, the research by Ventola and Mauranen (1991) and Mauranen (1993) has suggested that the writing of Finns, either in Finnish or English, follows a circular pattern of organization.

These diagrams are meant to show that coherence lies in the eye of the beholder and that one needs to exercise care in attaching identifying labels to others' writing.

In any case, Kaplan's earlier model, being concerned with paragraph organization, was useful in explaining essays written by college students for academic purposes. It also introduced the linguistic world to a real, if basic, insight: writing was culturally influenced in interesting and complex ways. However, the model was not particularly successful in describing writing for academic and professional purposes. Neither was it successful in describing composing processes across cultures. In fact, the original contrastive rhetoric was never intended to describe L2 writing for purposes other than essay writing.

Significant changes have taken place in contrastive rhetoric in the past 30-odd years. In my 1996 book, I suggested that contrastive rhetoric has taken new directions in the following domains: (1) contrastive text linguistics, (2) the study of writing as a cultural-educational activity, (3) classroom-based studies of writing, and (4) contrastive genre-specific studies, including a variety of genres composed for a variety of purposes such as journal articles, business reports, letters of application, grant proposals, and editorials.

Figure 9.4 summarizes studies in the four domains. A sample study from each of the above listed sub-genres of contrastive rhetoric illustrates the focus of each domain.

1. In text linguistics in the 1980s, perhaps the work with the most impact was by the late John Hinds, who compared patterns of coherence across Japanese texts and texts in English. Hinds found that many newspaper columns in Japan followed the ancient organizational pattern of *ki-shoo-ten-ketsu*, a four-step process that roughly

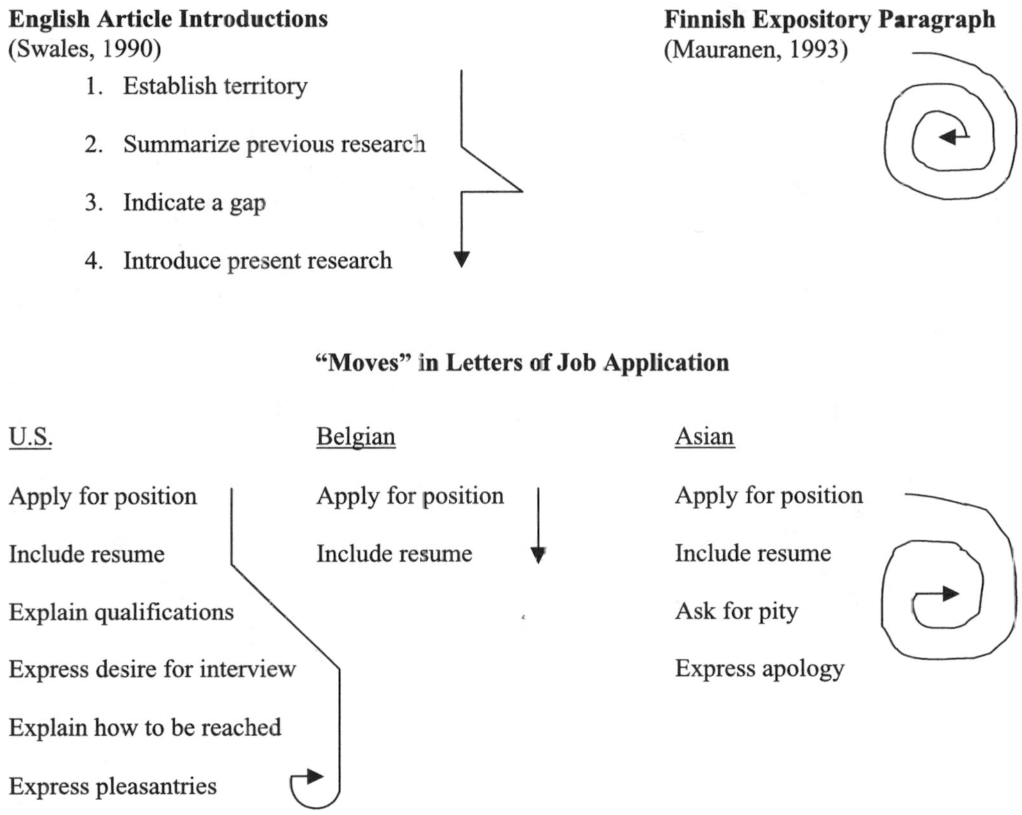

English Article Introductions
(Swales, 1990)

1. Establish territory
2. Summarize previous research
3. Indicate a gap
4. Introduce present research

Finnish Expository Paragraph
(Mauranen, 1993)

"Moves" in Letters of Job Application

U.S.	Belgian	Asian
Apply for position	Apply for position	Apply for position
Include resume	Include resume	Include resume
Explain qualifications		Ask for pity
Express desire for interview		Express apology
Explain how to be reached		
Express pleasantries		

Figure 9.3. New diagrams

1. Contrastive text linguistic studies examine, compare, and contrast how texts are formed and interpreted in different languages and cultures using methods of written discourse analysis. (See Clyne, 1987; Connor & Kaplan, 1987; Eggington, 1987; Hinds, 1983, 1987, 1990.)
2. Studies of writing as cultural and educational activity investigate literacy development on L1 language and culture and examine effects on the development of L2 literacy. (See Carson, 1992; Purves, 1988.)
3. Classroom-based contrastive studies examine cross-cultural patterns in process writing, collaborative revisions, and student-teacher conferences. (See Allaei & Connor, 1990; Goldstein & Conrad, 1990; Hull, Rose, Fraser, & Castellano, 1991; Nelson & Murphy, 1992.)
4. Genre-specific investigations are applied to academic and professional writing. (See Bhatia, 1993; Connor, Davis, & De Rycker, 1995; Jenkins & Hinds, 1987; Mauranen, 1993; Swales, 1990; Tirkkonen-Condit, 1996; Ventola & Mauranen, 1991.)

Figure 9.4. Summary of contrastive rhetoric studies in applied linguistics

translates (1) begin your argument, (2) develop it, (3) turn to material with a connection but not direct association with the text, and (4) conclude. In reading direct translations of Japanese writing in various genres, native English speakers found the introduction of the "ten" component of the *ki-shoo-ten-ketsu* pattern incoherent. Based on this research, Hinds (1987) suggested that Japanese writing is more "reader responsible," meaning that readers need to work harder to get the meaning of a text than in "writer responsible" writing such as English. In numerous publications, Hinds also argued that native English speakers prefer a deductive type of argument. Although English speakers are familiar with induction, they are not used to reading prose organized in ways other than induction and deduction.

2. Among studies investigating the development of academic literacy in L1 language and culture, the most comprehensive research was conducted by the late Alan Purves (1988) and others in the International Education Achievement (IEA) research group. Fourteen countries were included in an ambitious international study of writing achievement. The research yielded significant findings about the writing patterns of students at three age levels (12, 16, and 18) writing for three different purposes: narration, exposition, and argumentation. One major contribution was an increased understanding about the importance of the *tertium comparationis,* or the common platform of

comparison. One should compare only texts that are comparable by virtue of some shared equivalence. For example, expectations about what an argumentative essay entails vary from culture to culture. Thus, in some cultures, a good argumentative essay is a story. Therefore, insisting on exactly the same prompts – either in genre expectation (e.g., story vs. essay) or in content – may not be appropriate in cross-cultural research; and texts chosen for contrastive research should share comparable prompts.

3. Classroom studies have been conducted to study patterns of collaboration in writing groups in writing classes. The research of Joan Carson and Gayle Nelson at Georgia State University is the most extensive. Through text analyses and transcripts of collaborative writing sessions, Nelson and Carson (1998) have found, among other things, that Chinese-speaking ESL writers are more concerned about maintaining harmonious group relations than providing critical input on others' drafts, whereas Spanish-speaking students in the groups in the United States used more or less an opposite approach. (Peer interaction is discussed more fully by Ferris, Chapter 5 this volume.)

4. Genre-specific contrastive studies have extended the framework of contrastive studies. Sonja Tirkkonen-Condit (1996), for example, has contrasted the discourse of newspaper editorials in Finland, England, and the United States and has found, using various textual analyses, that editorials in Finnish newspapers are typically written to build consensus while in the United States they argue for a particular point of view.

What have we learned about writing across cultures in these 30 years of contrastive rhetoric research? We have found that all groups engage in a variety of types of writing, each with its own conventions and tendencies. Also, preferred patterns of writing depend on the genre (see Johns, Chapter 8 this volume, for a fuller discussion of genre conventions). We have also found that what constitutes straightforward writing depends on reader expectation. Thus, Kaplan's diagram of the linear line of argument preferred by native English speakers may represent what such speakers view as straightforward, but speakers of other languages do not necessarily interpret the features of English argument texts the same way.

Applications of contrastive rhetoric in English as a foreign language (EFL) situations

As the previous sections have shown, contrastive rhetoric has had an impact on the teaching of English as a second language in the United States

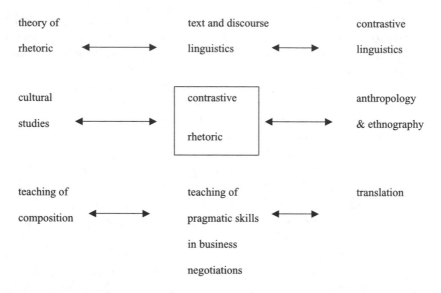

Figure 9.5.   Applications of contrastive rhetoric in Europe (adapted from Enkvist, 1997). Used with permission from the University of Durban Westville.

since its beginning 30 years ago. Recently, its influence is being recognized in the teaching of EFL in a number of countries. The Finnish text linguist Nils Erik Enkvist, in his 1997 article "Why We Need Contrastive Rhetoric," suggests that contrastive rhetoric could be pursued with varying aims and methods within different institutions at universities and outside EFL situations. He shows how contrastive rhetoric is of interest to many programs involved in training in foreign language skills at universities in the small country of Finland. First, Finnish universities, of course, have language departments, which teach language, literature, linguistic and literary theory, and applied linguistics. Second, for the past 25 years, Finland has had language centers at universities that teach languages for specific purposes and provide translation and editing services. A third type of language teaching establishment in Finland with potential for contrastive rhetoric is the School of International Communication. A fourth type of institution interested in contrastive rhetoric is the School of Economics. Figure 9.5 includes a diagram (adapted from Enkvist) to show the applications of contrastive rhetoric in Europe.

The following examples illustrate the use of the contrastive rhetoric framework in research relevant to academic and professional settings in Europe, including institutions mentioned by Enkvist. Following that is a discussion of the relevance of contrastive rhetoric for teachers of school and college students in many other EFL settings, in which the teaching of the school essay form is still very important.

Academic and professional writing in EFL

Research conducted in the contrastive framework appears in two academic genres: research articles and grant proposals. The research on EFL writing in Finland by Ventola and Mauranen (1991) has convincingly shown the value of text analyses in a contrastive framework. Their research relates to cultural differences between Finnish and English-speaking research writers. Their contrastive text linguistic project investigated language revision practices by native English speakers in Finnish scientists' articles written in English and also compared those texts to articles by native English-speaking writers. A contrastive systemic linguistic study found that Finnish writers used connectors less frequently and in a less varied fashion than native English-speaking writers. In reference use, the Finnish writers tended to use the article system inappropriately, and there were also differences in thematic progression. Other research by Mauranen (1993) found that in addition, Finnish writers employed less text about text, or "metatext," and also preferred placing the statement of their main point later in the text than do native English speakers.

In a project titled "Milking Brussels,"[3] in which analyses were done of research grant proposals written by Finnish scientists for the European Union research funds, the researchers discovered that Finnish writers had these same difficulties when writing grant proposals – such as not stating their theses at the beginning of the writing but preferring to delay the introduction of the purpose (Connor et al., 1995). Other textual differences in the Finnish writers' proposals included a lack of transitions and other metatext to guide the reader, differences similar to the ones found in Ventola's and Mauranen's research on academic research articles discussed above.

Differences between American English and Finnish were reinforced while my colleagues and I were producing a Finnish-language guidebook for grant writers (Connor et al., 1995) based on the team's research. Writing the guidebook using a team approach was an illustrative experience in contrastive rhetoric. In an intense discussion, I made the point that the guidebook describes how English writing differs from Finnish; therefore, it was important to state right at the start what the purpose of the book is and how important it is for Finns to learn to state their main points at the beginning, give examples, and provide transitions throughout the text and then to repeat the main point. The Finnish research assistant in the team wrote the first draft, which I as a Finnish-American found incoherent. I made suggestions in the margins, such as "we need to state the main point at the beginning of the paragraph," and "we shouldn't jump around with ideas, and leave the most important thing as the very last in the book." My summary comments on the draft to the Finnish research assistant and the team read (translated from Finnish): "Perhaps I'm reading this text as an American. It's all fine text but I find it incoherent in places, hard to follow. I expect the main point at the beginning of the paragraph. I expect a paragraph to contain examples about the main point – no jumping between several points. If others [the other researchers in the project] don't object to the current presentation, I must be completely Americanized."

With the globalization of business and professional communication, writing in such genres as letters, résumés, and job applications for readers with a different language and cultural background from their own is a reality for more and more people. Researchers have found that in these contexts, too, second language writers transfer patterns and styles from the first language to the second (Upton & Connor, 2001; Ypsilandis, 1994).

Predictably, differing reader expectations cause misunderstandings. For example, requests in letters can be interpreted as being too direct when directness is more valued in the first language than in the second. Résumés also differ in style cross-culturally and even intra-culturally, as in the difference between the functional résumé and traditional résumé in the United States.

The studies cited earlier, conducted in the contrastive framework in Europe in academic and professional writing, show how the contrastive rhetorical framework, originally developed for U.S. ESL settings, can be helpful in analyzing and teaching EFL writing in academic and professional contexts as well.

School essay writing in EFL: Examples from Japan and Senegal

Despite the increasing importance of academic and professional writing for increasing numbers of internationals around the world, the most frequently required writing for hundreds of thousands of students in the world is the school essay. The school essay in the mother tongue and in English is the most commonly used assessment instrument to measure writing achievement and performance. It is used in matriculation examinations at the end of high school years, and large-scale tests of English language proficiency, such as the TOEFL (Test of English as a Foreign Language), now include an essay task. Since no universally agreed-on assessments of writing processes exist, assessments focus on written products. The five-paragraph essay, much maligned in U.S. composition circles, is one of the most significant writing tasks that many, especially beginning-level students, can learn to produce in response to many assessment prompts.

Yoshimura (2001), a teacher/researcher in Kyoto, Japan, conducted an experimental study and taught the organizational pattern, coherence structure, and argumentative patterns of an English argumentative essay to beginning-intermediate level students in a private college in Japan. The experimental groups (one taught in English, the other taught to write the essay in Japanese first and translate it into English) outperformed the control group on a task of writing a "take a position and support it" argumentative essay. The treatment consisted of teaching paragraph and essay organization for a short period of each class during one semester; in many respects the study replicated the published work of Oi and Kamimura (1997) on the importance of explicit teaching of Western argumentative essay patterns to Japanese students.

Yoshimura reports that she is well aware of the criticisms raised against teaching the form of an essay instead of focusing on the process and content. However, the results confirm her belief after years of teaching English to Japanese students that these students benefit from being comfortable with a form of writing. She believes that the success students gain in the beginning stages of their writing can be transferred to future writing situations, such as writing a business letter or a company report.

In another dissertation, Mbaye (2001) examined the English essay writing styles of 22 international students from Senegal in ESL classes at a U.S. university through interviews and text analyses. He provides a fascinating discussion about the transport of the essay genre, originated by the writer Montaigne, 1533–1592, to England, to America, and to the current traditional rhetoric method of teaching writing in the United States in the last decades. He also describes the context of French L1 writing instruction in Senegal, which is characterized by the predominance of the "dissertation" (French equivalent of the essay) in pre-university schooling. The structure of the "dissertation" is totally different from the five-paragraph essay. First, the "dissertation" typically consists of four parts: introduction, "thesis," "antithesis" and "synthesis" (i.e., conclusion). Second, the introduction of the "dissertation" restates the essay topic in the form of a question rather than including a thesis statement and a controlling idea, as called for in the five-paragraph essay. Third, the writer may not take a position even though the prompt might require it. Finally, because "dissertations" are considered exercises in reasoned thinking, they tend to be longer than school essays written in English. A translation from French of a typical "dissertation" was shown by Mbaye and appears here in Appendix A.

The method of teaching essay writing in English emphasizes form, linearity, and final textual product. Mbaye argues for the importance of essay writing in English for Senegalese students and, based on a contrastive study, shows difficulties Senegalese students encounter when faced with the task. Learners of English in Senegal come to the writing task with two major obstacles: (1) many students' first languages are oral whereas English essay writing requires an Aristotelian, Western mode of thinking with a focus on style and organization; this includes a need for adequate supporting evidence and distinct beginning, middle, and end pieces of discourse with few digressions; and (2) students' first school language is French, through which they learn to write "dissertations." After learning the form of the "dissertation," students may transfer this structure to the writing of the English essay, which results in an unsatisfactory performance.

The results of Mbaye's study showed students had problems in relation to the basic paragraph and the structure of the concluding paragraph along with the absence of a thesis; these had been contributing reasons for the students in the study not to be tested out of ESL classes at the U.S. university they attended. Mbaye is cognizant of criticisms directed at teaching the essay form – for example, it discourages concern with process and content – but based on the results of the study, he strongly advocates using the essay as a practical instructional tool as it is "more adequate than anything the school may have for testing validly non-discrete items of knowledge" (p. 41). He also views the school essay as "a vehicle for an important function of language and literacy, i.e. the transaction of information" (p. 41). Finally, Mbaye makes a strong case for the essay as helping students from oral cultures in his country to develop some of the necessary skills for acquiring literacy. He writes: "By mandating a standard rhetorical structure, emphasizing linear logic, and the objectifying of language and thought, schooling and essay are laying the foundations for higher order cognitive skills" (p. 42).

In the past, I have stressed the importance of having bilingual researchers conduct contrastive rhetorical studies. Yoshimura and Mbaye are good examples of devoted, experienced EFL teachers and competent L2 writing researchers. Their viewpoints are valuable. In our Western, postmodern ideologies, we should not devalue the insights about essay problems that these teacher-researchers report on firsthand; nor should we insist on banishing the teaching of patterns and the essay form as form. Let us keep such issues in mind when we read the following section.

Criticisms and advances in contrastive rhetoric concerning culture, literacy, and critical pedagogy

Despite new developments in contrastive rhetoric and its contributions to teaching in ESL and EFL settings, both in instruction at the beginning and in the specialized writing instruction in the examples from Europe, the discipline has become the target of criticisms by researchers with varied disciplinary affiliations.

It is important for future teachers to find ways to tap into the real potential for classroom use suggested in previous sections. Future teachers should not be discouraged by recent criticisms of contrastive rhetoric but should treat them with a balanced perspective, as I attempt to show below.

In 1997, three published works in the *TESOL Quarterly* focused on the criticism of contrastive rhetoric. Two U.S.-born specialists, Ruth Spack and Vivian Zamel, who work with ESL students in the United States, were concerned about the labeling of students by their L1 backgrounds and the tendency of contrastive rhetoric to view cultures as "discrete, discontinuous, and predictable" (Zamel, 1997). Ron Scollon, in the same issue of the journal, criticized contrastive rhetoric research for being too concerned about texts and too neglectful of oral influences on literacy to consider EFL situations like the one in Hong Kong (Scollon, 1997). In an issue of the *TESOL Quarterly* in 1999, Ryuko Kubota is critical of the perception of a cultural dichotomy between the East and West (Kubota, 1999). According to her, researchers tend to create cultural differences that promote the superiority of Western writing – its supposed linearity, clarity, and coherence – and ignore the dynamic, more fluid nature of Japanese writing.

One could view all of these criticisms as stemming from different disciplinary backgrounds of the writers, somewhat apart from the mainstream of second language writing as a field. Zamel and Spack could be described as being closely aligned to L1 writing traditions with emphasis on process writing and individual expression (Ramanathan & Atkinson, 1999). Scollon comes from anthropology, a discipline whose major focus is not pedagogical applications, unlike contrastive rhetoric, which does address pedagogical concerns. Kubota, a Japanese native applied linguist, takes a position stemming from critical pedagogy and questions the teaching of Western norms of academic writing.

Instead of viewing their work primarily from an adversarial perspective (Belcher, 1997), I would like to use it to develop a more generous conception of the contrastive rhetoric framework, especially regarding changing definitions of culture. Both Spack and Zamel bring up the changing definitions of culture, in which forces of heterogeneity and homogeneity are juxtaposed, and the latter seriously questioned. In the last couple of years, the concept of culture has been discussed widely in applied linguistics with relevance to contrastive rhetoric. Atkinson (1999) provides a comprehensive review of competing definitions of culture as they relate to TESOL. According to Atkinson, two competitive views of culture in TESOL are (1) the "received view" and (2) alternative, nonstandard views. The received view refers to a notion of culture based largely on geographically and often nationally distinct entities that are relatively unchanging and homogeneous (e.g., Japan, Japanese). The alternative, nonstandard views stem from postmodernist-influenced concepts and have evolved from critiques of the traditional, received view of culture. In the latter camp, Atkinson discusses concepts such as those of "identity," "hybridity," "essentialism," and "power," all of which have been used to criticize traditional views of culture:

These terms indicate the shared perspective that cultures are anything but homogeneous, all-encompassing entities, and represent important concepts in the larger project: the unveiling of the fissures, discontinuities, disagreements, and cross-cutting influences that exist in and around all cultural scenes, in order to banish once and for all the idea that cultures are monolithic entities, or in some cases anything substantial at all. (p. 627)

Following Atkinson (1999), it can be argued that contrastive rhetoric largely adopted the notion of "received culture." For example, I defined culture as "a set of patterns and rules shared by a particular community" (Connor, 1996, p. 101). A great deal of traditional contrastive rhetoric has similarly viewed ESL students as members of separate, identifiable cultural groups and, as discussed by Deborah Tannen (1985), can come under the current criticisms directed at any research on cross-cultural communication. Tannen thus notes that "some people object to any research documenting cross-cultural differences, which they see as buttressing stereotypes and hence exacerbating discrimination" (p. 212). She argues, however, that ignoring cultural differences leads to misinterpretation and "hence discrimination of another sort" (p. 212).

Although contrastive rhetoric has often defined national cultures in the "received" mode, researchers in contrastive rhetoric have not interpreted *all* differences in writing as stemming from the first language or the national culture. Instead, they have tried to explain such differences in written communication as often arising from multiple sources including L1 national culture, L1 educational background, disciplinary culture, genre characteristics, and mismatched expectations between readers and writers. In this respect, contrastive rhetoric is similar to spoken intercultural research or intercultural pragmatics analysis, as described by the spoken discourse analyst Srikant Sarangi (1994). Sarangi suggests the term "intercultural" to refer to migrants' fluid identities and recommends that we consider reasons of language proficiency, native culture, and interlocutors' accommodation in explaining miscommunication between native and non-native speakers in immigrant language situations.[4]

Nevertheless, future contrastive rhetoric research needs to develop greater sensitivity to the view that sees writers not as parts of separate, identifiable cultural groups but as individuals in social groups that are undergoing continuous change.

Related to the discussion about culture is the issue of standards and norms. A major question in contrastive rhetoric deals with an ideological problem about whose norms and standards to teach and the danger of perpetuating established power roles. This has been raised as an issue in postmodern discussion about discourse and the teaching of writing (Kubota, 1999; Ramanathan & Atkinson, 1999). The discussion has, of course, been in the forefront in contrastive rhetoric; recent critics of contrastive rhetoric have blamed contrastive rhetoricians for teaching students to write for native speaker expectations instead of expressing their own native lingual and cultural identities.

Researchers working in the current contrastive rhetoric paradigm have maintained that cultural differences need to be explicitly taught in order to acculturate EFL writers to the target discourse community. Hence, they maintain that teachers of English and others, such as consultants in grant proposal writing, need to educate students or clients about the expectations of their readers. Thus, at workshops for Finnish scientists about how to write proposals in English, I taught a Western, generic style of grant proposal writing using a set of rhetorical moves (à la Swales, 1990) we had developed (Connor et al., 1995). I instructed the Finnish scientists that if they wished to get European Union (EU) research grants, they needed to follow EU norms and expectations, which, at least in the late 1990s, were based on an Anglo-American scientific and promotional discourse. When, on the other hand, Finnish scientists write grant applications in Finnish, I suggested that they would do well to follow the expectations of the Finnish agencies. Although the decision about language choice seems straightforward in the case of grant proposals in the project described above, it may be more complex with student writers in undergraduate colleges in the United States. Encouraging the preservation of the first language and style may be perfectly acceptable in an effort to preserve the national identity of immigrant students, for example.

In the EU project we became aware of another issue facing contrastive rhetoric – namely, that there may not be an English-language norm for the writing of EU grant proposals. It seems clear that there may be changes in the norms and standards of English in grant proposals because the raters of grant proposals for the EU in Brussels are not solely native speakers of English but are scientists from all EU countries with many different first languages and many different rhetorical orientations. In fact, something like a "Eurorhetoric" has probably emerged. This blurring of standards and norms in written language in this case is consistent with recent developments in spoken language. David Crystal (1997), for example, suggests that a new kind of English, World Standard Spoken English (WSSE), may be arising for use when the need is to communicate in English with people from other countries for purposes of business, industry, and diplomacy. Little, however, has yet been conjectured about the nature of this world English, and no theoretical model, as is the case with "Eurorhetoric," has been established.

Conclusion

Major changes are taking place in contrastive rhetoric. The influence of contrastive rhetorical theories has expanded beyond the teaching of ESL and EFL writing, as the Finnish, Japanese, and Senegalese examples show. Contrastive rhetoric is affecting teaching not only of business and technical writing in L2 situations overseas but also of "mainstream writing" in the United States. Woolever (2001), for example, recommends using contrastive rhetorical theory in teaching business and technical writing in non-ESL U.S. classrooms.

In addition to the expansion of contrastive rhetoric to classrooms outside traditional ESL and EFL classes, contrastive rhetoric itself is embracing new influences and thus revising its goals and methods. No doubt it will need to become even more responsive to new currents in critical approaches to culture, writing, and the internationalization of English. Consistent with postmodern indications, contrastive rhetoric needs to promote further research-situated reflexivity, to be more sensitive to local characteristics and particularity of writing activity, and to become more conscious of the influences of power and ideology in any setting.

Contrastive rhetoric also needs to become sensitive to feminist and minority concerns. Too often, contrastive rhetoric proceeds as if differences in gender did not make any difference in text, as was true even in the monumental and valuable IEA project. Various chapters in the previously mentioned collection by Panetta (2001a) present reflections about the usefulness of contrastive rhetorical theories for the research and teaching of writing to other "marginalized groups," such as African American and women writers. (See also Fox, 1994.)

In conclusion, contrastive rhetoric research continues to provide empirically testable models of cross-cultural texts and writing behaviors. Barton (2000) has noted that in the case of first language writing empirical discourse analysis is needed along with the current popular emphasis on theorizing about culture and cultural diversity. It is especially important for contrastive purposes. I would add that there is a continuing need, which I have stressed elsewhere (Connor, 1996, p. 163), to develop models for empirical comparisons and contrasts that would ensure impartiality. The goal would be a *tertium comparationis*, an inclusive frame of genre significant features drawn from the compared texts, from whose unbiased perspective local differences in individual texts could be measured.[5]

Notes

1. A third such conference is scheduled in 2003, and the organizers again expect to attract an international set of presenters and participants.
2. In an article arguing for the importance of including training in contrastive rhetoric for teachers in TESL programs, for example, Johnson and Duver (1996) illustrate the ways that cultural differences sometimes account for grammatical choices that create writing problems for learners. They note "people's cognitive interpretation of the external world differs and . . . these cultural thought patterns affect [second language learners'] production and understanding of . . . writing a second language" (Johnson & Duver, 1996, p. 117), but their examples all derive from a linguistic rather than a rhetorical perspective.
3. The European Union is based in Brussels.
4. The notion of "interculture" is suggested by Sarangi to describe the migrants' fluid identities of native and target cultures in immigrant situations, reminiscent of Selinker's (1972) concept of interlanguage, which refers to shared features of a speaker's native and target languages.
5. There is a directly analogous procedure in computer science (Langley et al., 1987), which employs the interpolation of inclusive frames of significant features in which the same comparable data sets can be mapped approximately well and from whose necessarily neutral perspective the distinctive features of such sets can be distinguished and thus contrasted (p. 53). This mathematical procedure might be developed into a model for some comparisons/contrasts in empirical contrastive rhetoric research such as the national or cultural differences in grant proposals noted above.

References

Allaei, S. K., & Connor, U. M. (1990). Exploring the dynamics of cross-cultural collaborations in writing classrooms. *The Writing Instructor, 10*(1), 19–28.

Atkinson, D. (1999). Culture in TESOL. *TESOL Quarterly, 33*, 625–654.

Barton, E. (2000). More methodological matters: Against negative argumentation. *College Composition and Communication, 51*, 399–416.

Belcher, D. D. (1997). An argument for nonadversial argumentation: On the relevance of the feminist critique of academic discourse to L2 writing pedagogy. *Journal of Second Language Writing, 6*, 1–21.

Belcher, D., & Connor, U. (Eds.). (2001). *Reflections on multiliterate lives.* Clevedon, England: Multilingual Matters.

Bhatia, V. K. (1993). *Analyzing genre: Language use in professional settings.* New York: Longman.

Brauer, G. (Ed.). (2000). *Writing across languages.* Stamford, CT: Ablex.

Carson, J. G. (1992). Becoming biliterate: First language influences. *Journal of Second Language Writing, 1*, 37–60.

Clyne, M. G. (1987). Cultural differences in the organization of academic texts: English and German. *Journal of Pragmatics, 11*, 211–247.

Connor, U. (1996). *Contrastive rhetoric: Cross-cultural aspects of second language writing.* New York: Cambridge University Press.

Connor, U., Davis, K., & DeRycker, T. (1995). Correctness and clarity in applying for overseas jobs: A cross-cultural analysis of U.S. and Flemish applications. *Text, 15*, 457–475.

Connor, U., Helle, T., Mauranen, A., Ringbom, H., Tirkkonen-Condit, S., & Yli-Antola, M. (1995). *Tekokkaita EU-projektiehdotuksia* [Successful grant proposals for European Union research funds]. Helsinki, Finland: TEKES.

Connor, U., & Kaplan, R. B. (Eds.). (1987). *Writing across languages: Analysis of L2 text*. Reading, MA: Addison-Wesley.

Crystal, D. (1997). *English as a global language*. Cambridge: Cambridge University Press.

Eggington, W. G. (1987). Written academic discourse in Korean: Implication for effective communication. In U. Connor & R. B. Kaplan (Eds.), *Writing across languages: Analysis of L2 text* (pp. 153–168). Reading, MA: Addison-Wesley.

Enkvist, N. E. (1997). Why we need contrastive rhetoric. *Alternation, 4*, 188–206.

Fox, H. (1994). *Listening to the world: Cultural issues in academic writing*. Urbana, IL: NCTE.

Goldstein, L. M., & Conrad, S. M. (1990). Student input and negotiation of meaning in ESL writing conferences. *TESOL Quarterly, 24*, 443–460.

Hinds, J. (1983). Contrastive rhetoric: Japanese and English. *Text, 3*, 183–195.

Hinds, J. (1987). Reader versus writer responsibility: A new typology. In U. Connor & R. B. Kaplan (Eds.), *Writing across languages: Analysis of L2 text* (pp. 141–152). Reading, MA: Addison-Wesley.

Hinds, J. (1990). Inductive, deductive, quasi-inductive: Expository writing in Japanese, Korean, Chinese, and Thai. In U. Connor & A. M. Johns (Eds.), *Coherence in writing: Research and pedagogical perspectives* (pp. 87–110). Alexandria, VA: TESOL.

Hull, G., Rose, M., Fraser, K. L., & Castellano, M. (1991). Remediation as a social construct: Perspectives from an analysis of classroom discourse. *College Composition and Communication, 42*, 299–329.

Ibrahim, Z., Kassabgy, N., & Aydelott, S. (Eds.). (2000). *Diversity in language: Contrastive studies in Arabic and English theoretical and applied linguistics*. Cairo, Egypt: American University of Cairo Press.

Jenkins, S., & Hinds, J. (1987). Business letter writing: English, French and Japanese. *TESOL Quarterly, 21*, 327–354.

Johnson, R., & Duver, M. (1996). The usefulness of contrastive rhetoric theory in training TESOL teachers and English-as-a-second-language students. *The Teacher Educator, 32*, 107–121.

Kaplan, R. B. (1966). Cultural thought patterns in intercultural education. *Language Learning, 16*(1), 1–20.

Kaplan, R. B. (1987). Cultural thought patterns revisited. In U. Connor & R. B. Kaplan (Eds.), *Writing across languages: Analysis of L2 text* (pp. 9–21). Reading, MA: Addison-Wesley.

Krashen, S. D. (1982). *Principles and practice in second language acquisition*. Oxford: Pergamon.

Kubota, R. (1999). Japanese culture constructed by discourses: Implications for applied linguistics research and ELT. *TESOL Quarterly, 33*, 9–64.

Langley, P., Simon, H. A., Bradshaw, G. L., & Zytow, J. M. (1987). *Scientific discovery: Computational explorations of the creative processes.* Cambridge, MA: MIT Press.

Mauranen, A. (1993). *Cultural differences in academic rhetoric.* Frankfurt am Main: Peter Lang.

Mbaye, A. (2001). *A contrastive study of EFL-ESL writing problems: Case studies of five Senegalese students in U.S. colleges.* Unpublished doctoral dissertation, Oklahoma State University, Stillwater, Oklahoma.

Nelson, G. L., & Carson, J. G. (1998). ESL students' perceptions of effectiveness in peer response groups. *Journal of Second Language Writing, 7,* 113–132.

Nelson, G. L., & Murphy, J. M. (1992). An ESL writing group: Task and social dimensions. *Journal of Second Language Writing, 1,* 171–194.

Noor, R. (2001). Contrastive rhetoric in expository prose: Approaches and achievements. *Journal of Pragmatics, 33,* 255–269.

Oi, K., & Kamimura, T. (1997). A pedagogical application of research in contrastive rhetoric. *JACET Bulletin, 28,* 65–82.

Panetta, C. G. (Ed.). (2001a). *Contrastive rhetoric theory revisited and redefined.* Mahwah, NJ: Lawrence Erlbaum.

Panetta, C. G. (2001b). Understanding cultural differences in the rhetoric and composition classroom: Contrastive rhetoric as answer to ESL dilemmas. In C. G. Panetta (Ed.), *Contrastive rhetoric theory revisited and redefined* (pp. 3–13). Mahwah, NJ: Lawrence Erlbaum.

Purves, A. C. (Ed.). (1988). *Writing across languages and cultures: Issues in contrastive rhetoric.* Newbury Park, CA: Sage.

Ramanathan, V., & Atkinson, D. (1999). Individualism, academic writing, and ESL writers. *Journal of Second Language Writing, 8,* 45–75.

Sarangi, S. (1994). Intercultural or not? Beyond celebration of cultural differences in miscommunication analysis. *Pragmatics, 4,* 409–427.

Scoggins, D. (2001). Contrastive rhetoric theory in an electronic medium: Teaching ESL writers to become bricoleurs in a computer-assisted classroom. In C. G. Panetta (Ed.), *Contrastive rhetoric theory revisited and redefined* (pp. 65–74). Mahwah, NJ: Lawrence Erlbaum.

Scollon, R. (1997). Contrastive rhetoric, contrastive poetics, or perhaps something else? *TESOL Quarterly, 31,* 352–363.

Selinker, L. (1972). Interlanguage. *International Review of Applied Linguistics (IRAL), 10,* 209–231.

Soter, A. (2001). Straddling three worlds. In D. Belcher & U. Connor (Eds.), *Reflections on multiliterate lives* (pp. 74–78). Clevedon, England: Multilingual Matters.

Spack, R. (1997). The rhetorical construction of multilingual students. *TESOL Quarterly, 31,* 765–774.

Swales, J. M. (1990). *Genre analysis: English in academic and research settings.* New York: Cambridge University Press.

Tannen, D. (1985). Cross-cultural communication. In T. A. Van Dijk (Ed.), *Handbook of discourse analysis* (pp. 203–216). New York: Academic Press.

Tirkkonen-Condit, S. (1996). Explicitness vs. implicitness of argumentation: An intercultural comparison. *Multilingua, 15,* 274–275.

Upton, T., & Connor, U. (2001). Using computerized corpus analysis to investigate the textlinguistic discourse moves of a genre. *English for Specific Purposes, 20,* 313–329.

Ventola, E., & Mauranen, A. (1991). Non-native writing and native revisiting of scientific articles. In E. Ventola (Ed.), *Functional and systematic linguistics* (pp. 457–492). Berlin: Mouton de Gruyter.

Woolever, K. R. (2001). Doing global business in the information age: Rhetorical contrasts in the business and technical professions. In C. G. Panetta (Ed.), *Contrastive rhetoric theory revisited and redefined* (pp. 47–64). Mahwah, NJ: Lawrence Erlbaum.

Yoshimura, T. (2001). *Formal instruction of rhetorical patterns and the effectiveness of using L1 in argumentative writing in an EFL setting.* Unpublished doctoral dissertation, Temple University, Japan.

Ypsilandis, G. S. (1994). Logomachia: Pragmatic failure in letters of application. In E. Douka-Kasitoglu (Ed.), *Logomachia: Forms of opposition in English language/literature* (pp. 331–346). Thessaloniki, Greece: Hellenic Association for the Study of English.

Zamel, V. (1997). Toward a model of transculturation. *TESOL Quarterly, 31,* 341–352.

Appendix A: Translation of a French-language "dissertation," as it appeared in Mbaye (2001)

Topic: Should one agree to baptism of offspring when personal convictions are against this tradition?

Convenience baptism

In every society, clashes of values are usual, since these values are often not shared by all the members of the society. The case in point is representative of this situation while highlighting another problem. The question at hand is tantamount to deciding whether it is preferable to act according to one's own principles, or whether, under given circumstances, it is better to repress one's standards, and sacrifice to a certain social conformism. This question is very important, because in this case, the potential victims of ostracism are innocent third parties, and our children, in this adult debate! This problem is an ethical one, for the freedom of worship is guaranteed by the law. Yet one cannot force others to be open minded toward our choices, and our children may well suffer from the exercise of our agnostic beliefs, by becoming laughing stocks at school and in the neighborhood, for that matter. Shouldn't we in this case compromise our convictions as the saying goes, in order to preserve appearances?

David Hume's moral philosophy may offer guidelines in this situation. For him, reason alone cannot guide our moral decisions, for even if it can be of help in making reasoned decisions, it does not establish our goals, which are essentially dependent on feelings. The only standard in terms of morals is the approval or disapproval of those around us. Consequently, any moral sense does not make sense unless it refers to a culture. This is why moral judgment can differ considerably from epoch to epoch or culture to culture. However, there are common points: the love for our children is an example. It is clear that in such a case, the love for one's children and the wish for them not to be ostracized should inspire a prudent conformism in us. For Hume, belonging to a community is an important value, and if one has to camouflage one's religious convictions to live up to the community, it is not a problem, for nothing in our deepest convictions can be affected by this attitude. We may, by the way, suspect that many in the community are already acting in this way.

Nonetheless, such a solution contains some part of hypocrisy. Being truthful to oneself and living one's own convictions are principles dear to us. Hasn't Nietzsche shown that conformism is the cause of the stifling moral of the herd? Is it good to transmit to one's children values of duplicity and of submission to the moral order of the majority? By acting in this way, are we condemning them to mediocrity, fear, and self-repression? Individualism is at the origin of all great inventions. It reinforces character and allows each to express their intrinsic will of power. Individualism substitutes hypocrisy for frankness and full self-affirmation. It develops autonomy, although this latter involves suffering. Under these particular circumstances, such a choice implies imposing something to one's children, but after all, isn't this what all parents do?

Put in such a situation, we realize that morals are social in character. To get one's children baptized is required from a good Catholic. Catholics will tend to believe that those who don't baptize children are ignorant or mean: only malevolent people may deprive their children of salvation. This is at least how the logic of the believer goes. But, as Nietzsche pointed out, it is fortunate that believers are not as strict as religion would demand, and cheat occasionally. In this way religious dissidence will be accepted by some of them.

It seems then that the best choice, the most honest, and also the most affirmative consists in defying public opinion and affirming one's difference. One however needs to be aware that such a choice implies courage and constant vigilance, so as to face up to the frustrations that may affect the family, and particularly the children. One also will have to depend on the more tolerant people in the hope that mentalities will change gradually.

10 Reading and writing relations: Second language perspectives on research and practice

William Grabe

In the past two decades, the role of reading-writing relationships has been a topic of increasing interest to both reading and writing specialists. Researchers from a variety of fields (e.g., education, composition, reading, learning psychology, and applied linguistics) have become interested in the ways that reading and writing might reinforce or accelerate the learning of content, the development of literacy skills, and the acquisition of language abilities. Interaction between reading and writing is thus a topic of concern in the academy as it relates to students studying in their first language (L1) as well as students studying in their second language (L2). Writing teachers in particular need to understand what has been learned through a variety of research studies on a range of topics related to the multiple ways in which reading and writing interconnect so that these teachers can develop a broad-based view to help them guide student learning.

In L1 contexts, a number of seminal studies on reading-writing relations appeared in the 1980s. In these studies, researchers examined correlations between learners' reading and writing abilities, the roles of author and audience in reading and writing contexts, and the ways in which students improve their learning by reading and writing together. By 1990, there was a solid body of research on these topics in L1 contexts that allowed researchers to ask more probing questions and extend the earlier work, and this range of research has continued into this century. Cumulative insights from this body of research have contributed to helping teachers find a variety of ways to exploit reading and writing connections in the composition classroom.

In L2 contexts, the study of reading-writing relationships has evolved more slowly. Through much of the 1980s, L2 researchers assumed that most L1 findings would apply to L2 learning contexts, with suitable modifications. At the same time, however, L2 researchers pointed out that cultural and language differences among L2 students create complexities that are not be accounted for by L1 research, including at least the following:

1. Differing senses of audience and author

242

2. Differing preferences for organizing texts
3. Differing ways to use texts as learning resources
4. Differing cultural socializations and belief systems
5. Differing functional uses for writing (Leki, 1991; Silva, Leki, & Carson, 1997)

In addition, L2 learning itself, involving knowledge resources from two languages, creates both problems and strengths for L2 learners engaged in writing from texts. These issues have led to a growing body of work on L2 learners, particularly since the 1990s. Two important reviews of reading-writing relations by Carson (1990, 1993) summarize much of the relevant research for L2 contexts up until the early 1990s. A recent collection of papers (Belcher & Hirvela, 2001) provides numerous individual perspectives on the topic.

This chapter provides an orientation to the earlier research as well as an outline of further developments from the 1990s onward, focusing on the type of information most critical for teachers to know. It also explores implications of this research for instructional practices and concludes by suggesting future directions for both research and instruction. For the most part, this chapter addresses post-secondary contexts because teachers in elementary and secondary settings often have considerable control over real academic tasks and reading-writing demands. However, much of what is reported on and interpreted in this chapter is applicable to many contexts other than university settings.

Before examining reading-writing relations in greater detail, however, I should comment on the relative roles of reading and writing as seen separately in research on reading-writing relations. Reading-writing relationships is an area that has more typically focused on the writing side of the relationship, both historically and currently. That is, this relationship is most commonly discussed in terms of the impact of reading on writing, the uses of readings to help students carry out writing tasks, and the ways in which student learning from texts is reflected in writing tasks. It is less common to assume that students, and most other people, write in order to read, though this is possible and occurs from time to time (cf. Zamel, 1992). Reading researchers also generally assume that students learn information from texts and, aside from summary writing, do not generally require extended writing from students in order for them to demonstrate this learning. The reverse position – that students learn content information from writing without involving the reading of text materials – is less easily accepted. Certainly, one of the most common tasks in school and academic settings is to read texts and then use that information for writing purposes. These trends highlight the real interest among writing researchers in issues of reading-writing relations; writing researchers who consider academic writing have to address these relations more directly in both theory and practice than do most reading researchers. In line with these trends, the present chapter places greater emphasis on writing issues associated with reading-writing relations.

Theories of reading, writing, and reading-writing relations

The study of reading-writing relations must be grounded in theories of reading and writing that can stand independently. Reading-writing relations should then build on these theories and offer a framework that explains the ways in which reading and writing together enhance language, literacy, and content learning. Such a framework can offer teachers a richer understanding of how to assemble a course designed to promote literacy and language skills.

The ability to read is typically assumed in many discussions of reading-writing relations. However, even in L1 settings, limited reading abilities sometimes make it difficult for students to carry out tasks that combine reading and writing. It is not possible to outline here a theory of reading that would provide all the background assumptions relevant to students' learning how to read and write in combination. However, some comments on L2 reading should be highlighted to point out the distinct L2 contexts in which L2 students engage in reading and writing together. In particular, L2 readers may have difficulties writing from textual sources simply because of weaker language skills and reading comprehension abilities, and these possible limitations need to be taken into account when students are asked to use text resources for writing tasks. Thus, it is not enough to apply L1 research about reading (and writing) to L2 contexts (Grabe, 2000; Grabe & Stoller, 2002; Silva et al., 1997; Urquhart & Weir, 1998).

A theory of L2 writing, in addition, must account for students' abilities across a range of tasks and writing contexts. Consideration needs to be given to the roles of language knowledge and background knowledge, cognitive processing, motivation, social context factors, and learning opportunities (Grabe, 2001; Grabe & Kaplan, 1997). The processing and problem-solving components of writing development can make intense demands on students, particularly when students are reading difficult L2 texts in order to collect or glean new information for their writing. In many reading-writing tasks, students are forced to make a number of complex decisions. Students need to decide the following:

1. How much information should be taken from the text; which information should be taken
2. How the information taken will fit with task and writer goals

3. How accurately the information should be represented when going from text source to student writing
4. What formal mechanisms should be used for transforming or using the textual information

All of these choices call for both writing skills and reading skills. As a final complexity, writing from multiple texts requires even more demanding planning, processing, and revising. The interpretation of task demands and the integration of textual information force critical decision making that requires much practice and consistent efforts to "traverse the topical landscape" from multiple directions (McGinley & Tierney, 1989). Simply put, students need a lot of practice with these types of tasks.

Reading and writing together: L1 research

Reading-writing relations have been a topic of L1 research for the past two decades (Tierney & Shanahan, 1991), and some familiarity with L1 findings can help L2 teachers develop greater awareness of the challenges that all learners face in accomplishing their reading and writing goals. Early work in the 1980s pointed out the importance of learning from reading and from writing, though demonstrating learning from writing has been somewhat harder to verify. This early research base has also argued that reading and writing together can lead to effective learning, though again the research studies are relatively few (cf. Perfetti, Britt, & Georgi, 1995; Tierney et al., 1989).

A set of articles by Shanahan and Tierney (1990; Shanahan, 1990; Tierney & Shanahan, 1991) summarize the 1980s decade of work and highlights three fundamental directions in L1 research on reading-writing relations: (1) shared processing and knowledge resources in reading and writing, (2) reading and writing as interaction, and (3) reading and writing to learn content. First, the goal of "shared processing" examines the overlap of processing skills. Students are tested in various reading abilities and writing abilities, and then they are compared on these abilities. Study results have generally shown that reading and writing abilities correlate between .50 and .70 (25% to 50% overlap). This line of research has demonstrated a moderate overlap in abilities; at the same time, it reveals considerable room for differences between reading and writing. Second, "reading and writing as interaction" highlights the notion of dialogue at a distance through the medium of the written text. Research studies have shown that envisioning an audience can improve writing, and to a lesser extent, considering the author assists critical reading (Tierney & Shanahan, 1991). Third, "learning content from reading and writing together" has been less thoroughly demonstrated, though early work by Langer and Applebee (1987) made persuasive arguments about such a connection (see also Tierney et al., 1989).

The L1 work on reading-writing relationships has continued under two major organizing issues: (1) reading to write, and (2) writing to learn from multiple texts. This organizing frame is intended to serve as a guideline only, since there is much overlap across these categories. In the area of *reading to write*, three issues play major roles: (1) the continuing observation that better readers tend to be better writers across a range of writing tasks; (2) the argument that recognizing and using the organization framework of the text leads to better writing; and (3) the argument that extensive exposure to print can lead to better writing over time. On the first topic, McGinley (1992) has demonstrated that better readers are, in general, better able to collect, organize, and connect information in their writing. On the second topic, studies have shown that the use of relevant models of task assignments leads to better writing (Charney & Carlson, 1995; Smagorinsky, 1992; Stolarek, 1994). On the third topic, there is now a range of evidence that extensive reading (over a long period of time) leads indirectly to better writing (Elley, 1991; Wagner & Stanovich, 1996).

Work on *writing from multiple texts* also suggests two interesting lines of research: (1) the cognitive processing required for such tasks (and the resultant learning), and (2) the interaction of reading and writing as tasks are carried out. Recent research on reading-writing interactions has demonstrated that students use the first reading to form a framework for summarizing when working with multiple texts, and they add relatively few main ideas after the second text (Gradwohl-Nash, Schumacher, & Carlson, 1993; Perfetti, Britt, & Georgi, 1995). Rouet et al. (1997) have demonstrated that expert readers in a discipline integrate and use multiple texts in very different ways from more novice students when composing an argument. A number of studies have reported that work with multiple texts forces students to become more flexible in their interpretation of information presented (McCarthy-Young & Leinhardt, 1998; Stahl et al., 1996).

Reading and writing together: L2 research

Second language research on reading-writing relations can be traced back to the 1980s, though this research tends to be tied to very specific issues, as is noted below. These issues remain important concerns for understanding reading-writing relations today, though more-recent studies have expanded that range considerably. Two early topics of research involved the Interdependence Hypothesis (or the Common Underlying

Proficiency Hypothesis), a theory proposing literacy transfer from the L1 to the L2, and the Language Threshold Hypothesis, a theory arguing against supportive transfer until a certain (variable) level of L2 proficiency is attained. Two further topics have also been sources of continued discussions. One is the argument that extensive reading directly improves writing abilities (Krashen, 1984, 1993). The second involves the role of directionality between reading and writing. (Is it better to go from reading to writing or from writing to reading for the most effective instruction?) Together, these four issues have dominated discussions of L2 reading-writing relations in the 1980s and 1990s, and they are explored in a number of sources (Campbell, 1990; Carson, 1990, 1993; Ferris & Hedgcock, 1998).

The Interdependence Hypothesis

The Interdependence Hypothesis, the notion that there is an underlying common proficiency across languages, was first proposed by Cummins (1979, 1981) and has been influential for more than two decades. The notion is actually quite complex since Cummins also suggested that students need a reasonable L2 proficiency to allow transfer of common literacy abilities. Moreover, while it is typically assumed that this hypothesis supports L1 literacy development that then transfers, there is also evidence that L2 literacy abilities can transfer back to a later developing L1 literacy (Wagner, 1998). Overall, there appears to be considerable evidence that certain types of literacy skills transfer to support L2 literacy development. For the most part, these abilities relate more to reading than to writing (see, e.g., Durgunoglu & Verhoeven, 1998), though contrastive rhetoric research is built on the assumption of L1 transfer in writing (e.g., Connor, 1996), and some of the L2 writers reporting on their case histories in the chapter by Silva et al. (Chapter 4 this volume) discuss this phenomenon. Research on writing that would support the Interdependence Hypothesis typically involves similarities in writing processes and strategies based on small groups of students engaged in think-aloud tasks, and a number of studies support this view (see Grabe & Kaplan, 1996).

At the same time, for both L2 reading and L2 writing, there are conflicting research results that limit the claims of the Interdependence Hypothesis. Carson et al. (1990), for example, found conflicting patterns of L1 influences on L2 performance. In addition, both Silva (1993) and Raimes (1987) have argued that certain aspects of L2 writing should not be directly attributable to L1 writing abilities. A reasonable position to adopt is that transfer is an important aspect of L2 literacy development, but it is not always clear which aspects of literacy abilities transfer readily, nor do we know which abilities do not transfer readily. This area of research is still open to much more exploration.

The Language Threshold Hypothesis

The Language Threshold Hypothesis has provided one of the strongest arguments that transfer is not the whole story for L2 literacy development and is probably not even the major influence on L2 literacy development. In its early formulation, this hypothesis argued that students must develop a reasonable L2 language proficiency before they will transfer L1 reading processes and strategies. Alderson (1984) formulated the issue for L2 reading in the form of a basic question: Is L2 reading more dependent on L2 proficiency or L1 reading skills?

In the 1990s, cumulative research evidence has persuasively supported the Language Threshold Hypothesis. Beginning with a study by Carrell (1991), a number of studies have converged across different student populations, tasks, texts, and general proficiency levels to show that L2 proficiency is a far more powerful predictor of student reading performance up to a level of reasonable L2 proficiency (Bernhardt & Kamil, 1995; Bossers, 1992; Lee & Schallert, 1997). Generally, L2 proficiency tends to account for 30% to 50% of the variance in L2 reading comprehension measures, while L1 reading often accounts for less than 20% of the shared variance. So, one could say that the relationship between L2 proficiency and L2 reading abilities is about twice as strong as the relationship between L1 reading abilities and L2 reading abilities. It is also important to note that the concept of a language threshold is a variable one. L2 researchers do not assume that there are specific structures or vocabulary that represent a fixed threshold for all settings and learners, or that a language threshold is suddenly passed, never again to be an obstacle to understanding.

In the field of L2 writing, there is less evidence of an L2 language threshold, though two studies provide persuasive support to the reading research. In one study, Johns and Mayes (1990) demonstrated that students with better L2 language proficiency wrote better summaries. In another, Sasaki and Hirose (1996) found that L2 language proficiency accounted for 52% of the variance with an L2 writing task, while L1 writing abilities accounted for 18% of the shared variance. Overall, it is fair to say that L2 language proficiency is a crucial element of L2 literacy abilities. Moreover, this language proficiency factor is central to L2 reading-writing relations.

The Extensive Reading Hypothesis

The Extensive Reading Hypothesis and its impact on L2 writing abilities is an area that continues to generate interesting research, arguing that considerable extensive reading, over time, will lead to better writing abilities. This argument was proposed early in the 1980s by Krashen

(1984), reiterated in Krashen (1993), and supported by further research (see Elley, 1991, 1996; cf. Flahive & Bailey, 1993). In parallel with the L2 perspectives, L1-based research on exposure to print has argued that extensive reading leads to language knowledge that supports better writing abilities. For example, research has shown that extensive reading leads to better vocabulary knowledge, better verbal fluency, better syntactic knowledge, better semantic memory, better metalinguistic awareness, and broader knowledge of the world (see Stanovich et al., 1996; Wagner & Stanovich, 1996). Based on a decade of persuasive empirical studies, Stanovich and his colleagues have argued that students who have much greater exposure to print over years develop a range of literacy-related skills and abilities. A major implication for reading and writing relations, for both L1 and L2 contexts, is that connections between reading and writing may be variable, but they can be interconnected more efficiently through extensive reading in combination with consistent writing practice.

An L2 study from Hong Kong adds further support to the argument that extensive reading contributes to better writing abilities. Tsang (1996) reported on a treatment study involving 144 Hong Kong secondary school students at four grade levels. Three groups at each grade level received 24 weeks of instruction: Group one received regular instruction plus math instruction as a control group; group two received regular instruction plus frequent writing practice; group three received regular instruction plus extensive reading. At the end of the six-month period, the group (at each grade level) with extensive reading wrote significantly better essays on a post-treatment task. The extensive reading group also learned significantly more content information. With further replications of studies such as this one, it would be possible to make claims about the impact of extensive reading on literacy development equally as strong as those that can now be made for the Language Threshold Hypothesis.

The directionality issue

Much of the discussion of L2 reading and writing research does not specifically address reading-writing relations, at least not in the ways that are common in L1 research (with the exception of the influence of exposure to print on writing). One early research area that drew more specifically on issues of reading-writing relations examined directionality; that is, either (1) reading improves writing, or (2) writing improves reading, or (3) reading and writing improve each other (bidirectionality), or (4) there is no direct relationship (no directionality). Current research seems to have reached a consensus on this issue: Without reviewing the details of this discussion, most researchers see reading-writing relations as mutually supportive for literacy development and content learning (Carson, 1990; Ferris & Hedgcock, 1998).

Writing from multiple texts and writing to learn

The L1 issues that have attracted the most interest in the past decade – reading and writing to learn content and writing from multiple source texts – have received much less attention to date in L2 contexts. The exception to this gap in L2 research is in the growing area of EAP (English for academic purposes) writing research. The best examples of this newly emerging emphasis in L2 settings are Carson and Leki's (1993) *Reading in the Composition Classroom*, the first L2 volume devoted to reading-writing relations, and the more recent Belcher and Hirvela (2001) volume (see also Campbell, 1990; Carson, 1990; Hirvela, 2001; Johns & Mayes, 1990).

In Carson and Leki's book, Flahive and Bailey (1993), for example, explored reading and writing correlations and found that the relationships are only modest, accounting for 12% of variance among measures used (leaving almost 90% of the relationship unexplained). They noted that L2 students may be much more variable in their reading and writing abilities; one cannot assume that a good reader is a good writer, and vice versa (cf. 25%–50% shared variance in L1 research studies). In another study, Basham, Ray, and Whalley (1993) found that students sometimes interpret texts from their own L1 cultural frameworks. Drawing on a small sample, they argued that their Chinese students studied the text closely and followed the text information very carefully; Latino students used the reading as a jumping-off point for their own personal experiences on the topic; and Native American students developed a personal orientation to the information in the text. These studies deserve to be replicated to determine the validity and the strength of their conclusions.

A key concern for teachers in academic environments relates to teaching reading and writing skills together. In a chapter on this topic, Johns (1993) makes a very strong argument for centering EAP literacy development on reading-writing relations. Surveys by faculty and students in EAP contexts demonstrate that teaching advanced students to write from text resources is essential for academic success. Johns's chapter highlights the need to examine disciplinary classes in universities and determine the most genuine academic tasks (via faculty surveys, classroom ethnographies), deconstruct tasks assigned to students for their reading and writing demands (analyze prompts, develop strategies), and compile resources that will help students complete these reading and writing tasks successfully (collect models and analyze them, use peer reviews, work with support groups). This approach is developed much more extensively in Johns (1997).

More recently, Carson (2001) provides an extensive description of the reading and writing tasks required in six different college courses at both the undergraduate and graduate levels. Her findings lead her to conclude that "an increased emphasis on reading and writing related to task preparation, not just production, [seems to be] in order" (Carson, 2001, p. 81), an important insight for teachers.

Needs analyses for reading-writing relationships in EAP settings

A final topic of concern for L2 reading-writing relations, and particularly for EAP, involves surveying L2 student perceptions, their own ESL classes, university content classes, and writing expectations in university EAP settings to understand the reading and writing demands placed on L2 students. This approach takes into account EAP literacy environments, the range of tasks that L2 students need to perform, and the need for both students and faculty to become more aware of L1–L2 differences. It should also lead to a rethinking and refinement of EAP instruction so that reading and writing are combined to reflect authentic demands.

Leki and Carson (1994) used student surveys to explore student expectations for EAP performance in university settings. They found that students expected more challenging literacy tasks, a wider range of tasks, tasks that combined reading and writing abilities, and assistance with deconstructing tasks and writing models. A second study by Leki and Carson (1997) argued strongly that L2 students need more practice with tasks that involve reader-responsible writing – that is, writing from texts in which the content is considered an important part of evaluation.

Both of the Leki and Carson studies complement recent work on analyzing EAP settings from the perspectives of language minority students in U.S. universities and deriving appropriate instructional approaches. Thus, Johns (1993, 1997) highlights many of the same points noted by Leki and Carson, stressing the need to determine genuine tasks for students to practice, promoting careful analyses of task prompts, examining models of successful task performance, and providing much practice and assistance with texts and genres that students will need to work with (cf. Johns, Chapter 8 this volume; and Spack, 1998). Carson (2000) offers a similar translation-to-practice through an extensive task-based EAP curriculum. In both cases, instruction is centered around the reading and writing of many texts that fit university expectations. Practical implications of reading and writing interactions have also been a long-standing concern of Swales (1990, 1998) as he expands from an ESP perspective into advanced EAP needs of L2 students who are engaged in graduate-level work. It should also be noted that Zamel (1992) provides a unique practical perspective on L2 reading and writing relations, adopting the position that these relations can lead to effective learning when students begin from writing tasks rather than from the reading of texts.

Further research issues

Two additional topics not typically addressed from a reading-writing perspective represent important areas for future research and synthesis. First, summarizing has been relatively neglected as a research area as applied to reading to write, writing to learn, and writing from multiple source texts. Johns and Mayes (1990) offer one important L2 study in this area, but many more are needed. Perhaps there is a perception among L2 researchers that summarization is no longer an appropriate issue to examine in detail. However, reading-writing relations in EAP contexts strongly suggest that summarization is a major issue for literacy development and content learning. The same can be said for synthesis writing (Spivey, 1990; Spivey & King, 1989), a topic that is virtually unexplored in L2 contexts.

Second is the role of cross-cultural expectations and assumptions for reading comprehension and writing performance. Particularly for L2 writing, the notion of contrastive rhetoric needs to be incorporated more fully into discussions of reading-writing relations. The fundamental claim of contrastive rhetoric is that L2 writing is influenced by L1 discourse preferences for organizing information in texts (Connor, 1996, Chapter 9 this volume; Grabe & Kaplan, 1996). However, contrastive rhetoric issues have not been associated with specific research on reading to write, writing to learn, or writing from multiple source texts. Over the past decade, it has been associated more with genre differences and genre expectations in differing disciplinary and professional writing contexts (for a recent review, see Hyland, 2002). These topics provide a natural bridge to reading-writing relations in advanced EAP contexts (e.g., Johns, 1997; Swales 1990, 1998). Contrastive rhetoric is also easily associated with the role of genre knowledge in writing, though less so for reading implications (see Johns, Chapter 8 this volume). The study of genre variation and its implications for writing offer additional major connections with reading-writing relations.

Reading-writing relations in L2 contexts are quickly becoming an important subfield for L2 writing and for EAP instruction in particular. There are many issues that deserve further exploration and many research questions that need to be addressed. The following list suggests some of these L2 issues that merit more attention:

1. A current synthesis of research findings on transfer
2. A detailed examination of the exposure to print argument
3. A greater exploration of reading and writing to learn
4. An expanded exploration of writing from multiple source texts
5. A reexamination of summarization from a reading-writing perspective
6. A synthesis of reading-writing relations with contrastive rhetoric issues
7. A stronger linkage of reading-writing relations with research on academic genre knowledge and its uses in academic writing
8. A detailed examination of reading-writing relations and its relation to academic success in various EAP contexts

These issues provide a partial list of opportunities for researchers as well as for teachers who might wish to engage in action research. One of the final research issues that remains involves ways to translate theory to practice in contexts that emphasize reading-writing relations so that pedagogical decisions can be derived from empirical findings.

Reading-writing instruction in L2 settings

From theory to practice

Reading-writing relations have taken on greater importance with the recognition that students must be prepared to engage in academically appropriate tasks and do so successfully. Research exploring academic settings and tasks has demonstrated that students are commonly asked to combine reading and writing activities. While these writing activities connected to reading are not universal across academic contexts or disciplines, they are sufficiently general to be a major component of advanced EAP curricula. Thus, apart from any intrinsic value that derives from literacy development through reading and writing interactions, there is a documented need for teaching specific instructional genres (e.g., summarizing, writing a response to a reading) keyed to a variety of academic contexts.

The development of students' language and literacy skills for academic success is not an easy task in itself. Student success requires a combination of factors: (1) extensive practice in the tasks that reflect literacy demands in disciplinary courses, (2) appropriate and effective guidance and support to carry out these tasks successfully, (3) student engagement in the learning process, (4) focused discussions around academic reading and writing tasks, and (5) critical reflection on the processes and tasks involved in language and content learning. A number of curricular approaches and instructional practices have been proposed and implemented for these purposes. The next two sections briefly review several of these options.

Curricular issues in L2 reading-writing development

Curricula for language and literacy learning require, at a minimum, a needs analysis and a coherent framework for meeting student needs. A needs analysis should identify student and institutional goals; academic task demands that represent an endpoint to instruction; tasks, texts, and topics that should be included in instruction; time and resources needed to ensure effective instruction; and appropriate means to assess effectiveness of learning and make adjustments as needed. At the level of curricular frameworks, four general options exist for implementing EAP instruction: (1) a language-emphasis program, focusing on specific language skills (generally disconnected from specific EAP needs analysis); (2) a program with a reading-and-writing emphasis (generally taught as separate courses with little coordination); (3) content-based instruction (emphasizing EAP contexts); and (4) task-based instruction (again emphasizing EAP contexts). Other possible options can be listed as variants under one of these four frameworks. The two frameworks that offer the best opportunities to incorporate reading and writing within realistic academic demands are content-based instruction and task-based instruction. In both cases, there are possibilities to build the foundational skills for reading and writing noted at the outset of this chapter and also to develop literacy abilities to advanced levels in a coherent curriculum, reflecting realistic academic expectations.

Content-based instruction can be implemented in many different ways (and with varying levels of success). When set up well in response to student needs and institutional goals, it offers an effective way to provide a coherent set of reading and writing experiences, and it can provide much practice in the specific literacy tasks expected in advanced academic settings. Content-based instruction, whether set up as thematic units or in an adjunct configuration, builds student motivation, offers a degree of student autonomy, allows for group planning and project work, and provides opportunities for many realistic reading-writing tasks. Frameworks for theme-based instruction that can support reading-writing interaction are presented in Johns (1997) and Snow and Brinton (1997). Kasper (2000) also presents chapters dealing with the theory and practice of providing college-level content-based instruction.

Much like content-based learning, task-based learning operates under various guises. The approach considered here assumes advanced academic contexts and tasks that work well to support reading-writing integration. Many discussions of task-based learning focus on lower levels of language learning and do not propose intensive reading-writing interactions for advanced academic purposes (see Skehan 1998a, 1998b). However, the approach proposed by Carson (2000) strongly emphasizes reading and writing tasks developed for students in transition to academic work in university settings. She notes the following as a set of goals for EAP task-based instruction:

1. Establish tasks that support real academic learning goals.
2. Cycle across fluency, accuracy, and complexity.
3. Vary familiar and unfamiliar tasks, more formal and less formal language.
4. Focus on meaning, form-control, and form restructuring.
5. Use tasks that reflect real-world language uses.

There are many options for organizing an EAP curriculum that will emphasize reading-writing relations, learning from texts and writing tasks, and working from multiple text resources. Even in curricula that are less innovative or focused less directly on academic task demands, numerous tasks and activities can prepare students for academic demands through reading and writing interactions. A number of these tasks are fairly traditional (e.g., summaries, writing responses, in-class essay writing, report writing), but they hold up well in developing skills needed for academic success; others are somewhat more innovative and directly responsive to academic demands and text-responsible writing (Hale et al., 1996; Johns, 1997).

Instructional practices in L2 contexts

Any discussion of important instructional tasks and activities to promote reading-writing relations can result in a catalogue of hundreds of ideas for writing instruction (cf. Ferris & Hedgcock, 1998; Grabe & Kaplan, 1996; Grabe & Stoller, 2002; Reid, 1993; White, 1995). Rather than repeat readily available techniques for instruction, this final section will offer ten general guidelines for instruction. This list is not intended to be comprehensive or universally applicable; rather, it suggests a starting point for building reading and writing foundations for academic success.

1. Reading and writing instruction should *begin from task analyses.* This perspective is the complement to creating effective prompts for writing (see Reid & Kroll, 1995). Both teachers and students need to collect tasks used in various courses and contexts and then analyze task expectations, plans for completing the tasks, and critical evaluations of what would be seen as an effective performance (and why).

2. Students need to *practice writing many types of relevant genres and tasks* (e.g., instructional genres: summaries, timed essay-exam writing, literature reviews, reading responses, research reports). The actual tasks and genres can reflect assignments in disciplinary courses or they can promote foundational skills for more advanced task demands. Important skills, instructional genres, and realistic tasks need to be recycled regularly so that students build effective and increasingly more complex problem-solving routines. Students need extensive practice – in particular, in writing from text resources if they are to develop this ability.

3. Students need to *develop rhetorical stances to tasks and texts* that will build reading-writing relations. Taking a rhetorical stance as a reader requires analyzing texts in at least the following ways:
   • Adopting critical perspectives on text resources
   • Becoming aware of author and textual choices for conveying information
   • Recognizing how a writer is shaping the text through linguistic choices to establish a position
   • Reflecting on the stances and perspectives taken in their own writing and connecting these positions to task expectations in appropriate ways

4. Students need to *develop an awareness of text structure* itself. They have to understand how written discourse is organized to communicate within genre and task expectations. They should be aware of the ways that coherence is signaled in texts, the ways that ideas are sequenced and linked effectively, the ways that larger units of information are combined to achieve the overall task goal, and the ways that texts open and end. Students also need to develop an awareness of how the language itself serves important communicative and writer goals; rhetorical goals and informational goals are not completely separable.

5. Helping students *become strategic readers and strategic writers* should be a major goal for any EAP curriculum. Accomplishing this goal requires extended attention to strategic processing and continual student awareness of planning, monitoring, and repairing. Student attention and awareness need to be built steadily and consistently by learning, modeling, and using many types of strategies: strategies for planning, for learning information, for monitoring comprehension and writing, for re-evaluating goals and plans, and for repairing and revising.

6. Helping students to collect and use *feedback from peers and teachers* is an essential component of any curriculum focusing on reading

and writing. There are many discussions of writing feedback, but the concepts also apply to reading comprehension and critical reading tasks. Both aspects need to be incorporated in EAP instruction.

7. Teaching students to *collect and interpret data* on interesting issues and topics may seem a bit unusual as an instructional priority, but in EAP settings there are many contexts in which simple data collection through surveys, interviews, observations, and peer canvassing provides resources to organize information, compare information to textual sources, and provide new information for writing tasks. In a curriculum that emphasizes reading-writing interactions, data collection and analysis provide important practice for analyzing information, critiquing content from texts, and planning ways to present information and make persuasive arguments.

8. A fundamental goal for an EAP curriculum should be to *use textual resources appropriately in writing tasks*. Aside from formatting, quoting, and plagiarism issues that are commonly noted in discussions of writing from resources, other important skills are needed for determining the strength of arguments, inferring the author's position, incorporating strong examples and illustrations, making effective links between ideas across texts, and presenting critical comparisons of conflicting information. The development of these abilities requires a considerable commitment to writing from texts. Part of the difficulties that students have with these skills is that they are not asked to practice them on a regular basis. Without consistent efforts to work out effective plans for writing from texts, they cannot be expected to achieve success regularly. However, being able to write effectively from texts is a major expectation in many academic settings.

9. An important early step for students to take in learning to work from texts is being able to *summarize main ideas* from a text and *synthesize main information* across two or more texts. These skills can be developed initially from fairly simple tasks and can be practiced enough times in varying settings to allow for the development of effective practices and problem-solving routines. They allow for reasonably straightforward feedback and support, and these skills are essential aspects of larger tasks requiring writing from text resources.

10. Finally, any reading and writing curriculum will need to *incorporate effective ongoing assessment practices* for reading and writing integration. This goal can be carried out partly through continual feedback on reading and writing tasks as well as discussion about

texts and writing tasks. Students also need more formal feedback mechanisms that will reflect the expectations of academic settings. Effective assessment can be provided by means of writing portfolios, timed essay writing that is graded (and then discussed), and larger projects (posters, reports, term papers, etc.) in which formal feedback mechanisms are used at stages along the way. Formal feedback approaches are often seen as punitive or discriminating, but they are serious components of the academic world that students will enter. Students are done a disservice if they are not fully aware of how their reading and writing abilities will be assessed in future academic settings. Formal feedback and assessment practices also provide exceptionally good opportunities for later discussions around texts and tasks (see Ferris, Chapter 5 this volume).

Conclusion

Many topics, research studies, and instructional implications could be addressed in a chapter on reading-writing relations, but the key to any discussion of reading-writing relations is to establish linkages across the many issues that drive research in reading, writing, and reading-writing interactions. These three areas form a complex network of information, theories, positions taken and arguments made, and collectively they provide a large body of curricular and instructional implications. In particular, since the focus of much student writing involves writing from text resources, informed decision making by teachers requires a thorough understanding of the instructional implications provided by the accumulation of research findings.

Attempts to teach students to write from texts is complex. Teachers and researchers must recognize that many layers of knowledge and skills are being combined in these tasks. Language knowledge, topical knowledge, and background knowledge are being called on; complex processing abilities are expected; L1/L2 differences will affect planning and production; individual differences, motivations, and social contexts will shape student performances; and the accumulation of experiences from engaging in such tasks is critical for successful performance.

In the final analysis, the importance of reading-writing relations depends on the varying goals of students. In academic settings, the literacy demands made in a range of real academic contexts should drive instructional planning. That can best be accomplished when teachers are aware of many of the issues that have been presented and reviewed in this chapter.

References

Alderson, J. C. (1984). Reading in a foreign language: A reading problem or a language problem? In J. C. Alderson & A. H. Urquhart (Eds.), *Reading in a foreign language* (pp. 1–24). New York: Longman.

Basham, C., Ray, R., & Whalley, E. (1993). Cross-cultural perspectives on task representation in reading to write. In J. Carson & I. Leki (Eds.), *Reading in the composition classroom* (pp. 299–314). New York: Newbury House.

Belcher, D., & Hirvela, A. (Eds.). (2001). *Linking literacies: Perspectives on L2 reading-writing connections*. Ann Arbor: University of Michigan Press.

Bernhardt, E., & Kamil, M. (1995). Interpreting relationships between L1 and L2 reading: Consolidating the linguistic threshold and the linguistic interdependence hypotheses. *Applied Linguistics, 16*, 15–34.

Bossers, B. (1992). *Reading in two languages: A study of reading comprehension in Dutch as a second language and in Turkish as a first language*. Rotterdam: Drukkerij Van Driel.

Campbell, C. (1990). Writing with others' words: Using background reading text in academic compositions. In B. Kroll (Ed.), *Second language writing: Research insights for the classroom* (pp. 211–230). New York: Cambridge University Press.

Carrell, P. (1991). Second language reading: Reading ability or language proficiency? *Applied Linguistics, 12*, 159–179.

Carson, J. (1990). Reading-writing connections: Toward a description for second language learners. In B. Kroll (Ed.), *Second language writing: Research insights for the classroom* (pp. 88–107). New York: Cambridge University Press.

Carson, J. (1993). Reading for writing: Cognitive perspectives. In J. Carson & I. Leki (Eds.), *Reading in the composition classroom* (pp. 299–314). New York: Newbury House.

Carson, J. G. (2000). Reading and writing for academic purposes. In M. Pally (Ed.), *Sustained content teaching in academic ESL/EFL* (pp. 19–34).Boston: Houghton Mifflin.

Carson, J. G. (2001). A task analysis of reading and writing in academic contexts. In D. Belcher & A. Hirvela (Eds.), *Linking literacies: Perspectives on L2 reading-writing connections* (pp. 48–83). Ann Arbor: University of Michigan Press.

Carson, J., Carrell, P., Silberstein, S., Kroll, B., & Kuehn, P. (1990). Reading-writing relationships in first and second langauges. *TESOL Quarterly, 24*, 245–266.

Carson, J., & Leki, I. (Eds.). (1993). *Reading in the composition classroom*. Boston, MA: Heinle & Heinle.

Charney, D., & Carlson, R. (1995). Learning to write in a genre: What student writers take from model texts. *Research in the Teaching of English, 29*, 88–125.

Connor, U. (1996). *Contrastive rhetoric*. New York: Cambridge University Press.

Cummins, J. (1979). Linguistic interdependence and the educational development of bilingual children. *Review of Educational Research, 49*, 222–251.

Cummins, J. (1981). The role of primary language development in promoting educational success for language minority students. In *Schooling and language minority students: A theoretical framework* (pp. 3–49). Office of Bilingual Bicultural Education, California State Department of Education, Sacramento. Los Angeles: Evaluation, Dissemination and Assessment Center, California State University.

Durgunoglu, A., & Verhoeven, L. (Eds.). (1998). *Literacy development in a multilingual context: Cross-cultural perspectives*. Mahwah, NJ: Lawrence Erlbaum.

Elley, W. (1991). Acquiring literacy in a second language: The effect of book-based programs. *Language Learning, 41*, 375–411.

Elley, W. (1996). Using book floods to raise literacy levels in developing countries. In V. Greaney (Ed.), *Promoting reading in developing countries* (pp. 148–162). Newark, DE: International Reading Association.

Ferris, D., & Hedgcock, J. (1998). *Teaching ESL composition: Purposes, process, and practice*. Mahwah, NJ: Lawrence Erlbaum.

Flahive, D., & Bailey, N. (1993). Exploring reading/writing relationships in adult second language learners. In J. Carson & I. Leki (Eds.), *Reading in the composition classroom* (pp. 128–140). Boston, MA: Heinle & Heinle.

Grabe, W. (2000). Reading research and its implications for reading assessment. In A. Kunnan (Ed.), *Fairness and validation in language assessment* (pp. 226–262). New York: Cambridge University Press.

Grabe, W. (2001). Notes towards a theory of second language writing. In T. Silva & P. K. Matsuda (Eds.), *On second language writing* (pp. 39–57). Mahwah, NJ: Lawrence Erlbaum.

Grabe, W., & Kaplan, R. B. (1996). *Theory and practice of writing*. New York: Longman.

Grabe, W., & Kaplan, R. B. (1997). Teaching the writing course. In K. Bardovi-Harlig & B. Hartmann (Eds.), *Beyond methods: Components of second language teacher education* (pp. 172–197). New York: McGraw-Hill.

Grabe, W., & Stoller, F. (2001). Reading for academic purposes: Guidelines for the ESL/EFL teacher. In M. Celce-Murcia (Ed.), *Teaching English as a second or foreign language* (3rd ed., pp. 187–203). Boston: Heinle & Heinle.

Grabe, W., & Stoller, F. (2002). *Teaching and researching reading*. Harlow, UK: Longman.

Gradwohl-Nash, J., Schumacher, G., & Carlson, B. (1993). Writing from sources: A structure mapping model. *Journal of Educational Psychology, 85*, 159–170.

Hale, G., Taylor, C., Bridgeman, B., Carson, J., Kroll, B., & Kantor, R. (1996). *A study of writing tasks assigned in academic degree programs* (TOEFL Research Report No. 54). Princeton, NJ: Educational Testing Service.

Hirvela, A. (2001). Incorporating reading into EAP writing courses. In J. Flowerdew (Ed.), *Research perspectives on English for academic purposes* (pp. 330–346). New York: Cambridge University Press.

Hyland, K. (2002). *Teaching and researching writing*. Harlow, UK: Longman.

Johns, A. (1993). Reading and writing tasks in English for academic purposes classes: Products, processes and resources. In J. Carson & I. Leki (Eds.), *Reading in the composition classroom* (pp. 274–289). New York: Newbury House.

Johns, A. (1997). *Text, role, and context*. New York: Cambridge University Press.

Johns, A., & Mayes, P. (1990). An analysis of summary protocols of university ESL students. *Applied Linguistics, 11*, 253–271.

Kasper, L. F. (2000). *Content-based college ESL instruction.* Mahwah, NJ: Lawrence Erlbaum.

Krashen, S. (1984). *Writing: Research, theory, and applications.* Torrance, CA: Laredo Publishing.

Krashen, S. (1993). *The power of reading.* Englewood, CO: Libraries Unlimited.

Langer, J., & Applebee, A. (1987). *How writing shapes thinking.* Urbana, IL: NCTE.

Lee, J-W., & Schallert, D. (1997). The relative contribution of L2 language proficiency and L1 reading ability to L2 reading performance: A test of the threshold hypothesis. *TESOL Quarterly, 31,* 713–739.

Leki, I. (1991).Twenty-five years of contrastive rhetoric: Text analysis and writing pedagogies. *TESOL Quarterly, 25,* 123–143.

Leki, I., & Carson, J. (1994). Students' perceptions of EAP writing instruction and writing needs across the disciplines. *TESOL Quarterly, 28,* 81–101.

Leki, I., & Carson, J. (1997). "Completely different worlds": EAP and the writing experiences of ESL students in university courses. *TESOL Quarterly, 31,* 39–69.

McCarthy-Young, K., & Leinhardt, G. (1998). Writing from primary documents: A way of knowing history. *Written Communication, 15,* 25–68.

McGinley, W. (1992). The role of reading and writing while composing from sources. *Reading Research Quarterly, 27,* 226–248.

McGinley, W., & Tierney, R. (1989). Traversing the topical landscape: Reading and writing as ways of knowing. *Written Communication, 6,* 243–269.

Perfetti, C., Britt, M., & Georgi, M. (1995). *Text-based learning and reasoning.* Mahwah, NJ: Lawrence Erlbaum.

Raimes, A. (1987). Language proficiency, writing ability and composing strategies: A study of ESL college student writers. *Language Learning, 37,* 439–468.

Reid, J. (1993). *Teaching ESL writing.* Englewood Cliffs, NJ: Regents Prentice Hall.

Reid, J., & Kroll, B. (1995). Designing and assessing effective classroom writing assignments for NES and ESL students. *Journal of Second Language Writing, 4,* 17–41.

Rouet, J.-F., Favart, M., Britt, M., & Perfetti, C. (1997). Studying and using multiple documents in history: Effects of discipline expertise. *Cognition and Instruction, 15,* 85–106.

Sasaki, M., & Hirose, K. (1996). Explanatory variables for EFL students' expository writing. *Language Learning, 46,* 137–174.

Shanahan, T. (Ed.). (1990). *Reading and writing together: New perspectives for the classroom.* Norwood, MA: Christopher-Gordon.

Shanahan, T., & Tierney, R. (1990). Reading-writing connections: The relations among three perspectives. In J. Zutell & S. McCormick (Eds.), *Literacy theory and research: Analyses from multiple paradigms* (pp. 13–34). 39th yearbook of the National Reading Conference. Chicago: National Reading Conference.

Silva, T. (1993). Toward an understanding of the distinct nature of L2 writing. *TESOL Quarterly, 27,* 757–67.

Silva, T., Leki, I., & Carson, J. (1997). Broadening the perspective of mainstream composition studies. *Written Communication, 14,* 398–428.

Skehan, P. (1998a). *A cognitive approach to language learning.* New York: Oxford University Press.

Skehan, P. (1998b). Task-based instruction. In W. Grabe et al. (Eds.), *Annual Review of Applied Linguistics, 18: Foundations of second language learning* (pp. 268–286). New York: Cambridge University Press.

Smagorinsky, P. (1992). How reading model essays affect writers. In J. Irwin & M. Doyle (Eds.), *Reading/writing connections* (pp. 160–176). Newark, DE: International Reading Association.

Snow, A., & Brinton, D. (Eds.). (1997). *The content based classroom: Perspectives on integrating language and content.* New York: Longman.

Spack, R. (1988). Initiating ESL students into the academic discourse community: How far should they go? *TESOL Quarterly, 22,* 29–51.

Spivey, N. (1990). Transforming texts: Constructive processes in reading and writing. *Written Communication, 7,* 256–287.

Spivey, N., & King, J. (1989). Readers and writers composing from sources. *Reading Research Quarterly, 24,* 7–26.

Stahl, S., Hynd, C., Britton, B., McNish, M., & Bosquet, D. (1996). What happens when students read multiple source documents in history? *Reading Research Quarterly, 31,* 430–456.

Stanovich, K., West, R., Cunningham, A., Cipielewski, J., & Siddiqui, S. (1996). The role of inadequate print exposure as a determinant of reading comprehension problems. In C. Cornoldi & J. Oakhill (Eds.), *Reading comprehension difficulties: Processes and intervention* (pp. 15–32). Mahwah, NJ: Lawrence Erlbaum.

Stolarek, E. (1994). Prose modeling and metacognition: The effect of modeling on developing a metacognitive stance toward writing. *Research in the Teaching of English, 28,* 154–174.

Swales, J. (1990). *Genre analysis.* New York: Cambridge University Press.

Swales, J. (1998, July). *Teaching the literature review to international graduate students.* Paper presented at the Second Language Reading/Writing Connections Conference, Columbus, OH.

Tierney, R., & Shanahan, T. (1991). Research on the reading-writing relationship: Interactions, transactions, and outcomes. In R. Barr et al. (Eds.), *Handbook of reading research* (Vol. II, pp. 246–280). New York: Longman.

Tierney, R., Soter, A., O'Flavahan, J., & McGinley, W. (1989). The effects of reading and writing upon thinking critically. *Reading Research Quarterly, 24,* 134–173.

Tsang, W.-K. (1996). Comparing the effects of reading and writing on writing proficiency. *Applied Linguistics, 17,* 210–233.

Urquhart, S., & Weir, C. (1998). *Reading in a second language: Process, product and practice.* New York: Longman.

Wagner, D. (1998). Putting second language first: Language and literacy learning in Morocco. In A. Durgunoglu & L. Verhoeven (Eds.), *Literacy development in a multilingual context* (pp. 169–183). Mahwah, NJ: Lawrence Erlbaum.

Wagner, R., & Stanovich, K. (1996). Expertise in reading. In K. A. Ericsson (Ed.), *The road to excellence* (pp. 189–225). Mahwah, NJ: Lawrence Erlbaum.

White, R. (Ed.). (1995). *New ways in teaching writing.* Alexandria, VA: TESOL.

Zamel, V. (1992). Writing one's way into reading. *TESOL Quarterly, 26,* 463–485.

11 Literature in the teaching of second language composition

Stephanie Vandrick

Writing instructors constantly face curricular decisions about which types of approaches, methods, and materials should be used to teach writing most effectively. Instructors have to explore many curricular possibilities and make conscious decisions based on their own prior training, the educational setting in which they teach, their goals for the classes, and the needs of their students. One such decision concerns whether, and how, to use literature in writing classes. These particular questions reflect an ongoing controversy in professional conversations in both first language (L1) and second language (L2) settings. This chapter summarizes arguments for and against the use of literature in writing classes, outlines the history of the controversy in both fields, and explores questions that arise when a choice is made to use literature, including the following concerns: Which genres of literature are appropriate in the L2 writing class? What is the place of multicultural and international literature in the L2 writing class? How can literature best be used to enhance writing instruction? Exploring these types of questions should prove helpful to teachers in training as well as to experienced teachers, all of whom want to make informed and productive decisions about the curricula and goals of their writing classes.

While the focus in this chapter is on adults, particularly college students, much of what is said also applies to younger students, especially high school students. Further, although the focus here is primarily on ESL writing classes in universities in North America, many of the points made could be generalized, with modifications, to academic English as a second language/English as a foreign language (ESL/EFL) settings in other countries, and thus any discussion regarding the use of literature in the composition classroom applies wherever there are composition classrooms.

Before turning to the question of the use of literature, we need to back up a step and address the question of the use of reading – whether literature or other types of materials – in writing classes. To some, writing is a separate skill, and spending "too much" time on reading merely detracts from the time and energy that could be devoted to the teaching and learning of writing skills. To others, it is clearly

263

impossible and undesirable to teach writing without reading. The two skills are inseparable. Carson and Leki (1993) point out that "for many years reading and writing in ESL classrooms were taught separately and as technical skills," but in recent years, the field has recognized "the extent to which reading can be, and in academic settings nearly always is, the basis for writing.... Reading and writing abilities are inextricably linked" (p. 1). Morrow (1997) points out that there is little research to "prove" that reading enhances writing skills, but she concludes that "as a teacher...my overarching goal is to demonstrate the variety of ways in which readers and writers negotiate meaning" (p. 470). Readings serve as models of good writing, and even more important, serve as sources of information and ideas that stimulate thinking, discussion, and responses, all of which are essential foundations of writing. (For more on reading in the writing classroom, see Grabe, Chapter 10 this volume.)

Although this chapter outlines arguments that can be and have been presented both for and against the use of literature in the L2 writing classroom, and further addresses potential problems in using literature, the main thrust of the argument is that literature has an important role to play in the writing classroom. (See Hirvela, 2001, for a similar argument constructed along somewhat different lines.)

Arguments for using literature in L2 writing classes

The reasons for, or benefits of, the use of literature in L2 writing classes can be summarized as follows. First, literature is intrinsically enjoyable. Most people naturally are drawn to story, to narrative. They like to read about human situations, concerns, problems, solutions, and emotions. Sometimes people (including students) like stories because they cover universal themes, such as family, work, loneliness, love, and mortality, and readers can thus identify with the stories and their characters. Sometimes people like stories that they, the readers, can identify with in a particular way, such as when the characters are the same age or of the same ethnic background as the readers or experience problems similar to those of the readers. For example, students of traditional college age often enjoy stories about the relationship between children and parents, and stories about romantic love, as these are subjects they are often dealing with in their own lives. Other times, readers enjoy stories that introduce them to new settings, new experiences; this literature expands their worlds, and they are hungry for such learning and expansion. In any case, when reading is enjoyable, pleasurable, it arouses interest and a sense of connection and in turn motivates students to respond in discussions and in writing. This kind of motivation is extremely important in facilitating students' investment in, and progress made in, improving their writing abilities.

Second, literature gives students information about other cultures, including the culture(s) of the country where they currently live. It also gives students a way to engage with cultural differences. Willoquet-Maricondi (1991/1992) states that "the natural tensions that arise when cultures meet can be dealt with productively in a literary context" (p. 11). Literature also educates students about "culture" in the sense of knowledge about the arts. This type of information is useful in and of itself, and in addition it is useful because it helps prepare international and immigrant students for other academic classes in which such cultural knowledge may be assumed and expected. For example, when an ESL student who has been exposed to some literature in her or his writing class takes a humanities, literature, or psychology class, and the professor mentions "Hemingway," "the Victorian novel," "metaphor," or "motive," perhaps the student will at least have some idea what the professor is alluding to, rather than failing to understand the references at all.

Now coming more specifically to the benefits of literature for learning writing, it seems that the complexity of fiction is a feature that will help students think and write in a more multidimensional and analytical way. Practice in analyzing and interpreting literature, teasing out its multilayered meanings and aspects, cannot help but make students more sophisticated in their own thinking and writing. Students responding in writing to literature also practice the important academic skill of supporting their opinions with information gained by a close reading of the text (McKay, 2001). Closely related to this contention is the argument that reading literature promotes critical thinking. After all, "ideas, language, readings are not cut-and-dried in their meanings; a thinking person must analyze, question, interpret, synthesize what she or he hears and reads" (Vandrick, 1996b, p. 27), and a good writer must be a good critical thinker. As I pointed out elsewhere (Vandrick, 1997b), an important part of this process is helping students to see that a piece of literature, such as a novel,

doesn't exist in a vacuum. It's a living, breathing entity, one with which the reader interacts, one which comes to life when read by a particular reader. Each individual reader brings her or his experience, knowledge, and feelings to the novel, and creates a unique relationship, a unique reality, as she or he reads and responds to it. (p. 106)

In addition, students can learn very precise, nuanced, and useful vocabulary in literature. They are also exposed to language patterns that help students see the many and complex ways that sentences and paragraphs can be put together. Grammatical patterns can be absorbed unconsciously in the course of reading literature as readers are exposed to complexity, variety, and subtlety in grammatical patterns. And Sage (1987) points out that in literature "the student encounters nearly every kind of communicative technique speakers use or think of using. Literature displays a broader range of such communication strategies than any other single ESL teaching component" (p. 6). Related to these points is the appeal to the aesthetic reason for using literature in ESL writing classrooms: literature provides texts that often show the English language in ways that non-literary texts do not.

Students who read literature are reading creative work, and exposure to creative work enhances the students' own creativity, which in turn enhances their writing ability. Reading good literature teaches them the importance of sensory and descriptive details, of close observation and reporting, of imaginatively entering into the mind and motivation of a character, and of creating with language a new way of expressing an idea or feeling.

Instructors in writing classes typically have a choice about which readings to offer students; there is generally no set "content" that must be covered in the sense that certain material must be covered in a biology or history class; therefore, at the very least, the use of literature should be one of the very acceptable options for those readings. My colleague Mary Burns (Personal communication, May, 2002) asks, "Why wouldn't we use literature in writing classes? Why wouldn't we want to share with them the best that our language has to offer?"

Arguments against literature in L2 writing classes

Several reasons have been given and arguments made against the use of literature in the writing class, and in particular in the L2 writing class. Here I summarize those arguments and offer counter-arguments as well as possible solutions to the difficulties some have outlined.

One common concern, as Spack (1985) points out, is the assumption by some instructors that students majoring in science and engineering will not want to read literature; however, she says, research shows that this is not necessarily true. These students need and often want to be exposed to the best that the language has to offer, and the best is often found in literature.

Others argue that literary English is not everyday English or practical English; it is not the English that students will generally be required to know and use. But surely being familiar with the language as it is used by its most creative and imaginative practitioners can only be positive. Students should, of course, not be expected to speak or write in the same way or as well as well-known writers of literary works. But they can learn a lot about the language from these models and the ways language can be used and can be effective. They can enjoy and savor these works, be motivated by them, and even be inspired by them when they are doing their own writing.

Another concern is that reading literature may be "too hard" for students. Some instructors fear that students in L2 writing classes will find the literature too difficult, will become discouraged, and will not be able to learn from the literature or the class. Clearly instructors must be aware of their students' language levels, choose appropriate literature for those levels, and adjust assignments accordingly. There are certainly many works of literature that are quite accessible, even to intermediate learners. Even students at fairly low levels can understand and enjoy very short stories with good support, such as glossaries and the provision of background pre-reading information. Although literature may be a "stretch," students need to be, and even relish being, challenged and stimulated by their assigned readings. And they generally feel proud of and gratified by being able to read "real" literature; literature is recognized in most languages as the "best" a language has to offer, something that L2 students who are highly literate in their L1 are most likely to be aware of.

Yet another concern raised by some, especially those who fear that some L2 composition instructors are merely frustrated literature instructors, is that all the class time will be taken up by literary analysis, criticism, and theory. This assumes that the focus of the class will be the same as that of a literature class. In fact, in a writing class, literature is generally read for enjoyment, exposure to good writing, and provision of ideas and information that students can then write about and/or respond to. Any literary analysis will generally be fairly straightforward – to help students discuss and understand the literature and in turn to understand and practice good writing. Good writing does not generally, in L2 writing classes, mean that the students themselves write literature or even write in a "literary" style.

In addition, because it is very unlikely that students, particularly students still learning a second language, could write as well as the literary writers, some instructors feel that it would be too discouraging for students to read these works. The literary works cannot be direct models for their writing, and they will become discouraged by the large gap between the unattainable level of the literary works and the lowly level of their own writing. This concern can be addressed by the instructor's talking to the students about the reasons for reading literature and explicitly telling them that the writings are for enjoyment, learning, the provoking of thoughtful discussions and analysis and response, and inspiration. Students already understand this; even in their own languages they are aware that, with very rare exceptions, they will not be able to write as well as their countries' great authors of fiction and poetry.

It is also true that some writing instructors prefer not to feature literature in their writing classes because they themselves were not literature majors or do not read much literature, and therefore they feel uncomfortable about or ill-equipped to teach literature. But as mentioned above, literature in these classes is not taught as literature but is used to facilitate the learning and practicing of writing. So instructors do not have to be very familiar with literary or critical theory or terminology to bring literature into their classrooms effectively. Of course, if an instructor feels a strong antipathy to using literature, then perhaps it is better for that person not to do so. Students of a teacher who is unenthusiastic about the literature he or she teaches will soon catch on to that lack of enthusiasm and will be unlikely to respond positively to the literature. All writing classes do not have to feature literature, but instructors can at least seriously consider the potential benefits of its use in their classes.

Perhaps the most common, most substantive, and most contentious reason given by some L2 writing professionals (as well as some L1 writing professionals) for not using literature in writing classrooms is their strong belief that the major goal of writing classes should be to prepare students for academic writing, or writing in their particular disciplines or discourse communities. For those who make this argument, literature is often considered a distraction from the work at hand. They believe that readings in a writing class should, for example, consist of selections from college textbooks, articles from journals and high-quality magazines and newspapers, and classic essays. Some advocate even more specificity, urging that students take writing classes particularly for their majors, such as "Writing for Biology Majors," and learn how to write reports and other types of writing specific to their disciplines. (See Johns, Chapter 8 this volume, for some discussion on this issue of disciplinary reading materials in writing courses.) Of course, it is appropriate that students should be prepared for the kinds of writing they will actually be doing, and it would be helpful to them to read selections that are examples of that type of discourse. But writing well cannot be easily pigeonholed into categories. And university students will be writing for many types of classes in the university, not just classes in their major. Furthermore, after their academic experience, they will be writing in many types of situations, not just situations directly related to their major field of study. As Knight (1993) puts it, "a characteristic of an educated person is the ability to transfer learning. Thus, those of us who teach the basics of composition do not have to teach different writing courses for every discipline within 'the academy'" (p. 676). So yes, writing students should be exposed to academic discourse of various sorts, but they should also be exposed to literature. And again, the kind of thinking, analysis, and interpretation they do when responding to literature will also be very helpful in any kind of advanced writing.

History of the controversy in L1 writing

Several of the arguments outlined above, for and against using literature in writing classes, have been threads in ongoing discussions in both L1 and L2 writing venues. First, let's examine the discussion that has taken place in L1 writing venues. Although there has been a particularly heated discussion in L1 composition in the past decade on whether literature belongs in the freshman composition class, the issue has actually been debated for at least six decades: Steinberg's historical research shows that "imaginative literature has not had a secure place in composition classrooms since at least the 1930s" (1995, p. 271). Tate (1995) states that surveys of freshman composition programs by both Albert Kitzhaber, in 1959–60, and Richard Larson, in the early 1990s, showed that only about one in five contained any literature.

The argument was reignited famously in 1993 when Erika Lindemann and Gary Tate debated the issue in their paired articles in the journal, *College English*. Lindemann (1993) argued that academic discourse, not literature, should be the focus of writing classes; that classes based on literature focus on consuming texts, not producing them; that studying literature requires students to assume an abstruse critical style, and silences students' own voices; and that focusing on literature slights the study of the discourses and natures of other disciplines. Tate (1993) countered that because literature was often misused in the writing classroom, rhetoric took its place there and in professional conversations in the 1960s and has stayed in ascendance ever since, causing the neglect of an essential element of the writing class and of life, namely literature. He believes that students should be trained not just to become good writers in their own fields but to write as educated people in the broader sense, "as people whose most important conversations will take place *outside the academy*, as they struggle to figure out how to live their lives... as individual human beings who will have private and maybe public lives that transcend whatever disciplines they associate themselves with while in college" (Tate, 1993, pp. 320–321), and this kind of broad education should include literature.

Lindemann's and Tate's exchange elicited a number of impassioned responses (Crain, 1993; Gamer, 1995; Jay, 1993; Knight, 1993; Latosi-Swain, 1993; Peterson, 1995; Steinberg, 1995) and reprise pieces from Lindemann (1995) and Tate (1995). Issues that were addressed included the different needs of different levels and types of composition classes; the question of whether teaching literature in composition classes is elitist; the increasingly blurred line between fiction and expository prose; the need to focus on the nature of reading rather than on the materials being read; and the value of literary texts in helping students understand multidisciplinarity.

In these interchanges, arguments for using literature in writing classes included the following. Latosi-Swain (1993) argues that the literature-versus-academic discourse dichotomy is a false one and that these "extreme positions are unnecessary given the creative compromises already in the field. The question is no longer whether there is or isn't a place for literature in a composition program, but how literature *on occasion* is to be defined, selected, and used" (p. 675). She says that "literature can lead students naturally into the discourse of the academy" and that in fact "literature is being used to study human life in fields as varied as business, management and abnormal psychology" (p. 675). Knight (1993) agrees that reading literature is in fact "practical" and that

> because literature is the subject matter that deals most directly with learning through metaphors, learning to read literature properly is the most direct (and, therefore, the most practical) way of learning to image properly what is read. The person who is able to read literature well will have the skills to read computer manuals. (p. 677)

Similarly, Gamer (1995) compares using literary texts to employing the case study method in education and other classes; "imaginative texts provide us with particularized material with which students can interact, and from which they can discuss ideas" (p. 284). Knight (1993) also makes the point that reading literature is one of the best and most efficient ways for students to learn critical thinking, a necessity for good writing.

Crain (1993) puts the controversy in perspective when she reminds us that just because literature is used in a class does not mean it will take over, and that "we should not allow the misuse of literature to discourage us from 'right use' "; she further says, sensibly, that "all of us probably agree that writing should be taught in a writing course, and once the emphasis is on writing, what literature we use should be a matter of teacher and student choice" (p. 679). And Koller (quoted in Tate, 1995) reminds us of something many writing instructors know intuitively: "Our experience in freshman composition has shown over and over again that the freshman writes much better papers after he has been studying great literature than before he has begun to read, experience, and look at the works of great writers" (p. 307). My own experience teaching both L1 and L2 students confirms this point.

History of the controversy in ESL/L2 writing

In the ESL/L2 writing field as well, over the years there has been spirited discussion of the use of literature. Initial discussion of this topic was about the use of literature in ESL classes in general, rather than specifically about the role of literature in L2/ESL writing/composition classes.

The prominence of literature in ESL in general has ebbed and flowed through the years. In the very early years of ESL teaching, literature was commonly included in the curriculum. Then the linguistics emphasis became predominant, and literature waned (Widdowson, 1982). Di Pietro (1982) expresses his disappointment that

> we concentrate so intently on the formal properties of language ... that we have nothing significant to say about the use of literature for higher levels of learning. ... Hardly ever does an article that deals with literary themes or with the use of literature in the classroom appear in the *TESOL Quarterly* or in any of the other journals we read regularly. (p. 216)

Until recently, there were very few exceptions to Di Pietro's claims; however, some ESL scholars throughout have argued persuasively for the use of literature in ESL classes. Povey (1967) and Marckwardt (1978) asserted that reading literary texts provides models of good writing as well as cultural information and understanding. Marshall (1979) writes of teaching ESL students about the joys of English literature, and how such literature contains universal themes that cross cultures. Widdowson (1982) decries the banality of many ESL lessons and recommends that literature be used more frequently in teaching ESL. McKay (1982) also advocates the use of literature in ESL classes, listing the following benefits: it develops linguistic knowledge; students enjoy it and therefore are more motivated to read and ultimately increase their reading proficiency; students learn more about other cultures; and students develop their own creativity and imagination, which will improve their writing ability. Although these scholars do not specifically advocate the use of literature in ESL writing (as opposed to reading or general ESL) classes, many of their arguments apply in the context of writing classes. The controversy about the usefulness of literature in general language classes is still very much alive; Edmondson (1995/6), for example, attempts to demolish, one by one, all the claims that literature promotes language learning.

The use of literature specifically to teach writing – as opposed to, more generally, teaching language – is finally addressed in two 1985 *TESOL Quarterly* articles. In the first, McConochie (1985) discusses ways to teach literary texts and argues that writing about literature will enhance the understanding and enjoyment of the literature; however, she does not state whether the reverse is true (i.e., that reading literature enhances writing skill). In the second article, Spack (1985) writes specifically about the positive effects of reading literature on students' writing. She states that "ESL students have much to gain when literature is the reading content of their composition course and the subject matter for their compositions" (p. 703), and she gives very specific examples of ways to incorporate literature into the teaching of writing. She lists the following benefits: studying and responding to literature in writing improves the ability to interpret, analyze, and think critically; it enhances vocabulary acquisition; and it helps students to absorb the linguistic and intellectual structure of the language. Oster (1989) further states that reading literature can help students understand and take varying points of view, thus leading to more-flexible writing and thinking and at the same time encouraging more-imaginative use of the language. Willoquet-Maricondi (1991–1992) writes about using short stories to promote better writing, and Nash and Yun-Pi (1992/1993) describe their research showing that extensive reading, including reading of literature, improves student writing. Gajdusek and van Dommelen (1993) advocate the use of literature to promote interest in writing topics as well as critical thinking.

Although writing of the benefits of literature for ESL students in general language acquisition rather than specifically about development of writing ability, Lazar (1996) includes some important benefits for students: literature is motivating, absorbing, and emotionally engaging; it is authentic language; it helps students understand different cultures; it develops students' interpretive abilities; it is enjoyable for students; it is highly valued by students and faculty and has high status, which in turn is motivating; and it develops language awareness, including sophisticated language. Maley (2001), also writing about literature in a broader framework than just the writing course, categorizes the typical reasons given for teaching literature in language classes: for cultural purposes, as a language model, and for personal growth. All of these, as suggested in this chapter, feed directly into a writing course. (For a more extensive, detailed discussion of the history of the controversy in both L1 and L2 settings, see Belcher & Hirvela, 2000.)

Choosing the literature

Which genres?

Writing instructors who decide to use literature in their classes still have several broad curricular decisions to make before choosing specific texts, specific literature. One important question concerns which genres of literature are most appropriately and effectively used in the ESL writing class. My own definition of literature is quite broad and includes not only novels, short stories, plays, and poems, but also essays, memoirs, and other variations of belletristic rather than expository prose, such as the "nonfiction novel" and "autobiographical fiction." It is useful to explain the differences among these genres to students, as well as what they have in common, and to discuss what makes them literature.

Short stories are the most commonly used form of literature in classes, as they are both interesting to students and "manageable." Because they are short, they can be read and discussed in a reasonable amount of class time and students can get a feeling of achievement and satisfaction quickly. Most of the literary analysis that can be done with novels can also and perhaps more easily be done with short stories, e.g., analysis regarding theme, setting, plot, characters, symbolism, and so forth. Short stories are very accessible; many textbooks feature them, and they are also available in many anthologies. Stories generally have many themes and topics packed into their few short pages, so there is much to discuss. They also provide useful vocabulary practice.

Poetry is also often effectively used, although students sometimes have trouble understanding poems and often are less interested in poems than in fiction. Reading poems aloud and having students read them aloud often markedly increase students' interest in and understanding of poetry. Discussing poetry provides useful lessons for writers, lessons about the importance of each word, about imagery, about brevity and density, about interpretation, and about expressing the universal in the particular. Even students who will never write their own poems can benefit from these lessons in all of their writing.

Novels, although long, can also be incorporated into ESL writing classes. Meloni (1994) advocates students' reading short novels, stating that they are interesting and motivating, provide continuity in a way a collection of short pieces cannot, and yet are short enough to be manageable for the L2 student. By short novels, she means those of about 100–150 pages, such as George Orwell's *Animal Farm*, John Steinbeck's *Of Mice and Men*, and Amy Tan's *The Joy Luck Club*.

Longer novels can also be read by advanced ESL students. In many cases, the instructor will have the whole class read the same novel, over a period of time, discussing it and writing about it as they go along. Alternatively, each student can choose a different novel and give periodic written and oral reports to the class. The instructor may want to provide students with a list of recommended novels but also allow them to choose their own, only asking them to check titles with the instructor so that she or he can steer them away from inappropriate novels (those that are too long, too short, too obscure, too difficult, or lacking in any literary value). For students of traditional college age, coming-of-age novels have particular meaning and thus are especially popular; examples include J. D. Salinger's *The Catcher in the Rye*, John Knowles's *A Separate Peace*, Betty Smith's *A Tree Grows in Brooklyn*, Elizabeth Bowen's The *Death of the Heart*, Carson McCullers' *The Member of the Wedding*, and Gish Jen's *Typical American*.

The essay is the most obvious form of literature to use in writing classes (although, as discussed above, some do not consider essays "literature").

These provide the closest "model" for the kinds of writing students are most likely to do. They incorporate many of the elements of any good literature: originality, vision, careful and creative use of the language, awareness of the reader (audience), purposeful organization and shaping of the material, and experimentation with style and tone.

Some have suggested the use of children's literature for adult students in ESL writing classes. Khodabakhshi and Lagos (1993) state that "carefully selected children's literature arouses interest and stimulates ESL students' oral and written expression. It can also be used to introduce more complex reading material" (p. 55). They caution that teachers need to point out to adult students that many authors intend "children's" literature for all ages. They believe that through this literature, "students re-examine their own experiences through the medium of powerful, meaningful stories, making connections to their own as well as their classmates' lives and to the human truths embodied in children's classics" (p. 52). Instructors should not dismiss such literature without investigating it; they may be surprised at the high quality, expressiveness, and power of many children's books.

A related question regarding which kind of literature to use is the question of whether to use abridged fiction. Some instructors, and publishers, favor abridged works as a way to make literature available to students with limited English, and perhaps with limited time. Other instructors argue that if students are to truly experience the benefits of literature, they should experience it in its undiluted form; cutting a writer's words seems disrespectful. Although abridged works should in general probably be avoided, it may be that in low-level classes, abridged stories can provide a useful preliminary stage to students' being able to read "the real thing."

The canon or multicultural literature?

Another important curricular question faced by instructors regarding which kind of literature to choose for L2 writing classes is whether to read literature from the "canon" (works that have traditionally been considered the "best" in a given language and have withstood the test of time) or from a more diverse multicultural body of literature. There are good arguments for each position.

Teaching students about the traditional great works of English and American literature gives students at least a little of the background that students who have attended school in the United States or another English-speaking country will already have, and thus helps ESL students be more prepared for their other university classes where such knowledge might be presupposed, and even for living in countries where this is the dominant literature. Also, most works in the canon are there because they represent a consensus (at least until recently) about which works are the best in English; thus students reading these works will be exposed to high-quality literature, with all the benefits that exposure entails. On the other hand, the United States and the world are becoming more multicultural, more diverse, more mixed, and it is entirely appropriate that students read literature by authors from various national, ethnic, and class backgrounds, and by women as well as men. It is also important that students, at least some of the time, read literature about settings, characters, and situations that they can relate to and even identify with, and that they may thus find sympathetic and validating. A carefully chosen mixture of literature, partially from the "canon" and partially from more recent, more multicultural literature, is probably the best solution.

In fact, in ESL textbooks and classes, in the past 15 to 20 years there has been a decided move toward increasing use of multicultural literature. Until the 1980s, when ESL scholars advocated the use of literature in L2 reading/writing classes, they generally referred to mainstream literature, literature mostly by white male writers. ESL textbooks featuring literature tended to focus on "classic" pieces that were part of the mainly European and European-American, mostly male canon. Di Pietro (1982) called for the use of multi-ethnic literature, but the literature readily available at that time was still quite limited, so the authors he recommended were still predominantly white males of European ancestry: Italian Americans, Russian Americans, Jewish Americans. The works of these authors did broaden the "canon," and they were especially effective in that they often portrayed immigrant lives and lives other than those of mainstream middle-class white America.

In the late 1980s, the selections in ESL reading/writing textbooks became much more multicultural. Fortunately, there was an increasing variety of literature in print and available to draw from. Diversity, multiculturalism, and multicultural literature were now popular, even trendy. Currently, textbook authors/editors clearly seek out literature by women and by writers from various countries and from various ethnic groups. They include stories and other literary selections by, for example, African, Asian, South American, and Middle Eastern writers as well as (in the United States) by African American, Asian American, Hispanic American, and other minority group authors. Unfortunately, however, virtually no commercially produced ESL reading/writing textbooks to date include literature portraying the lives of lesbian and gay characters or disabled characters (although there may well be locally produced exceptions).

Not only does multicultural literature help students learn about other cultures and allow them to identify with characters and situations that may be from their own or related cultures, but such literature also may promote tolerance and understanding. By learning from the literature about both similarities among cultures and people and differences among cultures and peoples, students can understand and write about what connects all people and what divides them. Reading multicultural literature also helps counter stereotypes that students may have about, for example, "the United States"; when they read literature by and about various ethnic and other groups, they will begin to realize that the United States and its culture(s) are far from monolithic. Reading literature about the themes described leads to deeper and more engaged thinking and writing.

In addition, as I have argued elsewhere (Vandrick, 1996a, 1997a), multicultural and diaspora literature serves as a kind of mirror to ESL students and is experienced by many of them as validating. Not only does this feeling of validation enhance students' comfort, but it also enhances their ability to focus on and succeed in their writing. Just one example of this occurred in a writing class where students read well-written descriptions in literature from their own country or one geographically nearby. These students were able to understand the concept of vivid descriptive details better, and this understanding translated into the use of more and better details in their own essays (Vandrick, 1996a).

Despite the value of multicultural literature, it is important for instructors to be critical in choosing such literature and textbooks that feature it for L2 writing classes. First, the principles of selection should be clear from the title and from the prefatory material. For example, a book of stories from around the world has a different emphasis and obviously will include different selections from those in a book of pieces from various cultures and groups within the United States. Then within those goals and limits, the selections in the book should be balanced, including literary selections by writers from a wide variety of backgrounds. Female and male authors should be approximately equally represented. The discussion questions and other apparatus in the books should be informative and sensitive about cultural differences portrayed. There should be attention to both differences and universal themes. Focus should not always be on "problems"; although it is important to discuss these, there should also be attention to positive aspects of each culture.

Teachers should also be careful about how they teach this multicultural literature. It is probably not enough simply to expose students to literature from various backgrounds; such exposure may simply reinforce students' preconceptions and prejudices. Shapiro (1991) suggests that there may be a danger of including selections from so many different cultures that "we risk trading depth for breadth" (p. 526) and at the same time risk "stereotyping a culture by limiting its exposure through single, short, excerpts" (p. 526). Sadarangani (1994) has a similar concern, feeling that some multicultural textbooks "suggest that foreign cultures are easily knowable through short pieces of writing, often ignoring the complexities of those cultures" (p. 48). Although selection of pieces included in the text is the responsibility of authors, editors, and publishers, it is also the responsibility of instructors to choose their class texts carefully and to guide students through them in a sensitive and positive way. This responsibility is one reason that teachers in training – and afterward – should learn as much as they can about the possibilities for incorporating literature into their curricula.

Literature and social issues

An issue related to choosing and using multicultural literature is choosing literature that focuses on social issues of various types. One of the many benefits of using literature in a writing class is that literature so often deals with social, political, and economic questions. Literary purists may question instructors' and readers' focusing on these questions, but they provide built-in interest-building and discussion-stimulating materials that are invaluable in writing classes. Spack (1994), in her textbook *The International Story*, points out that stories

provide a sense of social history. . . . Many of the stories reflect the concerns of the times: class distinctions, roles of women, immigration and acculturation, the American dream, social and economic limitations, World War I, racism and colonialism, post-World War II materialism, religious and cultural identity, Communism, poverty, violence, and effects of the Vietnam War. (p. 44)

Zandy (1998) points out a related benefit that might not spring to mind as quickly but is also invaluable: literature often serves to teach issues of class, including working-class issues, such as the heavy toll that hard physical work takes. For just one example, consider the class issues so exquisitely delineated in de Maupassant's short story "The Necklace" (collected in Spack, 1994). The main character longs to rise to a higher class, yet circumstance forces her to pay for her ambitions with the painful hard work of the poor. This story elicits students' knowledge and feelings about social class in a very visceral way, and the discussions and writing elicited by this story can be impressively analytical and complex.

There is a clear connection here to recent interest by ESL professionals in peace education, meaning teaching about issues related to social justice, issues relating to peace and war, violence, the environment, civil rights, gender, race, and so on (Birch, 1993; Vandrick, 1994, 1996b). Some instructors might be concerned that discussing social issues is somehow ideological, promoting certain political or social views, but surely examining stereotypes and increasing understanding is beneficial. Besides, Benesch and others have made the point that all teaching is in fact ideological "whether or not we are conscious of the political implications. Educators who do not acknowledge or discuss their ideology are not politically neutral; they simply do not highlight their ideology" (1993, p. 706). The beauty of literature is that it power-fully portrays social problems as they play out in people's lives; the issues are no longer abstract.

Using the literature

Instructors new to using literature in the L2 writing class may wonder how to employ it effectively. Its most important use is as a prelude and stimulus to writing. But before students read short stories, for exam-ple, they might benefit from learning some basic literary terms, such as plot, theme, conflict, resolution, character, protagonist, antagonist, set-ting, symbolism, metaphor, simile, and flashback. These terms are tools that will aid students in analyzing, understanding, discussing, and writ-ing about the stories. Some textbooks provide useful descriptions of these terms (e.g., Spack, 1994).

Before students read each story, it is useful for them to do some pre-reading activities, such as learning at least a little about the author, the time period, and the literary genre. Students can look at the title and speculate on what it might mean or predict. They can glance over the story to see how long it is and whether it has a lot of dialogue. They can read the first paragraph or two and then stop and discuss the material with classmates, perhaps identifying the setting and main characters and again speculating on what might happen. The instructor can urge stu-dents to read the story at least twice. She can also urge them not to look up too many words in the dictionary, especially during the first reading, but instead to try to immerse themselves in the story and not worry if they don't understand every word or every detail. Otherwise they will become too caught up with frequent stops to look up words and won't enjoy the story; in addition, they will lose the flow of the story and not see the forest for the trees.

This is not to imply that learning new vocabulary is not, for ESL stu-dents, an important part of reading literature. The teacher certainly can answer questions about vocabulary. In fact, it is helpful for the instruc-tor to identify and provide the students with a list of some of the most useful new words in each selection. In this way, students receive some guidance about which words of the many new words in any given piece they should focus on. Learning the words on the list can be enhanced by vocabulary exercises and perhaps quizzes.

Reading literature also exposes students to a rich variety of sentence structures and other syntactical and linguistic complexities. Although students' attention should be drawn to certain structures, this should be part of their understanding of the piece, rather than a sort of grammar exercise in isolation. (See Frodesen & Holten, Chapter 6 this volume, for a discussion of how this awareness promotes increased proficiency.) McKay (1982) makes the point that literature should not primarily be treated as a source of examples of usage; the aesthetic experience should be paramount, and "language usage should be explored only to the extent that it is relevant to that experience" (p. 533).

Class discussion should focus not only on "what happened" (although it is important to ascertain that students have in fact understood the basics of the plot). Discussion can include such questions as the following: What theme or themes are addressed in this piece? Who are the main characters, and what do you learn about them? Which details and dialogue help you understand these characters? Do you relate to any of the characters? Do they remind you of anyone you know? Do you have any strong reactions to any of the characters? Is the story believable? Which parts of the story and its themes are universal, and which parts are culturally bound? What do you learn about the culture of the time and place of the story? What is the tone of the story or piece? What do you notice about the type of language used? Is it dense, ornate, simple, complex? Is there a lot of dialogue? What is the role of dialogue in this story? Is there a lot of description? How much is explained and how much is left to the reader's imagination? Can you find symbols in the story? What do they represent? (See McKay, 2001, for an illuminating, detailed example of how classroom analysis of two specific stories might fruitfully be carried out.)

In discussion of a piece in class, it is often useful to have students read aloud selected passages, either chosen by the instructor or by the students. These might be passages that are particularly revealing about certain characters or particularly dramatic. Passages with a lot of dialogue can be read aloud almost as a dramatic play. Sometimes it is interesting to ask each student to pick a short passage – perhaps only a sentence or two – that is particularly meaningful to her or him, to read it aloud, and perhaps tell why she or he chose that passage. Other times it is helpful to have students pick out particularly vivid details and discuss how these details reveal setting, character, theme, and plot. This last exercise is helpful in reminding students of the importance of providing vivid details in their own writing. Reading passages aloud is not only useful but enjoyable; language read aloud comes alive in a way that it may not when read silently. As mentioned earlier, this is particularly true when reading poetry.

An extension of reading aloud can be role play. Students may imagine the characters after the story is finished, for example, and act out what they think might happen next. Or they can act out the story with the roles of the main characters reversed or with the characters older, or younger, or in a different time or place. Depending on the story, the instructor can design role play situations that help students to further explore the implications of the story.

After the students have read and discussed the literary selections, they are ready to write. Writing assignments based on such selections can range from response journals to short response pieces to reports to traditional "English papers" offering literary analysis and interpretation. Many writing instructors have found the response journal extremely useful. In its most common form, students divide pages in half, copy selected passages of interest on one half of the page, and write their own personal responses on the facing side of the page. Another variation is the 15-minute response paper in class, generally after a discussion. Students may be given a rather specific question to address, or they may be given freedom to address any aspect of the reading in any way they choose. Typical types of responses relate to such questions and directions as the following: What is the theme of this story? Describe one of the characters in detail. Does something in the story remind you of some aspect of your own life and experience? What did you particularly like or dislike about the story? Write a letter to one of the characters, giving the character your opinion and/or advice about her or his situation and actions.

Most of the activities discussed apply to literary selections that all the students in class have read. Regarding full novels, an instructor may also want to ask each student to choose a novel to read and report on. One way of organizing assignments on the novel is as follows. The students receive a loose format for reporting on the book, emphasizing not only summary and analysis but also personal responses. They can complete about three oral and three written reports during the course of the semester, thus keeping a steady pace in reading while being asked to stop and reflect regularly. Sharing their novels with their classmates in oral reports also widens the cultural knowledge of the students in the class, preparing them for future academic work and sometimes even motivating them to later read a novel recommended by a classmate. Students then respond in writing to one of their classmate's oral reports, thus provoking another layer of analysis and interpretation. (For a more detailed description of this assignment, see Vandrick, 1997b.) Thus, there is a strong interconnection between reading and writing with literature used as a base. Finally, various ESL researchers (e.g., Dupuy, Tse, & Cook, 1996; Nash & Yun-Pi, 1992/1993) have advocated "extensive reading," in which students read various materials individually, inside and outside class – materials that are generally literary selections such as novels. The point of this reading is to develop the habit of reading for pleasure, though Grabe (2001) cautions that there is need for much more empirical evidence to support a claim for improved writing skills resulting simply from pleasure reading in L2. Except for the benefits of group discussion of a particular selection that all have read, extensive reading provides many of the same benefits as a whole class reading selections together. This can be somewhat addressed by book reviews or reports, literature circles, and other small-group activities in which students share their readings and their responses to the readings.

Conclusion

It would be unfortunate if L2 writing instructors were to dismiss the use of literature in their classrooms without investigating the many important benefits of such use. Ideally the use of literature can be integrated with the use of other types of readings, all of which in combination provide students with a rich and challenging stimulus to good writing. In addition, exposure to literature helps students enter into and become part of the world of academe, of intellectual life, and of the life of the educated person.

References

Belcher, D., & Hirvela, A. (2000). Literature and L2 composition: Revisiting the debate. *Journal of Second Language Writing, 9*, 21–39.

Benesch, S. (1993). ESL, ideology, and the politics of pragmatism. *TESOL Quarterly, 27*, 705–717.

Birch, B. (1993). ESL techniques for peace. *CATESOL Journal, 6*, 7–16.

Carson, J. G., & Leki, I. (1993). Introduction. In J. G. Carson & I. Leki (Eds.), *Reading in the composition classroom: Second language perspectives* (pp. 1–7). Boston: Heinle & Heinle/Wadsworth.

Crain, J. C. (1993). Comment on "Two views on the use of literature in composition." [Letter to the editor]. *College English, 55*, 678–679.

Di Pietro, R. (1982). The multi-ethnicity of American literature: A neglected resource for the EFL teacher. In M. Hines & W. Rutherford (Eds.), *On TESOL '81* (pp. 215–229). Washington, DC: TESOL.

Dupuy, B., Tse, L., & Cook, T. (1996). Bringing books into the classroom: First steps in turning college-level ESL students into readers. *TESOL Journal, 5*(4), 10–15.

Edmondson, W. (1995/6). The role of literature in foreign language learning and teaching: Some valid assumptions and invalid arguments. *AILA Review, 12*, 42–55.

Gajdusek, L., & van Dommelen, D. (1993). Literature and critical thinking in the composition classroom. In J. G. Carson & I. Leki (Eds.), *Reading in the composition classroom: Second language perspectives* (pp. 197–217). Boston: Heinle & Heinle/Wadsworth.

Gamer, M. (1995). Fictionalizing the disciplines: Literature and the boundaries of knowledge. *College English, 57*, 281–286.

Grabe, W. (2001). Reading-writing relations: Theoretical perspectives and instructional practices. In D. Belcher & A. Hirvela (Eds.), *Linking literacies: Perspectives on L2 reading-writing connections* (pp. 15–47). Ann Arbor: University of Michigan Press.

Hirvela, A. (2001). Connecting reading and writing through literature. In D. Belcher & A. Hirvela (Eds.), *Linking literacies: Perspectives on L2 reading-writing connections* (pp. 109–134). Ann Arbor: University of Michigan Press.

Jay, G. S. (1993). Comment on "Two views on the use of literature in composition." [Letter to the editor]. *College English, 55,* 673–675.

Khodabakhshi, S. C., & Lagos, D. C. (1993). Reading aloud: Children's literature in college ESL classes. *Journal of the Imagination in Language Learning, 1,* 52–55.

Knight, L. (1993). Comment on "Two views on the use of literature in composition." [Letter to the editor]. *College English, 55,* 676–678.

Latosi-Swain, E. (1993). Comment on "Two views on the use of literature in composition." [Letter to the editor]. *College English, 55,* 675–676.

Lazar, G. (1996). Exploring literary texts with the language learner. *TESOL Quarterly, 30,* 773–776.

Lindemann, E. (1993). Freshman composition: No place for literature. *College English, 55,* 311–316.

Lindemann, E. (1995). Three views of English 101. *College English, 57,* 287–302.

Maley, A. (2001). Literature in the language classroom. In R. Carter & D. Nunan (Eds.), *The Cambridge guide to teaching English to speakers of other languages* (pp. 180–185). New York: Cambridge University Press.

Marckwardt, A. H. (1978). *The place of literature in teaching English as a second or foreign language.* Honolulu: University of Hawaii Press.

Marshall, M. (1979). Love and death in Eden: Teaching English literature to ESL students. *TESOL Quarterly, 13,* 331–338.

McConochie, J. (1985). "Musing on the lamp-flame": Teaching a narrative poem in a college-level ESOL class. *TESOL Quarterly, 19,* 125–136.

McKay, S. (1982). Literature in the ESL classroom. *TESOL Quarterly, 16,* 529–536.

McKay, S. (2001). Literature as content for ESL/EFL. In M. Celce-Murcia (Ed.), *Teaching English as a second or foreign language* (3rd ed., pp. 319–332). Boston: Heinle & Heinle.

Meloni, C. F. (1994). Reading for pleasure: Short novels in academic university ESL programs. *Journal of the Imagination in Language Learning, 2,* 50–54.

Morrow, N. (1997). The role of reading in the composition classroom. *JAC: A Journal of Composition Theory, 17,* 453–472.

Nash, T., & Yun-Pi, Y. (1992/1993). Extensive reading for learning and enjoyment. *TESOL Journal, 2*(2), 27–31.

Oster, J. (1989). Seeing with different eyes: Another view of literature in the ESL class. *TESOL Quarterly, 23,* 85–103.

Peterson, J. (1995). Through the looking-glass: A response. *College English, 57,* 310–318.

Povey, J. F. (1967). Literature in TESOL programs: The language and the culture. *TESOL Quarterly, 1,* 40–46.

Sadarangani, U. (1994). Teaching multicultural issues in the composition classroom: A review of recent practice. *Journal of Teaching Writing, 13,* 33–54.

Sage, H. (1987). *Incorporating literature in ESL instruction.* Englewood Cliffs, NJ: Prentice Hall.

Shapiro, N. (1991). [Review of *Across cultures: A reader for writers; American mosaic: Multicultural readings in context; Emerging voices: A cross cultural reader; Intercultural journeys through reading and writing;* and *Writing about the world*]. *College Composition and Communication, 42*, 524–530.

Spack, R. (1985). Literature, reading, writing, and ESL: Bridging the gaps. *TESOL Quarterly, 19*, 703–725.

Spack, R. (1994). *The international story: An anthology with guidelines for reading and writing about fiction.* New York: St. Martin's.

Steinberg, E. R. (1995). Imaginative literature in composition classrooms? *College English, 57*, 266–280.

Tate, G. (1993). A place for literature in freshman composition. *College English, 55*, 317–321.

Tate, G. (1995). Notes on the dying of a conversation. *College English, 57*, 303–309.

Vandrick, S. (1994). Teaching social justice issues through literature. *CATESOL Journal, 7*(2), 113–119.

Vandrick, S. (1996a). Issues in using multicultural literature in college ESL classes. *Journal of Second Language Writing, 5*, 253–269.

Vandrick, S. (1996b). Teaching critical thinking and reading for peace education. *College ESL, 6*(2), 27–36.

Vandrick, S. (1997a). Diaspora literature: A mirror for ESL students. *College ESL, 7*(2), 53–69.

Vandrick, S. (1997b). Reading and responding to novels in the university ESL classroom. *The Journal of the Imagination in Language Learning, 4*, 104–107.

Widdowson, H. G. (1982). The use of literature. In M. Hines & W. Rutherford (Eds.), *On TESOL '81* (pp. 203–214). Washington, DC: TESOL.

Willoquet-Maricondi, P. (1991/1992). Integrating ESOL skills through literature. *TESOL Journal, 1*(2), 11–14.

Zandy, J. (1998). The job, the job: The risks of work and the uses of texts. In A. Shepard, J. McMillan, & G. Tate (Eds.), *Coming to class: Pedagogy and the social class of teachers* (pp. 281–308). Portsmouth, NH: Boynton/Cook/Heinemann.

PART V:
EXPLORING TECHNOLOGY

There can be little doubt that computers have vastly altered how writers produce texts. From the obvious use of computer keyboards as alternatives to the typewriters that earlier replaced pen and paper as the most typical means of transcribing ideas into words, to the ease with which electronic mail facilitates communication across near and vast distances, technological advances continue to shape people's literate activities (see Kern, 2000, pp. 223–266).

The contributions of technology to the field of language learning go back a long way and extend well beyond the role of computers in writing courses (for brief overviews of numerous possibilities, see Hanson-Smith, 2001; Sokolik, 2001). Still, it is critical for writing teachers to remember that they have a vital role to play in helping their students find (new) ways to use computers effectively for writing and research purposes. For example, information available via the World Wide Web has altered and expanded the ways in which student researchers can access data and ideas (Slaouti, 2002), offering a path to greater control over their own learning.

For some teachers and students, creating an expanding role for computers will involve overcoming computer anxiety; this leads to a kind of resistance that can prove counter-productive to achieving improvement in academic writing skills (cf. Davidson & Tomic, 1994). In an online review of Jane Ward Schofield's book *Computers and Classroom Culture* (Cambridge University Press, 1995), Bump (2000) notes that "teacher resistance remains the primary obstacle to the advance of [computer use] in English," echoing Schofield's finding that many teachers enrolled in university courses reported fear, anxiety, and phobia in regard to computer use. Teachers need to see that computers are not a threat to the key role they themselves play in classroom interactions; rather, the computer is a tool of most value to those who can learn to tap into its potential.

How do computers and technology enhance (or hinder) the delivery of writing courses to second language writers?

To foster a broader understanding of how computers contribute to the second language (L2) writing class, and to counter potential insecurity on the part of novice teachers, Chapter 12, by Martha Pennington, addresses the role of computers and technology as specifically relevant in L2 writing contexts. In numerous settings, teachers of both first language (L1) and L2 writing courses make assumptions – or possibly require – that students will hand in computer-mediated written work using their own choice of word processing programs. In some settings, particularly in North America, many freshman composition courses are specifically designed to take place in a computer lab with the dual goal of (1) helping students become more proficient at using the computer to produce texts and (2) utilizing computer capabilities for interactive peer response, mastering research skills, and so on. Regrettably, in many other settings, some teachers might feel ill-trained or disinclined to address the issue of the computer in their writing class. Pennington's chapter shows how important it is for teachers to find ways to include a computer component in their pedagogical repertoire. She discusses various computer media, including word processing, networked computers, and hypermedia, suggesting that L2 teachers have a responsibility to be proactive in ensuring the optimal use of technology not only in promoting but also in transforming literacy.

References

Bump, J. (2000). [Review of Janet Ward Schofield, *Computers and classroom culture*]. *Currents in Electronic Literacy, Spring 2000, 3.* Available at http://www.cwrl.utexas.edu/currents/spr00/culture.html

Davidson, C., & Tomic, A. (1994). Removing computer phobia from the writing classroom. *ELT Journal, 48,* 205–214.

Hanson-Smith, E. (2001). Computer-assisted language learning. In R. Carter & D. Nunan (Eds.), *The Cambridge guide to teaching English to speakers of other languages* (pp. 107–113). New York: Cambridge University Press.

Kern, R. (2000). *Literacy and language teaching.* Oxford and New York: Oxford University Press.

Slaouti, D. (2002). The World Wide Web for academic purposes: Old study skills for new? *English for Specific Purposes, 21,* 105–124.

Sokolik, M. (2001). Computers in language teaching. In M. Celce-Murcia (Ed.), *Teaching English as a second/foreign language* (3rd ed., pp. 477–488). Boston: Heinle & Heinle.

12 The impact of the computer in second language writing

Martha C. Pennington

The computer in its many guises as writing tool and communications medium is changing the way we interact with information and with each other. Whether in the form of a word processor installed on a personal computer (PC), a group of PCs linked in a computer lab or a university network, or the Internet connecting people and electronic information sources around the globe, the computer is having a profound effect on literacy practices in the present age. It is, at the same time, contributing to an ongoing expansion of information and communication resources that has put English in the hands of more and more people around the globe.

These trends have created a great demand for literacy in English as a second language (ESL) as well as for literacy in computer writing tools, issues that are sometimes hard to separate. Many of our literacy practices in education, work, and social life have moved off the page and onto the screen: more and more people are doing the majority of their writing and reading on computer and transmitting messages electronically rather than on paper (Warschauer, 1999).

As the communicator of the present day and especially of the future is inevitably linked to electronic media, those charged with instructing ESL students in writing cannot afford to remain outside these developments, teaching without regard to the communication technologies that are increasingly at the center of their students' world; teachers should be prepared to bring computers into the center of their own pedagogical practice. The modern ESL writing teacher needs to understand the nature of electronic writing media, the kinds of impacts these media have on students' writing, and the ways they can best be employed in the teaching of writing. This chapter aims to raise the awareness of ESL writing teachers regarding electronic writing media, their effects on ESL writers, and their pedagogical applications, beginning with a review of some critical issues in word processing and then moving on to networking, hypermedia, and the use of the Internet as a research tool/assistant for writers.

Word processing

The basic writing tool provided by the computer is a word processor, with most word processors including a spellchecker and many including a grammar checker as well. Most people agree that word processors are useful for writing because they facilitate the mechanical processes of putting words on paper; revising text by substitutions, deletions, additions, and block moves; and producing attractive and readable finished copy. The word processor is not only a convenient tool combining an automated typewriter, editor, and printer; it is also a composing medium that with time and practice can significantly change the writer's process and product. Many studies have shown that beyond their facilitating effects, word processors have an impact on student writers' attitudes, the characteristics of their texts, their revising behavior and the attention they pay to form and mechanics, and the order and the type of writing activities in which they engage (for reviews and discussions of research, see Bangert-Drowns, 1993; Cochran-Smith, 1991; Pennington, 1996b, 1996c, 1999a, 1999b; Snyder, 1993).

Student attitudes

Most students have a good initial reaction to the computer and feel that it can help them in their work, though some users, especially older students, may be uncomfortable with the technology or may even be "computerphobic." Another minority of users may have their enthusiasm dampened if they experience technical problems early on, have difficulty typing or mastering computer commands, or have limited access to computers and to experienced users who can offer assistance when things go wrong. As a result, a few who try word processing will give up in frustration. Typically, however, after a period of weeks or months spent improving their keyboarding skills, most students persist and become regular computer users.

The mechanical capabilities of a word processor are especially valuable in a second language (L2) context, where the physical processes of putting words on paper and revising text to a finished product, and the cognitive processes underlying these, are more effortful and less automatized (Jones & Tetroe, 1987) than when writing in the first language (L1). Not only the actual capabilities of the machine but also the students' view of these as helpful for their writing are significant for L2 writers, who may, even more than inexperienced L1 writers, lack confidence in their writing ability (Betancourt & Phinney, 1988). Word processors can relieve the anxiety some L2 writers feel about writing the L2 script, about producing academic work in their L2, and about writing in general (Pennington, 1999a; Phinney, 1989).

Many studies conducted with L2 writers report positive attitudes associated with word processing (e.g., Neu & Scarcella, 1991; Pennington & Brock, 1992; Phinney, 1991; Phinney & Mathis, 1990). For example, in their comparison of word processing and pen-and-paper composing in English by Turkish university students, Akyel and Kamisli (1999) report that the use of the computer improved student attitudes toward writing and built up their confidence. In a longitudinal investigation of a group of mature ESL writers in Hong Kong who were able to use the computer as much or as little as they wished in their written work for a course (Rusmin, 1999), the majority of the students were positive toward the computer and adopted it for their writing from the beginning of the term or increasingly as the course progressed. On the basis of the different patterns of attitudes and computer use, Rusmin (1999) classified the 27 students in the class into six categories, which she labeled "devotees," "enthusiasts," "rededicateds," "positives," "converts," and "skeptics," categories that may be applicable to a host of students in a wide variety of locales.

Textual properties

Also related to attitude is self-consciousness. The student writer working in a computer medium is led to write in a less self-conscious way and with greater engagement, thus writing with a freer mind and less "rewriting anxiety." As a result, the student's greater involvement may lead him or her to write for longer periods of time and produce longer texts. Several studies with L2 writers (e.g., Brock & Pennington, 1999; Chadwick & Bruce, 1989; Pennington & Brock, 1992) document that longer texts are a general effect of word processing.

In addition to the production of longer texts, the physical easing of the writing process that results in a less constrained, more relaxed writing process may produce texts that are in a sense also "more relaxed." Written products generated on a word processor "are often unconstrained and experimental, being more likely to be in a non-generic form that sometimes amounts to what has been called 'train of thought' or 'spaghetti writing' – long strings of loosely connected strands of ideas" (Pennington, 2000, p. 14). In some cases, computer-produced text represents an unfinished, intermediate work that given sufficient time for continued development will result in a high-quality product (Pennington, 1996b, 1996c). In other cases, it may represent a new type of work, as when writing in hypertext – for example, for a Web page or in an e-mail context.

Revision strategies and accuracy concerns

Surface-level editing for spelling and mechanics is encouraged in a word processing environment, where the small size of text visible on one screen may engender an especially focused type of revision at word, phrase, and sentence level (Pennington, 1996b, 1999b). At the same time, the ease with which individual words can be searched and whole sections of text deleted, added, or moved suggests that word processing may have value as a macro-level revision tool. Rather than being a separate activity following the generation of a draft, revision in a computer context is closely linked to text generation. Pedagogical intervention aimed at increasing students' awareness of and ability to apply revision strategies in their own writing (e.g., Steelman, 1994) has demonstrated the value of the computer medium for helping learners increase the type and depth of their revisions.

In other research, L2 writers have been found to revise more when writing with a computer than when writing by traditional means (e.g., Chadwick & Bruce, 1989; Li & Cumming, 2001; Phinney & Khouri, 1993); to revise more dynamically and continuously (Phinney & Khouri, 1993); and to spend more time revising in a computer context, where they may "continue revising after planned changes [have] been made" (Phinney & Khouri, 1993, p. 271). Writers also make more revisions beyond the surface level. There is some evidence that word processing is more effective in stimulating meaning-level revision when aligned to a process approach to writing (Daiute, 1985; Susser, 1993) than when used without process support or with other computer writing aids such as grammar checkers (Brock & Pennington, 1999; Pennington & Brock, 1992). The research thus supports an approach that teaches the writing process in the context of learning to write and revise using a word processor.

Implications for planning

In pen-and-paper composing, writers often spend a lot of time in intensive planning before writing to avoid making mistakes or changing their minds about what they want to say and then having to undertake the tedious chore of rewriting or recopying text already written down. Under such conditions, pen-and-paper writers may habitually write a paper without any revision or with only a minimum amount of revision to avoid producing more than one draft. In sharp contrast to this paper-based mode of composing, the automated text-generation and revision tools provided on computer, coupled with the malleability of text on screen or disk, encourage a very different computer-based writing mode (Bernhardt, Edwards, & Wojahn, 1989; Haas, 1989; Williamson & Pence, 1989). In a contrasting "computer writing style," the writer generally begins writing immediately, soon after a topic is decided – or even before it is decided.

Instead of writing to fit a plan, computer writers plan as they are writing (Haas, 1989), an effect also documented for L2 writers (Akyel & Kamisli, 1999; Li & Cumming, 2001). Planning thus becomes more of a middle stage than a beginning stage activity, and the time and intensive cognitive activity that would have been involved in pre-planning is instead involved in writing itself. The sharp division of composing into the three stages of planning, writing, and revising breaks down in a computer context, in which planning as well as revision occurs as part of the writing process. In the computer-engendered approach to writing, cognitive effort is distributed throughout the writing process and writing is developed more on the basis of concrete text already generated than on an abstract plan; this procedure would seem to be especially valuable for L2 writers, who have less cognitive capacity available for writing than do L1 writers.

Weighing the advantages and disadvantages

In spite of the obvious advantages of the computer over pen-and-paper writing in terms of automation, flexibility, and cognitive demands, the results of research on the quality of writing produced in a computer context are not all favorable, as only some studies have yielded positive effects for student compositions produced by word processing in contrast to pen and paper (see Pennington, 1996b, 1996c, 1999a, 1999b, for reviews). A mixed pattern of findings can be seen in the L2 literature: in some studies, word processing gave writers an advantage in terms of writing quality (e.g., Lam & Pennington, 1995; McGarrell, 1993), while in others, word processing gave no advantage over pen and paper (e.g., Benesch, 1987; Chadwick & Bruce, 1989).

These mixed results from individual studies have often been used to caution teachers against an easy acceptance of word processing; however, three summative (meta-analytical) reviews of research results comparing word processing to pen-and-paper composing have demonstrated an advantage for computer-produced over pen-produced text in terms of traditional measures of writing quality (Bangert-Drowns, 1993; Roblyer, Castine, & King, 1988; Schramm, 1989). In addition, most studies showing negative results for word processing were carried out from the late 1970s to the mid 1980s, and some of the negative findings may have been related to the characteristics of early word processors, subjects' unfamiliarity with computers, the context of research, or the ways in which effects were measured in these early studies. Teachers are therefore cautioned against placing too much weight on the older studies of word processing; they are advised instead to base their decisions about computer use on more recent findings and the accumulated comparative evidence, which generally show a positive impact of word processing on students' writing. At the same time, teachers should always keep an eye out for the latest trends in computer use and research findings, bearing in mind that the focus and the results of research are likely to change as the context for writing on computers also changes – from word processed compositions to e-mail and Web pages.

As in all other cases in which new technologies or teaching approaches are introduced, teachers' and learners' behavior is dictated by their knowledge and understanding of the innovation. As students learn how to apply their word processing capabilities in their writing, they are likely to develop positive attitudes toward the computer writing medium and the context of writing, which may in the case of L2 writers extend also to their attitudes toward the English language. When the learners' knowledge and attitudes are favorable, that is, when their "cognitive-affective response" to word processing is positive, in the process of learning about the medium they will gradually experience effects on their writing behavior of three types (Pennington, 1996b, 1996c, 1999a, 1999b):

Manner Effects. A sense of the ease of writing and revising in a fluid writing process involving continuous and recursive write-revise cycles
Quantity Effects. Writing for extended periods of time, producing long texts with much content and many revisions
Quality Effects. Writing to a high standard in terms of topic development, formal characteristics, and writing goal

Given enough time and favorable circumstances for learning, these three types of effects, represented in Figure 12.1, may ultimately result in high-quality written products.

Under less favorable conditions, learners may not experience a positive cognitive-affective response to word processing if they have low awareness of computer potential that can help them in their writing, if they are intimidated by the computer or find it difficult to use, or if they experience frequent mechanical breakdowns. Consequently, under such conditions, their behavioral response is essentially the opposite of the learners' response found in more positive circumstances. This negative response consists of

Anti-Manner Effects. A sense of the difficulty of writing and revising, reinforcing a one-shot linear plan-write process
Anti-Quantity Effects. Limited time spent writing, producing short texts with restricted content and few revisions
Anti-Quality Effects. Writing to a minimal standard in terms of topic development, formal characteristics, and writing goal

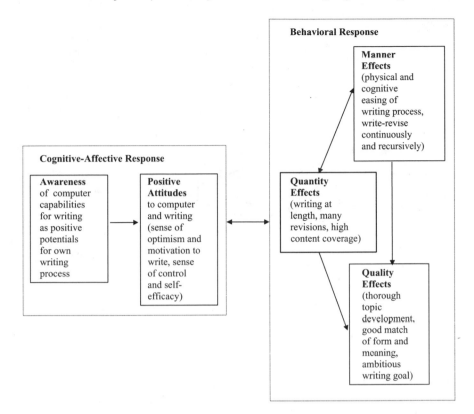

Figure 12.1. The positive path in computer writing effects (adapted from Pennington 1999a, p. 283). Used with permission from Swets & Zeitlinger.

These three types of behavioral effects, illustrated in Figure 12.2, represent disfavoring conditions that predict poor written products.

Whatever the research findings, the inevitable presence of word processors in L2 contexts and in the future of most of our students is undeniable, and any teacher who ignores this reality is avoiding a responsibility to teach to student needs.

Networking

Another way in which ESL writing teachers find that computers can play a key role in instruction is when they have the opportunity to teach in or have their students participate in a networked environment. A local area network (LAN or intranet), such as in a computer lab, or a wide area network (WAN), such as the Internet or World Wide Web,

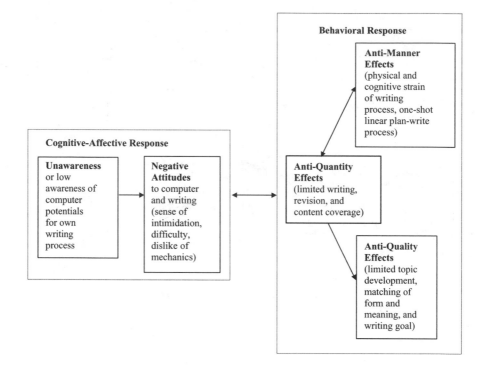

Figure 12.2. The negative path in computer writing effects (adapted from Pennington 1999a, p. 285). Used with permission from Swets & Zeitlinger.

makes it possible to extend the computer writing environment by linking student writers to other people with whom they may interact to develop their writing. Through a computer network, students' computers may be linked to those of their teachers as well as other students as a way to develop collaborative work or to gain input on their writing other than by face-to-face interaction (Bruce, Peyton, & Batson, 1993; Bruce & Rubin, 1993; Mabrito, 1991; Palmquist, 1993). All types of network arrangements have the potential for motivating L2 students to write and to revise in response to a real audience, for helping them to gain more input on their writing, for encouraging them to experiment in their writing, and for empowering them to seek out the resources they need for developing their ideas.

Within a computer network, students may participate in such novel activities as online feedback on classmates' work or "team editing" (Kaufer & Neuwirth, 1995) as well as the sending and receiving of e-mail "letters" or other sorts of messages (Howard, 1992). Where the students' computers are linked in a network, the potentials for collaboration and participatory interaction are increased (Warschauer, 1997). Some of this collaboration and interaction takes place around the computer; but increasingly it takes place in cyberspace, with the interactors being physically removed – often at great distances – from one another. As a result, the writer may be encouraged to experiment with ideas and with language because of the risk-free social access afforded by electronic connectivity. At the same time networks bring writers together to increase shared knowledge and produce collaborative work, they also seem to help student writers to create an individual voice. Moran and Hawisher (1998) observe that writers can use online space to create alternative selves and to experiment with roles that they might not assume in face-to-face interaction.

E-mail exchanges

In a departmental or university-wide network, writing teachers can use e-mail to contact their students, and students can have easy access to their teachers to ask questions about their work and to receive feedback on drafts. As a further advantage, e-mail aids students working together on team projects to fulfill written assignments (Hoffman, 1996). With a university-wide network, L2 students can be linked to L1 partners or more experienced L2 students on campus (Nabors & Swartley, 1999). With Internet access, L2 students can participate in information exchange with sister classes and e-mail partners overseas (Sayers, 1989; Slater & Carpenter, 1999; Woodin, 1997), such as via the International Tandem Network (available at: http://www.slf. ruhr-uni-bochum.de/email/stats-eng.html) or via the Intercultural E-mail Classroom Connections (IECC) service (http://www.teaching.com/iecc/). Woodin (1997) points out that in providing an opportunity for real communication one-on-one with speakers of the target language, e-mail functions "as a bridge between the language classroom and the natural setting. There is the opportunity for contact with a variety of native speakers, but from within the safety of one's own environment" (p. 31). In either type of partnering arrangement, the e-mail contact may allow writers to obtain information or input from a real audience in relation to their written assignments. Or the contact with other communicators over a network may itself function as stimulation for students' writing.

Lists, newsgroups, and bulletin boards

An additional possibility is to join a group that communicates by e-mail through a discussion list. Within each of these lists, many of which are available via Listserv, there is a wide range of topics that subscribers may access or participate in. Lists often serve the purpose of providing specialized information or the answers to questions in a field. For example, students or teachers might request information about language teaching from the ESL list, TESL-L (listserv@cunyvm.cuny.edu); about teaching ESL on a network from NETEACH-L (listserv@raven.cc.ukans.edu); or about linguistics, language acquisition, or a specific language such as English from the applied linguistics list, LINGUIST (listserv@tamvm1.tamu.edu). Such specialized lists can be used to locate experts and other sources of information in a specific field or on a specific topic. They also often serve the purpose of debating issues, generating different points of view, and comparing different (well-known or unknown) people's information or points of view. Windeatt, Hardisty, and Eastment (2000) have activities for introducing students to discussion lists (Activity 1.9, pp. 43–45) and for setting up an electronic list (Activity 1.11, pp. 47–49).

A newsgroup is a group of users networked by e-mail for specialized discussions through a service called Usenet, which has newsgroups of various kinds for different countries, such as in the UK (http://www.usenet.org.uk/) or Norway (http://www.usenet.no/). A bulletin board is like a list except that instead of receiving information via e-mail, the user goes to a specific Web site to read messages posted on the bulletin board. Bulletin boards thus allow for individual access to information and individual choice as to whether and when to participate. Students might visit bulletin boards as part of Internet searches (see Windeatt, Hardisty, & Eastment, 2000, for suggestions). A bulletin board can also be set up for a specific class or group of students (e.g., at a site called BeSeen, http://www.beseen.com/board/index.html), as a way to encourage their independence, full participation, and sharing of information. Bulletin boards are also of value to teachers for sharing resources and expertise and for building a sense of community. For example, in a study of students in a TESOL (Teachers of English to Speakers of Other Languages) methods course interacting on a World Wide Web bulletin board, Kamhi-Stein (2000) found that the electronic medium encouraged participants to take responsibility for learning both collectively and individually, as shown by a high level of student-led interaction, collaborative learning, and equal participation by native and non-native students alike.

Synchronous communication: Chat, MUDs, and MOOs

In addition to the asynchronous, or saved and time-delayed transmission of messages via e-mail and e-mail lists, networked communication includes several types of synchronous, or nearly immediate, real-time communication. One interactive writing program, *Daedalus Interchange* (Daedalus, Inc.), allows students in a networked class to send a message related to a writing task to other students simultaneously.

Teleconferencing and videoconferencing, though not widely used in instruction, are other examples of synchronous communication. An increasingly popular type of program is text-conferencing software, most commonly in the form of Internet relay chat (IRC) programs, such as *Microsoft Chat* (Microsoft Corp.) or *mIRC* (available free at: http://www.mirc.com/), which makes it possible for participants to have an online discussion or "chat" by typing at the computer keyboard while others who are also logged on to the same site can watch the interaction evolve. There are many open IRC "chat rooms," and a closed chat room can also be set up for selected participants.

An advantage is the equality of the interaction, as every participant has the same chance to initiate a topic and/or to respond to another's turn. There is also the possibility of any number of people composing input at the same time. These discussion programs therefore offer possibilities for expanding student writers' ability to gather and refine their ideas in interaction with others. They can also, like e-mail and other forms of net-worked communication, stimulate creativity and personalization. There are some disadvantages, however, as Windeatt, Hardisty, and Eastment (2000) observe:

Unfortunately, the more people join in a 'chat', the more disjointed the discussion is. In addition, the contributions to the discussion are often short and people tend to use abbreviations, and make a lot of typing mistakes. Nevertheless . . . IRC can be useful for discussion among a small number of people, especially as the discussion can be 'logged', i.e. a copy can be saved on disk, to look at more carefully later. (p. 113)

Such functions have utility for writing, for example, in interacting about ideas for writing and giving feedback on writing, and in general, for establishing and maintaining contact with a community of writers not only in a networked classroom but also beyond the confines of a classroom. Note, however, that IRC software (unlike, for example, the *Daedalus* package) is not specifically designed for composing-related use and in fact seems to promote a type of spontaneous playfulness that encourages the breaking of conventions.

Two additional types of synchronous communication are MUDs (multi-user domains) and MOOs (multi-user domains, object-oriented). Like text-conferencing, these involve multiple users interacting online by going to a specific Web site and typing information on a keyboard. Rather than chat sites, these are Internet-based specialized environments or virtual worlds where participants can interact with each other or ac-cess information. Unlike chat rooms, in which the interaction exists only as long as users remain online, these environments are structured to have continuity of characters, spaces (e.g., "rooms"), and objects from one session to another.

A MOO is similar to a simulation in which participants interact on-line. Since participants are generally linked from all over the globe, a MOO can be seen as a type of "global village" in which students can be linked with an international group of participants as resources for their ideas and their writing. MOO interactions have the special characteristic that users can assume one or more imaginary identities and keep their real identity hidden, thus encouraging playfulness and experimentation. MOO interactions may therefore have some value in stimulating student writers to develop ideas and "freeing" them to experiment with different authorial voices and writing styles.

An example of a MOO that incorporates properties of other sorts of Web sites is schMOOze University (http://schmooze.hunter. cuny.edu:8888/), which is described on the opening page of the Web site as

a small, friendly college known for its hospitality and the diversity of the student population . . . established as a place where people studying English as a second or foreign language could practice English while sharing ideas and experiences with other learners and practitioners of English. Students have opportunities for one-on-one and group conversations as well as access to language games, an online dictionary, virtual stockbroker and many language games.

The schMOOze University Web site includes an introduction to the MOO environment and the schMOOze University, a Virtual English Language Center, Internet TESL Journal pages for ESL students, a collaborative MOO project, teacher discussions on NETEACH-L, and a link to Dave's ESL Café (an ESL Web site run by Dave Sperling, an ESL instructor based in the United States).

Expanding peer response

Communication in a networked environment can change some of the dynamics of peer feedback sessions as found in traditional classrooms (discussed by Ferris, Chapter 5 this volume). Sullivan and Pratt (1996) discovered that the communication that occurred as peer feedback over the computer network was of a type that might have been especially valuable for students in improving their writing. They summarize some of the contrasts as follows:

[Face-to-face peer] discussions were often filled with personal narratives (students focusing on themselves rather than the task at hand) and short interjections of agreement (uh-huh) or repetition . . . [whereas, over the network] . . . the responses followed a pattern that consisted of a positive comment about the essay followed by one or more suggestions for revision. (p. 499)

Moreover, the networked feedback from more than one student tended to reinforce the same points and the same suggestions for revision, thereby perhaps focusing the writer's attention on certain points for revision. However, in a study carried out with EFL writing students in Hong Kong, Braine (2001) reports that the feedback given in a networked environment did not result in better written texts. He found that final draft essays written by students who engaged in traditional face-to-face classroom peer interaction received higher holistic scores and showed greater gains than final drafts written by students who carried out peer discussions via a LAN (Braine, 2001, p. 283). Thus, networking student writers electronically does not guarantee better writing.

Changing patterns of communication

There is some evidence that more focused use of language is a general effect of networked communication: "With more opportunities and different opportunities to negotiate input in a computer environment come not only a greater quantity of language, particularly, the second language, but also more focused, explicit, and specific uses of language" (Pennington, 1996a, p. 2). This is probably because the relatively "cueless environment" (Spears & Lea, 1992) of the computer context makes it necessary to invoke the context of the speech event more explicitly than would be required in face-to-face communication. In a study of ESL learners exchanging information by e-mail in Canada, Esling (1991) found that "in the initial exchange of notes, the communication is characterized by revelation of information about local setting which would not normally be exchanged but which would rather be taken for granted and left unsaid in face-to-face conversation" (pp. 126–127). A similar finding is reported by Nabors and Swartley (1999) in a study in which e-mail partners were provided for ESL students on an American university campus. Thus, the relatively cueless environment, coupled with the anonymity and ease of communication in an electronic network, may promote both a more content-rich and a more individual and creative form of writing.

Discourse implications

Writing over a network can add real audiences, input, and motivation to write; also, the online context changes the writing task to one that has some of the attributes of spoken interaction. Thus, for example, Nabors and Swartley (1999) found that the ESL e-mail penpals in their study used a range of strategies to build a relationship with their partner, many of which, such as giving personal information and sharing feelings, are also common in face-to-face relationships. As Moran (1995) notes:

"E-mail is, simultaneously, the most intimate and the most public form of correspondence" (p. 16). In consequence, discourse produced in an e-mail context shares characteristics with both personal and professional letters, as well as with some speech genres, particularly, public interviews (Collot & Belmore, 1996). At the same time, based on its unique contextual attributes, e-mail communication appears to be evolving as a new genre, which Baron (2000) describes as a "creole" that merges some properties of both speech and writing. The e-mail context may therefore contribute to improving the student's fluency and willingness to write even as it contributes to a breakdown of established writing conventions and genres. This breakdown of conventions appears to be even greater in synchronous network communication.

Hypertext / hypermedia

Another development of import to writers is the possibilities for creating hypertext, a computer tool for building "layered text":

Like Chinese boxes, text can be nested within text, and huge texts can reside within tiny fragments. With the combination of both hierarchical subordination and lateral links from any point to any point, hypertext offers greatly expanded possibilities for new structures characterized by layering and flexibility. (Bernhardt, 1993, p. 164)

In hypertext, writers create "mosaics of information" (Marcus, 1993) made up of chunks of information arranged on computer "pages." These chunks of information, which may be textual, visual, auditory, or any combination of these, are connected by electronic links in a Web page format. Users are then free to create their own paths to negotiate the information from one part of the screen to another or from one screen to another.

The possibility of linking a chunk of text to another to create "information layers" encourages a new mode of "layered thinking" and "layered composing." Because of its nonlinear properties, "hypertext ... may help support an enriched network of thoughts and associations that assists writers to explore and develop their ideas, thereby enhancing the cognitive potentials of [the computer]" (Pennington, 1996b, p. 23). The possibility of combining chunks of text with "sound bites," "video bites," and other "media chunks" adds creative potential for illustrating written work while also encouraging the creation of new modes of presentation using text, other visual media, and sound media. When all these potentials are combined with Internet access, the computer offers a distributed set of links and a highly creative, all-purpose hypermedia or multimedia communication tool.

Web pages and Web sites

The World Wide Web (generally referred to as "the Web") is a sector of the Internet made up of linked hypertext sites that can be accessed by mouse clicks. A Web browser such as Internet Explorer or Netscape Navigator is needed to read Web pages. Web searches can be conducted online using search engines such as Google (http://www.google.com/) and AltaVista (http://www.altavista.com/), which, among other things, allow the user to type in a word or phrase to find Web pages that contain all or some of the desired words or that match these most closely. Web pages can be created using various tools and then put up on a local-area network or placed on a public drive. Software such as Microsoft Inc.'s FrontPage or Macromedia's Dreamweaver will allow a teacher to manage a Web site (and also to author Web pages). In addition, Windeat, Hardisty, and Eastment (2000) have a Web site linked to their book with useful information for teachers regarding Web pages and anything to do with the Internet (available via the Oxford Teachers' Club at http://www.oup.com/elt/global/teachersclub/). Another useful resource is the WebCT (World-Wide-Web Course Tools) program (available at: http://www.webct.com/) used by Kamhi-Stein (2000) in her TESOL teacher education course. It offers Web-based bulletin board systems, group presentation and chat areas, conferencing tools, and e-mail.

Increasingly, hypermedia tools and the Web are defining new domains of communication and literacy, including a new emphasis on visual and combined-media literacy (Kress, 1998), extending to new dimensions some of the more conventional reading and writing connections important to L2 students (see Grabe, Chapter 10 this volume). An investigation comparing texts written by L2 French students in pen-and-paper, word processing, and hypertext modes (Marcoul & Pennington, 1999) found that the latter medium, when aligned to a student newspaper Web site, sparked students' creativity and drew their attention to visual aspects of design at the same time that it drew their attention away from surface correction of language. Interestingly, although the students in the Marcoul and Pennington (1999) study made fewer surface revisions, they made more content and paragraph-level revisions in hypertext than in the other two modes. This comparative study of writing media suggests that having students write in hypertext for a Web page may encourage them to spend more time refining their texts in terms of content and organization of information at the same time that it encourages them to focus on other aspects of presentation that take time away from the writing process per se.

In the instructional project investigated by Marcoul and Pennington (1999), readers could interact with student creators of Web pages to add comments to their text and to visit the links that writers had created to their Web pages. In this way, readers interacted with writers by collaborating in the ongoing development of texts and by exploring a part of the writer's world. The interactive creation of text, which is greatly facilitated by network and Web-based communication, is a major area of literacy innovation that has value for L2 writers.

In a study that involved Web explorations by junior high school students in Mexico, Romano, Field, and de Huergo (2000) report on the students' engagement with knowledge outside their community, including their engagement with the English language, finding "a strong tendency for Web literacy and literacy in English to converge, becoming nearly one and the same" (p. 204). An investigation by Lam (2000) of the e-mail and text-conferencing chat activities of a Chinese adolescent immigrant to the United States revealed that "the English he controlled on the Internet enabled him to develop a sense of belonging and connectedness to a global English-speaking community" (p. 476). In a discussion of Web communication in Australia, McConaghy and Snyder (2000) stress the interaction of local and global knowledge and perspectives that result from this type of communication. As they conclude: "Perhaps, in the final analysis, the possibilities for engaging the local in the global through the World Wide Web represent the new medium's greatest potential" (McConaghy & Snyder, 2000, p. 89).

The Internet and World Wide Web as resources

The Internet and World Wide Web provide students access to electronic resources online that may be helpful for their writing, such as journals, library catalogs, topical databases, search services, and resources on English language. Most journals' Web sites give access to contents and abstracts and in some cases, to articles in past issues. Bibliomania (http://www.bibliomania.com/) is a resource for searching reference materials and works of fiction, drama, poetry, and religious texts. Project Gutenberg Electronic Library (http://promo.net/pg/index.html/) offers free download of a variety of electronic texts, and Kidon Media-Link (http://www.kidon.com/media-link/) provides links to Web editions of thousands of newspapers. Online dictionaries are available for English and other languages at http://www.dictionary.com/, a Web site that includes a language discussion forum, *Roget's Thesaurus*, and writing resources such as grammar, usage, and style guides, including some for writing on the Internet. Many grammar references are also available online, such as Charles Darling's Guide to Grammar and Writing (http://cctc2.commnet. edu/grammar/), and Professional Training Company's Good Grammar,

Good Style TM Archive (http://www.protrainco.com/grammar.htm). The text by Windeatt, Hardisty, and Eastment (2000) contains a variety of structured activities for students to learn how to negotiate the Internet and to use different types of resources available on the World Wide Web, such as English language stories, films, and new sources.

The Web is also an excellent resource for teachers, offering quick access to professional organizations such as TESOL (http://www.tesol.org/) and IATEFL (the international Association of Teachers of English as a Foreign Language) (http://www.iatefl.org/); teaching materials and articles, such as those through ERIC Educational Resources Information Center (http:/www.askeric.org/); online journals, such as the monthly *Internet TESL Journal* (http://www.aitech.ac.jp/~iteslj/), and the quarterly *TESL E-J* (http://www-writing.berkeley.edu/TESL-EJ/); teaching sites, such as the Beaumont Publishers' Virtual Learning Community site for K-12 projects (http://www.cyberjourneys.net/), the English Through the Internet projects of Elaine Hoter (http://web.macam98.ac.il/~elaine/eti/), the Email Projects Home Page by Susan Gaer (http://www.otan.us/webfarm/emailproject/email.htm), and the Linguistic Funland TESL Page (http://www.linguistic-funland.com/tesl.html/), a rich site including everything from listings of job opportunities and graduate programs in TESL to teaching and testing materials and services for students. There are also useful individually-sponsored Web pages with information oriented toward teaching English as a second language, such as those of Dave Sperling (http://www.eslcafe.com/), Ruth Vilmi (http://www.ruthvilmi.net/hut/), or Mark Warschauer (http://www.gse.uci.edu/markw/). In addition, a good annotated compilation called "Internet Projects for Learners and Teachers of English" is available at http://www.wfi.fr/ volterre/ inetpro.html/.

Other electronic resources include concordancing programs, such as TACT (available at http://tactweb.humanities.mcmaster.ca/) or Athelstan, Inc.'s MonoConc (available at http://www.athel.com/); these allow student writers and their teachers to search their own or others' texts for the occurrence and contexts of specific words or phrases. With Internet access, they can search online corpora such as the British National Corpus Online (available at http://www. hcu.ox.ac.uk/bnc) and find out about others, such as those listed at the University of Lancaster UCREL (University Centre for Computer Corpus Research on Language) Web site (http://www.comp.lancs.ac.uk/ computing/research/ucrel/corpora.html). There are also online resources for preventing and detecting plagiarism, such as Plagiarism. org (http://www.plagiarism.org/) and the Indiana University Writing Resources Web page (http://www.indiana.edu/~wts/wts/plagiarism. html).

Potentials and issues

The computer offers a wide variety of literacy and communication tools that may assist more people to achieve literacy in one or more languages than ever before. At the same time, "the result of writing in an electronic medium may not be the written products of a pen-and-paper age but more ephemeral forms of *think-text* and *talk-text*" (Pennington, 2000, p. 21). In addition, in the contexts of computer-mediated communication, writing is moving in the direction of, on the one hand, a more social construction of the activity and interactivity of writing and, on the other, a more media-saturated construction of text as existing within a rich nexus of other resources.

The value of the computer for the L2 writer is considerable for helping to automate the production and revision of text, to encode ideas, and to spark and energize the writing process. With the additional resources of networking and hypermedia, it offers a veritable banquet of media and communication options. Figure 12.3 summarizes some potentials of the computer to aid L2 student writers.

In addition, as Warschauer (2000b) notes, computer media empower students and give them greater control over their own learning, thus increasing their *agency*:

Agency is really what makes students so excited about using computers in the classroom: the computer provides them a powerful means to make their stamp on the world. Think, for example, of the difference between authoring a paper (i.e., writing a text for the teacher), and authoring a multimedia document (i.e., creatively bringing together several media to share with a wide international audience), and even helping to author the very rules by which multimedia is created. . . . By allowing and helping our students to carry out all these types of authoring – toward fulfilling a meaningful purpose for a real audience – we are helping them exercise their agency. The purpose of studying English is thus not just to "know it" as an internal system, but to be able to use it to have a real impact on the world. (p. 7)

At the same time the computer offers all of these potentials to student writers, certain issues of literacy on the computer remain to be resolved, as summarized in Figure 12.4.

Those of us involved in teaching L2 writing can help to ensure computer access for all to avoid a division of the world into computer "haves" and "have-nots" that Warschauer (2000a) terms the "digital divide."

At the same time, we need to consider what effective limits might be on students' computer access, so as to keep work on the computer from taking up too much of their time and attention and from replacing human contact. There are also issues we need to address about how to assess the new types of work produced in computer contexts, such as group-produced essays, Web pages, and the illustrated texts and texted

Computer assistance in the way of mechanical tools and an

environment to help with writing, revising, and

dissemination of text

Increased writing *efficiency and effectiveness*

Increased *motivation*

Increased *amount of writing*

More *effective use of language*

Creative potential

Interactivity and collaboration

New *modes and genres* of writing

Flexibility of access to tools, texts, helps, and partners

Expanded access to writing resources, information, and the world

Figure 12.3.   Computer potentials for L2 writers

illustrations made possible by multimedia and hypertext. It is also important to consider what values should be stressed in evaluating students' computer-produced work. For example, should originality be emphasized over correctness and quality of layout emphasized as much as quality of content and linguistic form? Finally, there are important matters we need to consider about whether and how to control students' use of others' work and "unsuitable information" (e.g., pornography or violent material) available electronically.

Issues of access and control in computer contexts are matters that we in ESL need to be concerned about. As observed by Hawisher and Selfe (2000):

The Web is a complicated and contested site for postmodern literacy practices. This site is characterized by a strongly influential set of tendential cultural forces, primarily oriented toward the values of the white, western industrialized nations that were responsible for designing and building the network and that continue to exert power within it. Hence, this system of networked computers is far from world-wide; it does not provide a culturally neutral conduit for the transmission of information; it is not a culturally

Access

How to ensure computer access for all?

What (if any) is a reasonable limit to computer access?

Assessment

How to assess group-produced essays?

How to assess writing in hypertext / Web pages?

How to assess illustrated text / texted illustrations?

Control

How / whether to keep students from "using" the work

of others available on Internet?

How / whether to keep students from "surfing" the net

to find "inappropriate" material?

Figure 12.4.   Issues of literacy on computer

neutral or innocent communication landscape open to the literacy practices and values of all global citizens. But the site is also far from totalizing in its effects..., [as] [t]he Web also provides a site for transgressive literary practices that express and value difference; that cling to historical, cultural, and racial diversity; and that help groups and individuals constitute their own multiple identities through language. (p. 15)

How we make use of computer potentials with our L2 learners and how we resolve the issues surrounding the use of electronic media are matters of great interest and concern. Even more important than how these matters are resolved is that we take an active role in computer-affected outcomes, that we are directly involved in resolving computer issues and deciding the best ways to make use of computer potentials for our own population of students, that is, L2 writers. In the present day, no ESL teacher can afford to remain on the sidelines of these developments, which have transformed and are continuing to transform literacy, language, and all communication in very significant ways.

References

Akyel, A., & Kamisli, S. (1999). Word processing in the EFL classroom: Effects on writing strategies, attitudes, and products. In M. C. Pennington (Ed.), *Writing in an electronic medium: Research with language learners* (pp. 27–60). Houston: Athelstan.

Bangert-Drowns, R. L. (1993). The word processor as an instructional tool: A meta-analysis of word processing in writing instruction. *Review of Educational Research, 63,* 69–93.

Baron, N. S. (2000). *Alphabet to email: How written English evolved and where it's heading.* London: Routledge.

Benesch, S. (1987). *Word processing in English as a second language: A case study of three non-native college students.* Paper presented at the conference on College Composition and Communication, Atlanta, GA. (ERIC Document No. ED 281383)

Bernhardt, S. A. (1993). The shape of text to come: The texture of print on screens. *College Composition and Communication, 44,* 151–175.

Bernhardt, S. A., Edwards, P. G., & Wojahn, P. R. (1989). Teaching college composition with computers: A program evaluation study. *Written Communication, 6,* 108–133.

Betancourt, F., & Phinney, M. (1988). Sources of writing block in bilingual writers. *Written Communication, 5,* 461–478.

Braine, G. (2001). A study of English as a foreign language (EFL) writers on a local-area network (LAN) and in traditional classes. *Computers and Composition, 18,* 275–292.

Brock, M. N., & Pennington, M. C. (1999). A comparative study of text analysis and peer tutoring as input to writing on computer in an ESL context. In M. C. Pennington (Ed.), *Writing in an electronic medium: Research with language learners* (pp. 61–94). Houston: Athelstan.

Bruce, B., Peyton, J. K., & Batson, T. (Eds.). (1993). *Network-based classrooms: Promises and realities.* New York: Cambridge University Press.

Bruce, B. C., & Rubin, A. (1993). *Electronic quills: A situated evaluation of using computers for writing in classrooms.* Hillsdale, NJ: Lawrence Erlbaum.

Chadwick, S., & Bruce, N. (1989). The revision process in academic writing: From pen and paper to word processor. *Hongkong Papers in Linguistics and Language Teaching, 12,* April, 1–27.

Cochran-Smith, M. (1991). Word processing and writing in elementary classrooms: A critical review of related literature. *Review of Educational Research, 61,* 107–155.

Collot, M., & Belmore, N. (1996). Electronic language: A new variety of English. In S. Herring (Ed.), *Computer mediated communication: Linguistic, social, and cross-cultural perspectives* (pp. 13–28). Philadelphia: John Benjamins.

Daiute, C. (1985). *Writing and computers.* Reading, MA: Addison-Wesley.

Esling, J. H. (1991). Researching the effects of networking: Evaluating the spoken and written discourse generated by working with CALL. In P. Dunkel (Ed.), *Computer-assisted language learning and testing: Research issues and practice* (pp. 111–131). New York: Newbury House/HarperCollins.

Haas, C. (1989). How the writing medium shapes the writing process: Effects of word processing on planning. *Research in the Teaching of English*, 23, 181–207.

Hawisher, G. E., & Selfe, C. L. (2000). Introduction: Testing the claims. In G. E. Hawisher & C. L. Selfe (Eds.), *Global literacies and the World-Wide Web* (pp. 1–18). London: Routledge.

Hoffman, R. (1996). Computer networks: Webs of communication for language teaching. In M. C. Pennington (Ed.), *The power of CALL* (pp. 55–78). Houston: Athelstan.

Howard, T. (1992). WANs, connectivity, and computer literacy: An introduction and glossary. *Computers and Composition*, 9(3), 41–57.

Jones, S., & Tetroe, J. (1987). Composing in a second language. In A. Matsuhashi (Ed.), *Writing in real time: Modelling production processes* (pp. 34–57). Norwood, NJ: Ablex.

Kamhi-Stein, L. D. (2000). Looking at the future of TESOL teacher education: Web-based bulletin board discussion in a methods course. *TESOL Quarterly*, 34, 423–455.

Kaufer, D. S., & Neuwirth, C. (1995). Supporting online team editing: Using technology to shape performance and to monitor individual and group action. *Computers and Composition*, 12, 113–124.

Kress, G. (1998). Visual and verbal modes of representation in electronically mediated communication: The potentials of new forms of text. In I. Synder (Ed.), *Page to screen: Taking literacy into the electronic era* (pp. 53–79). London: Routledge.

Lam, F. S., & Pennington, M. C. (1995). The computer vs. the pen: A comparative study of word processing in a Hong Kong secondary classroom. *Computer-Assisted Language Learning*, 7, 75–92.

Lam, W. S. E. (2000). L2 literacy and the design of the self: A case study of a teenager writing on the Internet. *TESOL Quarterly*, 34, 457–482.

Li, J., & Cumming, A. (2001). Word processing and second language writing: A longitudinal case study. *International Journal of English Studies*, 1(2), 127–152.

Mabrito, M. (1991). Electronic mail as a vehicle for peer response. *Written Communication*, 8, 509–532.

Marcoul, I., & Pennington, M. C. (1999). Composing with computer technology: A case study of a group of students in computer studies learning French as a second language. In M. C. Pennington (Ed.), *Writing in an electronic medium: Research with language learners* (pp. 285–318). Houston: Athelstan.

Marcus, S. (1993). Multimedia, hypermedia and the teaching of English. In M. Monteith (Ed.), *Computers and language* (pp. 21–43). Oxford: Intellect Books.

McConaghy, C., & Snyder, I. (2000). Working the Web in postcolonial Australia. In G. E. Hawisher & C. L. Selfe (Eds.), *Global literacies and the World-Wide Web* (pp. 74–92). London: Routledge.

McGarrell, H. M. (1993, August). *Perceived and actual impact of computer use in second language writing classes*. Paper presented at the Congress of the Association de Linguistique Appliquée (AILA), Frije University, Amsterdam.

Moran, C. (1995). Notes toward a rhetoric of e-mail. *Computers and Composition, 12,* 15–21.

Moran, C., & Hawisher, G. E. (1998). The rhetorics and languages of electronic mail. In I. Snyder (Ed.), *Page to screen: Taking literacy into the electronic era* (pp. 80–101). London: Routledge.

Nabors, L. K., & Swartley, E. C. (1999). Student email letters: Negotiating meaning, gathering information, building relationships. In M. C. Pennington (Ed.), *Writing in an electronic medium: Research with language learners* (pp. 229–266). Houston: Athelstan.

Neu, J., & Scarcella, R. (1991). Word processing in the ESL writing classroom: A survey of student attitudes. In P. Dunkel (Ed.), *Computer-assisted language learning and testing: Research issues and practice* (pp. 169–187). New York: Newbury House/HarperCollins.

Palmquist, M. E. (1993). Network-supported interaction in two writing classrooms. *Computers and Composition, 10,* 25–57.

Pennington, M. C. (1996a). The power of the computer in language education. *The power of CALL* (pp. 1–14). Houston: Athelstan.

Pennington, M. C. (1996b). *The computer and the non-native writer: A natural partnership.* Cresskill, NJ: Hampton Press.

Pennington, M. C. (1996c). Writing the natural way: On computer. *Computer Assisted Language Learning, 9,* 125–142.

Pennington, M. C. (1999a). The missing link in computer-assisted writing. In K. Cameron (Ed.), *CALL: Media, design & applications* (pp. 271–292). Lisse: Swets & Zeitlinger.

Pennington, M. C. (1999b). Word processing and beyond: Writing in an electronic medium. In M. C. Pennington (Ed.), *Writing in an electronic medium: Research with language learners* (pp. 1–26). Houston: Athelstan.

Pennington, M. C. (2000). Writing minds and talking fingers: Doing literacy in an electronic age. In P. Brett (Ed.), *CALL in the 21st century* [CD-ROM]. Whitstable, UK: IATEFL.

Pennington, M. C., & Brock, M. N. (1992). Process and product approaches to computer-assisted composition. In M. C. Pennington & V. Stevens (Eds.), *Computers in applied linguistics: An international perspective* (pp. 79–109). Clevedon, UK: Multilingual Matters.

Phinney, M. (1989). Computers, composition, and second language teaching. In M. C. Pennington (Ed.), *Teaching languages with computers: The state of the art* (pp. 81–96). La Jolla, CA: Athelstan.

Phinney, M. (1991). Word processing and writing apprehension in first and second language writers. *Computers and Composition, 9,* 65–82.

Phinney, M., & Khouri, S. (1993). Computers, revision, and ESL writers: The role of experience. *Journal of Second Language Writing, 2,* 257–277.

Phinney, M., & Mathis, C. (1990). ESL student responses to writing with computers. *TESOL Newsletter, 24*(2), 30–31.

Roblyer, M. D., Castine, W. H., & King, F. J. (1988). *Assessing the impact of computer-based instruction: A review of recent research.* New York: Haworth.

Romano, S., Field, B., & Huergo, E. W. de. (2000). Web literacies of the already accessed and technically inclined: Schooling in Monterrey, Mexico. In G. E. Hawisher & C. L. Selfe (Eds.), *Global literacies and the World-Wide Web* (pp. 189–216). London: Routledge.

Rusmin, R. S. (1999). Patterns of adaptation to a new writing environment: The experience of word processing by mature second language writers. In M. C. Pennington (Ed.), *Writing in an electronic medium: Research with language learners* (pp. 183–227). Houston: Athelstan.

Sayers, D. (1989). Bilingual sister classes in computer writing networks. In D. M. Johnson & D. H. Roen (Eds.), *Richness in writing: Empowering ESL students* (pp. 120–133). New York: Longman.

Schramm, R. M. (1989). The effects of using word-processing equipment in writing instruction: A meta-analysis. (Doctoral dissertation, Northern Illinois University, 1990). *Dissertation Abstracts International, 50,* 2463A.

Slater, P., & Carpenter, C. (1999). Introducing e-mail into a course in French as a second language In M. C. Pennington (Ed.), *Writing in an electronic medium: Research with language learners* (pp. 267–283). Houston: Athelstan.

Snyder, I. (1993). Writing with word processors: A research overview. *Educational Research, 35,* 49–68.

Spears, R., & Lea, M. (1992). Social influence and the influence of the "social" in computer-mediated communication. In R. Spears & M. Lea (Eds.), *Contexts of computer-mediated communication* (pp. 30–65). New York: Harvester Wheatsheaf.

Steelman, J. D. (1994). Revision strategies employed by middle level students using computers. *Journal of Educational Computing Research, 11,* 141–152.

Sullivan, N., & Pratt, E. (1996). A comparative study of two ESL writing environments: A computer-assisted classroom and a traditional oral classroom. *System, 24,* 491–501.

Susser, B. (1993). ESL/EFL process writing with computers. *CAELL Journal, 4*(2), 16–22.

Warschauer, M. (1997). Computer-mediated collaborative learning: Theory and practice. *Modern Language Journal, 81,* 470–481.

Warschauer, M. (1999). *Electronic literacies: Language, culture, and power in online education.* Mahwah, NJ: Lawrence Erlbaum.

Warschauer, M. (2000a). Language, identity, and the internet. In B. Kolko, L. Kakamura, & G. Rodman (Eds.), *Race in cyberspace* (pp. 151–170). London: Routledge.

Warschauer, M. (2000b). The death of cyberspace and the rebirth of CALL. In P. Brett (Ed.), *CALL in the 21st century* [CD-ROM]. Whitstable, UK: IATEFL.

Williamson, M. M., & Pence, P. (1989). Word processing and student writers. In B. Britton & S. M. Glynn (Eds.), *Computer writing environments: Theory, research, and design* (pp. 93–127). Hillsdale, NJ: Lawrence Erlbaum.

Windeatt, S., Hardisty, D., & Eastment, D. (2000). *The internet.* Oxford: Oxford University Press.

Woodin, J. (1997). E-mail tandem learning and the communicative curriculum. *ReCALL, 9*(1), 22–33.

EPILOGUE:
EXPLORING OURSELVES

Historically, in language classrooms of about 50 years ago, writing was once seen as the "handmaid" of the other skills (Rivers, 1968), suggesting its purpose was to reinforce the "real" purpose of learning a language, namely, mastery of its grammar system. This issue is still subject to debate in foreign language (FL) classrooms (Kern, 2000), and some continue to argue that FL writing should be promoted as a tool in the service of other aspects of language learning (Homstad & Thorson, 2000).

However, specialized English-language writing courses for foreign students at American universities, for example, date back at least to the 1960s, with one of the early pioneer teacher-researchers being Nancy Arapoff-Cramer, who was based at the University of Hawaii. Around the same time that Rivers was relegating writing to the back bench, Arapoff-Cramer published numerous articles discussing the importance of teaching writing as a specific skill to EFL students (e.g., Arapoff, 1967, 1969; Arapoff-Cramer, 1971), as well as one of the earliest specialized textbooks in the field (Arapoff, 1970). In that era of first establishing a field of inquiry known as second language (L2) writing, it became important to point to ways in which L2 writers could be served by offering courses tailored to their special needs as both language learners and novice writers.

Today, rather than focusing merely on pointing to and identifying the distinct needs of L2 learners in terms of writing courses, specialists continue to expand their territories of investigation into such issues as research design, textual properties, and other broad-based issues, several of which have been addressed in this volume. A new line of inquiry is suggested by the work of Katznelson, Perpignan, and Rubin (2001); they suggest that enrollment in writing courses includes some positive by-products for students that have nothing to do with their writing but more specifically with changes that alter their "affective and behavioral processes" (p. 155). What is not often questioned, perhaps, is the extent to which the *skills* promoted in L2 writing courses actually assist the students enrolled in them with their long-term needs.

The final chapter in this volume, written by Ilona Leki, serves as a kind of epilogue to the entire book. The collective message of the previous

311

12 chapters is that the field of second language writing is a dynamic one with many facets to explore. Rather than closing with a chapter that exhorts teachers and scholars to go forth in their explorations of writers, writing classrooms, programs, and contexts for writing – all laudable goals – the final chapter sounds a note of caution. To truly serve our students best in terms of their academic needs, Leki suggests, we must also be prepared to question the value of what we do. This stance is similar to the premise behind a recent major study undertaken by Lillis (2001), in which she calls into question some of the pedagogical approaches used in the United Kingdom to address academic writing needs of non-traditional students (including non-native speakers of English) there. The voices of several other practitioners concerned about their institutions' difficulties in finding optimum ways to help student writers improve are anthologized in a volume designed both to "write [the] wrongs, and, then, to right [the] wrongs" (Wallace, Jackson, & Wallace, 2000, p. xii).

Writing teachers are sometimes so concerned with delivering what they perceive to be the best-designed course that they sometimes appear to have forgotten the importance of continually reviewing *why* we believe students need to take writing courses in the first place. Further, writing teachers, "content" area instructors, and L2 students do not necessarily agree on the desired outcomes of courses targeted to improve L2 student writing (Tait, 1999). Leki's chapter suggests that we have much to learn by working with our students to find out more about how writing serves their individual academic purposes.

Leki has been doing close case studies of individual writers, collecting large amounts of survey data, and paying especially close attention to what the students themselves say over a period of many years (Leki, 2001; Leki & Carson, 1994, 1997). With this chapter, she stands out as one of the first senior people in L2 writing to openly challenge some of the foundational ideas of curriculum planning. She asks us to consider the potential usefulness of material presented in our L2 writing courses and not to accept without question the importance of writing itself in the lives of our students. By encouraging all of us to take a close look at what we do so that we might learn to take a critical stance toward our beliefs and practices, Leki is not suggesting that writing is unimportant or that our courses do not serve a variety of student needs. She instead asks us to review our thinking so that we may better serve our students.

References

Arapoff, N. (1967). Writing: A thinking process. *TESOL Quarterly, 1*, 33–39.

Arapoff, N. (1969). Discover and transform: A method of teaching writing to foreign students. *TESOL Quarterly, 3*, 297–304.

Arapoff, N. (1970). *Writing through understanding*. New York: Holt, Rinehart and Winston.

Arapoff-Cramer, N. (1971). A survey of university writing assignments. *College Composition and Communication, 22,* 161–168.

Homstad, T., & Thorson, H. (2000). Writing and foreign language pedagogy: Theories and implications. In G. Brauer (Ed.), *Writing across languages* (pp. 3–14). Stamford, CT: Ablex.

Katznelson, H., Perpignan, H., & Rubin, B. (2001). What develops *along with* the development of second language writing? Exploring the "by-products." *Journal of Second Language Writing, 10,* 141–159.

Kern, R. (2000). *Literacy and language teaching*. New York and Oxford: Oxford University Press.

Leki, I. (2001). Hearing voices: L2 students' experiences in L2 writing courses. In T. Silva & P. K. Matsuda (Eds.), *On second language writing* (pp. 17–28). Mahwah, NJ: Lawrence Erlbaum.

Leki, I., & Carson, J. (1994). Students' perceptions of EAP writing instruction and writing needs across the disciplines. *TESOL Quarterly, 28,* 81–101.

Leki, I., & Carson, J. (1997). "Completely different worlds": EAP and the writing experiences of ESL students in university courses. *TESOL Quarterly, 31,* 39–69.

Lillis, T. (2001). *Student writing: Access, regulation, desire*. London: Routledge.

Rivers, W. M. (1968). *Teaching foreign language skills*. Chicago: University of Chicago Press.

Tait, J. (1999, March). *Multiple perspectives on academic writing needs*. Paper presented at the 33rd Annual TESOL Convention, New York. (Available through ERIC Document Reproduction Service No. ED432157.)

Wallace, R., Jackson, A., & Wallace, S. (2000). Introduction. In R. Wallace, A. Jackson, & S. L. Wallace (Eds.), *Reforming college composition: Writing the wrongs* (pp. xi–xxx). Westport, CT: Greenwood.

13 A challenge to second language writing professionals: Is writing overrated?

Ilona Leki

Writing researchers and practitioners in English as a first language (L1) have long assumed that writing does or should play a central role in tertiary education, and indeed in the lives of educated citizens in a democracy. In the case of English as a second language (L2), the argument for a privileged role for writing in L2 learning had to be specifically made in the 1960s and 1970s as a challenge to audiolingual methods of language teaching, which had relegated writing to the position of least important of language skills. (See Matsuda, 2001, and this volume, for a somewhat different account.) The place of writing continued to rise through the mid 1970s up to the present, as textbooks, teacher education materials, and other published work on L2 writing have obligatorily listed the benefits to L2 learners of developing writing skills and explained the overriding importance of writing in academic contexts. In the mid 1980s, as a tangible sign of the increasing significance of writing, the Test of Written English was added to the TOEFL (Test of English as a Foreign Language) battery of tests, increasing the number of possible hoops for L2 English learners to jump through to gain access to English medium universities.[1] Further underscoring the importance of writing, since the mid 1980s many tertiary institutions in the United States have required writing entrance, proficiency, and/or exit exams to ensure that those with weak writing skills would be weeded out of academic institutions, prevented from progressing within those institutions, or barred from graduating from them. Every indication is that L2 writing has arrived and that the development of skill in writing is considered to be extremely important.

But important for what? Are we now in fact overvaluing writing? What are the consequences, particularly for L2 English students, of placing such a high value on writing? Is writing overrated? These questions arose for me in the course of reading about writing and about how painful we make it for some students through our writing exams and through our insistence on certain ways of writing. In this chapter I would like to examine some of the claims we make for writing and then to note some of the consequences of those claims for our L2 writing students. That is, each claim that a teacher makes to students in a writing class about the importance of that course, or even of a particular assignment, and each claim a program makes about its writing courses to students, faculty, or the administration derives from a network of assumptions that are not without ramifications for these students.

Precisely because many L2 writing teachers and researchers function within an institutional power structure that can dramatically impact our students' lives and futures, I would argue that we have an ethical obligation to scrutinize our assumptions about what we do. It may be that, as Shor (1998) has remarked about L1 English basic writing courses, "Smart people with good intentions often find themselves working in structures with bad functions" (p. 107). We cannot move toward decisions about whether and/or how to work against those bad functions or structures until we first think through our foundational beliefs that undergird and support them. It is not my intention here to create a manifesto for doing away with writing courses. Rather my purpose is to ask, have we been so intent on winning a place of respect for writing in L2 education (and for those who teach it) that we make claims incommensurate with reality?

Our core, and I would argue insufficiently challenged, belief appears to be in the importance that writing will have in our L2 students' lives. In our courses and through our institutions, we insist on the importance of writing because, as we tell our L2 English students, they will have to pass writing entrance exams (Sternglass, 1997; Tucker, 1995) or they will face writing assignments in college (Losey, 1997) or on the job (Spilka, 2001). Or we suggest to students that their lives would be richer if only they would open themselves up and use writing to explore their thoughts and feelings (Mlynarczyk, 1998). Our apparent belief in the overriding importance of writing comes out even in written research portrayals that provide descriptions of successful/unsuccessful or experienced/novice student writers. The successful, experienced writers come off as robust, alert, sensitive while the unsuccessful/novice writers seem befuddled and pathetic (e.g., Murray & Nichols, 1992; Patton & Nagelhout, 1998), as though the totality of these people can be reduced to their writing skills.

Perhaps as L2 writing teachers and researchers, we might be expected to place great stock in the written word. As Roen (1989) states, for example, "We are, after all, professional wordsmiths – people with a special affection for writing. Most people do not share our affection for the written word" (pp. 194–195). In order to make a more convincing case for the importance of writing, we have recruited the testimony of others, particularly students. Examples of such testimonials appear in Sternglass's (1997) account of the long-term writing development of a group of college students, some of whom had begun their educations in languages other than English. In her account, as I read it, Sternglass asserts that it is writing – not reading, not attending classes, not talking to others – that became the prevailing promoter of her research participants' intellectual growth: "Their most significant development occurred through...writing" (p. 293); "Writing promoted the truest method for learning" (p. 293); and "Only through writing...did they achieve the insights that moved them to complex reasoning" (p. 295). In fact, speaking of one student (Jacob), Sternglass maintains, "Writing was his real life" (p. 74).

Sternglass's account was a turning point for me. The over-arching thesis of her study is that we should not give up on students our institutions initially designate as academically underprepared; with this assessment I completely agree, and I applaud Sternglass's project to keep a space open for these students at the university. But in reading her descriptions of the students in her study, students so motivated and so personally rewarded by their academic writing experiences, I simply could not recognize these students. Sternglass's descriptions were entirely discontinuous with my own experience with L2 writing students – in talking to them informally, as their teacher in writing classes, and in my ongoing case study research on the literacy experiences of English L2 writers at the university (Leki, 1998).

The students I encountered had a much broader range of reactions to writing requirements in courses than the students Sternglass worked with. My L2 students found their writing requirements occasionally satisfying and sometimes frustrating, but most often they regarded writing assignments as necessary evils they would have preferred to avoid. This disjuncture between my own experiences and those of Sternglass caused me to begin to see nearly everywhere in the literature on both L1 and L2 writing an unspoken baseline assumption that writing is so important, potentially so meaningful, so powerful that almost no amount of sacrifice is too much to ask our students to make for the sake of learning to write. And underlying that article of faith is perhaps another: Learning to write takes place once and for all, and it will happen, or must happen, in *our* classes – our basic writing course, our English Language Institute, or our freshman writing course.[2]

My hope is that after having considered the detailed features of L2 writing instruction and research discussed in this volume, such as the history of the field, the role of feedback, contrastive rhetoric, reading/writing links, and so on, the reader will use this chapter as a means of stepping back from the enterprise to view it as a whole. The point of this chapter, however, is *not* to argue that writing is unimportant, that L2 English writers should not be offered the opportunity to learn to write in English in ways that will promote their well-being in their academic, personal, and professional lives, nor that writing instruction should be abolished. The point of the argument presented here, rather, is to challenge the unexamined assumption of the centrality of writing in the lives of educated people and to examine what our belief in its centrality buys us. The point of the challenge is to encourage us as L2 writing professionals to take a more critical stance in relation to what we do and what we ask our students to do.

The claims we make

To judge by writing textbooks in both L1 and L2, far from seeing writing as their "real life," our students need to be convinced of the importance of writing by reading in their writing textbook or hearing on the first day of the writing class a litany of claims about how important writing already is to them in their daily lives (to write grocery lists, notes to friends and family, letters of complaint to landlords, e-mail messages) and how important writing will certainly be eventually to do such things as take an exam in a management course, write a biology lab report, work as an engineer, and participate in democracy by writing letters to the editor or to elected representatives.

We seem to make these claims for writing:

1. Writing can be, is, or should be personally fulfilling
2. Writing helps students to learn disciplinary content
3. Students will have to do a lot of writing in other courses in college
4. In the work world, employers look for or demand good writing skills and/or since English is the language of international communication, moving up in various professions will require writing well in English
5. In a democracy, writing is a powerful tool for justice

We make these claims repeatedly to our students, to our institutions, and to each other in the professional literature. The remainder of this chapter will examine each of them in turn.

1. Writing is personally fulfilling

My sister-in-law, who also teaches writing, teaches an elective course in writing as healing. She writes easily and well, and writing is personally fulfilling for her and probably also becomes so for the students who enroll in her courses. However, for many L2 English students, learning to write in English is probably less likely to become much of a source of personal fulfillment; it is more likely that if they turn to writing for self-exploration at all, they will turn to writing in their L1s (see, for example, several of the accounts in Belcher & Connor, 2001). Nevertheless, some of our writing classes do ask L2 students to open themselves up to us or to try to think through personal issues publicly by writing in a language that is not transparent to them, that they may still be struggling with. Perhaps we ask them to do this partly under the assumption that eventually this kind of writing may be cathartic. And in fact, even for some L2 students, writing in English actually does sometimes permit an exploration of personal questions that might be more difficult to explore in the writer's L1, but such an experience seems limited to a relatively small number. Even in L1 English, those who do not write easily or well or those from an orally oriented home culture turn to writing, as Brodkey (1996) says, only when for some reason our first line of healing, conversation, fails us (p. 140).

But from reading the professional literature on writing, it is possible to get the impression that no one talks, listens, or even reads, for personal growth, only writes. In the introduction to a recent L1 writing text, the authors state "We believe there is *no better way* to come to know yourself than through the process of writing" (Bridwell-Bowles, 1998, p. 1 [italics mine]). No better way? Given how hard it is for some, particularly L2, students to write and how negative some students' experiences with writing have been, it certainly seems that the power of writing to explore personal issues is exaggerated here. The argument that learning to write is important because writing serves a few people so well is reminiscent of parents' argument to coerce children into practicing violin – someday the learner will be grateful. But we are not dealing with children, and we are not our students' parents.

2. *Writing helps students learn disciplinary content*

"Writing to learn" has become an important concept in the field of writing (discussed in the L2 field by Zamel, 2000, among others). Unfortunately, the assertion that writing aids in learning course content has been asserted more often than demonstrated. In his review of 35 different studies that attempted to assess the impact of L1 English writing on learning, Ackerman (1993) concludes that writing has never been convincingly shown to be more effective than other methods of focusing students' attention on content matter, and in some cases students actually remembered more of the content they were trying to learn when they were asked to do something other than write about it. Writing about content appeared to focus students' attention on only a narrow band of the material to be learned, although Ackerman acknowledges that writing might in fact be conferring advantages that the research methodologies used in these studies were simply unable to capture. But if these studies were unable to capture what exact advantage writing conferred, it was not for lack of trying. As Ackerman points out, sometimes the researchers whose work he reviewed would come to unwarranted and overly optimistic conclusions about the power of writing to aid learning in the face of their own research evidence to the contrary; such is the force of the belief in the centrality of writing.

Furthermore, in research by Chenoweth et al. (1999) using pre- and post-testing, we find that the L1 English students in their study who took a lower-division writing course did not do better on the material to be learned in the course, such as critical reading skills and the ability to identify argument strategies, than did the control group of students who had not taken the writing course. Apparently, then, writing was not helping the students, at least in these courses, to learn the material even in the writing course, let alone the material in other disciplinary courses.

In fact, Geisler (1995) comments that "writing is a fairly poor tool" (p. 102) for students to use in "learning...knowledge made by others" (p. 102), suggesting instead that taking notes and working on study questions might be tasks that are better suited for preparing students to perform the "knowledge displays routinely required in academic settings" (p. 112).

In the area of upper-division writing courses, results have sometimes been more positive though not always in ways that were expected. Hilgers, Hussey, and Stitt-Bergh (1999) found that students in required upper-division writing-intensive courses reported that engaging in writing tasks was helpful to them more often to learn the research methodologies appropriate to their fields than to learn content and key concepts.

Finally, studies by Smagorinsky (1994) result in his contention that a variety of artistic and creative activities confer the same kinds of benefits for learning or understanding that appear to be claimed exclusively for writing. Students who dance, draw, create architectural constructions or music, for example, engage in the discovery of meaning, develop new understandings through these activities, and learn from dialectical interactions with peer viewers/listeners. Smagorinsky argues that if we continue to assume that such growth is reserved for the domain of writing alone, we ignore and implicitly devalue a rich "multiplicity of sign systems" (p. 31) that diverse students bring to classrooms.

A further problem with blind faith in the idea that writing helps students learn relates to what we do with that belief. Do we, in our writing classes, ever teach students *how*, exactly, to use writing to learn content? If we wanted to do so, it would appear necessary to actually ask students to learn content in writing classes. Some writing classes may well do that, but it seems more typical that we ask writing students not to *learn* but only to *explore* certain issues and then write about them, in the worst case scenario using relatively little information beyond what comes from an anthologized essay or two on euthanasia or sex-linked genetic traits or such. Then, when that writing is evaluated, the evaluation is most likely to be based on how well the material has been *used* in the writing, not on how well it has been learned. In fact, it is difficult to imagine a poorly written paper in a writing class that would receive a high evaluation based on the student's demonstration of having learned the content. What this amounts to, then, is that we say writing to learn is very important; but in our writing classes, we do not ask students to write to learn, and we do not show them how to do it. This is not to say that self-initiated note taking or thinking on paper does not help L2 students learn. It may well. But that kind of writing is hardly the obligatory English department, sustained essay writing taught in most writing classes.

3.   *College students do a great deal of writing*

This reason for emphasizing the importance of writing (college students must write a lot) and the next reason (the need to write on the job) both bring up the issue of student need. But need as defined by whom? On one hand, we tell students they need to become prepared for all the writing that they will be assigned to do in other classes, and then on the other hand, we lament among ourselves and to other faculty that other disciplinary courses do not take responsibility for teaching writing, that they do not have students do enough writing; we complain that teaching writing should be everyone's job at the university, not just the job of the writing teacher. In other words, we tell our students they need to learn how to write because they will do a lot of writing beyond our writing courses, but apparently we do not actually believe that is the case!

Is writing as central to L2 English undergraduate education as we say? My own case studies of four L2 English students throughout their undergraduate careers (Leki, 1998) suggest that writing, in the sense of composing long stretches of text for an audience as we teach it in composition classes, was not a prominent feature of their first two years (except in the writing classes they took), at least for these four bilingual students. Reading and listening were far more important to their development. Lamentably, these first two years were mostly filled with the kind of general education classes that enroll dozens of students in a single class; presumably the size of these classes discourages instructors from assigning much sustained writing. This means that for students who take freshman writing during their freshman year (or at language institutes before admission to college), all the information they get and skills they learn in the writing classes are unlikely to be put to use until two years later! My case study students' lived experience in courses outside the writing class directly contradicted what their writing teachers told them about how prevalent writing would be in their other courses. (However, see Reid, 2001, for counter-examples and reference to studies reporting ways in which some schools or departments do require writing.)

For the students in my case studies, once they entered courses in their majors that did include writing, one of two things happened. Either the disciplinary faculty began initiating students into the type of writing common or necessary in that major or they assigned papers that were entirely unlike anything that anyone practicing that discipline would ever do. In the first instance of specialized disciplinary writing, for example, a major part of the writing done by my research participant in the nursing curriculum consisted primarily of long, detailed, time-consuming nursing care plans requiring filling in matrixes with abbreviations, symbols, shorthand notations on patients' symptoms, and numbers. It was hardly the kind of extended prose we think of when we talk about writing in writing courses: something with an introduction, some central point, and arguments or evidence to support the point. There were barely any recognizable English words in these nursing care plans and almost no sentences. No writing class outside her major could have begun to prepare her for this writing, though preparing her for writing in college is, of course, one of the justifications for requiring writing classes.

For another of my case study participants, the writing assigned in his marketing major was nearly always group work projects, and my research participant, not liking to write and not feeling secure about his writing ability, made a point of getting himself assigned roles within the group that would allow him to avoid writing.

This is not to say that these students never wrote anything of the type that writing professionals have in mind when they refer to the power of writing, but rather just to suggest that much of the learning these students experienced came through a variety of sources and that writing cannot be privileged as the main source of their expanding knowledge and familiarity with their fields. Furthermore, if university students do not actually do much writing (outside their freshman writing courses) until they get to courses in their majors, whatever writing skills these students develop may not be engaged until some time down the road and so may degrade before they can be used. Finally, it becomes somewhat difficult to see how writing teachers can prepare students for that down-the-road disciplinary writing since we may not know enough about it. Perhaps writing across the curriculum (WAC) programs that work closely with disciplinary courses are better able to deal with disciplinary genres, but general writing courses do not appear to be very well positioned for overcoming this obstacle to making writing instruction relevant to students' academic lives.[3]

In addition to the specialized disciplinary writing assignments, the second type of writing assignment in the major that I found in my research was standard school-sponsored writing. This writing bore no relationship to anything disciplinary professionals might ever do outside of school, although it did have as its subject matter issues related to the major. It was the faculty themselves in these disciplinary courses who offered this characterization of their assignments as being unlike anything a nurse or social worker or engineer would ever do. When asked why they assigned such writing if it was unrelated to any real-world disciplinary writing, the instructors justified their assignments either as offering another evaluative measure of the students' progress in the course besides exams or as offering an opportunity for these students just to write because, as they said, they believed that writing in and of itself is very important. That is, writing for writing's sake, as an end in itself, is beneficial; it is the sign of an educated person, one who, in a kind of nineteenth-century notion of the educated elite, knows both how to write *and* play the harp.[4]

4. Employers demand good writing skills

The justification for (over)valuing writing because employers demand good writing skills begs the question of whether it is the job of the university to train people for the benefit of business and industry. But that ideological question aside, another question arises of what these employers mean when they say they want employees with good writing skills. According to Charney (1998), employers mean they do not want spelling and grammar errors, items not high on the list of most writing teachers these days. It seems demeaning, to say the least, to think that we are training students to spell correctly to make their employers happy. Furthermore, according to Belcher's (1991) research, although the L2 English writers she worked with were perceived by their employer, co-workers, and even themselves as needing to improve their writing skills, what proved to be more critical to their success than improved writing skills on the job was how they positioned themselves among co-workers – that is, their social interactions.

Even when writing is an important constituent of a particular work setting, writing for the job is the quintessential embedded activity, a skill that must be learned on the job, as we can see so clearly in Winsor's (1996) book-length study of four young L1 English engineering students in their work-study programs. In writing on the job successfully, what was central and crucial was, again, not the writing but a thorough familiarity with the history of the work site and with all the personalities there and their histories with each other, none of which, of course, can be known during the time we have these students in decontextualized writing classes and are telling them how important writing is.

Finally, it is not so clear how well we can actually estimate the amount of writing done at various work sites. When writing researchers go to a job site to investigate writing because they are researching writing, it is only logical that they would highlight the writing over the many other kinds of activities that take place at the work site. Because in these instances writing is such a focus of attention and described in great detail, it is possible that we inadvertently develop a distorted and exaggerated sense of the importance of writing in the workplace, coming to see practicing engineers, physicists, and biologists as spending most of their professional time writing. For example, in Winsor's (1996) study of the rhetorical education of the engineering students, although she notes that the amount of writing they did is probably more than practicing engineers would be doing, there still was not very much of it in the course of the five years she studied them. Nevertheless, because her book focuses entirely on writing, it is possible to come away with the impression that writing was much more central to their experience than it might in fact have been. As a result of this kind of predictable distortion, we may not have a very firm sense of how much writing professionals do in relation to other job-related tasks.

Even in academics, where writing does play a major gate-keeping role in professional advancement, surely faculty spend a great deal of time doing things other than writing, though much of that might be in preparation for writing. And, as we know from genre researchers, both biologists and physicists, to take these two disciplines as examples, certainly do write and must employ a complex set of rhetorical skills in order to position themselves and their work to their best advantage (Bazerman, 1985; Myers, 1985). But it is an open question whether these researchers might consider writing something of a necessary evil in their work, with the interesting or important part of the work already completed by the time they get to writing it down.[5]

What of the claim that increasing amounts of scientific and technical writing internationally is done in English (Connor, Chapter 9 this volume; Flowerdew, 1999; Swales, 1997)? According to Gosden's (1992) survey of editors of international scientific journals published in English, the suggestion that a scientist will be prevented from participating in journal-mediated professional discussions solely by the lack of writing skills may be an exaggeration, overemphasizing writing skills and underemphasizing such issues as material conditions in the writer's home country (Canagarajah, 1996), quality of the science reported, and prejudice on the part of editors and reviewers against submissions from certain regions. Gosden reports, however, that this bias is based not so much on linguistic grounds as on "the science culture" (p. 130). This means that although editors of journals with large submission rates may be looking for reasons to reject a submission, it would be disingenuous, to say the least, to suggest to L2 writers that good writing will save them from rejection and overcome prejudices.

5.   *In a democracy, writing is a powerful tool for justice*

At end of his chapter in the Roen, Brown, and Enos (1999) collection of autobiographies of prominent members of the discipline, Trimbur says that he wants his work to "bear witness to the 'appalling power' of late capitalism at a moment when the bosses are winning the class struggle on a global scale and working people everywhere need the intellectual and moral resources of literacy to find hope" (p. 141). I am moved by the statement and struck by the faith in literacy expressed here. I cannot tell for sure whether Trimbur means that literacy itself somehow brings hope for change, perhaps through solidarity with others who are struggling, or whether he means that reading and writing can actually be a means of successfully resisting the bosses. Nevertheless, I cannot help but wonder, when we link political power with the ability to write well, whether we are not telling our students another version of our standard lie about equality of opportunity: If you work hard and apply yourself – that is, if you learn to write powerfully – some day, Jose or Tyrunia or Shao Lin, all of this can be yours. In other words, we are telling them, in effect, that their success is in their own hands, they command their own fates; and logically, therefore, we are suggesting that if they do not some day succeed, the fault lies with them. Yet as Benesch (1996) has so cogently argued, language and writing alone will not bring power to the powerless irrespective of other factors, such as race, gender, and socioeconomic status.

To give students in writing classes a sense of a real audience, we sometimes encourage them to write a letter to the editor or maybe to a legislative representative, saying also that such writing constitutes active democratic participation. Yet, is it really people's facility with writing, their brilliant rhetoric, their ability to adjust their writing to the audience that convinces political officials and causes political roadblocks to melt away? My experience has been that it does not matter how rhetorically, logically, grammatically, orthographically excellent the letter is; what matters, if anything, is how many people write letters on the same issue. And do letters to the editor really ever sway a public? Ervin (1999) recounts an interesting town-and-gown battle over creationism in the letters to the editor section of the Wilmington, North Carolina, newspaper. After several rounds of exchanges, one of the participants said he was throwing a party for all those who had changed their minds on the issue as a result of the letter exchanges; he calculated that a phone booth would be big enough to handle the crowd. My point is not that writing letters has no role, but that it is one tool among others, and maybe we should not exaggerate what this tool can and cannot do.

Furthermore, there may be reason to believe that people develop the language and the level of literacy necessary for them to do what they need and want to do. For example, Cushman (1999) reported how a group of impoverished, L1 English-speaking women who were about to be evicted from their homes were able to defend themselves against the bureaucracy by learning and using the language of the oppressor (more oral than written, in this case). They did not take writing, or speaking, or vocabulary development classes. Rather, knowing very precisely what they wanted to get from the bureaucracy helped them figure out a means for trying to get it. The problem for writing teachers is that real needs and wants of the type that stimulated the kind of learning these women engaged in cannot be described and handed over to students before the fact in a writing course. Much like the development of language used in work settings and in fact like language acquisition in general, the language that is needed and wanted may be best and most easily learned on the spot through interaction with other participants in authentic speech events.

What you get for your money

When we buy into the idea of writing as the core of education, we generate at least two material and pernicious results: required writing courses like freshman composition and writing exams. The logic seems to be that if writing is so important we had better have a course in which we teach it; and to show how important we feel it is for people to learn how to write, we had better test students to make sure they can do it correctly. Crowley (1998) explores in great detail the reasons for getting rid of L1 freshman composition as a required course; Russell (1991) explores, also in great detail, the reasons that the freshman composition course cannot successfully teach writing, namely because the very existence of freshman composition implies that writing is a single generalizable skill that can be learned once and for all, rather than a situated social process and activity embedded in epistemological, ethical, personal, and historical contingencies that must be experienced in real time to be understood. The failure to understand writing as such an ongoing and continuing process accounts for many of the complaints on the part of non-writing faculty, and perhaps employers, that students cannot write.[6]

And with this misunderstanding comes the call for and acceptance of the validity of writing exams, the material evidence for and a logical consequence of our inflated views of writing, our belief in the centrality of writing, our love of words. The argument here is not that inflated views of the importance of writing are the primary reasons that writing exams exist; they are merely good excuses, easily swallowed justifications for these exams. Writing exams are convenient gate keepers with the political purpose of sorting and categorizing those who will and those who will not enjoy the privileges that may come with education. Nevertheless, emphasizing the importance of a decontextualized skill that leaves the test taker so particularly vulnerable to criticism, failure, and mockery makes it easier and more palatable for otherwise decent people to become complicit in the existence and sometimes ruinous results of these exams. It is important to recognize this complicity.

Writing exams have a high potential to be discriminatory, especially against L2 and language minority students, denying people an education *in the name* of the crucial importance of writing. They can also be capricious and illogical, exemplifying incomprehensible views of literacy. For example, at some West Coast institutions, apparently the working definition of "literate enough to be allowed to pursue a college education" is "able to produce a personal essay." At institutions in New York, the definition is "able to write an argument in 30 minutes on a topic the writer has not seen before, does not know about, and may not care about." Not only do these tests represent questionable choices for determining literacy, but potentially, a student literate enough to go to school in California might not be literate enough in New York and vice versa.

Furthermore, we need to be clear in our understanding that both the personal essay and the argument that define literacy in the two exam types mentioned above are English department genres. Why are they privileged? Why are they considered superordinate over other disciplinary genres? Are all those who knock at the door of the university planning to be English majors? Certainly that is not the case with most L2 English learners. Then how do we justify preventing someone from getting an education because he or she cannot write an English department genre? This makes about as much sense as it would to require future English majors to prove they are literate enough to be allowed to study English by showing that they can write a successful biology lab report.

Those who love writing, place it at the center of their intellectual lives, and want others to do the same have won out at the moment. Writing exams and required freshman composition courses are accepted by the educational community and by the public. But what do these courses and exams do to the people subjected to them? Over the last five years I have asked students to think of a writing experience that stands out in their minds and talk about it – actually, write about it. The majority of the stories they have told recount tales of trauma and cruel exposure of fragile egos. Those who did the hurting did so in the name of the importance of writing.[7]

I am hardly the first to say that there is tyranny in academic literacy. The challenge I wish to put to L2 writing professionals is not to discover how to avoid such destructiveness by building a better mousetrap, be it a writing course or writing exam. The challenge is rather an attempt to encourage some distance, a critical perspective that would allow us to ask ourselves if we are exaggerating the importance of writing and, if so, with what consequences to learners. We need, perhaps, to step back a bit to remember writing is a tool, not an end in itself. After all, in other academic settings – for example, in Europe – oral discourse, not written, plays the bigger role (Ivanic, 1998). Again, it is not that writing has no role to play in educational or professional or civic life; rather, because our professional interests as writing researchers and teachers lead us to focus on writing, we may ignore our own critical faculties and come to think of writing as rightfully occupying center stage for everyone. This seems particularly unjust toward L2 English writers, whose life agendas may or may not ever again include writing in English.

Writing is only one among several ways of becoming educated, doing our jobs, or making the world a better place to live. For most people, even some who lead perfectly fulfilling lives, writing is not the core activity to any of these ends. For this reason, those of us who teach L2 writing must keep what we do in proper perspective, not exaggerate the importance in our students' academic, work, or personal lives of what we have to offer, and perhaps think of our work more modestly in terms of its *potential* usefulness.

Notes

1. A particular composite score on the Test of English as a Foreign Language (TOEFL) is often required of English learners seeking admission to institutions of higher education in North America.
2. Over the years, in thinking through these issues, I have often asked (usually L1 English) graduate students in my classes whether they consider themselves good writers and, if so, where they learned to write. Writing classes are rarely mentioned as the source of their skill development.
3. Currie (1999) offers suggestions on organizing academic writing courses that focus on skills that might transfer from L2 writing courses to meet specific disciplinary requirements. For further discussion of this topic, see the chapter by Johns, Chapter 8 this volume.
4. It is true, however, that even when writing for writing's sake was assigned, the disciplinary instructors typically provided quite detailed instructions for completing these assignments and thereby did, in that sense, model elements of disciplinary discourse, perhaps most notably what the discipline values in its discourse.

   Furthermore, while these writing assignments did not reflect non-school-sponsored disciplinary writing tasks, obviously, this does not mean that they were without educational merit or effect. Assigning papers on an issue related to the courses certainly caused the students to spend time thinking, reading, talking – and writing – about the topic, although how they benefited from the time spent varied by student and by task. Arguably, it was the *time* spent focused on the topic, rather than the specific medium of writing, that promoted any learning that took place.
5. This may be why, according to interviews with graduate students, parts of the writing in these disciplines are left to the graduate students to do, partly to train them and partly to allow the faculty to avoid having to do the more pedestrian writing tasks, such as literature reviews, themselves (Leki, 1996).
6. Petraglia (1995) refers to the freshman composition course as offering "general writing skills instruction (GWSI)" (p. xi) and assembles an edited volume of chapters discussing its various inadequacies. Also see Lillis (2001).

7. This is not to say that no one has positive memories or experiences of learning to write (and read); see, for example, Brandt (2001). On the other hand, for an elaborate glorification of the possibilities writing can/should open up juxtaposed against how he assumes students experience writing, writing classes, and school generally, see Johnson (2001), whose article is, interestingly, entitled "School sucks."

References

Ackerman, J. (1993). The promise of writing to learn. *Written Communication, 10*, 334–370.

Bazerman, C. (1985). Physicists reading physics: Schema-laden purposes and purpose-laden schema. *Written Communication, 2*, 3–24.

Belcher, D. (1991). Nonnative writing in a corporate setting. *The Technical Writing Teacher, 18*, 104–115.

Belcher, D., & Connor, U. (Eds.). (2001). *Reflections on multiliterate lives.* Clevedon, England: Multilingual Matters.

Benesch, S. (1996). Needs analysis and curriculum development in EAP: An example of a critical approach. *TESOL Quarterly, 30*, 723–738.

Brandt, D. (2001). *Literacy in American lives.* New York: Cambridge University Press.

Bridwell-Bowles, L. (1998). *Identity matters.* Upper Saddle River, NJ: Prentice Hall.

Brodkey, L. (1996). *Writing permitted in designated areas only.* Minneapolis: University of Minnesota Press.

Canagarajah, S. (1996). "Nondiscursive" requirements in academic publishing, material resources of periphery scholars, and the politics of knowledge production. *Written Communication, 13*, 435–472.

Charney, D. (1998, October). *Workplace literacies.* Watson Conference on Rhetoric and Composition, Louisville, KY.

Chenoweth, N., Hayes, J., Gripp, P., Littleton, E., Steinberg, E., & van Every, D. (1999). Are our courses working? Measuring student learning. *Written Communication, 16*, 29–50.

Crowley, S. (1998). *Composition in the university.* Pittsburgh, PA: University of Pittsburgh Press.

Currie, P. (1999). Transferable skills: Promoting student research. *English for Specific Purposes, 18*, 329–345.

Cushman, E. (1999). Critical literacy and institutional language. *Research in the Teaching of English, 33*, 245–274.

Ervin, E. (1999). Academics and the negotiation of local knowledge. *College English, 61*, 448–470.

Flowerdew, J. (1999). Writing for scholarly publication in English: The case of Hong Kong. *Journal of Second Language Writing, 8*, 123–145.

Geisler, C. (1995). Writing and learning at cross purposes in the academy. In J. Petraglia (Ed.), *Reconceiving writing, rethinking writing instruction* (pp. 101–120). Mahwah, NJ: Lawrence Erlbaum.

Gosden, H. (1992). Research writing and NNSs: From the editors. *Journal of Second Language Writing, 1*, 123–139.

Hilgers, T. L., Hussey, E. L., & Stitt-Bergh, M. (1999). "As you're writing you have these epiphanies": What college students say about writing and learning in their majors. *Written Communication, 16,* 317–353.

Ivanic, R. (1998). *Writing and identity: The discoursal construction of identity in academic writing.* Amsterdam/Philadelphia: John Benjamins.

Johnson, T. R. (2001). School sucks. *College Composition and Communication, 52,* 620–658.

Leki, I. (1996, March). *Getting inside: Graduate NNES students' perceptions of academic literacy development in their disciplines.* TESOL Conference, Chicago, IL.

Leki, I. (1998, March). *Socialization into academic and pre-professional literacy among four NNES university students.* AAAL Conference, Seattle, WA.

Lillis, T. M. (2001). *Student writing: Access, regulation, desire.* London: Routledge.

Losey, K. (1997). *Listen to the silences.* Norwood, NJ: Ablex.

Matsuda, P. (2001). Reexamining audiolingualism: On the genesis of reading and writing in L2 studies. In D. Belcher & A. Hirvela (Eds.), *Linking literacies: Perspectives on L2 reading-writing connections* (pp. 84–105). Ann Arbor: University of Michigan Press.

Mlynarczyk, R. (1998). *Conversations of the mind.* Mahwah, NJ: Erlbaum.

Murray, D., & Nichols, P. (1992). Literacy practices and their effect on academic writing: Vietnamese case studies. In F. Dubin & N. Kuhlman (Eds.), *Cross-cultural literacy: Global perspectives on reading and writing* (pp. 175–187). Englewood Cliffs, NJ: Prentice-Hall.

Myers, G. (1985). The social construction of two biologists' proposals. *Written Communication, 2,* 219–245.

Patton, M., & Nagelhout, E. (1998, October). *Literacy and learning in context: Biology students in the classroom and lab.* Watson Conference on Rhetoric and Composition, Louisville, KY.

Petraglia, J. (Ed.). (1995). *Reconceiving writing, rethinking writing instruction.* Mahwah, NJ: Lawrence Erlbaum.

Reid, J. (2001). Advanced EAP writing and curriculum design: What do we need to know? In T. Silva & P. K. Matsuda (Eds.), *On second language writing* (pp. 143–160). Mahwah, NJ: Lawrence Erlbaum.

Roen, D. (1989). Developing effective assignments for second language writers. In D. Johnson & D. Roen (Eds.), *Richness in writing* (pp. 193–206). New York: Longman.

Roen, D., Brown, S., & Enos, T. (Eds.). (1999). *Living rhetoric and composition.* Mahwah, NJ: Lawrence Erlbaum.

Russell, D. (1991). *Writing in the academic disciplines 1870–1990.* Carbondale, IL: SIU Press.

Shor, I. (1998). Inequality (still) rules: Reply to Collins and Greenberg. *Journal of Basic Writing, 17,* 104–108.

Smagorinsky, P. (1994). Constructing meaning in the disciplines: Reconceptualizing writing across the curriculum as composing across the curriculum. (ERIC Document Reproduction Service No. ED366954)

Spilka, R. (2001). *Workplace literacy.* New York: Addison Wesley Longman.

Sternglass, M. (1997). *Time to know them.* Mahwah, NJ: Lawrence Erlbaum.

Swales, J. (1997). English as Tyrannosaurus rex. *World Englishes, 16,* 373–382.

Trimbur, J. (1999). Close reading: Accounting for my life teaching writing. In D. Roen, S. Brown, & T. Enos (Eds.), *Living rhetoric and composition* (pp. 129–141). Mahwah, NJ: Lawrence Erlbaum.

Tucker, A. (1995). *Decoding ESL.* Portsmouth, NH: Boynton/Cook.

Winsor, D. (1996). *Writing like an engineer.* Mahwah, NJ: Lawrence Erlbaum.

Zamel, V. (2000). Engaging students in writing-to-learn: Promoting language and literacy across the curriculum. *Journal of Basic Writing, 19,* 3–21.

Index